RANDOM HOUSE

LARGE PRINT

They Fought Alone

They Fought Alone

Alone

The True Story of the Starr
Brothers, British Secret Agents
in Nazi-Occupied France

CHARLES GLASS

RANDOM HOUSE
LARGE PRINT

Published in the United States of America by Random House Large Print in association with Penguin Press, an imprint of Penguin Random House LLC, New York, New York.

Cover photograph: Bettmann / Getty Images
Author photograph © George Glass
Cover design: Darren Haggar

Illustration credits appear on page 515.

The Library of Congress has established a Cataloging-in-Publication record for this title.

ISBN: 978-1-9848-2767-8

www.penguinrandomhouse.com/large-print-format-books

FIRST LARGE PRINT EDITION

Printed in the United States of America

10 9 8 7 6 5 4 3 2 1

This Large Print edition published in accord with the standards of the N.A.V.H.

To the grandchildren:

Leonora, Allegra, Eva, Zelda, Rose, Christian,
Arthur, Iris, Felix, Harriet, Theo, Isaac, and Orlando

with love.

CONTENTS

LIST OF CHARACTERS

Lieutenant Claude Arnault: Code name "Néron"; demolition specialist sent by Special Operations Executive (SOE) to assist George Starr.

Serge Asher: Cover name "Serge Ravanel"; Resistance leader and regional commander of the **Forces Françaises de l'Intérieur** (FFI).

Vera Atkins: French Section (F-Section) intelligence officer under Maurice Buckmaster in London.

Georges Bégué: Radio operator and first agent that SOE infiltrated into France in May 1941.

Denise Bloch: Code names "Danielle" and "Catherine"; French Jewish **résistante,** courier of the DETECTIVE circuit and then of George Starr's WHEELWRIGHT in Castelnau-sur-l'Auvignon.

Marcus Bloom: Code names "Urbain" and "Bishop"; SOE F-Section radio operator, arrived in southern France in November 1942 with George Starr, transmitted for Maurice Pertschuk of PRUNUS and for George Starr.

Jan Buchowski: Polish naval lieutenant and skipper of the **Seadog,** delivered George Starr to the French coast and took John Starr out.

Colonel Maurice Buckmaster: Chief of SOE's F-Section.

Buresie: Former member of the Foreign Legion, George Starr's bodyguard.

Peter Churchill: Code name "Raoul"; early SOE organizer in France.

Winston Churchill: British wartime prime minister, established SOE on July 16, 1940.

Yvonne Cormeau: Code name "Annette"; radio operator for George Starr's WHEELWRIGHT circuit.

Hugh Dalton: Minister of economic warfare, to whom SOE reported.

Général Charles de Gaulle: Head of the Free French in London from 1940 to 1944.

Lieutenant Charles Duchalard: Code name "Denis"; French Canadian sabotage expert sent by SOE to assist Maurice Pertschuk and George Starr.

Pierre Duffoir: Code name "Félix"; courier for George Starr.

LIST OF CHARACTERS

Maurice Maxime Léon Dupont: Code name "Yvan"; French soldier and WHEELWRIGHT circuit courier.

Colonel Léon Faye: Founder of the ALLIANCE network, captured by the Germans and held at avenue Foch.

Major Horace "Hod" Williams Fuller: Code name "Kansul"; American marine officer and commander of Jedburgh Team Bugatti, which parachuted into southwest France in June 1944 to work with George Starr.

Sergeant Fernand Gaucher: Code name "Gérard"; member of France's 150th Infantry Regiment, which formed the core of the **Réseau Victoire**.

André Girard: French chief of CARTE circuit until 1943, when he was recalled to London.

Général Henri Giraud: French Army officer, captured in 1940 and escaped to lead Resistance networks, preferred by the Americans over Charles de Gaulle as leader of the Free French forces.

Dr. Josef Goetz: Second in command of the **Sicherheitsdienst** (SD) radio department in avenue Foch, initiated and ran the SD's **Funkspiel** radio game in France with radio sets captured from SOE agents.

Philippe de Gunzbourg: Code names "Philibert" and "Edgar"; French Jewish aristocrat and landowner, operative of the homegrown **Combat** Resistance network before working for George Starr.

Captain George Donovan Jones: Radio operator for ACROBAT circuit in eastern France, captured by the Germans and imprisoned with Captain Brian Dominic Rafferty.

Corporal Alfred von Kapri: SD official at 84 avenue Foch.

Noor Inayat Khan: Code name "Madeleine"; SOE radio operator in Paris, captured by the Germans and held at avenue Foch.

Sturmbannführer SS Major Hans Josef Kieffer: German SD counterespionage chief in Paris, employed the imprisoned John Starr to draw maps for the Germans at avenue Foch.

Colonel Helmut Knochen: Paris commander of the **Sicherheitsdienst des Reichsführers-SS** (Security Service of the Reichsführer-SS) and the **Sicherheitspolizei** (SIPO; security police).

Pierre Labayle: Montréjeau brewer and SOE **résistant** with PRUNUS circuit.

Roger Larribeau: Mayor of Castelnau, Castelnau-sur-l'Auvignon, early **résistant** and confidant of George Starr.

LIST OF CHARACTERS

Louis and Théo Lévy: German Jewish exile brothers, early members of the Resistance, worked undercover for George Starr. Théo ran George Starr's intelligence branch, and both brothers conducted operations disguised as German soldiers. Théo later adopted his brother's code name, "Christophe."

Captain F. Lofts: Staff officer of SOE Group B Special Training School (STS) in Beaulieu, Hampshire.

Leo Marks: SOE signals chief and author of **Between Silk and Cyanide: A Codemaker's Story, 1941–1945.**

Pierre Martin: Résistant who betrayed John Starr to the SS and Gestapo.

Alfred and Henry Newton: Prewar circus performers, John Starr's classmates at SOE training school, and agents in occupied France.

Major Gilbert Norman: Code name "Archambaud"; PHYSICIAN circuit radio operator, imprisoned with John Starr.

Tomás Guerrero Ortega: Code name "Camilo"; exiled Spanish Republican army officer, chief of **Groupe Espanol de Résistance dans le Gers,** the 35th Spanish Brigade of Guerrillas, who were armed by George Starr.

Second Lieutenant Erich Otto: SD radio department chief in Paris.

LIST OF CHARACTERS

Captain Claude Joseph Maurice Parisot: Code name "Caillou" (Stone); organizer of **résistants** under the **Organisation de Résistance de l'Armée (ORA)**, cofounder of the Armagnac Battalion, George Starr's closest friend in the Resistance.

Lieutenant Dennis Parsons: Code name "Pierrot"; radio operator sent by SOE to assist George Starr.

Maurice Pertschuk: Code name "Eugène"; Anglo French F-Section operative, organizer of SOE PRUNUS circuit.

Maréchal Philippe Pétain: World War I French Army marshal, head of the French state in Vichy from 1940 to 1944.

Master Sergeant Josef Placke: SD organizer of hoax Resistance circuit north of Paris.

Maurice Poncelet: Painter and **résistant** under Captain Maurice Parisot.

Captain Adolphe Rabinovitch: Code name "Arnaud"; F-Section radio operator for Peter Churchill's SPINDLE circuit and for George Starr.

Captain Brian Dominic Rafferty: SOE organizer for ACROBAT circuit in eastern France, captured by the Germans and imprisoned with Captain George Donovan Jones and John Starr.

LIST OF CHARACTERS

Jeanne Robert: Schoolmistress in Castelnau, Castelnau-sur-l'Auvignon, also known as Madame Delattre, Maurice Rouneau's lover and cofounder of the **Victoire** network.

President Franklin Delano Roosevelt: President of the United States from 1933 to 1945, presided over the establishment of the Office of Strategic Services (OSS), the American wartime intelligence organization trained by SOE.

Maurice Henri Rouneau: Cover name "Captain Martin Rendier," code name "Albert"; Belgian **résistant,** cofounder of the **Réseau Victoire** resistance group, brought George Starr to Castelnau-sur-l'Auvignon near Agen.

Diana Rowden: Code name "Paulette"; courier for John Starr, later captured by the Germans along with John Young.

Odette Sansom: SOE courier for the DONKEYMAN circuit, arrived in France by sea with George Starr in November 1942.

Paul Sarrette: French Army officer, Resistance deputy to Henri Sevenet.

Henri Paul Sevenet: Code name "Rodolphe"; French Army officer during the German invasion of France, later SOE agent and lieutenant to Baron Philippe de Vomécourt, SOE's VENTRILOQUIST circuit organizer.

Maurice Southgate: Code name "Hector"; George and John Starr's childhood friend, Royal Air Force pilot, and SOE organizer in occupied France.

George Reginald Starr: Code name "Hilaire"; British Army lieutenant, dispatched to France by SOE in 1942, organizer of SOE WHEELWRIGHT circuit in Gascony.

John Ashford Renshaw Starr: Code name "Emile," later "Bob"; younger brother of George Starr, sent by SOE to France in 1942 and 1943.

Second Lieutenant Ernest Vogt: SD interpreter and interrogator at 84 avenue Foch.

Philippe de Vomécourt: French liaison officer with the British Army in 1940, SOE F-Section VENTRILO-QUIST circuit organizer.

Anne-Marie Walters: Code name "Colette"; courier sent by SOE to assist George Starr.

Lieutenant Colonel Stanley H. C. Woolrych: Commandant of SOE's Special Training School (STS) at Beaulieu, Hampshire.

Lieutenant John Young: Code name "Gabriel"; radio operator for the ACROBAT circuit in eastern France, captured by the Germans with Diana Rowden.

PROLOGUE

Courage was their common badge.

MAURICE BUCKMASTER, THEY FOUGHT ALONE:
THE TRUE STORY OF SOE'S AGENTS IN
WARTIME FRANCE

━━

The German occupation of France, as Dickens wrote of the French Revolution, was the best and the worst of times. The defeat of the French Army in June 1940 challenged Frenchmen and -women to choose between courage and cowardice, rebellion and compliance, freedom and slavery. The worst collaborated with their occupier to enjoy the rewards that power afforded. The best and bravest resisted, turning for support to the ancient enemy, England. The British sent arms and, just as important, men and women to organize disparate French ranks into effective forces.

As far as the public knew, the organization providing the resources for resistance, Special Operations Executive (SOE), did not exist. And until July 16, 1940, it didn't. Britain's new prime minister, Winston Churchill, created it, as has often been quoted, to "set Europe ablaze." SOE was something new for Britain, with its vast experience of counterinsurgency in the empire. When Germany seized most of the European continent, the British backed the kind of rebels they suppressed in their colonies. SOE's models were Lawrence of Arabia, organizer of Arab irregulars against the Ottoman Turks in Syria, and the Irish Republican Army that had expelled the British from southern Ireland twenty years earlier.

SOE's London headquarters at 64 Baker Street bore the innocuous name Inter-Services Research Bureau. Staff signed the Official Secrets Act that prohibited disclosure of their activities, even to their families. The organization, which reported to the minister of economic warfare, Hugh Dalton, became a rival of the older spy agency known as the Secret Intelligence Service (SIS), or MI6. MI6 resented the intrusion of amateurs onto its turf despite the clear demarcation of objectives: MI6 gathering intelligence in secret, SOE conducting violent operations behind Axis lines. MI6's method was "hush-hush," while SOE went for "boom-boom."

Every country under Axis rule, from the Far East to France, came under a "section" of SOE that recruited, trained, and armed local populations to oppose occupation. The chief of SOE's French Section (F-Section), Colonel Maurice Buckmaster, was an astute commander and a good judge of personnel. He had studied at Britain's elite Eton College and was about to enter Oxford University when his father's sudden bankruptcy interrupted his education. He moved to France and mastered the language so well that he wrote as a journalist for the French newspaper **Le Matin**. Later, as assistant manager of the Ford Motor Company in Paris, he studied the country's road and rail networks, information that later would serve him well. Buck, as friends and associates called him, enlisted in the army at the outbreak of war, did basic training in England, and returned to France as part of the British Expeditionary Force to deter a German invasion. When the blitzkrieg invasion came, he retreated with his comrades from Dunkirk to England in June 1940 and took command of F-Section in March 1941, at the age of thirty-one. One of his operatives wrote that he was a "tall man, with a gentle, slightly self-deprecatory manner and eyes which, later in his life, suggested he had seen nearly everything. . . . [He] worked on average some eighteen hours a day." His primary concern, wrote SOE signals chief Leo Marks, "was for the safety of the agent."

The first agent that SOE smuggled into France was radio operator Georges Bégué in May 1941, less than a year after Britain evacuated its armed forces and intelligence assets from the Continent. More infiltrations, of men and women, followed by para-chute, submarine, sailboat, and Westland Lysander light aircraft that landed on occupied soil at great risk. The typical SOE team consisted of an organizer, a radio operator (W/T for wireless telegrapher), and a courier. Wireless telegraphers tapped out letters in Morse code to maintain links with London, while couriers carried messages on bicycles, buses, trains, and cars from organizers to field agents. Couriers were often women, whom the Germans scrutinized less than military-age men. A French intelligence in-spector had doubts about the arrangement: "Only the English could have sent their agents out in teams of three, consisting of two men and a girl, without taking account of the fact that it raised a question of which should be the friend of the girl." The three-member teams ran regional circuits, named for professions that were capitalized in internal commu-nications: BUTLER, FIREMAN, AUTHOR, and so on. The circuits, or networks, recruited French-men and -women to conduct sabotage against the Nazis and, more important, prepare to attack the Germans from the rear when the Allies invaded France.

Among those dispatched in secret to France were the brothers George and John Starr, whose Ameri-can father and grandfather had resettled the family in the mother country before the First World War. Theirs would be a lonely struggle, cut off from the wives and children they loved, deprived of the comradeship of a regular military unit, and on their own behind enemy lines, far from sources of supply. If captured, F-Section would not be able to protect them from inevitable torture and probable execution. The title of Buckmaster's memoir, **They Fought Alone,** encapsulates George and John Starr's experiences in occupied France. Borrowing his title for this book is both an homage to Buckmaster and acknowledgment of the Starr brothers' bravery under the most adverse conditions. It adds poignancy to John's discovery of facts that undermined Buckmaster's glowing portrayal of his section's wartime achievements.

France teemed with traitors, informers, collaborators, and opportunists liable to betray them. Some Frenchmen cooperated with the Germans out of loyalty to their idea of a France cleansed of the corruption that led to the defeat of 1940. Others curried favor with the occupier in the hope of advancement. Many used the occupation to settle old scores. The Starr brothers could rely on only a handful of men and women whose patriotism or stubbornness made them risk savage torture, summary execution, or slow, humiliating, and anonymous death in concentration camps.

The occupation set French against French as brutally as had the Revolution, Dickens's age of wisdom and age of foolishness. The Armistice that France signed with Germany on June 22, 1940, partitioned

the country along a Line of Demarcation into regions of direct German occupation in the north
and an autonomous French regime in the south, the
so-called **Zone Libre,** or Free Zone, with its capital
at Vichy. The physical separation was only one of
many factors dividing the French after their defeat.
The others were political, ideological, and personal.
Navigating the ambiguous political landscape would
be as important to the Starr brothers' survival and
success as finding safe houses, caches for weapons,
and locations for shortwave radio transmitters.

"In the eyes of the French people," wrote Olivier
Wieviorka, one of the finest French historians of the
Resistance, "the regime certainly enjoyed a strong
legitimacy." France's Third Republic had voted itself
out of existence on July 10, 1940, and handed power
to the First World War "hero of Verdun," the aged
Maréchal Philippe Pétain. "Joining the resistance
therefore amounted to stepping outside the law, a
risk that Dutch, Belgian, and Norwegian citizens
did not face, since their governments had taken exile
in London," wrote Wieviorka. The United States
recognized the Pétain regime and appointed a senior
naval officer, Admiral William D. Leahy, as its ambassador to Vichy. Many Frenchmen believed that
fidelity to France demanded allegiance to the legal
government. Patriots who responded to the appeal
on July 18, 1940, from French general Charles de
Gaulle in London "to listen to my voice and follow

me" were rare. Indeed, most of France was unable to hear the general's broadcast. The French Army convicted de Gaulle in absentia of treason and sentenced him to death. Vichy declared its underground opponents "terrorists," subject to the death penalty.

The French people thus fell into three categories: **résistants,** who fought the Nazis and the Vichy regime; **collabos,** who worked with Germany and Vichy; and the great majority, **attentistes,** who waited to see who would win. The obvious pool of potential **résistants,** more than 1.5 million of the nation's young men with military experience, languished in German prisoner of war camps. SOE instead looked for support among the minority who had evaded capture or had not served in the army. Complicating matters were rivalries among the many Resistance movements. Some were loyal to de Gaulle. Others favored another French general named Henri Giraud, who escaped from a German prisoner of war camp to become America's preferred leader over de Gaulle, whom President Franklin D. Roosevelt detested. Many belonged to organizations affiliated with the Communist Party, which did not support resistance until Hitler attacked its Soviet sponsor in June 1941. There were also socialists, royalists, and Freemasons. Many factions stole weapons from one another, and they clashed violently over ideology, strategy, and territory.

While British agents like George and John Starr

learned how to kill, training schools could not teach them whom to trust. They had to understand the sentiments of the French and to rely on their feeling for human beings more than on anything in SOE's instruction manuals. Their lives and the fate of the Resistance depended on it.

ONE

An Unexpected Encounter

**It was no use trying to do things by the book.
There was no book.**

MAURICE BUCKMASTER

════

In late October 1942, autumn squalls and the impending Allied invasion of French North Africa, Operation Torch, confined ships in Britain's Gibraltar naval base to port. The Royal Navy interrupted the moratorium on Thursday, October 29, for an operation of such high priority that it had to go ahead—regardless of storms and the threat of attack by German U-boats. At eight thirty that night, a small sailing craft called the **Seadog** cruised out of Gibraltar's harbor with an unlikely assortment of British, French, and Italian passengers. Each of them, unknown to the crew and for the most part to one another, had an **ordre de mission** from London to spread throughout Adolf Hitler's Fortress Europe and galvanize nascent networks of resistance. They looked like ordinary men and women in their French-made civilian clothes, but they were newly trained experts in the black arts of assassination, sabotage, armed and unarmed combat, explosives, safecracking, burglary, counterfeiting, and cryptography. All had officers' commissions in the British armed forces, in the vain hope that the Germans would treat them according to the Geneva Conventions if they were captured. Half of them, their instructors had warned, were unlikely to return.

On Monday night, November 2, whitecaps lashed the **Seadog**'s wooden hull, hurling the flimsy craft from wave to soaring wave. Lightning flared in the night sky, and thunder rocked every timber. Belowdecks, a half-American, half-British passenger was plaguing the radio operator: where was his message from London? The man was thirty-eight-year-old Lieutenant George Reginald Starr, who seemed certain SOE would abort his mission. No one liked to argue with George. His wrestler's physique made him appear larger than his five feet six inches. Dark chestnut hair, light brown eyes, ruddy complexion, and callused hands gave him the look of a miner, yet he spoke like a gentleman. He was both. After leaving a strict Anglican boys' boarding school, Ardingly College in Sussex, at the age of sixteen, he had labored underground for years in the Shropshire coal mines to qualify as a mining engineer.

That night, George sensed something amiss, and he wanted out. Anything but a coward, he was one of the last Britons to make it out of Belgium ahead of the invading Germans in May 1940. He had outpaced younger men during SOE's elite commando course in the Scottish Highlands, and he overcame a lifelong fear of heights to make his first parachute jump. His queasy gut had nothing to do with fear or seasickness. "It was more than a hunch," he said. "It saved me many, many times. If I'm going to do something and my stomach goes funny, then I don't do it." He asked the ship's radioman again and again for a communiqué canceling the operation and ordering **Seadog** back to Gibraltar.

The **Seadog**'s skipper, Polish naval lieutenant Jan Buchowski, had weathered worse storms in seven months of evading German and Italian warships in the western Mediterranean Sea. In the absence of orders for George Starr and the others to abandon their missions, he sailed on toward France. He and his crew were, in the words of a Polish army general, "too rough even for the Polish navy." Buchowski detested the Germans, not only for occupying his country but also for murdering his entire family. His service with Britain's Royal Navy started with the rescue of Polish soldiers from France during the German conquest of June 1940, and since April 1942 Buchowski had run a clandestine ferry between Britain's Gibraltar colony and the French coast, delivering secret agents and tons of equipment to France and returning with agents at the ends of their assignments. **Seadog** was a 20-ton, 47-foot Mediterranean felucca, similar in shape to the classic lateen-rigged feluccas that plied the River Nile. Despite overcrowding and engines that were prone to break down, their disguise as a commercial trawler had so far spared them inspection by German, Italian, and Vichy French patrols. Passengers complained of the stench, residue of the ship's prewar service as a sardine trawler. George, although longing to see France for the first time since Germany occupied it over two years before, did not regard the **Seadog** as an ideal mode of transport: "It turned every way but upside down. It was rough. You couldn't stay there, the stern. I found a good place in the galley. I cooked myself bacon and eggs all the time." His voracious appetite staved off nausea, but it did nothing for his anxiety.

Everything in his baggage was Belgian or French, down to the razor and scraggly shaving brush. His old shoes were Belgian made, and a French tailor in London had sewn his wool suit. His communications equipment was concealed in cylindrical metal containers, along with explosives and supplies weighing 1,000 pounds. His wallet contained 100,000 French francs, equivalent to £500 or $2,500, and a forged identity card in the name of Serge Watremez. Watremez had been George's classmate during his youth in the Loire Valley and he had faith that the family, if questioned, would vouch for him. George's code name was "Hilaire." Making sure that nothing British remained in his bags before departing Gibraltar, he had discarded a gold cigarette case that Colonel Buckmaster had given him. Most agents carried cyanide to swallow in the event of capture, but George had rejected the poison with the words "My family motto is **live** in hope."

George's "Final Instructions," dated October 12, 1942, ordered him to contact agent "Rodolphe" after his arrival in France: "Rodolphe is expecting you. He will see that you are safely installed, attend to the cashing of your first food coupons and give you all the necessary information as to local conditions."

"Rodolphe" was Henri Paul Sevenet, lieutenant to SOE's VENTRILOQUIST circuit organizer, Baron Philippe de Vomécourt. SOE chiefs in London knew Vomécourt, who had served as the French liaison officer with the British Army in May 1940. After escaping in 1940 on the last ship to England from Cherbourg, he joined the newly formed SOE and returned to France. He recruited Henri Sevenet, his brother's godson, in early 1941. Sevenet, whose personnel file described him as "an extremely courageous officer," had fought in the regular army during the German invasion of France and escaped twice from German captivity, the second time with de Gaulle's rival, Général Henri Giraud. The five-feet-ten-inch Frenchman's Charlie Chaplin moustache and thick glasses gave him the look of a professor, but he was a ruthless clandestine operator whom the Gestapo was doing its best to apprehend.

At this time, all that George knew about Sevenet was his code name, "Rodolphe." Could he be trusted? Was his organization secure? It had to be for George to achieve his objective: "Prepare a widespread underground organization ready to strike hard when we give the signal."

The other agents on **Seadog** were, like George, amateurs when it came to intelligence work. One was Lieutenant Marcus Reginald Bloom, a likable and flamboyant Jewish businessman from the north London suburb of Tottenham. The others were Australian Thomas Groome, Frenchman Alfred Maurice Schouten, Italian Giacomino Giovanni Sarfatti, and three women, Marie-Thérèse Le Chêne, Mary Katherine Herbert, and Odette Sansom.

George took a dislike to Odette Sansom before the **Seadog** set sail. "I swear I had the surprise of my life," he said of the journey from Glasgow. "I was put in charge of three bloody women." Sansom was a beautiful young woman, whose long, shapely legs, bright brown eyes, and coquettish charm attracted most of the men she met. George, however, was not one of them. His antipathy may have grown on **Seadog,** where he and Odette spent long hours in the galley—George cooking and Odette cleaning.

Sansom was born Odette Marie Céline Brailly in Amiens, northeastern France, on April 28, 1912. Her father died while serving as an army sergeant in the First World War. Plagued by ill health, Odette went blind at the age of seven for a few years, then suffered a bout of rheumatic fever. Her mother moved to the Normandy coast in 1925 to give her the benefit of sea air. In 1932, by then a healthy and attractive twenty-year-old with dark, wavy hair, Odette married Englishman Roy Sansom. They moved to London and had three daughters. Sansom joined the army in 1939 and, like Odette's father, became a sergeant. While her husband was away on military service in October 1940, Odette fled the German bombardment of London with her mother and daughters to a tiny village in rural Somerset. There she heard a BBC broadcast in 1942 appealing for photographs, including holiday snapshots, of the French coast for intelligence purposes. Listeners were asked to write to "The Admiralty, London, S.W.1.", but Odette sent her letter by mistake to "The War Office, London, W." This led to an interview with an SOE F-Section recruiter, and then an assignment with SOE. She placed her daughters in a Catholic convent in Essex and trained in Scotland and southern England, but she suffered a concussion on her last practice parachute jump. To avoid injuring her again, SOE dispatched her on one of the Royal Air Force's (RAF) Lysander light aircraft to deposit her on a secret field in France. SOE was sending her as a courier to the DONKEYMAN circuit in Auxerre, Burgundy. Shortly after takeoff, her Lysander crashed in England, almost killing her. Determined to proceed, Sansom cruised from Glasgow to Gibraltar on the troopship that carried George.

On the morning of November 3, the skies cleared and **Seadog** sailed northeast toward the Riviera resort of Cassis. The unusual topography between Cassis and the port city of Marseille made it ideal for clandestine operations. Fingers of land jutted into the sea, sheer limestone cliffs protected inland waterways from the wind, and pine forests obscured the view from the ridges. The French called the narrow bays **calanques,** the Corsican word for inlets. Buchowski's preferred **calanque,** one of the three largest, was Port-Miou, where he had made previous drops. It lay two miles west of Cassis, far enough from town to avoid detection, yet within walking distance of safe houses and the train station. As **Seadog** neared Cassis, the crew switched the ensign from Spanish to French. The shore hove into view at nightfall.

"Arriving at the position on 3 November at 2130 hrs," Buchowski wrote in the ship's log, "I transferred command to [Captain] Pohorecki and made my way via the dinghy together with two other people

16

to the Port-Miou calanque. After an hour's searching the shoreline, I found the agents, who had not been waiting at the position agreed, and we exchanged the correct signals." The reception party's leader, André Marsac of the CARTE resistance circuit, welcomed the Pole with a bottle of whisky.

Buchowski returned to the **Seadog,** where the waiting agents lowered themselves into the skiff. They rowed into the **calanque,** passing little jetties of fishing boats and pleasure craft. Almost a mile upstream, the Resistance reception committee was waiting on the bank. One by one, the agents disembarked from the bobbing rowboat.

"We land, and someone gives me a hand up off the rocky shore," George recalled. "It's me own brother."

John Ashford Renshaw Starr gazed into the face of the man beside him on the rocks. It was his brother. Although both men were of short stature, John five feet five and George five feet six, they were physical opposites. John was slim and lithe, George stocky and well muscled. John was more handsome, with a fair complexion, light brown hair, and blue-gray eyes. George's rough features contrasted with his brother's delicate profile. John was the charmer, often a trait of second sons competing for parental affection. George was a man of action, not words. Yet both brothers were outstanding athletes, strong and dexterous, who shared a love of good food and wine. Their parents' only children, they had been close all their lives. John had not seen George since he left England three months earlier, on August 27, to parachute into France. This chance meeting on a French waterway between agents "Hilaire" and "Emile," John's code name at the time, was the first either knew of the other's presence in the country.

"Are you going now?" George asked. John thrust something into his brother's hand, saying, "Here's my ration card. It might come in useful." He jumped into the dinghy with five other men and rowed back to **Seadog**.

"And that was all," George recounted. "He got on the boat and went."

Lieutenant Buchowski recorded in the ship's log: "0200 hrs the operation was completed. We moved away from the shore and set our course for the next operation point."

As the **Seadog** sailed to base with a galley short of food, John grew hungrier by the day. George mused years later that his younger brother reproached him, "It was your fault, because you've eaten too much."

Buchowski docked in Gibraltar on November 13, ten days after depositing one Starr brother and ex-filtrating the other, and the next day John flew to England. His first meeting in London was with Colonel Buckmaster at his Orchard Court office in

London's Portman Square, near SOE headquarters. John gave Buck his view on F-Section's networks in France's so-called Free Zone: they were a mess. The group in which London placed its trust, CARTE, was little more than a fiction concocted by a Frenchman named André Girard. Girard was a veteran soldier and committed patriot, but there was little evidence to support his contention that the hundred thousand soldiers of the Armistice Army that Germany had permitted Vichy to maintain for internal security would rise up at his command. Some of the agents John had met, and on whom his brother would have to rely, were doing more to dominate the circuit than to challenge the Germans.

Although disenchanted with F-Section's field operations, John volunteered to return to France and try again. Before sending him to Loch Morar in Scotland for refresher commando retraining, Buckmaster granted him a short leave to visit his family in Newcastle-under-Lyme, Staffordshire. Britain's Official Secrets Act did not permit John to tell his mother and father that he had seen their other son in France, a difficult fact to conceal in a family as close as the Starrs.

TWO

Called to the Colors

Most of our agents were ordinary men and
women and it was their ability to maintain
that appearance of ordinariness while
performing extraordinary actions which most
distinguish them.

MAURICE BUCKMASTER

=====

The Starrs descended from American pioneer stock, having left England for the New
World, in George Starr's words, "not on
the **Mayflower**, but not long afterwards." In 1635, the
ship **Hercules** carried Dr. Comfort Starr, a sur-
geon and treasurer of Canterbury Cathedral, with
his wife and children to Massachusetts Bay Colony.
Dr. Starr donated land to build Harvard College
and was laid to rest in its Old Burial Ground. His
son, also named Comfort, was one of five signatories

of Harvard's Charter of 1650. Succeeding genera-
tions of Starrs gave America frontiersmen, soldiers,
industrialists, physicians, and businessmen.

In 1899, two and a half centuries after Comfort Starr settled in Massachusetts, his descendant
George Oscar Starr sailed back to England as the
manager of the Barnum & Bailey Circus. His son,
Alfred Demarest Starr, accompanied him as the
chief bookkeeper. In London, the five-feet-three-
inch bookkeeper met the daughter of an engineer
he commissioned to construct a metal safety curtain for performances in the Olympia auditorium.
She was Ethel Jemima Renshaw, whose father's firm
went on to manufacture rolling stock for the train
that carried the circus and its wild animals around
Europe. Alfred and Ethel married on October 16,
1902, in Stoke-on-Trent, Staffordshire. Buffalo Bill
Cody and the cowboy and Indian stars of his Wild
West show were among the witnesses.

The couple's first child, George Reginald Starr,
was born on April 6, 1904, in London. The boy
spent his earliest years on the Continent with Barnum & Bailey and then with Buffalo Bill's troupe.
He would later boast about his wartime exploits,
"People say I got the cowboy and Indian stuff from
Buffalo Bill's Wild West show. Up to a point, you
need showmanship in a job like that." One consequence of George's Continental infancy was a lifelong phobia of heights, acquired when his parents

took him at age two to the top of the Eiffel Tower. The family moved back to England after the elder George Starr became manager of the Crystal Palace exhibition center in south London. Alfred and Ethel's second son, John Ashford Renshaw Starr, was born in Heaton Moor, Lancashire, on August 6, 1908. Alfred went to work for his father at the Crystal Palace for a few years until he found a job managing a factory in France.

George and John studied in France at the Lycée Vendôme and went on to board at Ardingly College. Although George finished before John started at the Sussex school, differences in their characters emerged during their education. Rugged older brother George was practical and excelled at the sciences, while John was a dreamer who loved painting and music. The family believed John was his mother's favorite. Both boys became corporals in the school's officer training corps, but only George became corps bugler.

George left school to work underground in the Shropshire coal mines, an apprenticeship that introduced him to hardworking men. "Those men, they were salt of the earth," he said. "Those men made me a man." Then came an engineering degree from the Royal School of Mines at London's Imperial College and employment with Mavor & Coulson of Glasgow. The company sent him to install mining equipment in Britain, Tunisia, Belgium, and Spain, and on the side he provided intelligence to MI6. George at this time was briefly married to a French actress, a marriage that lasted only a year. It was in Spain that he met Pilar Canudos Ristol, a dark-eyed ingénue of undeniable beauty and self-confidence. Her father was the director of the local social club in Manresa, about forty miles from Barcelona, near the mine where George was working. They wed in 1934 and moved to Brussels. Two children, Georgina and Alfred, came soon afterward.

John studied art in London and Paris, where he made his living drawing advertising posters for Agence Yves Alexandre Publicité. Occasionally visiting his brother over the border in Belgium, he led the charmed life of a playboy in interwar Paris. He sported a close-cropped, full moustache, and his hobbies were fast cars, tennis, and fishing. He married a Frenchwoman named Michelle Vergetas from Rouen on June 30, 1934, and they settled into a flat in the Paris suburb of Issy-les-Moulineaux. Two years later, they had a baby girl and named her for John's mother, Ethel.

While George was working in Brussels for Mavor & Coulson, General Francisco Franco led troops from Morocco into Spain to crush the Republic. The civil war bled Spain and brought fascist Italy and Nazi Germany in on Franco's side, while the democracies of the West allowed Spain's elected government to lose more and more territory. Pilar's family sided with Franco. George recalled, "During the civil war, our house was like a fairground with people arriving from one side and staying with us and going back to the other side. Obviously, it was one-way traffic. There weren't many Reds coming."

In September 1938, after British prime minister Neville Chamberlain and French premier Edouard Daladier ceded Czechoslovakia's Sudetenland to Adolf Hitler at Munich, George and John hastened to volunteer for the Royal Air Force. The RAF rejected them on the grounds that their father was an American citizen. Instead, George joined the British Army in Belgium, and John did the same in Paris.

Franco's forces defeated the Republic in May 1939. George, who called the rightist victory "the liberation of Spain," went there soon afterward. He carried his nine-month-old son, Alfred, on foot from France over the Pyrenees. They arrived just in time for Pilar's father to see his grandson, and the old man died the next day.

George and his family were back in Brussels on September 2, 1939, when Britain and France declared war on Germany. "We heard Chamberlain tell us we were at war," George said, "and we went out to play cricket." Pilar took Georgina and Alfred, then aged two and one, back to her family in Manresa. When the static "phony war" produced no battles, she returned to George.

In Paris, the army delayed John's enlistment. Michelle and baby daughter, Ethel, went to live with his parents in Newcastle-under-Lyme. In early 1940, the army posted John first to the King's Own Scottish Borderers Regiment in Rouen before transferring him to the Field Security Police (FSP). With little for him to do in the FSP, he carried on with his work as a commercial artist.

The fighting war erupted on May 10, 1940, while George was working deep below the earth's surface in a coal mine in Liège, Belgium. Luftwaffe aircraft bombed the city, a prelude to the blitzkrieg invasion of Belgium by the German Army, the Wehrmacht. "I had been on the night [shift] and came out at about half past four in the morning," he recalled. "I was in the washroom, and all hell broke loose." He rushed back to Brussels, where Pilar told him the British Embassy wanted him urgently. The embassy sent Pilar and the two children to Paris. From there, she took the children to her mother's house in Manresa. George remained in Brussels at the British Embassy, which issued him a sergeant's uniform to work with Phantom, a battlefield intelligence unit. The embassy staff evacuated, George said, "after showing me the direct line to Downing Street and left me in sole charge." A British admiral knocked at the door and asked, "Where's the embassy staff?" George answered, "You're looking at it." When the German Sixth Army overran Brussels on May 17, George blew up the radio and the rest of the embassy's equipment before racing a truck westward through artillery barrages to Dunkirk. The retreat of British forces from France began the next day, and George boarded a ship across the Channel.

As the German invaders spread from Holland and Belgium to northern France, John stayed behind with the FSP. His unit gathered frontline intelligence for commanders who, amid the Wehrmacht's lightning conquest, had no chance to use it. The Germans overran the FSP in the town of Nantes, and John seized a motorcycle for a mad race to the Atlantic port of Saint-Nazaire in time for the last ship to England.

The defeat of Belgium and France left the Starr family divided. Pilar and her two children were in Spain. Michelle and her daughter were living with Alfred and Ethel in the north of England. The brothers made it to London, having lost their homes and livelihoods on the Continent. They determined to get both back.

The army granted Sergeant George Starr home leave after his evacuation from Dunkirk. He arrived at his parents' house in Newcastle-under-Lyme on June 17, 1940. The new head of the French government, Maréchal Philippe Pétain, was speaking on the radio to announce his country's capitulation to Germany and to request an armistice. It was a heartrending moment for France's friends to hear the eighty-four-year-old newly appointed head of France's government say, "I spoke last night with the enemy and asked him if he is ready to seek with us, soldier to soldier, after the honorable fight, the means to put an end to the hostilities." George recalled his father's reaction:

I remember him sitting there listening to it, and he turned to me. There were tears running down his eyes. And he said to me, "You know, they'll never forgive us. They'll never forgive us for this, the French." I said, "What do you mean **us**?" I used to pull his leg a bit about being an American.

Alfred Starr applied for British nationality and volunteered for civil defense work. His hope was that his native country would rescue France and Britain as it had in 1917. In 1940, that prospect was unlikely.

George reported for duty in London, where his unit, Phantom, became General Headquarters Liaison Regiment. His first assignment involved overseeing carrier pigeons in a loft beside St. James's Park. The birds took messages to and from France, a measure of the dearth of British intelligence in German-occupied Europe. Serving with Sergeant Starr were the actor David Niven, Sir Jakie Astor, and Hugh Fraser, brother of famed commando officer Lord Lovat.

The army posted John to the FSP training base in Winchester, where he employed his artist's skills drawing war propaganda posters and, unofficially, portraits of senior officers. It was there that the new and secret government organization, SOE, approached him, as it did others with military experience and language skills, to infiltrate occupied Europe and attack the Germans from the rear.

John trained at SOE's irregular warfare school at Wanborough Manor, Surrey, in early 1941. His classmates included the brothers Alfred and Henry Newton, entertainers who had learned French touring the Continent like the Starr family. Theirs was a vigorous course of physical exercise, martial arts, secret codes, and bomb making. Students took commando training at Arisaig in the Scottish Highlands and advanced instruction in the dark arts at Beaulieu, the Montagu family estate in Hampshire's New Forest. His superiors awarded John top marks and a second lieutenant's commission.

Lieutenant John Starr recommended two other French speakers to SOE: his brother and a childhood friend named Maurice Southgate, who had joined the RAF in Paris on the day war was declared in September 1939. The Starr and Southgate families had been close for years. "His father and mother were very, very old friends of my father and mother," recalled George. "I used to call his father uncle." Southgate was born in 1913 in Paris, where as an adult he managed an upholstery factory. Like John Starr, Southgate was evacuated from Saint-Nazaire in June 1940. His escape, however, was not as fortunate as John's. German dive bombers sank his ship, **Lancastria,** with the loss of more than 3,000 troops and sailors. Southgate managed to swim until another vessel rescued him and brought him with 2,446 other survivors to England. Since then, he had been flying RAF bombing raids over occupied France.

George received orders to report to room 304 of the Hotel Victoria on Northumberland Avenue near Trafalgar Square. "I go in there," he said, "dirty old room with a broken-down table and a couple of broken-down chairs and an officer sitting behind the table." The officer, who did not give his name, was Captain Selwyn Jepson. His interviews determined who qualified for clandestine service in occupied France. Jepson, himself a fluent French speaker, asked George, as he had John a few months earlier, whether he spoke the language. George answered in the affirmative, and Jepson told him, "You're going back to France, you are." George looked doubtful and, demonstrating the caution that would characterize his subsequent military career, he set a condition: he would work anywhere except Vendôme or the Belgian frontier, where old acquaintances might recognize him.

While waiting for his SOE assignment, George continued to work with the carrier pigeons in St. James's Park. In July 1942, the War Office promoted him from sergeant to second lieutenant and issued him vouchers for an officer's uniform. Back at the Liaison Regiment barracks, Sir Jakie Astor saw the new uniform and said, "I see you're an officer and a gentleman." George answered, "I may be an officer, but I've always been a gentleman."

The following Monday morning, SOE training began. Buckmaster described the course, listing "[t]he use of codes, unarmed combat, fieldcraft, shooting, sabotage (which included the use of explosive and the knowledge of where to use it to inflict the maximum damage on specified targets), methods of contact, psychological tests" as components of the curriculum. SOE tried to teach the veteran coal miner to handle dynamite, but, George said, "I taught the instructors in England a lot about explosives." George graduated to commando training at Loch Morar, where among other skills he learned to sail. Despite his acrophobia, he was forced to parachute from an aircraft near Manchester. In Cardiff, Wales, he practiced surveillance with such determination that the police detained him on suspicion of espionage.

John, who had completed the same course three

and a half months earlier, gave his brother tips that SOE felt he should have kept to himself. Lance Sergeant Ree wrote in George's training report on July 7, 1942, "He brought his brother to the Rendezvous at Euston [station]. The conducting officer expressed his disapproval and he went away." On July 21, Sergeant Ree added that John had provided George "with plenty of material" about training. Ree cautioned George about "the danger of giving away to other students, information about the course and the organisation which he had had from his brother." To Ree, George was "a self-confident know-all," but also, he admitted, "quite reliable."

Lieutenant John Starr turned thirty-four on August 6, 1942. F-Section considered him ready for deployment in France, where his mission was to buy and store food supplies in the south to feed Resistance bands. Colonel Buckmaster, who usually met agents for a final briefing before sending them into the field, offered this advice: "If you are arrested, try to last out forty-eight hours." Two days would give his colleagues time to evade arrest, but SOE could not determine which of its personnel could withstand forty-eight hours of pain. Captured agents would have to discover that for themselves.

Under the full moon of August 28, 1942, a Halifax heavy bomber of RAF 138 Squadron flew John from Tempsford Airfield in Bedfordshire across the English Channel. His would be a "blind jump," with no one to receive and assist him on the ground. Patches of farmland around the Rhône Valley town of Valence in Vichy's Unoccupied Zone appeared below, and John dropped from the plane. As he descended, wind blew him over a farmhouse. He narrowly avoided crashing into it by maneuvering into a forest. His parachute caught some high tree branches, and he dangled until he cut himself free and fell to the ground. The cylinder of supplies that followed him down proved too heavy to carry any distance, so he buried it with his parachute under a haystack. Then came a five-mile walk to Valence, where he took trains another two hundred miles south, first to Marseille and then to the Mediterranean resort of Cannes. In the Cannes station, where Vichy police were inspecting passengers, John attached himself to a large family in order to walk out undetected.

His destination was the Baron Henri Ravel de Malval's sumptuous Villa Isabelle in the Route de Fréjus on Cannes' western outskirts, where he would be met by one of SOE's first organizers in France, Peter Churchill. Churchill had worked with Malval early in the war, while Malval was serving as the French military attaché in London. When he returned to France as a rare **résistant** of "the first hour," he lent Churchill the villa as his base in the south of France.

Thirty-three-year-old Captain Churchill, code name "Raoul," was an experienced operative on his third mission. His résumé was impressive: star athlete, fluent in five languages, and graduate in modern languages from Cambridge University. Buckmaster's admiration was unconcealed: "Churchill was here, there and everywhere—testing methods of introducing our men into France, recruiting new agents and encouraging existing ones—in short, doing the work of ten men." With his round, horn-rimmed glasses and slim physique, Churchill could pass for an innocuous accountant, a useful cover for a secret agent. He was not, as some colleagues presumed, related to Prime Minister Winston Churchill.

When John arrived, no one met him at the villa. He waited in the garden for hours until, at midnight, Churchill and another F-Section officer, Nicholas Bodington, appeared at the gates. "What the hell are you doing here?" Churchill asked. He and Bodington had gone to the station to meet him, but John's deft evasion of the police had deceived the two Britons as well.

For the next week, John sunbathed by the villa's swimming pool to replace his telltale London pallor with a healthy southern tan. When his color was right, CARTE circuit chief André Girard moved him to another safe house in the nearby coastal village of Antibes. The landlady there seemed anything but safe when she introduced him to her neighbors: "He's an Englishman. He came by parachute." His hosts shared their rations with him, although they had little to spare. When he mentioned that he had concealed food in a container near Valence, they took him there by train to retrieve it, only to dig up the canister and see English labels on the food tins. That, as John would learn, was only one of SOE's many obvious errors.

After John arrived in Antibes, he sensed that his new location was not secure. There was a bench opposite where he was staying, and John began to see the same man there every day, watching the house. A police officer, a gendarme, who somehow knew that John was a British agent, warned him that his place was about to be raided. John told his hosts, who sent their British-branded food away in a truck, and moved to the Plage de la Garoupe, made famous in the 1920s by F. Scott Fitzgerald, beside Cap d'Antibes. Like Poe's "Purloined Letter," John hid in plain sight, erecting an easel on the beach promenade and painting seascapes. A loud pink shirt, bright yellow scarf, espadrilles, and unkempt hair marked him as a **zazou**. The beatniks of their era, **zazous** were countercultural youths with a passion for American jazz.

The rest of the time, he carried out his orders to negotiate the purchase of large quantities of wheat, chocolate, dried bananas, and a flock of sheep to store for Resistance fighters. In Marseille, underworld figures gave him French francs to finance his operations in exchange for pounds sterling that SOE deposited in their London accounts. A French Resistance report observed that, while he made contacts to obtain provisions in "significant quantities," his role as adviser made it impossible for him to purchase the goods. However, the report concluded, "He accomplished this mission with great diplomacy and much tact."

SOE approved his work, as evidenced by his promotion from second lieutenant to lieutenant on September 1. At the end of the month, he asked London to send a doll to his daughter, Ethel, for her sixth birthday. The message came back, "Doll sent."

John, by now disillusioned, complained to Churchill that he was wasting his time. The CARTE circuit barely existed, and the **résistants** did not need a food expert. He had not come to France for an easy life, but to wage a struggle against the Nazis. It was time to leave. Churchill later recalled, "London let him down by not authorising payments." Churchill asked John to take reports on CARTE to London and arranged for his passage to Gibraltar. Then, at Port-Miou early on the morning of November 4, John chanced upon his brother. He would tell London what was happening in France, but there was no time to warn George.

After John left the Port-Miou **calanque, résistants** carried George Starr's supply containers to a secret cache near Marseille. The thousand pounds of explosives and equipment included an S-Phone and a Eureka homing device. S-Phones enabled direct voice communication with aircraft or ships along a straight beam that was difficult for the Germans to monitor. Unlike shortwave transmitters sending dots and dashes of Morse code, S-Phones allowed an agent's voice to be recognized and verified. The Eureka was a device that transmitted an invisible beacon to an aircraft's Rebecca receiver for pilots to follow to drop zones in any weather. George's equipment did not include a shortwave wireless transmitter. This radio device, packed into a small suitcase, was standard issue for all F-Section teams and the only means for maintaining regular contact with London and ordering airdrops of supplies. F-Section expected the DETECTIVE circuit to provide him a radio when he went to Lyon.

George and his fellow agents followed André Marsac from the shore uphill through a dense forest of umbrella pines to a safe house in Cassis. They slept for three hours. "We had at six in the morning to go to the station," George recalled. The railway cashier, like George, was barely awake. Forgetting his training and revealing what everyone called his atrocious French accent, he asked for a ticket to Cannes. But he pronounced it like Caen, a city at the opposite end of France in Normandy. George recalled the man's response: "You don't want to go there. That's in the Occupied Zone. You want to go to **Cannes** [pronounced **Cahn**]."

In Cannes, Peter Churchill met the agents at a beauty parlor run by a **résistante**. The men from the **Seadog** moved into the Villa Isabelle, where John Starr had spent his first week the previous August acquiring a suntan, and the three female agents stayed at the Villa Augusta. Together, the new arrivals discussed with Churchill how to reach their destinations in the south or the German-occupied north. George, however, was not going anywhere. Remembering his feeling of unease during the trip over, he took Churchill aside and asked about the setup in Lyon at the northern fringe of the Unoccupied Zone. Churchill said a source in Marseille might have information and he could arrange for George to meet him, but he asked George to take Odette Sansom along. Churchill explained, "I want her to get into the swim of things and make some contacts for me."

On November 6, George and Sansom boarded a train for a 120-mile journey west to Marseille. In the train station, she claimed, a German soldier scrutinized her identity papers but allowed her to pass. At six o'clock that evening, she met with Marsac in a café near the terminal. However, he had forgotten to bring Churchill's documents. Marsac took her to his apartment, but the nightly curfew was in force by the time he found the papers. For her safety, she said, Marsac lodged her in a brothel whose private rooms the Germans did not check closely.

George told a different story of their trip to Marseille. Unlike Sansom, he saw no Germans at the station, which accorded with the fact that Marseille was in the Vichy-ruled Unoccupied Zone. After they arrived, George searched out a hotel for the night. At the hotel reception desk, one story above the ground floor, he requested separate rooms. The receptionists gazed at the attractive young woman beside him, and George repeated, "**Two** rooms." Sansom's room was near the lobby and George's on the third floor at the rear. When they met downstairs to go out to dinner, she demanded to know why they had separate rooms. "Look, chum," he replied, "even in France brothers and sisters don't share a room to my knowledge."

After dinner, they walked through the city with its beautiful Old Port glimmering in the darkness before returning to the hotel. In George's account, Sansom was wearing "one of these organdy blouses that were damn near transparent, and it buttoned all the way down the back." He claimed that she led him to her room and asked, "Aren't you coming in to undo my blouse for me?" He snapped, "You buttoned it up. You can unbutton it, chum." When he called at her room for breakfast, she told him to come in. "There she was," he said. "She hadn't got the blouse on or anything. She said, 'Won't you help me to get dressed?' I said, 'Look, chum. You've got the wrong man.' And I walked out."

George was as prudent as he was prudish. Although Pilar Starr lived just over the Spanish border with their daughter and son and Odette's husband was serving in the British Army, his focus was on security. Affairs between agents opened them to pressure if they were captured, with one liable to say anything to save the other.

More important for George than Odette, though, was his rendezvous with Peter Churchill's Marseille contact. The source confirmed the "hunch" that had plagued George on the **Seadog**: Vichy police had penetrated the circuit to which George had been assigned in Lyon. Five days before George left Gibraltar, on October 24, police captured its British radio operator, Brian Stonehouse, and Blanche Charlet, a French courier trained by SOE in Britain. "Lyon was blown sky high, and everybody was on the run," George said. "The Germans were waiting for me with a password and everything else." His queasy stomach had saved his life.

George and Sansom returned to Cannes on the coastal train via Toulon, passing for local French travelers to deceive suspicious French gendarmes. George remembered their arrival:

And we got out of the train at around ten at night, and she went through the side gate like you do into this courtyard. Peter Churchill was waiting for her. She threw herself in his arms and [made] all sorts of advances. God, she was a dreadful lady.

On November 8, American and British forces invaded French Morocco and Algeria in Operation Torch. When the senior French commander in Algeria agreed to an armistice with the Allies, the Germans responded by occupying southern France. They awarded their Italian allies the island of Corsica and the southeastern Mediterranean coast, including Cannes. George was there when the Italians arrived on November 11: "I remember one morning we woke up and the Italians had landed and marched into Cannes. I watched them through the window. We were on the main road. The Italians were in lorries, playing mandolins."

After the parade, George and three other agents left the Villa Isabelle for lunch at a small restaurant down the coast. "There were four of us, and we were having a meal. A great car came driving up. An Italian officer, little bloke, dressed up, medals all over him, came in to have a meal with his chauffeur." The Italians were too busy celebrating their unopposed victory to notice the British saboteurs in their midst.

As CARTE circuit chief, André Girard was gathering the names, addresses, and other details of more than two hundred potential Resistance sympathizers to help SOE recruit operatives. He gave the list to Marsac to deliver, but on the train from Marseille to Paris, Marsac fell asleep. When he woke, the case containing the list was gone. Buckmaster lamented later that "massive arrests followed." SOE, dissatisfied with Girard's record, would recall him to London in February 1943. Girard, who felt the British had betrayed him, ended his short Resistance career by immigrating to the United States.

Henri Sevenet, the "Rodolphe" in George's orders, traveled to Marseille searching for a wireless operator to replace the captured Brian Stonehouse. Learning that his new deputy, agent "Hilaire," had arrived in France, Sevenet found George in Cannes on November 12 and offered him an alternative to the blown Lyon operation. Dedicated but unarmed **résistants** in the town of Agen in southwest France needed an organizer, trainer, and arms supplier. Agen was in the heart of Gascony, a sparsely populated region of hills, rivers, and forests bordering Spain's Pyrenees to the south and the Atlantic Ocean to the west. The Gascons were known as much for their belligerence as for their fine Armagnac brandy and foie gras. It may have been a good omen that the

Gothic church in Agen was named for Saint Hilaire. Two days later, George left for the remote Gascon countryside.

"That's where it all started," George would recall. "My empire in the southwest, as they say."

THREE

A Beautiful Friendship

Hilaire typifies the sort of person who was best suited to our work. He appeared on the surface a man of the most unassuming character and you would certainly pass him without a second glance; this was something we were not unwilling to have the Germans do to our men.

MAURICE BUCKMASTER

═══

Henri Sevenet took George Starr from the Italian Zone over more than four hundred miles of territory that the Wehrmacht was occupying. They traversed Toulouse, the "pink city" on the River Garonne and capital of the Midi-Pyrénées region, and stopped in the medieval town of Agen. Sevenet gave George dinner in a restaurant on Boulevard Carnot, where he usually ate on his own. Before they finished, a Belgian-born **résistant** named Maurice Henri Rouneau joined them. Rouneau, who went by the cover name Captain Martin Rendier, did not sit down at first. He was wary of the stranger whom Sevenet introduced only as "Hilaire." The Belgian journalist-turned-printer had reason to suspect those he did not know. Having spied before the war for French intelligence on German agents operating in northern France, he was arrested soon after the invasion for publishing anti-Nazi tracts. A French court in Arras convicted him of sedition. He escaped from jail and had been in hiding ever since.

George and Rouneau had little in common. Rouneau was tall and slim, while George was short and stocky. Raymond Escholier, a Gascon historian who knew them both, observed a "curious contrast" between them. In the extravagant language characteristic of his region, he wrote that Rouneau "with a large nose, deep and calm eyes, with his sober gestures" was the opposite of George, "the foreigner, short, all steel, clean shaved, with a look like water, water that runs deep." Yet Escholier felt both men "sought silence and shadows."

Rouneau remembered George's "profound gaze that examined everything, hard, but not worried." His description, while contradicting Escholier's account of the "clean shaved" British agent, reflected the profound impression George made on everyone he met: "With his hair so brown and abundant, his lip graced with a moustache like Clark Gable's, he made one think more of a Balkan who had escaped from his arid native mountains than of a son of Albion."

The meeting at the restaurant in Agen between Rouneau and George was to have profound consequences for both men, as well as for the Resistance. When Sevenet called George "**un ami très sûr**," Rouneau relaxed and sat at the table. He later wrote about the meeting to a fellow **résistant**, remembering, "Henri Sevenet asked me to help Hilaire, to house him and to assure his security, and I did." His help extended to placing George in a safe house that belonged to a colleague from his printing factory, Madame Hélène Falbet. Her flat was on a narrow street of two- and three-story gray stone buildings around the corner from the city hall. George stayed for eight nights, rarely venturing into streets patrolled by German troops and only with Rouneau. On November 22, Rouneau and George bicycled seventy miles along rough country tracks toward a hamlet where Rouneau's girlfriend lived. George, unaccustomed to cycling, strained up the hills. "How many times did he ask me, 'Is it still far?'" Rouneau wrote. At nightfall, they reached the ancient stone settlement of Castelnau-sur-l'Auvignon.

Castelnau-sur-l'Auvignon, perched on a hill about twenty-five miles south of Agen, had barely three hundred inhabitants. Life for its small farmers and artisans had not changed in at least a century. As if to emphasize its desolation, locals called it "Castelnau-des-Loups," Castelnau of the Wolves. Water came from a well, and electricity had yet to reach this isolated corner of rural Gascony. Castelnau boasted a stone castle from which it took its name. Its only other notable buildings were a small twelfth-century church, the chapel of Abrin, and a two-story school that doubled as the **mairie**, or municipal town hall. Its square dwellings of Gascon limestone nestled on either side of a road between Condom on the River Baïse in the west and tiny La Romieu, with its ancient Benedictine abbey, in the east. The road was poorly paved, increasing the hamlet's isolation. The beautiful setting five hundred feet above sea level afforded a magnificent view of forested land around a river called Le Grand Auvignon. The Gascon food was hearty and more plentiful than in the towns, where Vichy enforced strict rationing. There were geese and ducks, as well as eggs, to eat. Wine and Armagnac never ran short. Best of all, the nearest Germans were far away in Agen.

Castelnau's only light shone from the stars that guided Rouneau and George through the darkness to a farmhouse at the hamlet's edge. Rouneau knocked at the door. It opened, and the two men slipped inside. Rouneau introduced George to the mayor of Castelnau-sur-l'Auvignon, Roger Larribeau. "Age 47," stated an SOE report on Larribeau, "height about 1.75 [meters] [five feet nine inches]; dark brown hair; medium build, rather thin; farmer, and mayor of Castelnau-sur-l'Auvignon." The British agent and the French mayor became instant friends. "I cannot tell you what a feeling we had for each other, Hilaire and me," Larribeau later confided to Raymond Escholier. For his part, George saw Larribeau as a colorful, enthusiastic rebel from his farmer's boots up to the beret that he never took off.

Larribeau sent someone to the school to bring Rouneau's girlfriend, an attractive twenty-eight-year-old widow named Jeanne Robert. Robert, the village schoolmistress, ran to the Larribeau house. The mayor was waiting outside for her. "We have a visitor," he said. She recalled:

> So I went in, and he introduced Colonel Hilaire. And then I saw him. He noticed my look, and we looked at each other for I don't know how long. And I had the impression he was undressing me, inspecting me with a look that was very impressive. And then, when he'd had enough, he smiled, and I smiled back.

George remembered his introduction to Castelnau-sur-l'Auvignon, recounting, "On my first day in the village, I met the mayor and everybody else. I was a refugee from the north. As the schoolteacher came from Lille, I was accepted as a friend of her friends. No question of any problems." In Castelnau, George was discovering a hamlet with a wide field of fire in all directions, level farmland on the plain below for parachute drops, and, most of all, inhabitants who were loyal **résistants**.

"I moved in there," George boasted later, "and the spider began spinning his web."

The web was already half spun when he arrived, all due to a past incident when a German soldier had attempted to rape Jeanne Robert. The Germans had occupied her home region of the Pas-de-Calais in northern France in June 1940 and subjected it to German military control from Belgium. No one could enter or leave that Forbidden Zone without permission. Surveillance was stricter and German troops more numerous than in the rest of occupied France. Robert's husband had died in 1937, eighteen months after their wedding, and, as the widowed Madame Delattre, she taught school in a hamlet called Bucquoy amid dull farmland about fifty miles from her parents' village of Hasnon. Living with her were a twenty-year-old colleague, Loulou, and Loulou's sixteen-year-old brother, Fernand.

One evening in late 1940, two burly German privates and a noncommissioned officer entered the house uninvited, demanding food. Robert remembered the noncom as a gentleman, but the other two were crude. They drank wine while she fried eggs and potatoes. She put the plates in front of them and said, "Stay here. We are going to sleep." She, Loulou, and Fernand shared a room that night, and they bolted the door from inside. As they lay together on the only bed, one of the soldiers bashed the door open with his shoulder. He pounced on Loulou and tore at her nightdress. The second private jabbed his rifle into Robert and pressed his body against hers. "I screamed," she remembered. "I called the non-commissioned officer to plead with him. And he said, 'Get out!' They obeyed him and left."

In the morning, villagers pretended they had not heard her screams. Robert, refusing to accept fear and silence as the norm, sought out her cousin Léon Degand. He was a First World War veteran with a lifelong hatred of the Germans, or as he called them, **les Boches**. As the French railways' chief clerk in Lille, Degand was helping Allied soldiers stranded after the June 1940 British retreat from Dunkirk. With his connivance, they hid in boxcars and mail wagons traveling south to the Unoccupied Zone. "I began searching for clothing for soldiers in hiding," Robert recalled. "There were English soldiers, French soldiers, obviously in uniform, hiding out, who wanted to leave." Her mother, a seamstress, assisted her. "But my father, not at all," she said. "I had no trust in him, because he was in the war of 1914 to 1918 and for him Pétain was a god." Aiding Allied troops to evade capture was a dangerous enterprise. The penalty was death.

Jeanne Robert met Maurice Rouneau just after his escape from jail. "He arrived at my parents' house," Robert recalled, "because he knew my mother." Robert gave refuge to Rouneau, ten years her senior, and they became lovers. He was estranged from his French wife, Madeleine, in Bertincourt, about twenty miles west. Rouneau aided Robert with the escaping soldiers, until someone denounced him to the Germans. He fled to the Lower Pyrenees in the Unoccupied Zone on March 21, resuming his work as a printer at the Imprimerie Collet in the town of Pau.

Three months later, in June, it was Robert's turn to be denounced. "I was hunted by the Gestapo," she said. "They were waiting for me at the exit of the school." Thanks to the warning of a fellow teacher who spotted a Gestapo car, Robert left through a back exit and bicycled out of the village. Her faithful cousin Léon Degand smuggled her onto a train bound for Paris. Another train took her to Orthez, a checkpoint between the Occupied and Unoccupied zones. "At Orthez," she remembered, "an old German let me cross the Line of Demarcation."

She stopped in Castétis, a village a few minutes southeast of Orthez, where another teacher who had fled from the north gave her a room. Robert applied to teach in a school in Pau to be near Rouneau, but there were no vacancies. She went to Auch, the departmental capital of the Gers, and tried again. A school inspector, himself a refugee from Alsace-Lorraine, told her about an opening in Barbotan-les-Thermes. However, the teacher's quarters there were in a hotel that housed German soldiers. Then he mentioned a small hamlet in an isolated corner of the Gers, Castelnau-sur-l'Auvignon. "But the place there is completely destitute," he warned. "There is no water, no electricity." She accepted at once. He said, "I repeat. No water. No electricity."

The teachers' residence in Castelnau's schoolhouse had a kitchen on the ground floor and bedrooms upstairs. Robert taught twenty-seven children of all ages. "I had such gentle students!" she wrote, and years later she recalled, "Everyone was very kind to me." Villagers called her Madame Delattre with the respect due a teacher and a widow. A shepherd gave her a heavy quilt to keep warm at night. A horse dealer offered her the use of his telephone, one of two in the hamlet. Robert came to know the families through their children and to distinguish the Pétainists from potential **résistants**. The preeminent patriot turned out to be Mayor Larribeau, who had five children, aged between nine and twenty, and who did not hide his anti-Nazi and socialist beliefs.

Meanwhile, Maurice Rouneau was forging identity documents and ration cards for the **résistants** he was recruiting. As more volunteers joined him, he moved in October 1941 from Pau to Agen to work in a larger print factory twenty-five miles closer to Robert. Agen, with a population of about thirty thousand and as the capital of the Lot-et-Garonne department, offered greater scope for underground activity. The River Garonne flowed through the medieval town, famed for plums and the sixteenth-century sorcerer Nostradamus. Agen lay at the center of communications in the southwest: the Canal du Midi took barges to the Mediterranean, and a highway linked Agen ninety miles northwest to Bordeaux and the same distance southeast to Toulouse. The Germans established military and security bases in Agen, where England's Plantagenet kings had ruled in the Middle Ages.

An intelligence report noted that Rouneau took "most of his meals in a small restaurant there, frequented particularly by N.C.O.s of the 150 Regiment d'Infanterie," part of Vichy's 100,000-man Armistice Army. "He discovered that their opinions for the most part were the same as his." A group of noncommissioned officers at its Agen headquarters had already formed a secret cell, based on their membership in a Freemasons' lodge called **Victoire**. Pétain, as part of his antirepublican "New Order," had banned Freemasonry on August 27, 1940. Rouneau befriended one of their leaders, twenty-five-year-old Staff Sergeant Pierre Wallerand. Jeanne Robert called Wallerand, a native of Picardy in the north, "the soul of that clandestine military action."

On April 12, 1942, Rouneau and Wallerand ate a sumptuous Easter Sunday lunch in Jeanne Robert's kitchen at the school in Castelnau-sur-l'Auvignon. By the time they finished, they had founded a Resistance network, the **Réseau Victoire**. They invited Roger and Alberta Larribeau to join. The couple accepted at once, the mayor declaring, "My house, my buildings, myself, all is at your disposal. Act as you think right. Ground for parachute drops are here and my friend Pino [Novarini] has the best."

Rouneau and Wallerand spent the night at the mayor's house, discussing until dawn their plans and hopes for the new network. Larribeau recruited his neighbors, Joseph and Argentina Novarini, known to everyone as Pino and Tina. As Larribeau had said, their farm on the flatlands below the village provided ideal ground for **parachutages**, parachute drops, of supplies and agents. A report on the Resistance in Castelnau stated that the Larribeaus and Novarinis "jumped with both feet into their clandestine organization."

Rouneau recruited civilians, while Wallerand concentrated on soldiers. Among the first Rouneau enrolled was the former divisional chief of the Prefecture of the Upper Rhine, Alsatian refugee Maurice Jacob. Vichy had made Jacob the director of its Service des Réfugiés et Expulsés, responsible for settling refugees like himself from the Occupied Zone. Many Vichy officials used their positions to aid the Resistance in secret. Wallerand enlisted the support of his 150th Infantry Regiment comrade Adjutant (Sergeant) Fernand Gaucher. Gaucher, code name "Gérard," spread the recruitment drive north of the Gers into the South Dordogne department.

Volunteers, however, were few. Most Resistance networks at this time numbered no more than a hundred men and women. Rising up against the occupation seemed futile while the Nazis dominated Europe, and France's own government collaborated with them. Although the United States had entered the war on Britain's side in December 1941, the Allies were losing on all fronts. General Douglas MacArthur retreated from the Philippines in March 1942, abandoning more than twenty thousand American and Filipino soldiers to their fate on the Bataan Peninsula. The Japanese consolidated their hold in Southeast Asia, conquering the Dutch East Indies and Malaya, moving into Burma, and threatening British India. The Axis was expanding, not retreating. The Allies, apart from bombing Germans cities and staging occasional commando raids against German ports, were not shaking Hitler's dominance. The German Navy laid siege to the British-held island of Malta to expel the Royal Navy from the Mediterranean Sea. To join the underground Resistance while Allied prospects remained dim required more than courage. It took faith.

Those with sufficient trust to join **Victoire** were mainly refugees with firsthand experience of direct German rule in Alsace, Lorraine and other annexed areas. These exiles found in the Gascon hills fertile terrain for resistance. The region's history was rich in war and rebellion. The Gers, at the center of Gascony, boasted 146 castles, relics of a past when rival nobles battled for suzerainty. The stone fortifications had evolved into villages called **castelnaus,** like Castelnau-sur-l'Auvignon. Gascony resisted the English in the Hundred Years' War between 1337 and 1453, and its soldiers had fought for and against their French overlords. French literature romanticized the swaggering and courageous, though impoverished, Gascon swordsmen. Edmond Rostand's Cyrano de Bergerac was a classic Gascon noble, with a flaming feather, his **panache,** concealing the hole in his threadbare hat. Another was Alexandre Dumas's musketeer d'Artagnan. Dumas wrote,

> "Among ourselves, we say 'Proud as a Scotsman,'" murmured Buckingham.
> "And us, we say 'Proud as a Gascon,'" d'Artagnan replied. "The Gascons are the Scotsmen of France."

In the First World War, the two French commanders who defeated the Germans at the River Marne, Marshals Joseph Gallieni and Ferdinand Foch, were Gascons.

The Gascon Resistance in Castelnau-sur-l'Auvignon needed Britain, almost the sole provider of weapons to Frenchmen and -women willing to fight the Germans. George Starr needed a base. **Victoire**'s partisans gave him an ideal nucleus on which to build a network that SOE dubbed WHEELWRIGHT. Jeanne Robert appreciated the significance of his presence: "We knew that he was and would be our chief and that we and our network, the **Victoire** network, had passed to the command of SOE." He promised them weapons, explosives, military training, and, most of all, an invasion by Allied armies who would help them to liberate their country. By the chance assignment of Robert to teach in Castelnau, **Victoire** and George found each other. It was, as the American hero of a wartime Hollywood movie said, "the beginning of a beautiful friendship."

FOUR

"I Was a Human Being"

Hilaire built up his series of **Réseaux** with the
patience of a genuine strategist, never bothering
about any fireworks, reserving his best and final
effect for the days when it would best serve
the cause to which we were all devoted—the
extirpation of the German forces in France.

MAURICE BUCKMASTER

===

G eorge Starr spent his first night in Castelnau-
sur-l'Auvignon at Mayor Larribeau's house
and his second in a guest bedroom at Jeanne
Robert's school. "I feel good here," he told her that
Wednesday morning, November 24, 1942. "I'd like
to stay." Robert described her guest's behavior as im-
peccable: "There was the men's laundry and iron-

ing, and I had a class of twenty-seven students as well. In the evenings, I had to prepare the lessons for the next day. And Colonel Hilaire said to me, 'If you need me to do anything, just ask.'" He cooked, washed dishes, and shined shoes until they glistened. George became her "real companion," who, despite a reputation for creative profanity, rarely uttered a vulgar word in her presence.

Maurice Rouneau also remembered George doing household chores and being "a perfect comrade." Raymond Escholier noted, "No one was more unobtrusive than Hilaire. Not only did he reveal an aptitude for his work, he turned his hand to hoeing and tending the vines, the Armagnac vines whose purple one day produces its dark gold liqueur." George mingled as an equal with the peasants as he had with coal miners in his prewar career. "We'd go to bed like the French peasants," he said, "to bed with the animals and up with them." Rouneau observed that George fit into village life: "He was a man who gave himself to everything, who adapted to any environment. In Castelnau, we saw him alternately as a man of the world . . . [and] a peasant."

George's bushy moustache made him look like a local, but it served another function. "You can shave it off in five minutes," he said. "If somebody's used to a little dark man that wears a beret, and he's got a moustache and he always wears a brown suit, that's what they're looking for. They're not looking for a clean-shaven man wearing glasses and wearing a gray suit." Like most men in the village, he dangled a cigarette from his lips, always a cheap French-made Balto with its advertised **goût americain**. However, in a hamlet where strangers aroused suspicion, George's English-accented French was no help. "We said he came from Belgium," Robert explained, "that he was a friend of my parents, an engineer who was bored up north, the life being difficult, and that he found a comfortable place and came to stay there. This worked like a letter in the post." They called him Gaston, nickname Tonton, although the underground militants promoted the lieutenant to "Colonel" Hilaire or **le patron**. No one knew his real name.

Gaston the Belgian feigned pro-German sympathies: "I had deliberately given the impression that I was [a collaborator], saying the Germans were all right, supporting Pétain and the New Order, not overdoing it, just allowing them to get that impression." This insulated him from accusation by pro-Vichy Frenchmen, a common occurrence under occupation.

"In this little village he could live in perfect security," noted an SOE report. "I never locked anything," George said. "I don't think we could have locked it anyway."

A week before George's arrival, SOE had promised to send Henri Sevenet a consignment of arms and other supplies. George's first task therefore was to prepare for the expected **parachutage** on the night of November 24 with a reception committee of eight. "All these eight people knew each other, have done since childhood," he said. "You can't penetrate, because you're not one of them." The team comprised George, Mayor Larribeau, Maurice Rouneau, Pino and Tina Novarini, Jeanne Robert, and, from the 150th Infantry Regiment, Sergeants Pierre Wallerand and Maurice Maxime Léon Dupont. They met at the Novarini farmhouse, lit the drop site with flashlights, and drank Armagnac to warm themselves against the bitter cold. At dawn, though, they went home empty-handed. Bad English weather had stopped the plane from taking off, but the RAF would try again.

The next night, the moon was on the wane and the temperature below freezing. Pino Novarini set an enormous log ablaze in his field, a beacon no plane could miss. Rouneau recalled that Pino then went inside and "set on the table a decanter of white wine from his own harvest and the inevitable bottle of Armagnac." George amused them by telling stories. "From time to time, a man would get up and go out to listen to the night sounds," Rouneau wrote. They thought they heard an engine purring in the sky, but each time it was a false alarm.

The reception committee kept watch at the Novarinis' for several nights without result. On November 27, night four of their vigil, the clock struck midnight. Rouneau remembered, "White wine, Armagnac, stories, time was passing, when, all of a sudden, at one o'clock in the morning, a loud noise interrupted our conversation." The **résistants** held their breath. An engine rumbled in the night sky, growing louder as it came closer. Everyone dashed outside.

George, dressed in a fleece-lined canadienne jacket with the S-Phone strapped to his chest, positioned himself against a hedge. A triangle of two red lights along the base with a white lamp at the apex enclosed a target zone of about a hundred square yards. Rouneau ran to the top of the field, ready to shine his flashlight skyward. The others sheltered in a pine grove. One minute, two minutes passed. George called out, "There it is!"

Rouneau spotted an aircraft cruising into a moonlit gap in the clouds and flashed the letter **R** in Morse code, short-long-short. The plane circled and swooped to about three hundred feet. It was poised for a perfect drop when, suddenly, it banked upward and flew away. George called the pilot on the S-Phone, commanding him to release the desperately needed weapons and explosives. The pilot did not respond.

A few minutes later, the engine roared again. The plane approached as if to release its cargo, but it flew off. The only sound in its wake was George's enraged voice bellowing into the S-Phone. Apparently taunting George's team, the plane reappeared and made yet another approach. Rouneau flashed the Morse **R**. George shouted at the pilot to release the cargo. Robert heard George crying out, "**Putain, putain, putain**. What are they doing?" Rouneau recalled him entreating, "Answer me, you bastard! Good God, answer me!" There was no answer. No parachutes, no containers, no weapons. Despite George's curses and Rouneau's signal, the plane vanished into the clouds. It did not return.

From five miles away in the town of Condom came the shrill blare of an air-raid siren. The Germans had also seen the plane.

One hour and twenty minutes from the moment George's reception committee heard the engines, the six men and two women went home. "That was the first disappointment," George said. The fault was not his, but the S-Phone's, either his or the one on the plane. A disconsolate George strode to Mayor Larribeau's house. Rouneau recalled the next morning in Castelnau:

Hilaire went out slowly from Larribeau's, a cigarette between his lips, crossing the village in small steps, and came to me in the school where I had gone before him. He was again a stranger to the people of Castelnau. Apart from a modest "**Bon-**

jour," he didn't take the chance of speaking with the villagers.

George knew that the aircraft's motors must have alerted the inhabitants, not all of whom were sympathetic to the Resistance. At that time, he told his SOE handlers, "the population as a whole was neutral, neither for one side nor the other, they only wanted to be left in peace." British planes dropping weapons disturbed that peace and risked German reprisals. Yet luck was on George's side. Jeanne Robert went out to sample village opinion. The first person she encountered told her that **six** planes had flown over during the night. No, said another, **twelve**. A third insisted there had been **twenty-four,** in three groups of eight. No one mentioned a lone British plane. A pro-Vichy youth, who feigned omniscience about military matters, told Robert, "They were German planes on their way to drop mines in front of the port of Toulon!" That became the accepted version, which Robert did not contradict.

Adding to George's woes, the S-Phone batteries died. Rouneau bicycled across five miles of rocky rural trails to charge them in Condom, which had the electricity that Castelnau lacked. He returned them to George that afternoon in the hope the S-Phone would work next time.

On the same evening as the failed arms drop, November 27, the Germans demobilized Vichy's Armistice Army because most of the French Army in Algeria and Morocco had gone over to the invading Allies. German forces seized the French troops' weapons, including those of the 150th Infantry Regiment in Agen. Rouneau went to Agen on November 29 to find what remained of the 150th's **Victoire** cell. He soon realized, "That put an end to the military organization of **Victoire,** from which only the best members continued the struggle." The moving force in **Victoire,** Sergeant Pierre Wallerand, was leaving France for London to train with the British Army. Others were following his lead. When Rouneau returned to Castelnau with the bad news, Robert gave him worse. Vichy gendarmes were searching the nearby village of La Romieu for a man "who said he was a refugee from the North, but was in reality an Allied agent who was communicating by radio with London." Rouneau told her not to inform George, whose lack of a radio meant the police might have been seeking someone else.

George saw an advantage in the dissolution of the 150th Infantry Regiment: its men were no longer tied to Vichy's military command. "And then, of course, they became full Resistance," he said. Some hid their weapons for future use against the Germans and dispersed them among peasants around the village of Manciet, about an hour southwest of Castelnau.

While basing his WHEELWRIGHT circuit on the 150th Infantry Regiment's remaining veterans, George also welcomed untrained civilians, many from networks the Germans had broken up. Although deprived of weapons and communications, he set out to forge a guerrilla and sabotage force to support the Allied invasion of France. No one knew the date of D-Day, **Jour-J** to the French, but George's network had to be ready whenever it took place.

In late 1942, the liberation of France was barely a dream. The American and British armies were struggling to secure their hold on North Africa. The British were moving forward from Libya in the east, while the united Anglo-American forces had a long way to go from Algeria to squeeze the Germans out of Tunisia. Until the Allies secured the southern shore of the Mediterranean, they would be in no position to take the war to Europe. The Resistance in France organized and trained, but it had to be invisible until the real armies arrived to drive the Germans back into Germany.

To keep his network intact until the invasion, George reduced the risk of betrayals that had destroyed WHEELWRIGHT's predecessors. His method, he said, was to recruit only those known to people he trusted and to work slowly: "You build a step and you stand on it. And it holds. Then you jump on it, and it still holds. Then you jump on it again, and it still holds." When the ladder was complete, he would stop. "Then you protect your people that way. People begin to have confidence in you."

George's other precaution was to relay messages only by word of mouth. If a German roadblock stopped a courier, there would be no written evidence. "I never wrote anything," George said. "It was strictly forbidden. You had to learn it by heart. As soon as they get it [the message], forget it. No passwords at all. I didn't believe in passwords." Raymond Escholier observed George at work: "No paper. No pen. No pencil. He did not want to be tempted to write." George's security rules were strict but necessary, requiring an agent or courier, in his words, "never to find out more than he was told, never to try to find out who a contact really was, what he was doing or where he was living." He prohibited his operatives from using their real names and talking to anyone they did not know. "There was a very strict code of discipline with the severest penalty always for disobedience."

George allocated sectors of his realm to trusted deputies. He began with the former noncommissioned officers of the 150th Infantry Regiment, placing Sergeant Fernand Gaucher in charge north of the River Garonne. Gaucher would receive arms drops there, when they took place. He moved to the village of Fieumarcon, while his wife and children lived in Castelnau-sur-l'Auvignon. Twenty-one-year-old Sergeant Maurice Dupont, "Yvan," became a

WHEELWRIGHT courier. Circuit members met from time to time in a commercial building with multiple exits that George had rented in Agen. A trusted few gathered in Castelnau around Jeanne Robert's kitchen table, usually by candlelight over a bottle of Armagnac, to provide George with intelligence or to receive instructions. George presided at the table with stories, true or imagined, from his prewar life.

"Some days," wrote Rouneau, "the schoolhouse was transformed into a veritable command post." Henri Sevenet and his twenty-two-year-old deputy, Paul Sarrette, paid frequent visits for "councils of war." Sarrette, who earned the Croix de Guerre for his courage as a frontline sergeant resisting the German invasion of 1940, began work for SOE at Sevenet's urging in Lyon in September 1942. Under the pseudonym Amédée Gontran, the handsome young Frenchman worked as Sevenet's courier between Marseille and Lyon and often accompanied him to meet George in Castelnau-sur-l'Auvignon. "The school had become the command post of the 'terrorists' who were going to take the hard life to the German," Rouneau commented.

In the weeks after the failed **parachutage** of November 27, George stayed close to the hamlet. He sent verbal orders via courier to operatives miles away. His agents established dead letter drops in Agen and other Gascon towns, where they left coded messages for one another. One of Fernand Gaucher's more imaginative spots was the poor box in an Agen church. George did not use dead letters, preferring "live letters," intermediaries with oral communiqués to pass along and forget.

As Christmas 1942 approached, Sevenet came to Castelnau to tell George that the Gestapo was hunting for a former Lyon courier, Denise Bloch. The twenty-six-year-old Frenchwoman was vulnerable both as a **résistante** and because she was Jewish. Having fled the Nazi anti-Jewish regime in Paris in June 1942, her family had taken refuge in the Unoccupied Zone. Bloch joined the Resistance in Lyon as a courier for the DETECTIVE circuit. Sentenced in absentia to ten years' hard labor, Bloch had evaded capture during the Vichy police arrests of radio operator Brian Stonehouse and courier Blanche Charlet just before George's arrival. She had watched in silent impotence as the police marched a bloodied Stonehouse through Lyon's streets. Paul Sarrette rescued her on October 26, taking her on a train two hundred miles south to Marseille and then to the Mediterranean fishing village of Villefranche-sur-Mer. There, Sarrette left her in a safe house that belonged to the mother of his cousin's wife.

Denise Bloch's beauty and stature of five feet ten inches made her easy to recognize. She bleached her auburn hair blond in a Nice beauty parlor and changed her cover name from "Danielle" to "Catherine." Sevenet went to Villefranche in early January to tell her that she was **brûlée**, burned, known to the Gestapo. Sarrette soon brought her by train to Toulouse.

Sevenet conferred with George about Bloch, warning him that she was jeopardizing their security. A telegram she had sent to her mother enabled Vichy police to identify her and some of her contacts. Sevenet added that Bloch's indiscretion was responsible for the police learning about George's presence in France, as well as his code name. If he had gone to Lyon as ordered the previous November, they would have arrested him the moment he stepped off the train. Bloch's SOE file contains the note "Sevenet not impressed by her," but another SOE report further underlined the severity of the situation:

After discussing the matter HILAIRE said that the only solution was to liquidate her. Source [Sevenet] made no reply and the affair was arranged by HILAIRE. At the last moment, however, source felt that he could not allow her to be killed just because she was a nuisance, and decided to pass her over into Spain.

In early January 1943, Bloch and Maurice Dupont traveled by bus to the town of Oloron-Sainte-Marie on the Spanish border. From there, they climbed the Pyrenees. "But DUPONT was stopped twice as he was reconnoitering for her," an F-Section report noted, "and the snow was much too heavy for her thin shoes, so he took her back to Toulouse." Hélène Falbet gave Bloch a room in her safe house in Agen, and from there, Bloch went to Toulouse to meet the man who had been prepared to liquidate her.

Speaking with the attractive young woman for the first time, George decided not to send her away. Instead, he made her his courier, and Bloch moved into the school in Castelnau-sur-l'Auvignon. "I installed her in a little bedroom on the first floor," recalled Robert, who gave another room to Sergeant Dupont, while she slept on a sofa in the kitchen. Dupont taught gymnastics to her students, giving Robert an hour off each day. The patriotic sergeant erected a flagpole in front of the school and, in violation of German dictates, raised the French tricolor every morning for the children to salute.

Most evenings, Robert made dinner in her kitchen for George, Bloch, and Dupont as well as, on occasion, the Larribeaus and Novarinis. George adapted to the Gascon diet:

> The only thing about the Gascons, they don't eat vegetables. I mean if you were invited to a Gascon dinner, it's an insult to have vegetables of any description, even a chipped potato. No, a Gascon dinner is separate pieces of meat, different sauce, but no vegetables at all, not even salad.

Bloch's discipline and undoubted bravery made her an effective **résistante**. Obeying George's instruction never to write messages, she memorized every word she carried to his people in the field. A later SOE assessment concluded:

> An experienced woman with a knowledge of the world. She has courage and determination and hatred of the Boche. Has complete self-assurance and is capable of handling most situations.

Sevenet disapproved the appointment, but George trusted Bloch more than he did Sevenet. The two men were becoming rivals. George, though a lieutenant, bridled at taking orders from Captain Sevenet, and Sevenet for his part suspected George's motive for retaining Bloch. An F-Section debrief of Paul Sarrette contains the note: "SARRETTE says that soon after 'HILAIRE' had been introduced to 'DENISE' she became his mistress." If true, George was violating his own order against agents becoming lovers. Bloch, whether mistress or colleague, became George's dependable link to the operatives in his expanding realm. Sarrette described Bloch as an "unscrupulous adventuress," and his debrief added, "DENISE disliked both 'RODOLPHE' [Sevenet] and himself and, having HILAIRE's ear, persuaded him that the true story of her recent activities was wholly to her credit and their discredit."

George's lack of wireless contact with London forced him to rely on couriers to deliver his messages to the SOE stations at Britain's embassies in Spain and Switzerland, which sometimes took weeks. A breakthrough came in January 1943, when Sevenet turned up in Castelnau to tell George that another SOE organizer had moved to Toulouse, only sixty miles away. The organizer was the head of the PRUNUS circuit, Lieutenant Maurice Pertschuk.

Pertschuk offered what George needed most: a radio operator. His was Captain Marcus Bloom, the former businessman who had come ashore from the **Seadog** with George in November. Bloom, son of Orthodox Jews from Poland and Russia, was born in Britain on September 24, 1907. His father sent him to Paris in the 1930s to run the French branch of the family's mail-order textile firm, and in March 1938 he married a Frenchwoman, Germaine Février. When the business collapsed in early 1940, he returned to London, but the German invasion trapped Germaine, who had been visiting her family in France. Bloom volunteered for the Royal Artillery in 1941 and received an officer's commission, but his fluent French soon attracted the notice of SOE. He was recruited, and then sent to Thame Park, Oxfordshire, where he trained in Morse code and secret cyphers in order to be a wireless telegrapher. His instructors, despite one who described the five-foot-eight-inch recruit as "this pink yid," placed him near the top of his class. Bloom's assessment after the combat course in Scotland stated, "He has plenty of guts and is an extremely able man." Bloom used two code names, "Urbain" and "Bishop."

His original assignment had been to work with Anthony Brooks, code name "Alphonse," of the PIMENTO circuit near Lyon. Twenty-year-old Tony Brooks was F-Section's youngest British field operative and was bilingual in French and English. Brooks had expected Bloom to meet him the moment he arrived in Toulouse, but it was only three days later that, in Brooks's words, "a chap wearing a nice sort of hairy tweed suit and a pork pie hat with a pheasant's feather in the ribbon and smoking a pipe came breezing in." Brooks greeted him in French, but Bloom replied in English, "'Ow're you, mate?" Brooks berated him for smoking pungent Balkan Sobrani pipe tobacco with an aroma unknown in wartime France, and claimed that when Bloom was asked where he had been for two days, he answered, "I've been staying with a friend who wants to meet you, chap called Eugene." Bloom took Brooks to a black market restaurant called the Trouffe de Quercy to meet Pertschuk, code name "Eugène." George Starr, whom Brooks described as "one of the finest guerrilla leaders SOE had in France," was also present. Pertschuk asked Brooks whether he could borrow Bloom for occasional transmissions. Brooks, relieved to be rid of Bloom, said, "Look, I don't need a wireless operator. You, Eugene, can have Urbain as your wireless operator. I will clear this with London."

"While waiting for a radio," French Resistance archives summarized, "Starr recruited, mainly in Condom, where he met PRUNUS [Maurice Pertschuk], [Philippe de] GUNZBOURG and Louis LEVY, 'CHRISTOPHE.'" Pertschuk, Philippe de Gunzbourg, and Louis Lévy, together with Lévy's younger brother Théo, were destined to become George's most valuable allies. All were Jewish, although from different backgrounds. Twenty-one-year-old Pertschuk, born of Russian Jewish parents in Paris and raised in England until age twelve, was one of F-Section's youngest agents. Denise Bloch described him as "about 5' 10" or 5' 11", very thin, looks half dead, face as if cut in wood, filthy dirty hair falling over his nose, could easily pass as French, looks like an artist's model." Bilingual in French and English, he had undergone SOE training in England with Sevenet and returned to France the previous April to organize the PRUNUS circuit.

A judicious recruiter of top agents, Pertschuk found Gunzbourg, code-named "Philibert" and "Edgar," through Gunzbourg's cousin, whom he knew from childhood summers in the Boy Scouts. Gunzbourg was a dashing, dark-haired, French Jewish aristocrat. Rejecting the chance to escape to the

United States as his younger sister Aline had done in 1941, Gunzbourg bought the Château de Barsalou at Pont-du-Cassé near Agen to use as a Resistance base. His clandestine work began with the home-grown **Combat** network in January 1942, but he transferred his allegiance to George. A French Resistance report on Gunzbourg stated:

> He regarded two groups as serious: the Communists and the English. He did not want to work with the Communists, not that their ideas were not very advanced, but because nothing in his origin or his education had prepared him to work with them, then that he had more points in common with the English.

A Resistance colleague wrote that Gunzbourg "was a Frenchman, although due to his bearing, he was sometimes taken for an Englishman."

The Lévy brothers joined George's organization without hesitation. Louis, code name "Christophe," was thirty and Théo twenty-seven. German by birth, they had fled Nazi persecution at home only for it to follow them to France. When George needed agents to pose as Germans, the brothers filled the roles in stolen German uniforms. They lived in hiding, as Jews and as **résistants,** in the village of Vic-Fezensac, about twenty miles south of Condom, with the family of an ironmonger named Lac and his wife, Marie-Louise. One leading **résistant**, Henri Monnet, wrote of the Lacs that from the end of 1942 they "established contacts, housed agents and the radio transmitters with their operators and rendered innumerable services to the cause." Marie-Louise Lac, though, concealed many of her activities from her husband. With her typewriter, she forged identity cards for the Lévy brothers and other Jewish exiles, and one of her neighbors lent Pertschuk his meadow for the first parachute drop of arms to PRUNUS.

When Bloom attempted to operate his radio for Pertschuk, it failed to transmit. As with George's S-Phone, it may have left London without being checked. Pertschuk asked another radio operator, Captain Adolphe Rabinovitch, an Egyptian-Russian-Jewish W/T, to fix it. Rabinovitch was both a multilingual scholar and, at 180 pounds, a former light heavyweight boxer. The twenty-five-year-old stood five feet nine inches in his bare feet and had a build that his SOE file called "solid." John Starr had studied with him at Wanborough Manor, where his trainers noted his popularity and determination. Rabinovitch's friends called him Alec, and his code name was "Arnaud." Since parachuting into France on August 28, 1942, the same night John Starr jumped on his first mission, he had been transmitting for Peter Churchill. Rabinovitch repaired Bloom's radio at the Château d'Esquiré near Fonsorbes, about twenty miles south of Toulouse, where Bloom had based himself.

On Mondays and Thursdays, George and Bloch took turns bicycling twenty-two miles to Agen and taking the train to Toulouse to see Pertschuk. The young agent met them at the Café Riche, where he provided funds for George's circuit, and picked up Bloch's and George's shopping lists to pass on to courier Jeanine Morrisse. With the messages sewn into the lining of her clothes, Morrisse bicycled twenty miles to the Château d'Esquiré to give them to Bloom. Bloom transmitted George's requirements, drop sites marked with code numbers like "T-25," and meaningless sentences in French for the BBC to broadcast when the planes left England.

This was the communication connection that George needed in order to fund, equip, and arm the secret army that would play its part in the Allied liberation of France. His recruits, however, doubted that he could deliver. In the absence of tangible support from Britain, his **résistants** were susceptible to blandishments from the communists and other Resistance groups that were not part of Allied planning. If George could not pay and arm his networks, he had little leverage to keep them under the military discipline necessary to fight the Germans at the decisive moment. Thankfully, Bloom's radio transmissions, coinciding with German defeats in Tunisia and Libya, were strengthening George's hand,

and **résistants** began to believe that the Allies could win and George could deliver. No weapons, however, arrived.

Maurice Rouneau expressed his comrades' bitterness: "Winter, that awful winter, which with its rain, its snow, its fog, blocked every operation." The strain on George emerged in the form of psoriasis, patches of red and itchy skin over much of his body, rather than insomnia or nervousness. His three closest colleagues, Rouneau, Robert, and Bloch, feared he was also succumbing to depression. Robert attempted to console him, saying, "Listen. You can tell me when you are worried, when you have problems, when you miss your family. You can speak to me, and I won't tell anyone." However, George did not complain.

On Sunday morning, January 10, 1943, George woke in a dark mood. Rouneau assumed he missed his wife and children, who, while just over the border in Manresa working for SOE, were unaware he was living only 260 miles north of them. Before George departed for France, F-Section had asked him about his wife, Pilar, "Do you think she'll help us with a safe house in Manresa?" He answered, "I'm sure she would if you just asked." With the help of an uncle whom George called "one of the biggest bloody smugglers in Spain," she passed messages between France and London, provided papers to escapees and helped them to reach Gibraltar. SOE, which called her network the Stutz Line, did not tell her that some of the messages she relayed came from her husband. George said, "She never dreamt that I wasn't very far away." It was hard for him to be so close to his family, but unable to communicate with them.

Jeanne Robert tried to raise George's morale that January morning by offering him a bottle of **vin de Noa,** dry white wine from American vines planted after the mid-nineteenth-century phylloxera blight destroyed the native varieties. Robert recalled that George told her, "I believe that today I'm going to drink." She said, "Listen, serve yourself. It's yours." George remembered that one of Robert's students had brought the wine, not just one bottle but three, strong enough to "kill about 2,000 mules." He "began to feel on top of the world." When he finished the wine, he needed coffee, "but there wasn't any coffee in the rations." Thinking Mayor Larribeau had coffee, he proceeded to the Larribeaus' house. The chicory-flavored, ersatz coffee of the German occupation tasted foul, so the mayor gave him homemade Armagnac. "A superior Armagnac," Rouneau wrote, "but rough, like they drink it in the country. A bottle went, then two! Hilaire spoke a little too much, for him."

George was on a roll. Rouneau recalled Gaston the Belgian leading a procession through the village: "He went out, invited everyone to a house he had never entered, Monsieur Maupomé's. More white wine, more Armagnac, and our man became more and more talkative." Robert urged George to be quiet. From Maupomé the cattle trader's, George paraded to the Novarinis' farm. "And the libations continued," Rouneau wrote. Rouneau feared the alcohol was making George too talkative, yet admitted that "the agent never lost his sense of reality or himself. When he felt the game had gone on long enough, he went to sleep at Larribeau's."

In George's telling, though, he did not go to bed so quickly: "So, then I decided to ring the bloody church bells, pull the ropes. So, I climbed up the outside and started pulling the bloody bells." The Germans had banned the ringing of church bells, but they were too far away to hear. "They fed me with black coffee and then I suddenly got up and went straight to my own bed. Nobody saw me [leave], and they found me fast asleep in the bed. But that made me in the village. I was a human being."

George became so popular that Roger Larribeau named him the village's **adjoint du maire,** deputy mayor.

FIVE

A Cursed Day

You had to use your head.

MAURICE BUCKMASTER

═══

By the beginning of 1943, the war was turning against Germany in French North Africa and the Soviet Union. British and American forces that landed in Morocco and Algeria in November 1942 were pushing into Tunisia, Germany's last foothold on the African continent. The German siege of Stalingrad, begun in July 1942, was collapsing as Soviet forces encircled the German Sixth Army. By January, German dreams of defeating the Red Army were freezing on the banks of the Volga.

The Allies held a conference at Casablanca in French Morocco on January 14 to plan the next phase of the war. Franklin Roosevelt and Winston Churchill conferred for ten days with a French leadership then divided between Generals Charles de Gaulle and Henri Giraud. Joseph Stalin was absent, due to the fighting around Stalingrad, but the other Allies felt the presence of the dictator whose country was bearing the heaviest burden in the war against Germany. The leaders agreed, despite American misgivings, to invade Sicily and the Italian mainland before attempting an amphibious landing in France. Roosevelt declared at the conclusion of the Casablanca Conference on January 24, "The elimination of German, Japanese, and Italian war power means the unconditional surrender by Germany, Italy, and Japan." This was the first enunciation of "unconditional surrender," a term Roosevelt borrowed from Union General Ulysses S. Grant's war on the Confederacy. Unconditional surrender meant no negotiated armistice of the kind that ended the First World War and led to the Second.

In late January 1943, good fortune was favoring the Allies in Africa, Russia, and, at last, George Starr's corner of southwest France. A break in the weather allowed lumbering RAF Halifax bombers to deliver a load of weapons and explosives to Castelnau-sur-l'Auvignon. George's reception committee hid the matériel in a medieval dungeon under the ancient village church, the chapel of Abrin. The successful operation raised **le patron**'s prestige among wary Frenchmen, and **résistants** from other areas sought him for arms. WHEELWRIGHT was becoming a force in Gascony.

While clear skies and Marcus Bloom's diligent radio transmissions altered George's fortunes, every minute on the air exposed Bloom to the Germans' ubiquitous radio detector vans. Disguised as laundry trucks and other civilian vehicles, the vans patrolled urban and rural roads to pinpoint the radio waves' source. Bloom proved ingenious at finding inaccessible sites, sometimes posing as a fisherman with a rod for an aerial. He helped to receive 35 tons of heavy weapons, light arms, and ammunition and bury it under the vegetable garden at Château d'Esquiré. "Urbain [Bloom] never missed a radio transmission or reception for us," wrote Rouneau. A French intelligence report stated, "He assisted in many acts of sabotage, notably the destruction of an enemy train in January 1943."

Bloom, however, violated security by inviting his wife, Germaine, to stay in the château. Informing her of his presence in France, as well as of his base, risked exposing PRUNUS to the Gestapo or the Nazi's intelligence agency, the Sicherheitsdienst (SD). Philippe de Gunzbourg was already concerned about the Château d'Esquiré, because of the many résistants who were hiding there. Gunzbourg wrote, "The place was spotted by the Germans, who were based nearby and it was obvious that Michel

[Bloom], encouraged by his wife, preferred to spend this honeymoon in a setting more luxurious than that in [the town of] Auch."

The French called the battle of wits between the Resistance and the German security services **la guerre des ombres,** the war of shadows, where treachery reigned. Men and women met in dingy alcoves, conspired to sabotage Germany's occupation, and gambled their lives in a contest few of them understood. A rendezvous with a fellow **résistant** could lead to surveillance, arrest, and death. An agent's most trusted source might be working for the other side. The Gestapo had agents in the Resistance, and the Resistance had its people in the Gestapo. This was the dark realm in which George operated, an environment that bred suspicion and fear.

Dangers came in unexpected forms. While waiting to meet a contact in a Toulouse café, George heard someone say to the cashier, in a strong British accent, "**Nous, officers RAF, pouvez-vous nous aider?**" The speaker and his companion were wearing RAF blue battle dress uniforms. A startled waiter dropped his tray of drinks, crashing the glasses onto the floor. Undercover **résistants** hustled the airmen out. It was not long before George was asked to smuggle the two aviators to Spain, which he did.

WHEELWRIGHT also facilitated the escape

to Spain of two American pilots. Rouneau wrote that an official of the French government tobacco monopoly, who was also "our first recruit in this little city of the Gironde," came to tell him that two American airmen shot down over Saint-Nazaire had made their way to him in La Réole. "I went to see them," Rouneau recalled. "They did not know a word of French." Rouneau photographed the men and forged identity cards for them at his old print factory in Agen. For intelligence on the Spanish border, he consulted a Resistance leader in Agen named Antoine Merchez. The forty-six-year-old Belgian told Rouneau that his daughter, Maguy, had already scouted the safest passes for escaping undetected through the Pyrenees and could guide the two men to Spain. Two days later, Fernand Gaucher delivered the airmen to the prohibited zone astride the frontier, and from there, local guides led them through dense forests and mountain trails to Spain.

While securing the Spanish escape line, George recruited new members to his network and acquired more weapons from London. However, the work exposed him to capture every time he left Castelnau-sur-l'Auvignon. In early 1943, after a rendezvous with Pertschuk in Toulouse, George met up with Rouneau. "At the agreed day and hour," wrote Rouneau, "I found myself in front of the station in Toulouse at the Café Regina."

George ran past, giving Rouneau a sign to go in

another direction. When Rouneau walked to the corner, George stepped behind him and whispered, "You have the tickets?" Rouneau had two tickets for the train to Pau, about 120 miles east of Toulouse. "Good," George said. "Let's go to the café and wait for the train." In the café, George expressed doubts about Henri Sevenet. Rouneau remembered George accusing Sevenet of "playing a dangerous game. He frequents constantly a Gestapo agent from whom he hopes to get interesting information." George claimed that Sevenet wanted to introduce him to the German, but he refused to meet him. He was sure the Gestapo was trailing him.

From Toulouse, George and Rouneau took the train to Pau for a rendezvous that evening with a **résistant** from the lower Pyrenees. The operative was suspicious and demanded proof that George was a British agent. George wrote a few words on a piece of paper for him to verify. When the three separated, each left in a different direction. The next day, the **résistant** asked Rouneau, "Are you sure about the man you were with yesterday?"

"Absolutely. Why?"

"But he had a strong German accent."

Rouneau laughed. "Don't you know how to tell an English from a German accent?"

"He wasn't English," the man insisted. "He was German!"

Later, Rouneau repeated the conversation to

George, who smiled and said, "They want to do great things, but they do not want to run any risk. The two don't go together."

After the rendezvous, Rouneau and George waited for the next train to Toulouse in the café of Pau's Hotel Continental. Glancing toward the entrance, George said, "There he is! The Gestapo man from Toulouse." A tall, trim German in a dark suit was standing with an equally sinister companion. "We looked relaxed," Rouneau remembered. "I slowly put my hand on the revolver in my pocket." Rouneau did not say what type of revolver he had, but George always carried a semiautomatic German Mauser pistol. The two Germans walked over to George and Rouneau's table and sat down. No one spoke. "Ten minutes," Rouneau wrote. "Ten centuries!" Unable to bear the tension, Rouneau decided to go to the men's room. "Excuse me, monsieur," he said to one of the Gestapo agents. "Would you let me pass?" The agent followed Rouneau to the lavatory and back to the table. The four men resumed their frosty silence. At last, Rouneau turned to George and asked, "Shall we go?"

They walked outside, Rouneau gripping the weapon in his pocket. "This time," he thought, "it's going to get hot." A cat and mouse game began. The Gestapo agents paused to speak with German soldiers on the terrace. George led Rouneau away from the café, employing countersurveillance techniques that SOE had taught him in Britain. Normally, the walk from the Continental to the train took fifteen minutes. Instead, George led Rouneau in another direction, ambling along the sidewalk and feigning nonchalance. "We stopped at shop windows," Rouneau wrote, "and we seemed to be discussing the things in the windows. In reality, we were observing [in the reflection] what was going on behind us." Putting distance between themselves and their pursuers, they turned onto a side street. When the Germans were out of sight, George and Rouneau ducked into a tea shop called La Minaudière. George, eating cakes that "were not bad at all," kept a discreet eye on the street outside.

An hour later, they paid and walked toward the station. No one followed. They boarded a train to Toulouse, but disembarked early at Lourdes. At a hotel there, they saw "some fat Boche officers who were feasting and making a lot of noise. We felt we had escaped a great danger, but we were not so sure." The next day, they returned to Castelnau-sur-l'Auvignon.

That spring, George installed Eureka homing devices in the church steeple and along a line of trees to help guide planes directly to the drop zones, whatever the visibility. In early April, RAF Halifaxes made two more deliveries to Castelnau-sur-l'Auvignon. The nine containers and two packages included machine guns, ammunition, and a replacement for the S-Phone that failed in November.

Sevenet and Rouneau expanded their networks of **résistants** north and west of George's area in Gascony. An SOE field report criticized Sevenet:

RODOLPHE [Sevenet] went to pick up the threads of the old set up in LYON and LE PUY, while Hilaire carried on in the southwest. While he was building up an excellent circuit, Rodolphe did little or nothing at his end, as witness a very disgruntled report from the local leaders, ETIENNE, ROLAND and HUBERT. Hilaire himself saw RODOLPHE during this period only two or three times.

The enmity between George and Sevenet was boiling over. Sevenet reported to F-Section that George visited him in Toulouse to warn that "he had seen at Agen a warrant for source's [Sevenet's] arrest on which was his name and photograph." F-Section questioned George's credibility, noting that "it was difficult to understand how HILAIRE could have seen a warrant in the Gestapo office at Pau. Source does not think that HILAIRE deliberately lied, but rather exaggerated certain suspicions in order to make sure source leave the country." George, it appeared, was trying to frighten Sevenet out of France.

The capture of one of Sevenet's Toulouse contacts, the owner of the Hôtel de Paris, and of his deputy, Paul Sarrette, only added urgency to George's desire for his departure. If either man succumbed to torture and revealed Sevenet's location, Sevenet was finished. The police had shot Sarrette while he resisted arrest and had taken him to a prison hospital in the industrial city of Clermont-Ferrand. Before anyone could interrogate the Frenchman, he escaped. German border patrols blocked his way into Switzerland, so he slipped back to Toulouse to see Sevenet.

Sevenet and Sarrette decided to flee together to Spain and on to England. Sevenet paid a final visit to Castelnau-sur-l'Auvignon. "Before he left," recalled Rouneau, "he had an unusually violent discussion with Hilaire. Their points of view were totally divergent, and it was impossible for Sevenet to accept Hilaire's aid."

Their first attempt to leave in February failed, because the Germans had just broken up the Pat Escape Line. The Pat Escape Line was operated by the SOE's French escape network, DF Section, and was made up of safe houses and guides to smuggle agents, downed aircrews, refugees, and Resistance volunteers to Switzerland, Spain, and coastal sites where ships could pick them up. On April 22, with anti-Franco Spanish guides and a party of French refugees, they made their way over the high Pyrenees in blinding snow. Their trek took thirteen days. Their first stop in Spain was Manresa, where the SOE contact was Pilar Starr, though records do not show whether Sevenet used her safe house or sought her help to go on to Barcelona.

Sevenet was now out of the way, but it became clear George should have been more concerned about PRUNUS organizer Pertschuk. Pertschuk was living at Gunzbourg's château at Pont-du-Cassé near Agen with Gunzbourg's two children and his beautiful wife, Antoinette Cahen d'Anvers. Gunzbourg sensed the young man was falling in love with Antoinette, and he detected that the young organizer had changed since they began working together in November 1942: "I was worried, because Eugène [Pertschuk] was physically exhausted." Exhaustion could lead to mistakes, mistakes to capture.

George needed Pertschuk to send messages through Bloom to London, above all for supplies to begin sabotage operations. By April 1943, other Resistance networks were launching more than one hundred attacks a month on the rail lines. WHEEL-WRIGHT needed to play its part.

London had radioed that in addition to arms containers and supply parcels, the next **parachutage** would carry a French Canadian sabotage expert named Lieutenant Charles Duchalard, code name "Denis." Rouneau wrote, "Lieutenant 'Denis' would turn would-be fighters into '**résistants et maqui-**

sards.'" A **maquisard** was a guerrilla who operated in the **maquis,** from the Corsican word **macchia,** for scrubland. SOE planned to parachute Duchalard into PRUNUS territory to assist the overworked Pertschuk and to help George with sabotage.

Born in Saskatchewan on June 3, 1915, to French immigrant parents, Duchalard moved to Paris as a teenager, where he became an electrician and joined the French Army. After the defeat of June 1940, he fled to England and joined SOE. His instructors had reservations about him, noting he had a "decided English (or Canadian) accent" in French, an obsession with women, was "too fond of talking," and exhibited an "anti-Semitic bias." They reported none of their misgivings to Pertschuk and George.

SOE informed George that Duchalard would parachute into Pertschuk's region in the Lot-et-Garonne on the night of April 11. Needing a reliable **résistant** to receive the Canadian and guarantee his security, George contacted a heavyset brewer from Montréjeau named Pierre Labayle. Forty-seven-year-old Labayle had worked for PRUNUS with Pertschuk from the early Resistance days. His duties for George included hiding gasoline in beer casks and assisting downed fliers to escape. Along with four men he trusted, Labayle went to the drop site and welcomed Duchalard to France. Duchalard hid in one of Labayle's safe houses to await George's

order to move him. However, April 11 was a dangerous time to arrive.

Maurice Pertschuk, while organizing his PRU-
NUS circuit, receiving arms drops, and re-
laying supply orders to Bloom for his and George's
circuits, rarely slept. His restless expeditions throughout the Lot-et-Garonne and Landes departments
under threat of capture could not but affect the
young man. The strain was evident when he met
Denise Bloch for their regular Monday rendezvous
at the Café Riche in Toulouse on April 12. She recalled that he looked "rather worried." They planned
to meet again at the same café the following Thursday, April 15. Pertschuk did not know, as a French
military investigation later concluded, "PRUNUS's
days were numbered in all ways, because an enemy
agent had infiltrated it."

On the evening of April 12, the Germans surrounded the Château d'Esquiré. They arrested
Marcus Bloom and the other **résistants** hiding
there. Bloom's wife had left for Normandy and
thus avoided capture with her husband. The Gestapo found Bloom's radio, but they overlooked the
35 tons of armaments under the vegetable garden.
SOE records stated that the Gestapo captured nine
PRUNUS members, although Gunzbourg put the

figure at fifteen. Bloom and another **résistant** were able to escape, and a report based on Bloom's testimony recounted, "BLOOM and a Spaniard, whose Christian name is ROBERT, were arrested by the Gestapo and handcuffed together. While they were being led away, BLOOM made an agreed sign to the Spaniard, who threw himself between the legs of the Gestapo and they managed to escape." The two prisoners ran for miles, crossing and recrossing a river to hide their tracks. When the Spaniard was too fatigued to carry on, the men traveled to the gendarmerie in a village near Toulouse that the SOE file called Marray, probably Muret. The Spaniard had heard that the gendarme captain there was sympathetic to de Gaulle.

They reached the gendarmerie at five o'clock in the morning. The Gaullist captain was absent. A brigadier promised to help, but instead called the Gestapo, who rearrested them. An SOE report noted, "In BLOOM's opinion both the Capitaine and the Brigadier were guilty." Another SOE communiqué stated, "URBAIN [Bloom] was seen shortly after his arrest being escorted through TOULOUSE by Germans. His face was covered with blood."

Back at the Château d'Esquiré, the SD found Bloom's radio, his documents, and a photograph of Pertschuk wearing a British Army uniform. No one was able to warn Pertschuk.

In the evening, Antoinette de Gunzbourg met

Pertschuk for dinner in a restaurant called Le Frégate in Toulouse. She discreetly passed him documents from her husband that were "particularly dangerous." Gunzbourg recounted, "The Englishman and the Jewish woman had a good dinner and, twenty minutes after leaving Antoinette, at eleven in the evening, he fell into a trap at the Pills' house." The "Pills" were the family of Robert Vuillemot, who lived in Toulouse at 22 rue des Pyrénées.

Armed agents of the German security services broke into Vuillemot's house and held the family at gunpoint while waiting for others to arrive. Pertschuk's courier wrote that a cactus plant in the window signaled when it was safe to enter the house. The Germans must have known, because the plant remained in place. Assured by the telltale cactus, Robert Vuillemot, who had not been at home, and Pertschuk went inside. The Gestapo grabbed Pertschuk, and though Vuillemot's daughter Catherine explained his presence by claiming he was her fiancé, the Germans took everyone for interrogation.

Tony Brooks, the young British agent in Lyon, later informed F-Section that the Gestapo had discovered Vuillemot's name and address in the notebook of Roger Bardet. Although Bardet was a double agent, one of many to bedevil the Resistance throughout the war, some in the Resistance believed the traitor to have been Jacques Megglé. Megglé, who later worked for Gestapo chief Klaus Barbie in Lyon, had attended a meeting at 22 rue des Pyrenees.

The day and night of April 12, 1943, seemed cursed and not only in France. In London, newly promoted Lieutenant Commander Jan Buchowski, the **Seadog** skipper who had carried George Starr to Port-Miou and taken John Starr out in November 1942, was on a well-earned leave. For his daring Mediterranean service, the free Polish exile government had awarded him the Cross of Gallantry and Golden Service Cross with Swords, and Britain the Distinguished Service Order. Late that night, Buchowski visited a flat in Pimlico belonging to the wife of a naval colleague. The colleague came home unannounced, saw Buchowski with his wife, and shot him dead.

Three days after he was arrested, Maurice Pertschuk failed to appear for his regular Thursday rendezvous with Denise Bloch at the Café Riche in Toulouse. Bloch told SOE that she waited for him and "made enquiries of the proprietress [of the café], but was told that he had not been seen since Monday." Her next stop was the house of one of Pertschuk's friends, but she had also disappeared.

Bloch drew the obvious conclusion and returned to Agen to inform George.

Tony Brooks had also scheduled a meeting with Pertschuk in the Trouffe de Quercy restaurant to give him a radio set. He later stated:

And when I went in, a woman who had served us, who was the boss of this black market restaurant, very small one, came up to me and she said, "Are you looking for your friend?" . . . whom we call Jean-Louis Barrault because he looked like the French film actor. And I said, "Yes, I was just looking for him. Funny chap." I said like that, terribly casually. And she said, "Well he's been arrested. You knew he was a British intelligence officer?" And I said, "Good heavens, no, I didn't." And I walked out and left.

The capture of Pertschuk and Bloom was the end of PRUNUS. George lost his funding and his radio contact with London, and was in danger of losing his life if Pertschuk or Bloom cracked under torture. Although the Germans subjected the two men to weeks of sadistic ill treatment, neither revealed anything of importance.

The head of PRUNUS's escape network, Dr. Fernand Hanon, told SOE that the Germans had found a large cache of Pertschuk's papers in a bathroom. These documents, although there was no corroboration of Hanon's claim, would have implicated George and the other WHEELWRIGHT activists in the Gers. Rouneau called this time **heures d'angoisse à Castelnau,** hours of anguish at Castelnau, when they all feared capture.

To notify London about the arrests, George found Peter Churchill, his and his brother John's contact in Cannes, and asked for the loan of wireless operator Adolphe Rabinovitch. Rabinovitch, after repairing Bloom's radio set four months previously, had moved with Churchill and Odette Sansom from the south of France to an Alpine hideaway astride the Swiss border. From a safe house a few miles from Churchill's base, he transmitted messages and ran a courier service to Switzerland for Churchill's SPINDLE circuit. Churchill gave him George's communiqué about the arrest of Pertschuk, Bloom, and the others to send to London. To his surprise, SOE replied, "Mind your own business. We know what we are doing." London assured Rabinovitch that, contrary to his message about Bloom's arrest, Bloom's radio was transmitting as usual and the RAF planned to deliver the supplies he was requesting.

Someone was operating the radio, but it wasn't Marcus Bloom.

SIX

"It Literally Rained Containers"

We could never have functioned at all had it not
been for the brave and unflinching support which
the ordinary French civilians rendered to us.

MAURICE BUCKMASTER

━━━

Bloom's radio gave the Nazis' Sicherheitsdienst
counterintelligence service the chance to rep-
licate in France the success its rivals in the
Abwehr, military intelligence, had achieved in Holland. Major Hermann Josef Giskes of Abwehr Section IIIF, counterespionage for Holland, Belgium,
and the Forbidden Zone of northern France, had
operated SOE radios since the arrest of Dutch SOE
agent Huub Lauwers on March 6, 1942. His messages deceived SOE and convinced it to parachute

weapons and personnel to the Abwehr in Holland. By the end of 1942, Giskes controlled fourteen SOE radio transmitters and had received three thousand Bren guns. The project, over which he gloated in his postwar memoir, **London Calling North Pole,** functioned under the name **Englandspiel,** "England game." Leo Marks, SOE's signals chief, called Giskes "SOE's most regular penfriend."

The SD counterespionage chief in Paris, Sturmbannführer (SS Major) Hans Josef Kieffer, dispatched his radio expert, Dr. Josef Goetz, to interrogate Bloom in Toulouse. Goetz, a former schoolteacher, was nominally the interpreter for radio department chief Untersturmführer (Second Lieutenant) Erich Otto but, in fact, he ran the service. On his arrival in Toulouse, he used Bloom's radio to initiate the SD's own **Funkspiel,** radio game, in France. Tony Brooks recalled, "Goetz, the famous German playback man from Paris, came down to Toulouse and tried to force URBAIN [Bloom] to play back his radio set, but he refused and, although terribly badly smashed about, never cooperated in any way with the Germans." Dr. Goetz had Bloom's codes, but not his "security checks," usually a redundant letter inserted at regular intervals in each transmission. SOE's security check system was designed to ensure London that the enemy was not operating its radios. Leo Marks wrote that these included a "bluff" check, which the operator was "allowed to disclose to the enemy and a 'true' check which was supposed to be known only to London." In addition, each operator had his or her own style of tapping the Morse keys that alert listeners in London recognized.

Even without the full security checks, Goetz's first transmissions from Bloom's radio fooled SOE and made it doubt George's report that Bloom and Pertschuk were prisoners. An internal SOE report admitted that "London refused to believe this and said they were still in contact with EUGENE [Pertschuk] through his wireless telegrapher. In fact, the Germans were playing him back and as a result a number of landing grounds were blown."

Subsequent messages aroused London's suspicions, and in line with procedure, SOE asked Bloom personal questions that only he could answer. One concerned "the Green pub," the Manchester Arms in Baker Street. When Goetz failed to respond, London understood that their wireless operator was a captive. Goetz admitted, "The decoy transmission went on for about four weeks but had no practical value." His deception had failed, but there would be others.

In March 1943, John Starr and Peter Churchill met in London. John, freshly promoted to captain, confided to his old comrade that he was "anxious to get out again into the field." SOE at last gave him an assignment: to organize the ACROBAT circuit in eastern France, far from his brother in the southwest. The region was an important SOE base, covering the Alps, Burgundy, and much of the French border with Germany. More densely populated than George's Gascon hills, it had a greater concentration of German troops and security agents. Despite the added dangers, John enjoyed an advantage George lacked when he arrived: a radio operator with a working wireless set. The W/T was thirty-five-year-old Lieutenant John Young, code name "Gabriel," a native of Newcastle upon Tyne in the north of England.

At the end of April, John Young and John Starr, whose code name SOE had changed from "Emile" to "Bob," boarded a Halifax bomber at RAF Tempsford. When they reached their drop zone in the Alps, the pilot saw no Resistance lights on the ground and returned to England. Two weeks later, on May 15, they tried again. German antiaircraft blasted an engine of their RAF Halifax bomber, forcing the pilot to jettison his surplus cargo to limp home. A third attempt took place on May 19. The pilot guided his Halifax over the English Channel and past the German coastal defenses. The plane circled over pine forests near Blye in the Jura department of the French Alps, until a triangle of light marking a Resistance drop zone appeared in a clearing at an altitude of about 1,600 feet. The crew opened the hatch, and the two agents leaped into the dark night.

Unlike his first **parachutage** into France, John landed without entangling his parachute in the trees and received help from local **résistants**. The Frenchmen disposed of the parachutes and loaded fifteen crates of weapons, supplies, and a radio transmitter onto a truck to take to a churchyard in the mountains. Young asked why the SOE organizer, Irish-born British captain Brian Dominic Rafferty, was not there to meet them. The **résistants** did not know, but one of them told Young his Geordie accent would give him away and to stay quiet. That night, John and Young went with the Frenchmen to a safe house to wait for Rafferty.

Giving up on Rafferty after two days, the two newly arrived agents proceeded two hundred miles west to Clermont-Ferrand, with its famed automobile factories. There, SOE comrades put them up in the apartment of a French family named Neraud. John was carrying 300,000 francs and secret radio codes for Rafferty's radio operator, Captain George Donovan Jones. While waiting for Jones, John contacted the childhood friend he had recommended to SOE recruiters, RAF Flight Lieutenant Maurice Southgate. Southgate, code name "Hector," had parachuted into France to a reception arranged by George Starr four months earlier, on January 21,

1943. Buckmaster regarded Southgate, chief of F-Section's STATIONER circuit, as one of his best organizers. Southgate informed John the Nerauds' flat was insecure, because too many agents gathered there. Rafferty and Jones, Southgate explained, "made frequent use of the place and MICHEL [Rafferty] used to go there four times a week, seeing five people each time."

Captain Jones arrived in Clermont-Ferrand three days later. John knew him by his training name, "Guy," from their SOE course in Britain. He recalled that the captain "was English, about 5'6" in height, aged 32 (then), fair hair, thin on top, and was blind in one eye." John gave him the 300,000 francs and new radio codes. After lunch together in a black market restaurant, John took a train two hundred miles back to the Jura in order to acquaint himself with other members of his circuit. One of the Frenchmen from his reception committee met him at the station with grave news: the Germans had captured Brian Rafferty while he was on his way to John's **parachutage**. The Irishman was under interrogation in Dijon's prison.

Lacking a courier to run errands, John risked another lengthy train trip back to Clermont-Ferrand to warn Jones. When he neared the apartment, he stopped. Already suspecting the flat's security, he tiptoed upstairs, rang the bell, and ran down again. From a distance, he watched to see who would open the door: Madame Neraud or a German officer. Madame Neraud peered out. John went upstairs to find her and her daughter in tears. They said that an SD radio detector van had homed in on Jones's wavelength at a safe house outside the city. Jones was now in prison with Rafferty. An SOE report noted, "ISIDORE [Jones] transmitted for many circuits, and, as already stated, too many times from the same house." John found 100,000 of the 300,000 francs he had given Jones, sharing it with the Nerauds to take into hiding. The radio codes, however, were missing.

It was time for John to make his getaway. He crept through Clermont-Ferrand's dark, deserted streets to the rail station. While he waited for the first train to anywhere, French gendarmes demanded to see his papers. These passed muster. Then they asked him to open his attaché case. John said:

In the case the police found a wad of 100 and some odd 1,000 francs, which I had recovered from Guy's [Jones's] letterbox. The police said I should have to accompany them and explain. I broke through the queue, which was waiting for tickets, and ran outside the station and returned immediately through the next door. The police apparently ran after me into the streets.

He jumped onto the footboard of a moving train and rode it to the next station, where he climbed inside. Via a succession of trains, he went back to his first safe house in the mountains, where Young was waiting for him. Young encoded and transmitted John's message that the Germans had arrested Captains Rafferty and Jones. Someone was betraying British agents to the Germans, making John's second mission to France even more perilous than the first.

George Starr's troubles in the southwest differed from his brother's, but they were just as threatening. In the final days of April 1943, his mission was on the verge of collapse. Only five months before, he recalled, "I'd arrived with a suitcase full of clothes and money, nothing else, except an S-Phone for talking to planes." Now, his clothing was ragged, his money spent, and his S-Phone uncertain. No organizer could build a Resistance network without communications, funds, and supplies. As he pondered whether to admit failure and go home, the strain affected his health. "You're doing too much," a local doctor told him. Directed to cut out white wine, George explained, "They [the Gascons] wash their teeth in it. They drink it all the time, the wine. Then he says cut out the white wine completely . . . And I've never drunk white wine since. Well, barely." His psoriasis grew worse: "And the skin goes all white and dead, dead nerves." He summarized the diagnosis: "Eating too well, drinking too well, sweaty ass on a bicycle."

When he was not cycling, George took buses and trains to meet agents in Condom, Agen, and Toulouse, as well as farther afield in Lyon. Using public transport had its dangers. He remembered an incident on a bus, when, once again, his sixth sense protected him. After he boarded the bus through the rear door, another passenger began talking about Pétain. George didn't like the sound of him and got off at the next stop. "When it got to Agen," George heard later, "everybody got out and had to show their credentials. Good thing I wasn't there. I had to walk back to Castelnau."

George bicycled to Condom on shopping expeditions with Jeanne Robert, who spoke for him lest his accent betray him. While pedaling along the country roads, the pair sang. "Then, yes," she admitted, "some dirty songs." One was a folk tune, "**Les filles de Camaret**":

Les filles de Camaret se disent toutes vierges
[The girls of Camaret say they're all virgins]
Mais quand elles sont dans mon lit
[But when they're in my bed]
Elles préfèrent tenir mon vis
[They'd rather hold my screw]

Qu'un cierge.
[Than a candle.]

"He joked like that," Robert remembered, "but was never, never vulgar."

In Castelnau-sur-l'Auvignon, Mayor Larribeau was doing all in his power to assist George. Having made him deputy mayor, he issued him identity documents to facilitate passage through police and German checkpoints, and applied to the regional government, the Prefecture, for George's appointment as **Inspecteur pour le Ministère du Ravitaillement,** inspector for the ministry of supply. This entitled him to the use of a car, rations of gasoline, and permission to circulate everywhere in the region. Under the occupation, cars were restricted to the Germans, Vichy officials, and collaborators. An SOE report noted the post's advantages: "This was an ideal cover job as a car was put at his disposal and he have [sic] every reason to circulate round the area as freely as he liked, not only in the daytime but also at night, on Sundays, and on jours de fete." George's cover and passes were useless, however, without a radio and supplies.

George was desperate. If London did not supply his basic needs, he would have to abandon his mission and leave **résistants** in the southwest without means to resist. "The position grew so serious that STARR decided to send Mlle. Denise BLOCH," commented SOE, "with a report on the situation to LONDON via Spain." Bloch would be not merely his messenger, but his advocate. London had to understand that the Germans had cut his communications twice. First, the Gestapo arrested Marcus Bloom on April 12, 1943. Then, four days later, German military intelligence lured Peter Churchill, who had only recently returned to France, and Odette Sansom into a trap in the French Alps. Rabinovitch went into hiding. London advised the wireless operator to flee to Spain, but he went to Cannes to warn the new F-Section organizer who had arrived in March to assume Churchill's duties as liaison to the CARTE circuit. Rabinovitch was now out of reach, and George did not have a third operator.

Violating his policy against committing anything to paper, George wrote a lengthy situation appraisal and an appeal for supplies, money, and his own radio operator. On April 29, 1943, George gave Bloch the report. They said good-bye at the safe house in Agen. Her departure was hard on them both. Bloch wanted to stay to resist the Nazis, who occupied her country and declared her, as a Jew, unfit to live. George was losing his closest companion. They had lived for four months on the upper floor of Jeanne Robert's schoolhouse and cycled together over miles of Gascon countryside. One report stated that "she always travelled everywhere with him." She had willingly risked her life for **le patron**. Whether they had been lovers, as Paul Sarrette alleged to SOE, the two were close and respected each other. She regretted leaving George in "a terrible mess."

George asked Maurice Dupont to take Bloch to the border as Dupont knew the route, having accompanied her on the aborted crossing to Spain in January. The plan called for guides to lead her over the high Pyrenees to neutral Spain and for Dupont to return to Castelnau. When the pair reached the frontier village of Cier-de-Luchon, however, Dupont did not have the heart to abandon her to the freezing mountains. "We were at the end of our strength," Bloch later told Rouneau. "Our clothes were in tatters. On my own, I'd have just stayed there. But 'Yvan' [Dupont] was so admirable. So many times, he said to me, 'Let's go, my little sister, have courage! Think of what you can do when you get there.'" Two local men in Cier-de-Luchon helped her to avoid German patrols in the Forbidden Zone. "She left at 12.30 A.M. and walked for seventeen hours in the snow, with bare legs and wearing a thin, half-length coat," stated a subsequent SOE report. Her ascent of the Pyrenees took her to nearly 11,000 feet above sea level. SOE noted, "Her guides were excellent, one accompanied her and the other went on ahead to see that the way was clear." The guides built a fire to keep her warm during the night and plowed ahead in the morning. A snowstorm made it so hard to see that she feared wandering back to

France. At last, she and Dupont reached the Catalan village of Bausen, where they waited three days for a bus to Lerida.

In Lerida, Spanish Guardia Civil interned Dupont. "Me, I was recognized as a British subject," Bloch later told Rouneau, "and, thanks to the Spanish gallantry towards a weak woman, I was not worried." The Spaniards, however, were not so gallant that they neglected to seize George's report. Bloch was concerned that the papers "gave information too precise not to be dangerous if they were communicated to the Germans." Her subsequent SOE debrief report added, "Regarding the loss of her papers in Spain, DANIELLE [Bloch] said that HILAIRE told her that if they were to be taken off her they would be forwarded direct to the British Embassy." The frontier guards in Bausen who seized George's report, however, did not send them to the British Embassy. And despite Spain's official status as a "nonbelligerent" nation, General Francisco Franco was a friend of Abwehr chief Admiral Wilhelm Canaris and owed his civil war victory to Germany. Bloch's fear that the Spaniards would pass the report to the German Embassy in Madrid was well founded, but records don't indicate what happened to George's report.

While waiting in Lerida, Bloch met the British consul from Barcelona, Sir Harold Farquhar, who was visiting. They had dinner together, and Farquhar issued papers enabling her to travel on to Madrid. Farquhar may have also had a hand in the release of Dupont, who was reunited with Bloch for the rest of her journey. After five days in Madrid, Bloch and Dupont went to Gibraltar, where they saw Sevenet and Sarrette. The two Frenchmen, furious to be kept waiting so long for transport, were determined to reach London to lodge complaints against George. Bloch spent three days in Gibraltar before flying to Lisbon and then, on May 21, to England. Bloch's entire journey took twenty days.

The next day, Vera Atkins, Buckmaster's intelligence officer, debriefed Bloch in F-Section's London Reception Center. Bloch pleaded for George: "He needs someone to help him as soon as possible, because he is now the only one left to control five departments (he is taking on LYONS and TOULOUSE), and if he is arrested there is no one else." Atkins's account of the interview provided insights into the circumstances confronting George: "Apparently his position is almost desperate as he is quite out of touch with London. He asks most urgently—hoping that it might still be done during the May Moon—for a W/T operator and for funds." Bloch told her that George enjoyed the cooperation of many pro-Allied mayors and officials in the Gers and had established reliable reception committees among local peasants. But not all was positive, as Atkins noted: "It would appear, however, that

HILAIRE himself is in great danger owing to the many arrests all round, and he may also be gravely endangered by the loss of his Report."

Bloch urged F-Section to send to George, in addition to military equipment, basics the region lacked: "3 shirts, 3 pairs of pants, 2 pairs of pyjamas, socks, handkerchiefs, toothbrush (they are unobtainable in France, and nail brushes, etc., are very acceptable), soap (wanted very badly) . . . [and] leather to sole shoes and extra shirts for the other men."

F-Section chiefs were unsure what to do with the young Frenchwoman, but she convinced them to train her for another deployment in France.

The last part of the message Bloch gave SOE from George was that he "would like his Mother to be informed that he is well, and he would like to have news of his family—also whether his sister-in-law's baby has arrived."

John Starr's wife, Michelle, gave birth to their son, Lionel, on January 17, 1943, in Burslem, Stoke-on-Trent. John, now back in France, decided to tell his in-laws about their grandchild and traveled to their home in Rouen, more than 250 miles from his base in Burgundy. He hazarded a personal journey, something his brother, George, would not have done. Although George's wife and children were just across the border in Spain, he never attempted to visit them, send them a message, or tell them where he was. John took a series of trains all the way to Rouen, which, as the capital of the Normandy region beside the English Channel, was under heavier German supervision than either George's Gers or John's Burgundy and Jura. He evaded German surveillance to tell Michelle's parents about Lionel's birth and to stay overnight with them. On his return to Dijon, he stopped in Paris and saw friends. If anything characterized the difference between the two Starr brothers, it was John's flagrant personal contravention of SOE procedures. John also visited his apartment in Issy-les-Moulineaux, something that had an operational justification: if he or another agent needed a safe house in the capital, it would be ready.

George Starr sent London a follow-up message, via a courier link through Irun and Madrid, to confirm he had sent Denise Bloch and Maurice Dupont to England. The dispatch also requested that a plane fly over a site designated as "London T25," a farm belonging to a family named Coulanges, relatives of courier Pierre Duffoir, "to speak with me by S-Phone." George asked that the plane "drop me a radio-telegraphist with set so that we may maintain constant contact," and pleaded that he had no funds to support his "vast organisation" and needed "at least 200,000 French francs a month and supplies to keep his circuits going."

At the end of May, word came from F-Section via a BBC announcement on its **Messages personnel:** **"Les giraffes sont les canards."** Giraffes are ducks. This coded message meant that F-Section operations officer Major Gérard "Gerry" Morel was taking off for London T25 with an S-Phone. Morel had trained with George and knew his voice. The plane circled, as the two SOE officers spoke to each other. George recalled, "They said there was no mistaking me, and I started cussing them up and down. 'There's no doubt about it, it's him all right.'" Morel went back to London and confirmed George was alive and all too well. F-Section promised a radio operator and a courier at "the next moon or the moon after."

Meanwhile, George absorbed stranded members of Pertschuk's PRUNUS and Churchill's SPINDLE circuits and expanded his area of operations. One of the first to join him was Pertschuk's fellow operative Philippe de Gunzbourg. "He was a very brave man," George said. "He did a wonderful job." Gunzbourg similarly admired George as "a professional . . . a great leader of the caliber of Lawrence [of Arabia]." George put Gunzbourg in charge of the southern Dordogne and northwest Garonne, where he prepared reception grounds, recruited partisans, and instructed young men in the use of modern weapons.

The infiltrations and betrayals that had destroyed VENTRILOQUIST, PRUNUS, and SPINDLE forced George to reassess WHEELWRIGHT's security. "Then I started taking a leaf out of the communists' book," he said. "Cells, so if one gets caught, they don't know where the others are. That's the only good thing I ever got from the communists." His seven-member cells were not permitted contact with one another. He appointed Captain Fernand Pagès, chief of the gendarmerie in Condom, to run a new security section. His counterespionage agents kept watch on the Gestapo and SD. The subprefect of Bergerac provided George with information on Gestapo movements, imminent arrests, and radio detector van routes. Aldo Molesini, a landowner in Montréal-du-Gers whom George met through Mayor Larribeau, also gave George intelligence. As the engineer for a big public works company that undertook projects for the Germans in the southwest, he had access to German military installations. Lastly, two Gestapo typists, a man and woman, kept George abreast of impending **rafles,** or raids.

In late spring 1943, Gunzbourg took George to the village of Vic-Fezensac, famed in the region for its bullring and springtime toreador festival. They walked along the village's narrow, dark streets to the home of Marie-Louise Lac, who was sheltering Louis and Théo Lévy. Gunzbourg introduced his friend, whom Madame Lac described:

The English colonel was a little chap, sporting a little blond moustache, three hairs on one side and two on the other; he had a beret; when I saw him for the first time, he wore a beige pullover, without a jacket; his sleeves had holes at the elbows, having been darned—certainly by him—with green wool. No one could have believed he was an English colonel endowed with courage and a will of iron.

"From that moment," she felt, "the Resistance was well organized." Madame Lac continued to hide **résistants** and began locating **parachutage** sites for George, but he still needed a radio.

In the spring of 1943, George made his courier Pierre Duffoir, code name "Félix," responsible for his communications with Switzerland. Duffoir's wife, Paulette, was the sister of Madame Hélène Falbet, landlady of George's safe house in Agen, and most of the Duffoir family participated in Resistance activities. Duffoir made frequent trips to the border zone and to the British Embassy in Berne with George's reports for the SOE station. Rouneau recalled, "The devil of a small man went everywhere."

During one of Duffoir's missions to Annecy on the French side of the Swiss border, Rabinovitch emerged from hiding. "After the RAOUL [Peter Churchill] affair (his arrest and the break up of his circuit)," stated an SOE report, "ARNAUD [Rabinovitch], his W/T operator who escaped arrest, got in touch with HILAIRE." Rabinovitch remained free thanks to the heroism of the woman George had dismissed as "a dreadful lady," Odette Sansom. Despite brutal torture at the Fresnes Prison south of Paris, which included having her toenails ripped out with pliers, she refused to disclose Rabinovitch's location. George's reports and interviews did not mention this debt to her. After Rabinovitch saw Duffoir, he transmitted from Annecy for George while Duffoir continued to take messages to Berne.

The two avenues of communications produced a sea change in George's fortunes. "Then it literally rained containers," Rouneau rejoiced. Arms, ammunition, and explosives poured onto drop zones all over Gascony, constituting what Rouneau called the "embryo of the arsenal that would allow us to arm the groups we had been supervising." Fernand Gaucher's reception committees collected the containers on balmy, moonlit nights in the Gironde, Gunzbourg received them in the Landes, and George attended drops in the Gers. In June, SOE finally sent him two radio transmitters, though one smashed as it hit the ground.

"The partisans understood that the war matériel had arrived," Rouneau wrote, "but they had completely ignored where they would hide it." Maurice Jacob, who ran Vichy's Service des Réfugiés et Expulsés, offered to conceal the weapons at Château de la Clotte near Agen. The château, which Jacob had rented as a home for French people banished by Germany's annexation of Alsace, became a weapons storehouse. Another Vichy official in Agen's Prefecture lent George a truck to carry the equipment from drop zones to the Château de la Clotte and other caches.

Moving the equipment required not only trucks, but also fuel to run them. George said he had little option but to steal it from the Germans, sending **résistants** disguised as Wehrmacht troops to the fuel depots: "I wanted at least two German officers' uniforms, I said, to be complete with the pistols and everything." SOE dispatched captured German clothes and sidearms. "I kept the pistol, and my German-speaking boys put the uniforms on." The **résistants** who went to steal the fuel were those who spoke the language. "We had a German section, the Alsatians. Théo [Lévy] and his brother [Louis] were German Jews . . . ," remembered George. "We had quite a gang who spoke German as their mother tongue, so they were the ones who did that." WHEEL-WRIGHT was coming together with vehicles, fuel, disguises, a radio, and tons of equipment.

Raymond Escholier wrote that George, Théo Lévy, "and some hardy Gascons, transformed Castelnau into an arsenal." Escholier imagined George's thoughts as he "inspected the treasures in the old square dungeon of Castelnau."

119

If the parachutages accelerate at this rate, we'll have enough to arm several divisions. Yes, but these arms, what can they do? Not politics! Nothing but war . . . Yes, but these arms, to whom shall we give them?

One Resistance leader in need of weapons was Claude Joseph Maurice Parisot, a former French Army officer. Captain Parisot, code name "Caillou," or "Stone," had organized nearly a thousand **résistants** under the banner of the **Organisation de Résistance de l'Armée** (ORA). The ORA comprised military officers who, while seeking to expel the Germans, did not answer to Charles de Gaulle. Parisot's base was in the village of Panjas, about sixty miles from Castelnau. A tall, handsome agronomist with dark hair and a clipped moustache, Parisot was, in Escholier's words, "an ardent Catholic, but a freethinker" and a "chief among chiefs." His father had been a professor of ancient history and his mother a French colonist from Algeria. During the First World War, he followed his older brother into the army and ended as a lieutenant. He studied farming after the war and worked for the Ministry of Agriculture until 1938, when he rejoined the army as a captain. The military based him in Corsica. When the Germans invaded northern France in May 1940, he demanded a transfer to the front. Instead, his superiors sent him to Algeria. He wrote from there to Raymond Escholier when Pétain announced his armistice with Germany, "I refuse to be complicit in this infamy." He planned to join de Gaulle's Free French in London, until Britain bombed the French fleet at Mers el-Kebir, Algeria, on July 3, 1940. Although Britain's objective had been to prevent Germany from using the French warships, Parisot and other French officers condemned an "ally" that killed more than twelve hundred of their comrades. Parisot left the army and returned to France to manage farms in the southwest's wine country.

After Germany occupied Vichy's Free Zone and disbanded its Armistice Army, Parisot, Captain Maurice Moureau of the 2nd Dragoons, Captain Henri Monnet, and an Armagnac distiller named Abel Sempé established an underground unit they dubbed the Armagnac Battalion. Its rank and file were **réfractaires,** men whose refusal to work as conscripted laborers in Germany under Vichy's **Service du travail obligatoire** (STO) forced them to live underground. Raymond Escholier wrote that volunteers included "the men from Flanders, the Belgian and the Alsatian **réfractaires** who had found refuge in Saint-Gô." Saint-Gô was a small village about forty miles southwest of Castelnau-sur-l'Auvignon. Parisot's Armagnac Battalion, lacking any connection to SOE, received no British arms.

While waiting near Saint-Gô for one of George's weapons drops, Théo Lévy met a painter named Maurice Poncelet. Poncelet asked him, "Why no arms for Caillou?" Lévy had no idea who Caillou was. Poncelet said Caillou, Captain Parisot, commanded the largest force in the southwest. Lévy, one of the few men George trusted to meet him in Castelnau, promised to ask **le patron** about supplies for Parisot. A few nights later at another arms drop, Poncelet demanded an answer. Lévy explained his boss distrusted people he didn't know. But Poncelet persisted, and Lévy said he would ask again. "The arms must not serve political ends," Lévy added. "No one can use them, except against the Boche." Poncelet assured Lévy that there was "no better Frenchman than Caillou."

That evening, Lévy told George about Parisot and the captain's sterling reputation. George said, "So be it. We can parachute him some arms. But I don't want to see him." Escholier wrote that the religious Parisot had been praying that weapons "would fall from the sky . . . And, in effect, they did." The RAF dropped its first consignment to Parisot's men near Saint-Gô on the night of April 9.

Without warning **le patron**, Lévy brought Parisot to meet George six days later in his Condom safe house, a building with three exits that belonged to a fellow **résistant**. After introducing Parisot to George, Lévy vanished rather than risk his chief's anger.

"It took me a long time to make up my mind that Parisot was okay," George recalled. "By the grace of God, there was an immediate spark. We were two men with the same idea." George instructed London to send more arms to Parisot, and the RAF dropped as many as three loads a night to him.

Parisot had made Panjas a center of resistance in large part because of its priest, Abbé Laurent Talès. The fierce Basque cleric rejected all compromise with the occupier, declaring from the pulpit, "Freedom of thought overrides borders, and the diktat of a Führer will never change that." Parishioners likened Abbé Talès to the Basque **pili-pili** hot peppers that he left to dry on his window shutters. George found in him a kindred spirit:

> The abbé was a jovial old boy, ready to fight anybody or anything so long as he was German. He was taken prisoner and escaped in Poland and escaped again, and got this living in Panjas. He was the complete and utter spirit of the Resistance. He carried a .45 revolver under his soutane. A patriot to the core. A good Christian and a good man. He was wonderful. Tell a good story, take a good drink, fight like hell, pray like hell. He was a Friar Tuck.

Abbé Talès had no qualms about hiding tons of SOE weaponry and explosives under the altar of the

Eglise de Saint-Laurent. He named one Resistance unit the **Groupe de Saint Laurent** and declared, "We will be the guardians of the church's treasures. And to save all that remains, we will, if necessary, burn at the stake as Saint Lawrence did to save our land." George had more confidence in him than in the local priest from the nearby village of Blaziert, Abbé Boë, who, he said, "talked too much." Abbé Boë's loyalty was never in doubt, only his discretion. His sermons condemning the Germans were known for their vehemence and excessive length. Escholier referred to Boë as "the classic poilu ["hairy," a First World War French Army enlisted man] type in a greenish cassock." One woman who knew him recalled, "He tore about the countryside on a bicycle, his soutane flying in the wind and his bare feet in the dirtiest pair of worn-out old sabots." George's renegade band had two Friar Tucks, but, since Denise Bloch's departure, no Maid Marian.

The flow of weapons for George's outlaws came to an abrupt halt in June, when a traitor informed on Rabinovitch. An internal SOE memo stated, "He was eventually considered to be so badly compromised that he was instructed to return to England. He reluctantly acquiesced, leaving France in June 1943." Rabinovitch escaped with a fellow F-Section agent to Spain, where Spanish authorities interned them until the British negotiated their repatriation to England.

George contacted London, by means that his file left unspecified, to declare: "All means of communications now cut." The same message requested a radio operator, one million francs, and the return of Denise Bloch and Maurice Dupont.

George grew impatient with matters that diverted him from his primary objective of preparing for D-Day. One was the sabotage expert, Lieutenant Charles Duchalard, who had complained to SOE that George and Rouneau gave him no support. Duchalard spent a third of the 100,000 francs London had given him for George on his own travels to Marseille and elsewhere, and Rouneau went to investigate. After questioning some of Duchalard's colleagues, he concluded that he had become a "burden . . . indiscrete [sic]" and in touch with "inappropriate people."

Rouneau traveled south to confer with George. Agreeing with Rouneau's assessment, George sent his courier to the SOE station in Berne with a message requesting that Duchalard "not remain long in the region." London settled the affair by ordering Duchalard back to England. Rouneau met the Canadian near the lower Pyrenean village of Luc-Harmeau, lectured him on security breaches, and told him that

London wanted him out of France. Rouneau sent Duchalard "to a place where we would take control of him," Mazères-de-Neste, where the family of a **résistant** gave him a room until George arranged his passage back to England.

Events outside France were bringing the country's liberation closer. On May 12, the Allies completed their conquest of North Africa, capturing 250,000 German, Italian, and other Axis soldiers. Allied shipping through the Suez Canal was secure, and the Germans had lost their chance to turn the Mediterranean into an Axis lake.

The Allies' next step had to be the invasion of Europe. Military commanders led Buckmaster to believe that meant his fiefdom in France. "In the middle of 1943," he wrote, "we had a top secret message telling us that D-Day might be closer than we thought. This message had been tied up with international politics on a level far above our knowledge and we, of course, had acted on it without question."

Believing the French offensive was imminent, Buckmaster ordered George to prepare aircraft landing strips in the southwest. The clearings had to be large enough for cargo aircraft to deliver thousands of Allied soldiers, tanks, jeeps, weapons, and other supplies on D-Day. It was a massive undertaking and a morale booster for the **résistants**. George organized the operation in the Gers, while Gunzbourg and his men chopped trees north of the River Garonne to receive "troops, machines for transporting light tanks, jeeps, a large quantity of light arms" at the start of the invasion. They worked on plans to destroy telephone installations and roads as well as to provide intelligence and "aides and guides" to the invading Allies.

When the landing fields were ready, Gunzbourg wrote, Allied headquarters "decided not to use these landing sites . . . This created difficulties for those who had made promises in good faith. The right-wing Resistance as well as the left-wing fell hard on Hilaire's organization and sought to stir up public opinion against it by pretending that the action had begun too soon, that all this was a trap, etc. . . . Naturally, after a few days, these sites were abandoned."

The Americans had argued all along for a cross-Channel landing in France. The British, with bitter memories of trench warfare in France during the First World War, resisted. Prime Minister Churchill had made the case at the Casablanca Conference for invading Italy first, but American senior officers, including Army Chief of Staff General George Marshall, believed Italy would rob resources from the main objective of taking the war to Germany through France. In May, however, at a meeting between Roosevelt and Churchill in Washington, the leaders confirmed they would invade Italy and put off the French landings until May 1, 1944. That date became one of the most closely guarded secrets of the war.

The premature D-Day planning led to a change in direction for F-Section's field organizers. Until then, SOE had answered to the minister of economic warfare with a mission to cripple Germany's economic infrastructure and war-making capacity. It now acquired a second master, the Allied military command, whose objective was to have the Resistance sever German communications and distract German troops when the United States and Britain invaded Hitler's Fortress Europe.

By July 1943, SOE noted, George's WHEEL-WRIGHT had organized "28 teams for railway destruction and a military group of 1,200 men for guerrilla activity." Its area of operations extended, George said, to "South Dordogne, Lot-et-Garonne, Gers, Landes Libre, Gironde Libre, Haute-Pyrenees, Bas-Pyrenees Libre, half of Haut Garonne and part of Tarn-et-Garonne," in effect, most of southwestern France. WHEELWRIGHT's main priority was to amass weapons for the guerrillas to use when the Allies invaded. More weapons stores, more volunteers, and a wider area of operations meant more dangers, at a time when the Germans were becoming more efficient at infiltrating SOE's Resistance circuits.

SEVEN

Arrests and Arrivals

War is no exact science.

MAURICE BUCKMASTER

═══

John Starr returned to Burgundy from his in-laws' in Normandy in time for a rendezvous with fellow SOE agent Harry Rée. A former secondary-school language teacher, Rée had para-chuted into eastern France the previous April, and his handiwork with explosives was making him one of SOE's most accomplished saboteurs. Rée intro-duced John to a **résistant** from Dole named Pierre Martin. "He was a cheerful ex-garage keeper, very energetic, who managed to get things done," Rée said. Martin seemed an ideal candidate to assist John. He had a car and fuel to keep it running. Rée later admitted, "I should have been suspicious by all this of course." He added that he "told BOB [John

Starr] that he had grounds for suspecting Martin, but BOB was unwilling to believe evil of MARTIN, who had done extremely good work for the organisation in providing transport for material." John, however, later insisted that he also had begun to doubt Martin, "as it appeared to him that MARTIN was accomplishing his tasks with rather too much facility."

Martin drove John and radio operator Young to a new hideout a few hours from Clermont-Ferrand in a medieval château above Saint-Amour-Bellevue. While John roamed the countryside in search of recruits, parachute drop sites, and targets for sabotage, Young stayed out of sight in Saint-Amour to prevent his accent from giving him away.

On June 16, F-Section sent John a new courier. Squadron Officer Diana Rowden, code name "Paulette," landed in a Lysander light aircraft near Le Mans in western France with two other female agents. Twenty-eight-year-old Rowden was the daughter of a British Army officer. She had grown up in southern France, spoke the language without an accent, and had survived combat as a Red Cross volunteer during the German invasion of 1940. Her arrival completed John's standard SOE team of organizer, radio operator, and courier.

John's efforts in the Jura and Burgundy mirrored his brother's in the Gers: establishing cells, arranging **parachutages**, and, one report noted, conducting a sabotage operation "near DIJON." Rowden carried messages for John's circuit, ACROBAT, as far as Marseille and Paris, and Young radioed messages from Saint-Amour. John extended ACROBAT's reach over a large swath of the Jura and Burgundy. The volunteers he armed and trained were, like George's in Gascony, standing by for deployment during the Allied invasion of France.

However, neither John nor George knew that Allied commanders had postponed the French invasion in favor of taking Sicily from Germany's vulnerable ally, Mussolini's Italy. At 4:45 on the morning of July 10, 1943, what was until D-Day the largest amphibious invasion force in history hit the Sicilian shore. More than 117,000 American, British, and Canadian soldiers under the command of U.S. Army general Dwight Eisenhower landed on the beaches and moved inland. The campaign, however, was anything but a pushover. The Germans reinforced the Italians and mounted a vigorous defense. The Allies pushed them back, but most of the German and Italian forces were evading destruction or capture by retreating intact to the Italian mainland. One military analyst noted that "Operation Husky was a valuable proving ground where shortcomings in leadership, doctrine, training, equipment and command and control were revealed." The Allies had to learn from mistakes in Sicily, if the much larger invasion of France were to succeed.

On July 18, John and Martin met for lunch in Dijon. They left Dijon for a short drive of about thirty miles to Dole, but as Martin's truck rolled into the Burgundian countryside, a roadblock appeared. Schutzstaffel (SS) troops ordered them out of the truck, demanded their identity cards, and asked why they were carrying 35,000 francs. Agents of the SS security department, the Sicherheitsdienst, took custody of the two men, handcuffed them together, and drove them back to their headquarters in Dijon. Then a curious thing happened. At headquarters, the SD men let John overhear them asking about Martin on the telephone. They returned and told him that local police confirmed Martin's identity and the Frenchman was free to leave. But John's papers stated he lived in Paris and "it was impossible for them to 'phone to Paris and that I should have to go to prison . . ." John reported, "I realised that MARTIN had given me away through the stupidity of the S.D. interrogators." Recognizing the deception for what it was, he asked for permission to smoke, since "all my notes and messages for home were burnt in a cigarette, which I kept for that purpose."

Later, John would write, "I was sold by a French double agent to the Sicherheitsdienst ('Gestapo') as a resistant and 'terroristen.' He led me into a prearranged roadblock guarded by SS and Gestapo agents."

A police van took John to a Wehrmacht prison in Dijon. As it passed through the ancient gates into the courtyard, John seized a chance to signal to Young and Diana Rowden that Martin had betrayed him. SOE recorded that, when the vehicle stopped, John "got out, pretended to be stiff with sitting, and then, catching his captors unprepared, took to his heels and ran at top speed down the yard and out through the gates." The SS men fired. A bullet pierced his left thigh. He ran, trailing blood, into a side street. The SS shot again, wounding his left foot. "I continued to run into the next road right," he said, "which was again a cul-de-sac, and finally entered the third turning right, and was about to turn left again, when through loss of blood my strength gave way. I was recaptured." He hoped that neighbors who saw him and heard the shooting would alert the Resistance, so Young and Rowden could avoid his fate and keep the ACROBAT circuit alive. It appeared to work, because a short time later the BBC broadcast to France, "Bob, contagious illness at the hospital, don't contact him."

The SS dragged him, with blood spurting from both wounds, into the prison. "One bullet went through my left thigh from buttocks to knee," he wrote. "I was thrown into a cell in solitary confinement." A prison doctor fixed a rough dressing and left him shackled to a wooden pallet. Two hours later, interrogators entered the cell.

They demanded to know who he was and who worked for him. He did not reply. The more he held out, the more they beat him. For three days without respite, they kicked him and threw him against the walls. The doctor reopened his thigh wound, intensifying the pain. He insisted that he was a French businessman, but the Germans repeated their questions about his courier and radio operator. He abandoned his cover story for what he called "his reserve cover story," which explained that "he had lived in France previous to the war (which was true), that he had been left behind when the B.E.F. [British Expeditionary Force] evacuated (untrue), and had consequently taken to civilian life again."

The Germans did not believe him, saying they had heard the same tale from other British prisoners. Then, John recalled, "I admitted everything that was known to them through Martin, which enabled me with little difficulty to hold back the part which was known only to myself." The admissions did not stop the torture.

On his fifth day of imprisonment, the SS drove him to a security office for more rigorous interrogation. He recalled that "when my answers were not 'satisfactory' as often, my wounded thigh was beaten up untill [sic] it was just a huge mass of pus and bruises." One day, John's interrogators left him alone in the interrogation room with an open dossier on the desk. He suspected they wanted him to see the file, which contained a list of SOE schools in Britain, along with the names of senior staff. The Germans had penetrated SOE's apparatus, but how? When the interrogators returned, they demanded descriptions of his instructors. He complied, saying that one was "about five feet nine inches, thin and dark." He said the same of the next, and the next. All his teachers were "about five feet nine inches, thin and dark." The interrogators gave up for the evening and returned him to his cell in the prison.

The next morning, he was taken back to security headquarters. The Germans showed him photographs of Captains Rafferty and Jones, who had been captured earlier that summer. They asked for the men's real names, which John refused to give. This provoked more torture of his infected thigh. The interrogators sent him again to the prison, where a doctor and several warders came into his cell during the night. They ripped off his trousers and held him down, while the doctor forced a long steel rod into his wound. The spike came out the other side of his thigh, and he fainted.

The Germans kept him in solitary confinement on bread and water, unable to wash, shave, or change his blood-drenched trousers. There was no toilet paper. His infected wound left him with a high fever. Yet his obstinacy served a purpose: it bought time for his comrades to disappear.

Not every German approved the mistreatment.

"The governor of the prison was a Wehrmacht officer (Oberleutenant)," noted an SOE report. "He used to come to see STARR practically every day, giving him first of all a military salute, then shaking hands." One night, a Wehrmacht medical officer changed John's bandages and told him about the progress of the war in Sicily, where most of the German and Italian forces were retreating across the Strait of Messina.

A few days later, guards woke John at three in the morning. For the first time during his five weeks of confinement, he showered and shaved. The reason soon became evident. They were moving him.

On Thursday night, August 16, 1943, as the Allies completed their conquest of Sicily, George Starr was expecting to receive twelve containers and two packages of weapons and other supplies. Louis Lévy and several of George's other **résistants** watched a British plane fly over the Landes department about twenty miles northwest of Condom. The drop site was a field near the hamlet of Arx. The plane was about to jettison the cargo, when it suddenly fell from the sky and crashed. George recalled, "It was a Lancaster with a crew of mad Poles." The plane was in fact a Halifax, which was too badly damaged to take off again. The reception team drove their trucks under the wings to siphon the valuable fuel. At the same time, the pilot prepared to blow up the aircraft rather than leave it for the Germans. "Some of the Polish crew were like schoolboys," George said, "and they threw a life-raft out, curious to see if it really did work." The men draining the gasoline heard the hiss of air from the life-raft and, thinking the plane was about to blow, fled. The rest of the reception committee and the Poles carried on, drinking a jeroboam of Armagnac to keep warm. "And after they blew up the plane," George said, "they all went off in enemy territory in a convoy of trucks, the Poles singing their heads off in the middle of the night. It was a miracle that nobody got caught."

Maurice Rouneau had been on an operation in Miramont when the Poles crashed. Jeanne Robert told him about it when he arrived in Castelnau the next morning, adding that Louis Lévy needed him at once in Condom. Rouneau hurried to the town, where Lévy asked for identity cards, ration books, and civilian clothing so the Poles could escape to Spain. Rouneau put his **résistants** in Agen to work. Former colleagues at the printing factory forged documents, while other friends dipped into stocks of old clothes.

George was reconnoitering routes to England for the Poles when a sudden crisis distracted him. The arms from the Poles' plane had been hidden in the house of a **résistant,** and one weapon accidentally went off and killed his wife. Unable to explain her death to the authorities, George sent the **résistant** to Spain, an easier proposition for a Frenchman than for a crew of Poles who did not speak the language. Meanwhile, the police launched a manhunt for the woman's killer.

On Friday, August 20, 1943, Rouneau moved some of the arms to Maurice Jacob's Château de la Clotte. He returned to Castelnau that evening. As he went into the schoolhouse, a car screeched to a stop outside. Fellow **résistant** Antoine Merchez jumped out and shouted, using one of Rouneau's code names, "Quick, my old Albert. You have to come to Agen. Things are bad. Gérard has been arrested!" Gérard was Fernand Gaucher, George's senior agent in the Gironde, whose wife and children lived in Castelnau-sur-l'Auvignon. Gaucher knew more about George, WHEELWRIGHT, and the Castelnau **résistants** than anyone the Germans had so far captured. Merchez told Rouneau that Hilaire, as he always called George, was waiting for him in Agen.

Rouneau asked for time to pack his and Jeanne Robert's belongings, but Merchez said that Hilaire wanted to see Rouneau alone. Rouneau refused to leave Robert behind. "I emptied Hilaire's cupboard," Rouneau wrote. "There was nothing compromising there except a journal with entries like 'subsidy for a Resistance group,' 'expenses for trip to Lyon, to Toulouse, to Agen, to Montélimar, etc.' I took the book with me."

As Rouneau went out to see Mayor Larribeau, Gaucher's wife stopped him in the street. He explained he was leaving the hamlet and added that her husband might want her and the children to depart as well. "But what's happening?" she asked. He lied, "Nothing extraordinary, but it's probable he'll quit the Gironde for some time and he would prefer to have you near him." When she asked if it was serious, he lied again, "No. As soon as the storm passes, we'll return."

Mayor Larribeau assured Rouneau, "It's better this way, because if the Boches come here and can't interrogate any of you, it will be easier for me to say I knew you as refugees and nothing more." The two men shook hands, and Rouneau left with Robert in Merchez's car.

George in the meantime had moved from his usual Agen safe house, which was known to Gaucher, to the house of his courier Pierre Duffoir. Rouneau and Robert arrived there after dark. George saw Robert and said to Rouneau, "I said Albert only. Madame Delattre should have stayed in Castelnau." Rouneau defended his lover: "She was in at least as much danger as the rest of us, so I decided she needed shelter as much as the rest of us. Understand?" According to Rouneau, George backed down, saying, "Okay. That's fine."

Gaucher's arrest threatened to blow their entire organization. The sad tale had begun that morning with a **Message personnel** from the BBC: "Jacqueline has a red and green dress." It meant SOE was finally sending George a wireless operator. Gaucher assumed the operator would need a radio when she landed. "I found Gérard on Tuesday in La Réole," George told Rouneau. "He had brought the radio that we received a few weeks ago. I was not pleased by that, because I had given him no instruction to do it. And I did not want the radio in La Réole. I ordered him to take it to Agen." Rouneau remembered that he had seen Gaucher just before George did, and Gaucher had told him he was bringing a radio for the new operator. Rouneau "tried to dissuade him by saying Hilaire had not given him any instructions about this and, in addition, whether any radio was needed there." He blamed himself for not having stopped Gaucher: "I gave my hand to my colleague and friend who went to his destiny."

That day at two o'clock, Gaucher left to store the radio at La Réole's railroad depot until the train left for Agen at six o'clock. "He was on his way to the station," George recounted, "and, because it was very hot, he was not wearing a jacket and so had no papers. I followed him at 100 meters." George watched as gendarmes looking for black marketeers ordered Gaucher to open his briefcase. He refused, and they took him to their headquarters.

"He thought he was doing the right thing," George said, "but it was strictly against my orders."

Someone assured George that Gaucher would not talk, but he cut him short: "I might talk. Anybody could talk when they get a hold of you. A man that says he's never going to talk, well, he's a fool." George dashed out on what he called his "Paul Revere ride" to warn everyone known to Gaucher to go into hiding. SOE's report on the debacle stated that George ordered his operatives to "cease all activities until 15 Sept when the Chiefs were to meet him in Auch."

George plotted a jailbreak to spring Gaucher at night, when pro-Resistance guards were on duty. But Gaucher preempted him with a daylight escape attempt. Vichy police recaptured him and gave him to the Gestapo. "If he'd waited till dark," George complained, "we would have had him out with no problem at all."

The Germans tortured Gaucher into providing some, though not all, information about his Resistance circuit. He gave the Germans their first eyewitness description of **le patron**: chestnut hair, five feet six inches tall, brown eyes, speaking French with a pronounced accent.

Following Gaucher's interrogation, the Germans arrested a journalist with the Resistance group **Combat** in Agen. They set up new roadblocks and raided Gunzbourg's Château de Barsalou. While the Germans were there, Gunzbourg nonchalantly strolled into the house wearing gardening clothes and said, "Good afternoon." He told them he was looking for something, gathered a few belongings, and disappeared. When the security detachment realized who he was, they chased him to Agen. Gunzbourg ran into the post office to mail a card to his wife. While his pursuers searched for him outside, he left by the back door.

Gunzbourg rode a bicycle out of Agen, past the town of Condom, and through endless farmland for forty miles to the village of Vic-Fezensac. Marie-Louise Lac opened her door to see an old friend who looked, she recalled, "completely exhausted." He explained, "The Germans came to my house. They were all shaken up, taking everything they wanted and causing a lot of damage." He remained in hiding at Madame Lac's for three days, and sent his wife, their two children, and their nanny to safety in Switzerland. The Germans, as with George Starr, offered a large reward for his capture.

An SOE after-action report on Gaucher's arrest stated, "He was interrogated and beaten up as a result of which he gave away the AGEN HQ, the MARMANDE HQ and the location of arms depots. This resulted in the AGEN HQ being liquidated with about 15 arrests and the remainder of the personnel sent out of the country." George, fearing that Gaucher had told the Germans about Castelnau, sent a **résistant** to evacuate Madame Gaucher and her children.

Rouneau and Jeanne Robert took refuge on Saturday, August 21, with a prominent rugby player and **résistant** at his Château de la Peyre. The place gave them, in Rouneau's words, "total hospitality and relative security." At five o'clock on the evening of their arrival, a weary George rode up on his bicycle. "This big empty house depresses me," he said. "I want to go back to [Maurice] Jacob at [Château de] la Clotte and spend the evening with him." Rouneau advised against it, reminding him that German roadblocks were everywhere.

A violent storm the next day shook the house. George and the others were eating, when an apparition on bicycle emerged from the mist. The man, an assistant of Maurice Jacob, related a tale as if from the **Ancient Mariner**: A detachment of German security personnel had raided the Château de la Clotte the previous evening. They arrested Maurice Jacob's wife and young son, as well as the wife of Jacob's associate, Paul Blasy. They "then went direct to the places where the arms were hidden and uncovered all of them." Jacob and Blasy, who were walking back from the forest, surrendered when they saw their families under arrest. The Germans seized hundreds of Tommy guns, thousands of cartridges, scores of antitank rifles, and other vital equipment that George had carefully buried in Jacob's garden over the previous three months. Only empty containers remained. Security personnel imprisoned the Jacob and Blasy families in Agen.

"**Merde!**" George muttered, forgetting his usual decorum around Jeanne Robert. Rouneau reflected, "All the fruit of long and patient work was dead."

George decided they all had to leave. Rouneau gathered his pistols and ammunition, but he abandoned a stock of 7.65mm cartridges as too heavy to carry. "I had a large quantity of false identity cards, kept a dozen and destroyed the rest," he wrote. "And then I consigned Hilaire's account book to the flames."

The Gestapo dragnet forced George to miss the reception of the new radio operator that SOE had promised in May. George appointed a **résistant** named Marius Bouchou, a farmer who owned the field where she would drop, and four other men to oversee the arrival. All he knew about the W/T was her code name, "Annette."

On Sunday evening, August 22, 1943, F-Section intelligence officer Vera Atkins reported to the RAF's Tempsford air base in Bedfordshire to bid farewell to agent Annette, thirty-one-year-old Flight Officer Yvonne Cormeau.

Born in Shanghai as Beatrice Yvonne Biesterfield to a Belgian father and Scottish mother, Cormeau grew up speaking English in Britain and French in Belgium. She and her husband, Charles Edouard

Cormeau, whom she married in 1937, lived in Brussels, where Cormeau had given birth to a daughter named Yvette. At the outbreak of the war, her husband enlisted in Britain's Rifle Brigade and was wounded during the German invasion. The family fled to London, where Cormeau became pregnant with another child. During the Blitz, a Luftwaffe bomb demolished their house. Cormeau, saved by a cast-iron bathtub that fell on top of her, woke in a hospital bed to learn that her two-year-old daughter was unharmed but her husband and unborn baby were dead. She enlisted in the Women's Auxiliary Air Force (WAAF) in November 1941 and joined SOE three months later. She later explained, "I was willing to do whatever I could. This was something my husband would have liked to do. And, as he was no longer there to do it, I thought it was time for me to do it."

Cormeau, like George, declined the standard SOE cyanide pill, though her reasons were more practical: "I admitted to Colonel Buckmaster that I did not take it with me because, if it had been found on me at any cursory search, that would have been signing my own death warrant too." In her pocket, instead, was a silver powder compact from Buckmaster that she could pawn when she needed money.

At the air base, Atkins handed her an envelope for Hilaire, and Cormeau boarded the Halifax bomber. She wore a regulation jumpsuit over a demure black curtain skirt and silk blouse. Her ankles were bandaged for protection against a rough landing, because she felt simple black shoes would be less conspicuous than paratrooper boots. Strapped to her back was a black handbag with a .22 revolver inside.

"We took off on a beautiful sunset in England," she reminisced years later. The moon was half full, bright enough to see the ground but also for German shore batteries to spot the plane. The pilot flew in silence over the English Channel and deep into occupied France. Cormeau's recollection of the journey contains none of the bravado usually associated with secret agents: "I was given a nice hot drink by the dispatcher. And then I saw he opened the hole in the floor of the fuselage, so it told me that we were soon going to do something." The dispatcher attached her silk cord to a rail and told her to be ready. A red light turned to green, and the dispatcher gave a signal. Then, she said, "I had to slide through the hole."

Her parachute snapped open, and she floated three hundred feet onto French soil. Containers and packages of weapons, ammunition, and radio equipment followed her down. The drop zone, seventy-five miles north of Castelnau, was a field outside the hamlet of Saint-Antoine-du-Queyret near Bordeaux's famed Saint-Émilion vineyards. "I could have put out my hand and picked some of the grapes," she remembered. Her subsequent F-Section debrief noted, "The landing was perfect although the ground was an extremely difficult one, being a strip of grass just beside a house, and blocked at one end by a high cyprus [sic] tree, the grass strip being not more than 100 yards in width." Her landing was not quite perfect: a falling canister grazed her leg, and she lost a shoe. She cut a patch of her white silk parachute to keep as a souvenir. The reception committee took her to Bouchou's farmhouse. Thirty-two members of the local Resistance circuit, who had come from a dance to "see what the new arrival was like," greeted her in the kitchen. The report continued:

> It was the first operation that had taken place in the area, and no-one had the slightest idea what to do. Everyone turned out to assist in bringing in the containers, and all this equipment (13 containers and four packages in all) was brought into the farm kitchen, together with the parachutes.

Later that night, one of the **résistants** bicycled with her five miles to a safe house in the village of Pujols.

The same evening, Antoine Merchez drove George, Rouneau, and Robert from the Château de la Peyre to Layrac, a village about five miles from Agen. There, they boarded a train to Auch.

En route, a gendarme checked the passengers' identity cards. Robert's was genuine, but the men's were counterfeit. Robert smiled at the gendarme, whom she knew, and he ignored the forgeries. When they reached Auch, Rouneau wondered, "From Auch, where could we go? No idea. We were going into the unknown." Rouneau telephoned Montréjeau brewer and **résistant** Pierre Labayle for help. At four in the afternoon, Labayle met the group and took them about thirty-five miles north to a clothing merchant named Marius Sorbé in the village of Seissan. They remained with him while Labayle sought longer-term quarters.

"At dinner," Rouneau recalled, "Hilaire astonished us with his prodigious memory." A dog came into the house, and George said, "I know that dog." The others were skeptical, but he insisted, "I know that dog." He said its owner was "a large, young blond woman, elegant, who wears shoes with flat heels." Sorbé said, "That's right. They came here to her parents' a few days ago." George explained, "I saw them on the train between Agen and Toulouse last February." At that moment, a woman fitting George's description walked into the house looking for her pet.

Labayle returned after dinner to take them to a small village, Montesquieu-Volvestre, about fifty miles southeast through sparsely populated countryside. They were about to leave when a mounted police patrol set up a checkpoint outside. "**Merde!**" George blurted. They waited, but the police did not budge. Unable to delay, they ventured out. One of the policemen ordered them to stop, but they scrambled into Labayle's car and drove off. Twenty miles down the highway, a car filled with Luftwaffe field police pulled alongside. A gunfight seemed imminent, but the Germans overtook them without stopping. It transpired that they were searching for the eight-man crew of an Allied aircraft that had come down in the area.

Labayle drove them along deserted roads to Montesquieu-Volvestre, a village of timber and brick houses on the banks of the River Garonne. George, Rouneau, and Robert moved into rooms that Labayle had rented in the best hotel. At dinner, the hotel proprietor asked why they were there. Rouneau concocted a story about buying timber to make charcoal. Due to wartime shortages and German requisitioning, the French used charcoal not only to cook but to run their cars. The proprietor responded by regaling Rouneau with technical details about local forests and qualities of wood. As Rouneau's boredom grew, George pressed a napkin to his lips to contain his laughter.

The next morning, the five men who had received Yvonne Cormeau came to Pujols to offer her their services. Seeing them for the first time in the daylight, she sensed something strange about one of them: "I didn't like the way he looked at me . . . [in] a very underhand way. I wouldn't have trusted him with anything." She suspected he was a traitor or a German in disguise.

The son of Cormeau's host in Pujols bicycled thirty miles to Montesquieu-Volvestre to tell George that his radio operator, Annette, had arrived. George arranged to meet her in the foothills of the Pyrenees. Cormeau provided several accounts about her encounter with George, including a 1945 SOE debrief and an interview with the Imperial War Museum in 1984. A Resistance liaison officer, said by George to be a sympathetic police inspector, brought her to where George was waiting.

The policeman introduced them, but George interrupted, "I've known this lady for a long time, known her before she was married." Cormeau's description matched the impact George had on most who met him:

Physically he was small, he was no taller than I am. Man who had celebrated his 40th birthday in the field. His main features were his eyes. He really hypnotized people into doing what he wanted by looking at them. Nothing disagreeable, but he sort of had a forceful way. . . . His main defect, if I can call it that way, he smoked too much, always had a cigarette.

George remembered speaking with her in a café, but Cormeau said their conversation took place on a long walk. She handed him the envelope from Atkins. It contained a letter and a photograph of his wife, Pilar, with their young children, Georgina and Alfred, that Pilar had sent to the British Consulate in Barcelona. "She was given a letter and photographs of the children," George recalled. "Of course, you're supposed not to look at them, but being a bloody woman, she bloody looked. So she knew what she was doing." Cormeau had not told Atkins that the Starrs and Cormeaus had been friends in Brussels, where George and her husband had played cricket together.

George read Pilar's letter and asked Cormeau, "By the way, what the hell are you doing here? Your husband has been killed. You've got a little girl. What's she going to do without a mother or a father? Because I guarantee you're never going to get out of here." He added that she had arrived at a difficult time. Since Gaucher's capture, the Gestapo were hunting him and had put a price of one million francs on his head.

He asked her to return to the farm where she landed. "He thought it was a good spot for getting ready," she said. She mentioned her suspicions about one of the men who had received her.

> I told him about this other chap and he said, "Well, you'll only stay there three days and mention what you think. You have my permission to mention your feelings to the leader of the group."

Cormeau's accounts of their conversation differ as to the duration, but after meeting with George, she boarded a train to Montréjeau. The 1945 debrief stated that "she stayed in a safe house" in Montréjeau, though in her 1984 interview she said she returned to the Bouchous' farmhouse and hid her radio in a false-bottomed wine barrel. She made her first transmissions from the bedroom of the Bouchous' teenage daughter.

Cormeau's instinct about one of the men who received her proved right. He was a traitor. The only name given for him in the records was "Rodolphe," who was most likely to have been a double agent named Rodolphe Feyton. An SOE report on Cormeau's activities in France commented:

> The owner of this house at Pujols and his family were soon afterwards arrested and taken to Germany through the same denunciation as caused his cousin's arrest, and the man responsible for

the blowing of the circuit was actually in charge of the reception committee to which informant landed, and was the first person on the field to greet her, so that within a few days of her arrival in the field, the Police were in possession of a very good description of her.

A follow-up SOE report stated that another member of her reception committee was arrested, after which police searched the man's house and found documents incriminating others: "As a result of this nine men were shot and four others tortured." Among the names revealed during the torture sessions were Maurice Rouneau and Pierre Duffoir.

Cormeau moved from one safe house to another every few days, until George retrieved her from Montréjeau on Monday, August 30, and brought her by train to Pujols. Thanks to him, she always stayed in the safest of safe houses. He advised her to hide the .22 revolver she had brought from England: "Look, if you are found carrying any weapon, that's signing your death warrant." His tenderness toward her did not go unnoticed, as she later recalled.

Knowing that my husband had been killed, he looked after me extremely well indeed. And I am very grateful for all the work he did looking after me. And that's why he wouldn't let me have a pistol, and that's why he gave me so many identity cards. That's why he arranged houses very safely all the time.

She reflected, "I never thought before when I met him casually, I must admit, in Brussels, that I would trust this man Hilaire with my life." But she did trust him and embarked on a clandestine life with **le patron** as his wireless operator, courier, **confidante**, and, a few alleged, his lover.

EIGHT

Avenue Boche

In secret wireless work under far from perfect conditions,
we were quite unable to ask for repetitions of doubtful
passages and to employ all those aids to accuracy and
checks which are so easy in peacetime work.

MAURICE BUCKMASTER

═══

In Dijon's Wehrmacht prison, SS guards roused Captains John Starr and Brian Rafferty from their cells, handcuffed them to each other, and shoved them into the back of a car. The Germans drove all day through the barren summer landscape without telling the prisoners their destination. After about two hundred miles, the car turned south toward the Parisian suburb of Fresnes. Its late-nineteenth-century penitentiary was by then notorious for the torture and execution of **résistants,** Jews, and hostages.

The SS handed the British agents over to the prison warders, who locked them in separate cells at opposite ends of a corridor. John's three cellmates were "a Polish officer [Zbigniew Jablonsky], subsequently shot, the second was a French student [Jean-Claude Comert] whom informant had previously met, the third was a man called JEAN ARGENCE, a garde forestier [forest ranger] from VIEUX CHENES, near LISEUX." Argence, who had worked with the PHYSICIAN circuit under Francis Suttill, told John the Germans had penetrated PHYSICIAN. His interrogator had shown him a map of the circuit's arms caches and photostatic copies of correspondence between London and PHYSICIAN. Neither Argence nor John knew that French double agent Henri Déricourt had copied the documents before aircrafts took them to London with returning agents. Argence said that the Sicherheitsdienst knew more about F-Section than he did.

At the end of September, three weeks into John's stay at Fresnes, SS guards came for him. His cellmates, knowing the drill, asked him to bring cigarette butts from the interrogation room ashtray. The guards drove him north across Paris to the fashionable 16th arrondissement and stopped at an imposing eighteenth-century mansion on avenue Foch. The broad thoroughfare, designed in 1866 by Baron Haussmann as the avenue de l'Imperatrice, stretched from the Arc de Triomphe to the Bois de Boulogne.

Sundry and competing German security services had commandeered the stately residences along the north side, numbers 58, 72, 82, 84, and 86, as well as another house just behind. Standartenführer (SS Colonel) Helmut Knochen, chief of both the Sicherheitspolizei (SIPO) and Sicherheitsdienst, had requisitioned one of the homes for himself, as had the Paris Gestapo chief. So much of the elegant thoroughfare hosted Germans that Parisians called it "avenue Boche."

John, weak from his wounds and torture, hobbled on crutches up the steps of 84 avenue Foch. Number 84, the middle of the SD's three adjoining belle époque mansions, was its counterespionage headquarters. One British detainee wrote of the establishment, "It was incongruous to think that this lovely building in this equally elegant and majestic Avenue should now house the most brutal elements of Nazi Germany." The first person John encountered was a man who introduced himself as "Ernest." Half-Swiss, half-German Ernest Vogt had moved to Paris in 1920, working first in a bank and then in a patent office. The French interned him as an enemy alien at the beginning of the war, and the Germans freed him when they occupied Paris. His color blindness and poor eyesight disqualified him from army service, but the SD hired the French and English speaker as an interpreter. He held the rank of Untersturmführer, second lieutenant. Yet like most other officers at headquarters, he dressed in a civilian suit and tie. Vogt's talent for winning inmates' confidence led to his conducting interrogations on his own. Having lived in England, he gave British detainees tea with milk instead of violence. His methods were unlike anything John had endured in Dijon.

During their first interview, Vogt ordered lunch for them both and spoke as if to a friend. Vogt's chief, Sturmbannführer Hans Kieffer, joined them soon afterward. A former policeman in the city of Karlsruhe, he had joined the Nazi Party in the 1920s. On June 27, 1940, just after the German conquest of France, the Wehrmacht ordered him to Berlin, where it issued him a military field police officer's uniform. The Reichssicherheitshauptamt (RSHA, Reich Main Security Office) sent him to Paris, and his wife and their three children remained at home in Karlsruhe.

One detainee at avenue Foch described Kieffer as "square-headed, not tall, hair cut short, strongly built, energetic, about 40, rather dark—could not speak French." Kieffer asked John a few questions, which Vogt translated, and then left the room. While Vogt resumed working on him politely and subtly, John dissembled as he had under the earlier brutality. Vogt recalled that John "had the sense to keep the Dienstelle [department] in Dijon in the dark about his activities until he was certain his collaborators knew of his arrest and were able to get to safety."

Vogt attempted to succeed with courtesy where the thugs in Dijon had failed with cruelty, but he admitted that his technique was not working with John:

> He made it appear that he was the only one it would be worth trying to get anything out of, and this impressed me very much. He told it with so much conviction and so many elaborate and supplementary details that he even made our men believe it for some days. I admired his inventiveness as well as his courage.

The first interview, more conversation than third degree, went on for most of the afternoon. In the evening, Vogt brought another prisoner, Major Gilbert Norman, to meet John. SOE had parachuted Norman into France on October 31, 1942, as the radio operator for Francis Suttill's PHYSICIAN circuit, the same circuit John's cellmate Argence had worked for before it was infiltrated. Eight months later, the Germans arrested Norman and most other members of the circuit. Norman believed Suttill had given Kieffer his agents' names in return for Kieffer's promise that none of them would be executed, though some suggested that either Norman himself or a double agent had handed over the names. Vogt left the room, and the two agents spoke to each other in whispers. Norman said the SD knew all about SOE and "it was no use to attempt to hide anything." The Germans had shown him copies of his own radio traffic with F-Section, and Norman was convinced that "there was a leak high up in London."

Vogt returned to resume his interrogation of John, asking whether he worked for "the French Section." Realizing that Vogt knew the answer, John confessed that he did. "You see," Vogt said. "There is no point in keeping anything back."

John slept that night for a few hours in the guardroom on the fifth floor. Early in the morning, guards brought him to Vogt for more questions. The verbal sparring lasted most of the day. Despite the absence of torture, the session was draining. Vogt spotted inconsistencies, and John had to stay alert for hours without letup. Vogt showed him correspondence between London and F-Section agents in France to demonstrate the futility of lying. He did not tell him that Henri Déricourt had obtained the documents in France, leaving John to share Norman's suspicion that the SD had a mole in London.

Kieffer joined the evening interview. Vogt translated as his chief unfurled a large map of France. The SD had demarcated twelve of SOE's operational areas, each marked with the names of captured F-Section officers. Kieffer asked John to draw a line around his zone of operations. John complied, expanding ACROBAT's borders in the hope of sparing neighboring SOE organizers SD scrutiny. Kieffer told him to put the number 13 and his code name, Bob, over his region. John did so in the clear calligraphy he had used as a poster artist.

Kieffer said something in German to Vogt, who translated, "He likes the way you print." The major asked him to redraw the map with his professional flourishes. In a statement made shortly after the war, John said he "decided to comply with the Germans' request." However, a few years later, he claimed that he agreed to **consider** the offer. Guards returned him to Fresnes at ten thirty that night. His pocket was full of cigarette ends from Vogt's ashtray.

While he and his cellmates smoked, John told them about Kieffer's proposition. Should he accept? They thought he should. If he gained the Germans' trust, he could discover what else they knew about SOE. The question troubling them was: who had betrayed them? John was inclined to work for Kieffer, as his debrief stated, in order "to glean a lot of information which would be extremely valuable if he could get it back to London." The same debrief conceded a more personal reason: "At the AVENUE FOCH, the food was good, being the same as that served to the German personnel in charge."

There may have been a third consideration: staying alive. After the Germans condemned one of his Fresnes cellmates to death, another recalled John saying, "That's what's waiting for me."

Three days later, the SD took John back to 84

avenue Foch and locked him in a sealed room. Keeping suspects on the premises was more convenient than bringing them every day from Fresnes, where they could pass messages to the outside world through other prisoners or sympathetic French staff. The cell in which John stayed was one of seven in the fifth floor attic that had been **chambres de bonnes,** maids' rooms, before the SD occupied the house. The only natural light in the cells came through shafts leading to skylights in the roof, and each shaft was barred at the base to prevent escape. The only furniture in his cell was a single bed with a blanket. Near the cells were two larger rooms, one for the guards and the other Vogt's office. A bathroom and a separate lavatory were at the end of the hallway. Below, on the fourth floor via white wooden stairs, was Kieffer's apartment. It had a bedroom, a kitchen, an imposing office lit by a crystal chandelier, and a small lobby for Kieffer's secretary. The radio unit was on the second floor, while the first floor housed other SD offices. A magnificent marble staircase led to the foyer and the front door.

The original arrangement was that John would remain at avenue Foch for three or four days to complete the map and some charts, but the drawing led, as he had hoped, to other tasks and a longer stay. Kieffer and Vogt provided tables of all the F-Section networks they had neutralized for John to redraw. "Eventually," recalled Vogt, "BOB was given various graphical drawings or sketches and representations to do, which were drawn up by KIEFFER and his collaborators owing to arrests or from captured documents." One captured SOE agent who saw John's scrolls described them: "The charts consisted of two large rolls of paper (one showing the German estimate of the S.O.E. organisation and the other that of the PROSPER [PHYSICIAN] organisation, the latter with photographs)." The SD sent photographs of the maps and charts to Berlin. The documents became instruments to break the morale of prisoners at avenue Foch by convincing them that the SD knew everything about F-Section through a German agent in London.

John worked in the guardroom, where the open door gave him a view of other captured agents on their way to Vogt's interrogation room. The warders kept him under surveillance and, during air raids, checked the cells to make sure that prisoners were in their beds and not signaling to the planes above. The guardroom had a small library from which prisoners borrowed books.

"Sometimes, he would be taken into the guardroom in the morning," one SOE report stated, "at other times, he would have to wait until the afternoon, according to the position in the guardroom." Life atop 84 avenue Foch was more comfortable than in any other prison of the Third Reich. Cooks provided meat, vegetables, bread, fresh butter, desserts, and wartime France's most prized commodity, real coffee. "Prisoners were better fed at the Avenue Foch than the guards, the prisoners being on officers' rations, while the guards had 'other ranks' rations," one inmate observed. Another SOE prisoner said, "I was amazed at H.Q. GESTAPO, to see the quantities of British food, guns, ammunition, and explosives which they had at their disposal; this was quite easy to understand owing to the contacts they had with ENGLAND." The coffee, tea, and many of the foodstuffs were unintended gifts from SOE in London. The Germans permitted inmates at avenue Foch to wash and shave. John wore a shirt and tie rather than prison clothes.

While working in the guardroom, John came to know the German staff and the East European guards. In addition to Kieffer and Vogt, he met Hauptscharführer (Master Sergeant) Josef Placke. A Catholic school alumnus and First World War veteran, he had worked for the German Field Police and the Abwehr before transferring to the SD in avenue Foch. Another official he met was Unterscharführer (Corporal) Alfred von Kapri. Kapri worked in the radio department, assisted at interrogations, and went on raids to capture résistants. Interpreter August Scherer sometimes accompanied Kapri to make arrests. Scherer's wife, Ottilie, also worked as an interpreter and was a friend of Kieffer's secretary (and lover), Käte Goldmann. Michel Bouillon, a

French collaborator, was a driver and odd-job man. The cleaner, Rose Marie Holwedts, was a French-woman whom one SOE prisoner called "dark, dirty and very vulgar." John came to believe she was the mistress of another staff member, Master Sergeant Karl Haug.

While Norman was alone with John one evening, he educated him about the **Funkspiel,** which the SD's radio section on the second floor was playing with SOE. It had begun with Marcus Bloom, who by this time languished in Fresnes Prison. Neither Norman nor John knew that Bloom had transmitted for George Starr. Norman said he, like Bloom, had refused to operate his radio for the Germans. Somehow, though, Goetz convinced London that the transmissions were genuine.

Dr. Goetz recalled later that he revived the **Funk-spiel** in Paris as soon as he returned from his failure with Bloom in Toulouse:

> When I came back from this there were two decoy transmissions in PARIS which I had to take over. One of these lasted only a short time; the other, much longer. Later a whole series of decoy transmissions followed of which some lasted a considerable time.

Dr. Goetz made good use of Norman's radio. Norman, like Bloom, had kept back his "security check" through which London authenticated all transmissions, disclosing only the "bluff" check. He assumed London would spot the absence of the "true" check. Goetz sent a test message. According to Norman, "Dr. Goetz was furious the day he received a message from London reminding him that he [Norman] had forgotten 'his double security check.'" Goetz bellowed: "You have forgotten your double security check. Be more careful." Goetz's subsequent messages contained both security checks, ostensibly from Norman, requesting **parachutages** of supplies and agents to designated drop sites north of Paris. Norman blamed London for lethal incompetence.

Norman also told John that Master Sergeant Placke ran a hoax Resistance circuit around Saint-Quentin, about one hundred miles north of Paris. Placke recruited unsuspecting French patriots and received supplies and agents that the SD ordered via the captured radio sets. "When STARR arrived at the Avenue Foch," stated an SOE report, "the Germans had already started to work at least one circuit." SOE was sending the Germans weapons, explosives, food, and other supplies. As Norman unfolded this terrible saga, John grew more desperate to inform SOE that it was playing the Germans' game. But how could he tell them?

NINE
Word of Honor

Our men were lonely in the field, that
was inevitable.

MAURICE BUCKMASTER

━━

In the early fall of 1943, George Starr brought
Yvonne Cormeau to the hotel in Montesquieu-
Volvestre where Jeanne Robert and Maurice
Rouneau were hiding. The four soon realized the
town's inhabitants were becoming suspicious. "On
our walks," wrote Rouneau, "the curtains twitched
and we had the conviction that conversations and
gossip about us were spreading." They left the village to avoid denunciation and drove about forty
miles west to Aventignan, a modest hamlet of simple
stone houses with terra-cotta roofs and fewer than
three hundred souls. "Thanks to the patriotism,
to the devotion of these brave people to the cause

of France," Rouneau wrote of the villagers, "we had found a center of action." However, he reflected, "Despite all the help and sympathy, we could not achieve the level of security we had during the previous ten months in Castelnau-sur-l'Auvignon, where the villagers were used to our presence."

In Castelnau, their cover stories had passed without question: Robert was the schoolteacher, Rouneau her printer boyfriend, and George Gaston the Belgian, her family friend. Convinced that returning to Castelnau was more practical than starting again with new false identities in an area they did not know, Rouneau decided to find out what Fernand Gaucher had told the Gestapo about the village. He and Robert risked a reconnaissance trip by train through Toulouse to Auch and by bus to Condom, where they looked for a taxi. A local garage owner was willing to drive them to Castelnau, but he warned, "It's forbidden now to hire a car without authorization." Rouneau submitted an application at the Department of Bridges and Highways, and when the official there said permission would take several days, Rouneau presented documents from a former member of Parliament with the signature of Vichy's minister of agriculture and supply. The papers authorized Rouneau to circulate without hindrance to buy materials for coffee production in Abyssinia. The pass was issued at once.

While waiting in Condom for the garage owner

to bring his taxi, Rouneau and Robert met a family from Castelnau. They told him no Germans had come and no one had been arrested. Gaucher had not betrayed them. Rouneau wrote, "Hilaire could return and reestablish his command post."

Reinstalled in the familiar schoolhouse, WHEEL-WRIGHT's activists resumed their clandestine work. The hamlet, however, was not free of dubious Frenchmen. Yvonne Cormeau recalled, "You never knew which man or woman was willing to give information to the Gestapo. Sometimes it was a personal vendetta between two families. Other times it was just for money, which was serious." Jeanne Robert told Rouneau that one of the peasants, wary about people coming in and out of Castelnau, was spreading stories that her house was "a veritable nest of spies!" Neighbors told the man to mind his own business, but George feared he might go to the police. Rouneau went to Condom to meet gendarme captain Fernand Pagès. The gendarme promised to deal with the would-be informer, and to assure WHEELWRIGHT's next **parachutage** by preventing the police from establishing checkpoints nearby. "I shook the hand warmly of this man, this soldier, who in fulfilling his unrewarding functions, wanted to continue serving the real France," Rouneau wrote.

When Rouneau returned from Condom, George was pacing the village square with the perpetual Balto burning between his lips. "Well?" he asked.

They went inside. Rouneau told him what Captain Pagès had proposed. George had one hesitation: "Provided that the gendarmerie doesn't come here now and burn me."

Pagès visited the gossiping peasant's farm the next day to demand evidence for his accusations. The peasant backtracked. He did not know the people in the school and, anyway, he had been drinking. Pagès left to make an inquiry and returned two days later to confront the farmer:

I know now what calumnies you have made against the teacher and her guests. Do you know who these men are? Okay, I'll tell you. They are important controllers of supply. And these are men you call spies. You deserve a beating and to be put away. Do you know that, if she wanted, the teacher could send you to prison for defamation?

"From that day," Rouneau wrote, "we lived without fear of denunciation."

George was secure again in his hilltop redoubt with his comrades Roger and Alberta Larribeau, farmers Pino and Tina Novarini, and the faithful Jeanne Robert. He resumed recruiting agents, teaching youngsters to fire rifles and use dynamite, receiving arms drops, and augmenting an underground arsenal that became one of the largest in

France. On September 15, as he had promised before he left Castelnau, he reactivated his sector. An SOE assessment noted that by that date "the security section reported that Gestapo activity had quieted down. The meeting between STARR and various heads took place at different times and places. They were given orders to build up their groups all over again."

Yvonne Cormeau established herself as one of SOE's most adroit "pianists," as SOE called its wireless operators. This did not prevent her from taking on other chores, including, in her words, "the ordinary work of finding out the fields that the people could put at our disposal and sending the latitude, longitude . . ." Thanks to Cormeau's faultless Morse transmissions, George's groups received from sixty to seventy containers by parachute at each full moon.

Despite the successful arms drops, arrests in Agen and other centers of WHEELWRIGHT activity made the partisans wary of one another. In September, George went to Montréjeau to meet with resourceful Pierre Labayle, who was holding funds for him. When George arrived in the village, Rouneau and Robert were waiting to tell him that Labayle had just been arrested. "He did not flinch at the news," Rouneau wrote, "but clenched his eternal cigarette more tightly between his lips." George broke into Labayle's office and took the money from the safe, and the three returned to Castelnau.

Arrests continued with the capture of Jean-Marcel Cazeneuve, a merchant in Agen's boulevard de la République. The Gestapo took him to the Saint-Michel Prison in Toulouse, where they were already interrogating Fernand Gaucher, Maurice Jacob, and Paul Blasy. The Germans then arrested Louis Lévy in Marmande. As they drove the young partisan from Marmande to the Saint-Michel Prison, Philippe de Gunzbourg appeared alongside the truck on his bicycle. Louis threw a crumpled piece of paper at him. On it were the words "Guérin, rue Cassaignol-les, Vic-Fezensac." The address was Madame Lac's, where he lived, and the name Guérin was the pseudonym she had typed onto his identity card. Marie-Louise Lac later wrote, "It is probable that without his presence of mind, you would not now be reading these 'Memoires of My Resistance.'"

Louis' brother, Théo, rushed to Castelnau to tell George about his brother's arrest. The younger Lévy insisted on taking Louis' place and using his code name, Christophe. George agreed and made Théo his liaison to Philippe de Gunzbourg. Together, with Yvonne Cormeau, they began an operation to exfiltrate the seven Polish airmen who had crashed near Arx on August 16.

George sent Théo Lévy and Cormeau to the

men's safe house in Fourcès, from which they took the men to the border. A smuggler warned that reaching Spain was nearly impossible at that time. Germans patrolled the road night and day, and the most direct footpath was teeming with ferocious tracker dogs. "So," recalled Cormeau, "you had to go through the snow on a snowy night so that your traces were quickly covered, and you had to go from bush to bush." Evading the hazards, the Polish fliers made it to Spain and returned to England for further missions over occupied Europe.

Meanwhile, at the crash site near Arx where the burned hulk of the Poles' plane lay in the snow, Vichy officials ordered foreign prison inmates to collect the munitions that the Resistance had left behind. They turned the matériel over to the Milice française. The Milice was Vichy's version of the Gestapo, established on January 30, 1943, under the operational command of a World War I veteran and fascist demagogue named Joseph Darnand. The paramilitary group presented a more insidious threat than the Gestapo, because its French miliciens knew the country better than the Germans and could discern a Belgian accent from one like George Starr's. Fanatically anti-Resistance and anti-Semitic, they employed traditional weapons of repression: tapping telephones, housebreaking, extortion, torture, and murder. Their brown shirts, blue jackets, and berets became part of the French scene, but many worked in plainclothes to infiltrate Resistance networks. Yvonne Cormeau said these "French traitors" were "worse than the Gestapo."

The Polish crew's crash and the frequent arms drops put the Milice and the Germans on high alert. They deployed on roads and hilltops in the Gers, Landes, and Lot-et-Garonne to watch for **parachutages** at each full moon. "These movements were such as to obstruct us, and the reception teams were in great danger," wrote Rouneau. George changed tactics, instructing London to make the drops on moonless nights. Instead of navigating by landmarks, the RAF crews homed in on George's Eureka radio beacons. This delighted Rouneau: "It was amusing to hear during the full moon the buzz of German motorcycles racing along the roads to try to suppress the flagrant crimes of the 'terrorists' who received their arms from the sky."

On September 24, George confirmed that Castelnau was secure. He wrote to London that he had

received news from an eyewitness that on being tortured by the Gestapo, E [code letter for Fernand Gaucher, "Gérard"] told them, "Vous pouvez me faire ce que vous voulez, je dirais jamais rien, et je vous emmerde tous" ["You can do what you want to me, but I will never tell you anything, and I shit on all of you"]. With all the information we have now it is absolutely clear that

E has been splendid and has acted as an officer and a gentleman. A true patriot.

George sent Gaucher's wife and two children, aged nine and five, "about 500 kilometers from here where they are lodged in a friendly house."

The Gestapo hunted down more of George's associates, capturing a member of the Agen **parachutage** reception committee. An SOE report on the arrest noted, "During his subsequent interrogation he gave away the names of the whole AGEN reception committee. As a result of this nine men were shot and four others tortured."

Perhaps as a response to the arrests, on September 25, George dispatched a report to London concerning Maurice Rouneau: "As regards this man, it is quite true that he gives a very good impression to everybody, but believe me when I say that if you send him back to France for us you will have trouble." Rouneau was still in France, but the warning not to send him back indicated that George intended to exile him, just as he had Henri Sevenet. In the dispatch, George listed Rouneau's "faults": "too fond of women," problems with money, too much drinking, "loves to give orders," and "no idea of security." He also blamed Rouneau for several of the arrests that had taken place. He concluded the condemnation, "If you send him back to France you will never stop him from going to Paris to see his wife and kids who are watched by the Gestapo or from going to C. to brag to his pals or from visiting his mistress at D."

While recommending that SOE keep Rouneau out of France, he did admit Rouneau was "full of courage" and "above all a soldier and an excellent soldier in a fight," but concluded: "If you should decide to send him back to France, suggest that he should be sent as an instructor to somebody that can hold him and make him follow instructions to the latter [sic]."

The report reached London on November 13, six weeks after George wrote it. In the meantime, he decided to deal with Rouneau his own way.

Also in September 1943, the SD brought Peter Churchill and Odette Sansom to 84 avenue Foch. The couple's arrests the previous April had crippled the SPINDLE circuit in Haute-Savoie. Since then, they had undergone rigorous interrogation. Their bluff that Churchill was related to Britain's prime minister won him immunity from torture, but that did not spare Sansom from merciless brutality at Fresnes Prison. Lovers by this time, they told the Germans they were married. As Churchill entered the SD portals, he noticed that a "tall man of maybe forty, in a dark lounge suit, looked up at me out of a grey intelligent face. His high forehead and protruding ears gave him an intellectual aspect, but his cold eyes gave me the shivers." This was Ernest Vogt, who questioned Churchill in his usual friendly manner. Afterward, he asked John Starr whether the agent was really a nephew of Britain's prime minister. John played along, answering, "Certainly." Vogt then asked if Sansom and Churchill were man and wife. "Of course," John said. "They're a very well-known couple in English society." Vogt interrogated Churchill without breaking him during two short stays at avenue Foch. The SD later sent Churchill and Sansom to Berlin and on to a series of concentration camps.

Prisoners who gave their word of honor not to escape from avenue Foch enjoyed a certain freedom of movement on the fifth floor. They went to the bathroom unaccompanied, an arrangement that Ernest Vogt said "freed the Russian guard from having to stand beside the lavatory open door." Asking agents for their **parole d'honneur** had been Vogt's idea. The British writer Jean Overton Fuller, who interviewed him after the war, rendered his rationale in blank verse:

> I suggested to Kieffer we offer
> selected English prisoners a measure
> of freedom from surveillance on
> their Word of Honour
> not to attempt to escape, he said,
> "We should have them all climbing out

of the windows!" I said, "Not
the English. I would not offer
it to the French."

The SD did not ask John for his **parole**, but his
relaxed pose in the guardroom made new prisoners
suspicious of him.

The next F-Section agents that the SS brought to
84 avenue Foch were the brothers Alfred and Henry
Newton. John recognized the former circus and
music hall performers from SOE training school.
After they parachuted into France with wireless operator Brian Stonehouse on June 30, 1942, an informer betrayed them. The Germans arrested the
Newtons in Lyon on April 4, 1943, and the Gestapo
chief in Lyon, Klaus Barbie, tortured them before
dispatching them to Fresnes Prison. On the brothers' arrival at avenue Foch, they were surprised to see
the comfort in which John was living. The SD interrogated them for a few days before sending them to
Buchenwald concentration camp.

Officials at avenue Foch did not require John to
inform on other prisoners. Vogt recalled, "BOB always declared to me that he would never become an
agent or informer of our Dienststelle [department]
and on no account would he denounce anyone else."
John instead passed the time in the guardroom
drawing maps, charts, and tables for Major Kieffer, as well as greeting cards for other Germans to

send to their families. For a joke, he made some un-flattering caricatures of Kieffer. When the major saw them, he did not take offense. He laughed.

Kieffer commissioned John to paint his portrait as a present for his wife in Karlsruhe. John had no can-vas, brushes, or oil paints, but he offered to retrieve all he needed from his flat in Issy-les-Moulineaux. Kieffer let him go on his word of honor as a British officer not to attempt an escape during the excur-sion.

One cold morning, Ernest Vogt and two SS guards drove John through Paris's mostly deserted streets. They stopped just beyond the 15th arrondissement, on the Left Bank of the River Seine, at a massive apartment building. "The Gestapo's behind me," John warned the concierge, who was about to greet him with affection. While John gathered his brushes, paints, and canvas, Vogt confiscated his household radio. The SS men began stealing pans and other things from the kitchen. John said, "The wireless is fair game. But my wife is coming back here to live in a few months, when the Allies have returned to France, and she will need her frying pans and sauce-pans. I want them put back." Vogt ordered the men to return everything, but he kept the radio.

Kieffer gave John a photograph of himself, because he did not have time to pose, and John painted the portrait in the guardroom, while also performing his regular duties. The SD had asked him to take on additional work that until then had been done by Gilbert Norman. "From about September or October 1943," Vogt stated, "Dr. Goetz obtained the help of the above-named Captain STARR alias BOB for the setting of transmissions. As far as I know BOB only corrected the text of the transmissions devised by Dr. GOETZ so that it was not known that they were German translations." This involved correcting English grammar in SD messages to London. Vogt pointed out, "However, this wireless traffic was already in existence before BOB helped Dr. Goetz and it would have certainly been maintained properly without the assistance of BOB." John's assistance made the SD's deception of London more plausible, but it also gave him deeper insight into what the SD knew about SOE. This was information that he planned, one day, to escape with to London.

Mass arrests occurred frequently during the summer of 1943, and the capture of Francis Suttill's PHYSICIAN circuit members left only one SOE radio operator in Paris. She was Noor Inayat Khan, code name "Madeleine." Born of an Indian Muslim father and an American mother from New Mexico, she grew up in Paris. Her father's Sufi order regarded her as a princess. In England, Leo Marks and most of the other SOE men who met the ethereal, dark-haired beauty fell in love with her. Her training reports were divided on whether she should go into the field at all. Although determined and devoted, her innocent otherworldliness left her vulnerable.

An RAF 161 Squadron Lysander had flown Khan with Diana Rowden, John Starr's courier, to Le Mans on June 16, 1943, only days before her circuit ceased to exist. She evaded arrest and eluded German radio detectors while sending messages from a variety of houses in Paris. "We were pursuing her for months," recalled Major Kieffer, "and as we had a personal description of her we arranged for all stations to be watched. She had several addresses and worked very carefully." Dr. Goetz shared Kieffer's assessment of the importance the SD placed on capturing Khan: "It was, naturally, of the greatest interest to us to arrest her as we suspected that she carried on wireless traffic with London, but [we] could not close in on her as the place of transmission was constantly changing."

Maurice Buckmaster ordered her, for her own safety, to return to England. She was reluctant to abandon her post, but SOE authorized an RAF Lysander to pick her up in mid-October 1943. Only days before her scheduled departure, a Frenchwoman contacted Major Kieffer offering important information.

As described later by Dr. Goetz, the woman asked for a large sum of money, and in return she would hand over a British radio operator calling herself "Jeanne-Marie Renier" and code-named Madeleine. Kieffer ordered Khan's immediate arrest. Early in the morning on October 13, Khan left her flat at 98 rue de la Faisanderie for one of the safe houses from which she transmitted. Vogt instructed a young French **résistant**-turned-collaborator named Pierre Cartaud to wait inside the flat in case she returned. At the same time, Kieffer sent Corporal Werner Ruehl of the SD's radio department to capture her at one of her safe houses. Ruehl recalled:

[Master Sergeant Karl] Haug and I followed her. She was wearing a blue tailored dress trimmed with white, was about 1.60–65m., slim with dark hair, about 24 [Khan was 30] years old and wearing a dark hat. Madeleine turned suddenly and saw us. She quickly disappeared round a corner and we did not see her again.

Khan went back to 98 rue de la Faisanderie. When she opened the door, Pierre Cartaud seized her from behind. She fought, scratching his face and lacerating his wrists with her teeth. He threw her onto the sofa and pointed a pistol at her. He threatened to kill her if she went on struggling and called Kieffer, who sent Vogt and some other SD men to his aid. Vogt arrived and saw a bloodied Cartaud standing a safe distance from his prisoner. Khan, as distressed as she was angry, said, "Another few days and I should have been in England."

Vogt took Khan, along with her radio and codes, straight to his interrogation room at 84 avenue Foch. She was a big fish whose capture gave the SD control of an important radio link. "You know who I am, and what I am doing," she told Vogt. "You have my radio set. I will tell you nothing. I have only one thing to ask you. Have me shot as quickly as possible." She expected torture, but Vogt proceeded in his usual sympathetic fashion. She refused to answer his questions. Frustrated, he ordered a warder to lock her in one of the cells. She asked to take a bath first, and Vogt agreed.

A few minutes later, John Starr heard a commotion. The warders told him that a new prisoner had attempted to escape through the bathroom window. They said the woman had asked her guard to close the door to give her privacy while she was in the bath. As soon as he did so, she climbed through the window and walked along a narrow rain gutter. Vogt, suspecting her intention, was waiting on a triangular roof within the internal courtyard. " 'Madeleine,' don't be silly," he said. "You will kill yourself. Think of your mother. Give me your hand." He took her to her cell, where she sat down and wept. "I ought to have let myself fall." She sighed.

Khan refused to eat over the days that followed. When she finally accepted tea and cigarettes from

Vogt, she went on ignoring his questions. Dr. Goetz took her downstairs to his radio room for a similarly fruitless interrogation and returned her to Vogt. Vogt did not give up, cajoling and flattering her for days. He occasionally sent Pierre Cartaud to her flat to bring clothes and toiletries, but even then, Kieffer noted, "Madeleine, after her capture, showed great courage, and we got no information whatsoever out of her." Khan's steadfast refusal to reveal anything impressed Vogt. "I suppose," he recalled, "that she was the best human being I have met." All she told Vogt was her cover story that she was Nora Baker of the RAF. Vogt, who never learned her real name, instructed John to write on his map of captured agents "Nora Baker, Royal Air Force."

John's cell was opposite Khan's. Although he could not see her, he heard her crying at night. When guards brought her past his workspace for his first glimpse of the beautiful young woman, he noticed she had "light brown hair with some red lights" and wore navy blue slacks, a polo-neck sweater, and sport shoes. She looked French to him. Seeing her anguish, he wrote her a note, "Cheer up, you are not alone, perhaps we shall find a way out of here." Passing it to her was difficult, because the guards did not leave them alone. He used the ruse of asking for permission to use the lavatory, dropping a pencil and "accidentally" kicking it around the corner toward Khan's cell. Out of sight of the guards for a second, he pushed the paper under her door. No one noticed. The note asked her to exchange messages by pressing them into a crack in the wall under the lavatory basin. In the morning, when John went to wash, her reply was waiting.

This written correspondence was their only means of communication, John later explained, because they did not utter "more than forty or so spoken words in all her stay in Av. Foch. All we could say was 'Hello' 'Cheer up' 'Good morning' and the most she ever said to me was, 'Carry on, you're doing a great job, more than any prisoner I ever heard of.'" Their hidden notes, exchanged almost daily, drew them closer to each other than their few spoken words. Through them, they worked on a goal that was crucial to them both: escape.

Khan also communicated in secret with a prisoner in the cell beside hers, tapping in Morse on their shared wall. He was Colonel Léon Faye, a forty-four-year-old French veteran of the First World War, a career officer, and a founder of the ALLIANCE network. As an intelligence-gathering circuit, ALLIANCE liaised with Britain's MI6 rather than SOE. Faye was on his third mission in France when the Germans captured him on September 16 in Aulnay-sous-Bois.

Khan asked John if she could tell Faye about their plans. He agreed, and Faye also secreted notes under the basin. John recalled, "He asked me if I thought we could make a getaway by going down the main stairs at night to which I replied impossible." The safest route out of the cells was up, through the light shafts to the roof. Iron bars, however, blocked the way.

John examined the bars in his ceiling. They were three parallel struts secured in a wooden frame. To squeeze through, all he had to do was loosen the screws and remove one bar. He needed a screwdriver. His next notes to Khan and Faye asked about their skylights. Their bars, unlike his, had no frames. Rods went straight into the walls, which required digging out the plaster. They too needed a screwdriver, a knife, or some other metal implement.

There was no obvious solution to the lack of tools until an unexpected opportunity presented itself. The cleaning woman, Holwedts, asked the guards to fix her carpet sweeper. None of the East European warders wanted to help, so John volunteered. He laid the machine on the guardroom table and took it apart, spreading dust in every direction. The guards grew impatient as he tinkered, and they told him to hurry. It would take less time, he said, if he had tools. The guards sent Holwedts to bring her box of cleaning paraphernalia. John rummaged through it and found a screwdriver. The guards were too vigilant for him to pocket the tool, so he took the precaution of doing a halfhearted job to give himself a second chance at it. This came five days later when the cleaner knocked at the guards' door to say her sweeper had broken again.

The guards told John to fix it, and when he finished, he slipped the screwdriver into a panel inside the fireplace behind him. If Holwedts complained it was missing, no one would find it in his cell. If anyone found it in the guardroom fireplace, he would not be suspected. John waited a few days, during which Holwedts did not mention the screwdriver. He then hid it in the lavatory for Khan, and she and Faye took turns with it, gouging bits of the plaster holding their bars in place.

As Khan chipped away late one night, she fell off the bed. The crash roused the guards, who rushed to her cell. She claimed she had attempted to hang herself, which earned her more sympathy from Vogt.

John's skylight was too high to reach. He moved his bed from its place against the wall to the middle of the floor below the shaft, but leaving it there would be suspicious, so he slid the bed to the opposite wall. One of the guards noticed the change and called Vogt. John explained that he wanted a different view. Vogt got the joke and said, "That's all right." In the following days, he shifted the bed to another wall and then another. The guards lost interest in his eccentric behavior. Soon he positioned the bed under the skylight in the center of the room. It was still not high enough for John at five feet five inches to touch the ceiling. He took the chance of moving a chair from the guardroom to his cell. A guard again informed Vogt, who asked John what was going on. John explained that he wanted something to hang his clothes on rather than leave them on the bed or the floor. This seemed fine to Vogt, who told the guard to ignore it. Alone in his cell that night, John put the chair on the bed and stood on it. The shaft was within reach.

John next convinced Vogt to let him connect an extension wire from the switch outside his cell so that he could turn his light on and off without asking permission. Vogt thought it would mean less work for the guard, and he let John keep the switch. When he was ready to escape, John could turn off the light without having to ask the guard. Slowly, the plan's elements were falling into place.

While working alone in the guardroom, John noticed a truncheon and hid it in the fireplace where he had secreted the screwdriver. Unsure that a wooden baton would be effective against armed guards, he left a note about it for Faye. The Frenchman answered that it might come in handy, and John left it for him in the lavatory.

Khan and Faye replaced the plaster they were digging out of their walls with kneaded bread. The dough, Khan wrote to John, was not the same color as the plaster. He recommended she use her makeup to tint the bread. Vogt then became an unsuspecting accomplice when, at her request, he sent Pierre Car-

taud back to her flat for cosmetics and more clothing. Vogt was doing all he could to humor her in the
vain expectation that she would operate her radio
for Dr. Goetz or give him information. Her makeup
arrived, and she mixed face powder into the bread
to achieve the right shade of beige. In one of her
coat pockets, she found tickets for the Paris Metro.
If and when she and the others got out of the building, they could rush into a train without wasting
time queuing for tickets.

When Faye's bar was loose enough to pull out, he
passed the screwdriver back to Khan. Their prepara-
tions had yet to attract their captors' notice.

The SD, however, tightened its watch on John.
Major Kieffer ordered the duty warders in the guardroom to keep him in sight at all times. He explained
that he had given John "drawing tasks whose subject matter was to be kept secret," and went on to
note: "Since in the eventuality of an escape he posed
a great risk to my office I impressed upon the guards
again and again that however affable and oblig-
ing 'Bob' might be his lodging was to be carefully
guarded and secured." After all, John's work for
Kieffer, checking the English in the SD's messages
to London, gave John what Kieffer called "a great
insight into our counterespionage work and [he] got
to know numerous arrested agents, W/T operators,
and organisers of hostile intelligence services."

While the three prisoners prepared their break-

189

out, avenue Foch was hosting more British agents. One was John's former radio operator, John Young, who was captured along with John's former courier, Diana Rowden, on November 18, 1943, in Clairvaux-les-Lacs. The SD put him in John's cell, saying, "Here's your old chief." The two men whispered to avoid being overheard. Young told John that his interrogators in Dijon tortured him to find out where his radio was. He pulled up his shirt to show John the scars on his back. Despite the pain, Young did not tell them anything. That meant, to John's relief, one less radio for deceiving London.

Guards moved Young to the cell beside John's in the morning. A few nights later, when they thought it unlikely anyone would hear, they tapped Morse messages to each other. John invited Young to join the escape. Young declined, saying he had given Kieffer his word of honor not to flee. The other three agreed to make the attempt without him. In the meantime, John compiled a written record on tissue paper of everything he was learning about the SD's penetration of SOE in France. If he could get it to London, the **Funkspiel** would be over.

TEN

Sabotage

Women were as brave and as responsible as men; often more so.

MAURICE BUCKMASTER

⸻

In the wilds of southwest France, George Starr was following the war's progress to determine when to tell his impatient followers to take up arms. Britain's Eighth Army, by this time famous for defeating German general Erwin Rommel's Panzers in North Africa, invaded the Italian mainland from Sicily on September 3, 1943. Six days later, the Americans landed at Salerno. Italian partisans popped up to assist the Allied invaders. The Red Army on the Russian front was deploying local partisans behind German lines to disrupt the rails, roads, and telephones, hastening the Soviet defeat of the Wehrmacht along the River Dneiper.

On September 11, Free French troops liberated a little piece of France, the island of Corsica. Circumstances in Gascony, however, were turning against the Resistance. For more than a year, they had kept the secret of thousands of people organizing and training to fight, but this provided time for the Germans to infiltrate the Resistance and disable it. On October 17, 1943, George's courier Pierre Duffoir bicycled to Castelnau-sur-l'Auvignon in panic. George was away, so Duffoir gave his ominous tidings to Maurice Rouneau: the Germans had captured a truck driver carrying supplies from a recent **parachutage**. The man had revealed, under torture, the location of drop site London T25, the farm where George had spoken by S-Phone with Major Gerry Morel. Vichy police and German Feldgendarmen, military policemen, raided the farm. They tortured its owner, Coulanges, Duffoir's relative, in front of his family. When he refused to reveal anything about **le patron** and the **parachutages,** they shot him dead and arrested his young son. Rouneau, whose growing animosity toward his chief may have colored his memory, wrote that Duffoir accused George of confiding in Coulanges secrets about Castelnau, its mayor, and the pro-Resistance gendarmes in the nearby village La Romieu. If the Germans had subjected Coulanges to more torment, he might have revealed all they needed to destroy WHEELWRIGHT.

Duffoir also said that unknown men had called at his house in Agen. Fearing for his wife, Paulette, and eleven-year-old daughter, Josette, he left to bring them back to Castelnau. George returned soon afterward, and Rouneau challenged him over his alleged indiscretions. The confrontation exacerbated tensions between them, but they had to cooperate to avoid catastrophe. If the Germans knew about London T25 and the Coulanges farm, they might raid Castelnau at any moment.

George stuffed a few clothes into a suitcase and said, "Now I'm going. I hope nothing bad happens today. Tomorrow morning at eleven, let's rendezvous near the Auvignon bridge at the edge of the village on the chemin de Caussens." Rouneau dug radio sets and money out of the castle dungeon and hid them at Mayor Larribeau's. He also assembled documents and valuables to store in metal cases. "I looked in vain for a newspaper cutting relating to the conviction by default [for sedition] that I received from the [Vichy] tribunal in Arras in 1941," he wrote, suspecting George had destroyed the paper. "I found this bizarre, because the teacher had filed it to show after the liberation that the affair had been manipulated." He and Jeanne Robert buried the crates in her garden behind the school.

Pierre Duffoir returned to Castelnau with his wife and daughter at nine o'clock that night. They were discussing with Rouneau what to do, when they heard knocking at the door. George slipped in and said, "I'm returning from Agen, where [Olivier] Prieur [butcher in Condom] took me. We're completely finished! We have to be out of here quickly." George claimed that a colleague from Rouneau's old print factory in Agen said that the Germans questioned another printer, "Tortillon," about safe house owner Hélène Falbet, Pierre Duffoir, and Rouneau. Rouneau wrote that George added, "So, they know everything now, and it's likely they won't delay in coming here, where the employees of the print factory know you come frequently." Rouneau had doubts, because the colleague from the print factory would not have known the nickname "Tortillon," which only he and Madame Falbet used. Despite that, he asked George, "So, what do you think should be done?"

"Leave immediately, tonight or before dawn."

Jeanne Robert protested that she had to teach in the morning. "How will that happen without me?"

"We'll have to find something to explain your absence, but you cannot stay here," George said. "I won't allow it, because, if you come to harm, I'll consider myself responsible."

Rouneau wrote that George lamented, "You don't know there are nights during which I cannot close my eyes when I think of poor Jacob, whom I did not force to leave." Maurice Jacob, head of the Service des Réfugiés et Expulsés, following his arrest at the

Château de la Clotte on August 21 with his family and friends, had been tortured in Toulouse's Saint-Michel Prison. The Germans then sent him, with Fernand Gaucher, to a series of concentration camps in Germany, the last of which was the death camp at Bergen-Belsen. Rouneau called George's reference to Jacob "pathetic."

Jeanne Robert, who would marry Maurice Rouneau, sympathized with both men. "Before Hilaire's arrival, Albert was the boss. And when he arrived, it was Hilaire who was the boss. It's necessary to understand that it was a little difficult."

While resentful at being sent out of France, Rouneau had no choice. He and George could not work together. Jeanne Robert packed her linen, silver, and personal items to store at the Novarini and Larribeau houses, and Rouneau stole six packs of cigarettes from George's stock, "over which Hilaire expressed extreme discontent the next day." They finished emptying the school at two o'clock in the morning. After trying but failing to sleep, Rouneau, Robert, and the three Duffoirs were on their bicycles at six.

Jeanne Robert said that, as they were leaving, George revealed to her his real name. It was not Serge, Gaston, or Hilaire, but George Reginald Starr. She recalled the poignancy of their parting: "We were almost brother and sister. Yes, because we complemented each other. We were good, never an affair, never anything. He was always content with what he had. Really, I have nothing bad to say about him, nothing but good." Her lover Rouneau, however, later savaged George in his memoir and in letters to SOE and to Philippe de Gunzbourg.

Rouneau, Robert, and the Duffoirs bicycled first to the Novarini farm to bid farewell to Pino and Tina, their comrades from **Réseau Victoire**'s founding at Easter 1942. The Novarinis cried as their friends left to cycle thirty miles south to Auch. There, Robert resigned her teaching post, explaining to an education official that her mother was ill and needed her in the Pas-de-Calais.

Their underground railroad depended on patriotic comrades to help them from post to post. They went on to Seissan and the house of Marius Sorbé, who had sheltered them in August and was regularly supplying George with civilian clothes for escapees to Spain. The next day it was to Tajan, where they stayed with the mayor and learned that Spanish police were interning all unmarried male refugees under the age of forty. The mayor gave Rouneau false papers under his cover name Martin Rendier that raised his age to forty-one. Pierre Duffoir, also under forty, was exempt from Spanish internment as a married man with a child.

On Wednesday, October 20, they stopped at the house of Roland Mansencal in Mazères-de-Neste. Mansencal urged them to stay, warning that a blizzard threatened to engulf the mountain. Rouneau refused. As a soldier in a Resistance army, he obeyed orders. Anyway, he believed that George Starr was also leaving France, a charge George confirmed:

> He fell out with me because I sent him home, which was the way to do it. But he thought the place couldn't run without him. And I got him to go, telling him I'd be following in a short time, which I never did.

George's antipathy to Rouneau emerged in the same interview: "In the village they had a funny duck. It wasn't a normal duck and it walked very funnily. We called it 'Rouneau run-run.'" When the interviewer asked George whether he considered himself "a martinet," he laughed and answered, "Oh, by Christ, yes. You had to be."

Rouneau's escape route took his small group to Loures-Barousse in the foothills of the Pyrenees. There, other men and boys were waiting to leave the country with them. At nine that night, a guide led them to the tiny Saléchan-Siradan train station. The stationmaster took them into his house, where more men were desperate to depart. They took stock of their weapons: one Tommy gun and a few pistols to face well-armed German border patrols. The friends who had accompanied them thus far said tearful good-byes and went back to Mazères-de-Neste. Rouneau's party set out on foot at one in the morning. Rain beat down on them as they followed the rail line south toward Luchon.

The refugees ascended the mountain, and rain turned to snow. The freezing trail became treacherous. They climbed all night and morning, resting only at noon. Their bread was frozen, but Jeanne Robert shared her few cans of paté. One of their guides urged them to tread quietly at the summit; a German border post was close by. The same guide picked up the nearly frozen eleven-year-old Josette Duffoir and carried her over the top. As they descended the other side, Paulette Duffoir collapsed in the snow. A few of the party went ahead to reconnoiter, while the rest remained with Paulette. She pleaded with them to abandon her, but they refused. An hour later, the two groups reunited at the edge of an abyss. It was so steep that there seemed no alternative but to return to France. A red-haired young Alsatian declared he would never go back. He forged ahead, the others following along the edge of the chasm. Rouneau recalled, "The slightest misstep, a little snow collapsing underfoot and we were finished." One of the local guides said, "This is the worst crossing I've ever made."

Rouneau slipped in the snow, which brought a laugh from little Josette Duffoir. This broke the tension, and they became hopeful as they trudged through the ice. Finally, on Wednesday, October 27, they reached Spain.

In Castelnau-sur-l'Auvignon, George was rebuilding his organization brick by brick. He had disposed of Rouneau, as he had his nominal commander, Henri Sevenet. None of the colleagues left in the Gers could challenge his authority. Indisputably **le patron**, George moved from the empty school into the house of Roger and Alberta Larribeau. His office remained in the kitchen of the shuttered school, while Robert's students transferred to classes in a hotel room in Condom. An SOE report for October 18, 1943, the day of Rouneau's departure, noted that George arranged for Roland Mansencal to replace Rouneau and for Gunzbourg to assume Duffoir's duties.

His untested fighters were growing impatient. They had joined the Resistance to harass German troops, destroy railways, cut telephone lines, and demolish bridges. What was SOE waiting for? In other areas, communist partisans were attacking the German troops. Yet provoking the Germans before D-Day brought retaliation, the capture of **résistants**, seizure of arms, murder of hostages, and loss of fighters who would be needed to support the Allied troops when they landed.

On November 10, 1943, George was promoted to captain. This did not alter his status in the field, where he did not wear a uniform or answer to a chain of command. The promotion made little difference to his **résistants**, who regarded him as their chief already, but it showed SOE's trust in its man in southwest France. Much, however, remained to be done.

The winter was one of the coldest on record. One night in December, while George's **résistants** were waiting for an arms drop in a field south of Vic-Fezensac, the temperature dropped to 20 degrees below freezing. The containers floated down and crashed deep into hard snow. The men cracked the ice to break them free. As they carried the heavy metal cylinders, they stopped every twenty steps to catch their breath. When they finished, one of them, Georges Dumont, said, "These are the days."

Late December was also hard on the Allied forces in Italy, whose offensive had stalled in the face of German reinforcements and strong defenses. The Wehrmacht kept the American beachhead at Salerno under artillery bombardment, delaying a breakout. Behind the lines, Italian guerrillas, many supported by SOE, were attacking the Germans and cutting their communications. The exploits of Italy's **partigiani,** like those of anti-Nazi partisans on the Russian front, set precedents for **résistants** in France.

Toward the end of 1943, Captain George Starr, like the men and women he commanded, was spoiling for action. Preparation was no longer enough. The **résistants** did not want to wait for the invasion. George asked London on December 13, SOE recorded, "for permission to make concentrated attacks on all Gestapo headquarters in his area, to take place after attacks on locomotives which were timed for the morning of the 1st January [1944]. This permission was granted on 14th December." London seemed willing to let him risk reprisals against civilians so long as he crippled German supply lines.

SOE promised to send a demolition specialist, Lieutenant Claude Arnault, to replace the unfortunate Charles Duchalard. Arnault was coming with a courier, although George had not requested one. Yvonne Cormeau recalled, "We had our courier service established." The new courier would be a young Englishwoman named Anne-Marie Walters. Arnault and Walters were both twenty years old and spoke fluent French, Arnault because he was French and Walters because she had grown up in Geneva. Walters's field code name was "Colette" and Arnault's "Néron."

A Halifax bomber took Walters and Arnault to France on the night of December 16, but severe weather prevented the pilot, Flight Lieutenant Stanley Nicholson Gray, from reaching the drop site. On the return to RAF Woodbridge in Suffolk, Gray's aircraft crashed in the Tangham Forest. Gray and two members of his crew were killed. An internal SOE document of December 17 noted Walters and Arnault "suffered shock and concussions" and had abrasions and sprained ankles. The medical officer recommended "complete rest." George would have to wait for his explosives expert.

As Christmas approached, George asked London for English 555 cigarettes and Scotch whisky. SOE could not commandeer special transport for luxuries, so it added George's presents to one of his regular **parachutages**. But the RAF "made a mistake and shoved it all down into a German barracks." George was mortified that the German soldiers were enjoying his cigarettes and whisky, until a few days later when a plane dropped the Christmas package in the right place. George stashed the whisky in a beehive.

Soon afterward, a radio message from London informed George that King George VI had awarded him the Military Cross for "exemplary gallantry." He decided to celebrate: "I went out in the dark, got the bottle of whisky, opened it and said, 'What muck!' I'd completely lost the taste, having drunk so much Armagnac. I put it back in the beehive. As far as I know, it's still there."

On November 19, 1943, Major Kieffer sent Ernest Vogt and interpreter August Scherer to arrest a French SOE wireless operator in an apartment in a suburb south of Paris. Master Sergeant Josef Stork drove them there at 11:00 P.M. and waited in the car with another SD man while Vogt and Scherer went up to the third floor. They broke into the flat and saw André Dubois, code name "Hercule," sending messages from a radio on the kitchen table. The Frenchman jumped up and fired his handgun at the intruders. His first shot killed Scherer. Vogt, a civilian who had never used a weapon, pointed his revolver at Dubois and fired. He wounded Dubois, who shot back and hit Vogt in the chest. Both men kept firing. Vogt described the scene of two bleeding adversaries trying to kill each other at close range: "When both our pistols were empty, we stood looking at each other, across the table, weaponless, since all our bullets were in each other's bodies. Then I felt myself fainting." Josef Stork and the other SD man, whom Stork called only "Untersturm- führer X," heard the shooting and ran up to the flat. Vogt lay unconscious and bleeding. Dubois, though seriously wounded, "ran as quickly as he could with a weapon in his hand to the door and down the stair- case and outside." The Germans chased him until he collapsed about one hundred yards away. They took both men to the Hôpital de la Pitié-Salpêtrière, where surgeons cut seven bullets from Vogt's body, including one over his heart.

While recovering, Vogt managed to get out of bed and stagger to the next ward to find Dubois. He sat on Dubois' bed and said to the bandaged prisoner, "You should not have fired. When you fired, I fired." Dubois answered, "I hoped to kill you and escape."

Vogt was still in the hospital on Thursday night, November 25, when John Starr decided the time had come to leave 84 avenue Foch. "After [a] three months stay," he said later, "I knew exactly the names of our agents, grounds, dumps, etc., known to the S.D. I also had all the dope on the [General Henri] GIRAUD and DE GAULLE organisations. In possession of this knowledge, I attempted my escape." He worked late in the guardroom on his oil portrait of Kieffer, while Faye and Khan were locked in their cells. To mask the sound of iron spars scraping their walls, John chatted with the guards and made a racket with his paints. When all seemed quiet, he asked a guard to take him to his cell. The door closed. The guard locked it, as always. John put the tissues with intelligence on the **Funkspiel** in his pocket and a letter for Major Kieffer on the bed. He switched off the light and, with the chair perched on his mattress, reached for the loose bar and slid it out. He strained not to make a sound as he climbed through the shaft to the skylight. Faye was waiting for him on the roof. Khan, however, was not there.

John and Faye walked in silence along the rooftop to her skylight. Khan was inside, struggling to remove the bar at the base of the shaft. The two men reached in and took turns with the screwdriver. Faye, who had the longer reach, did most of the work. After two hours of strenuous effort, he pried the bar out of the plaster. Khan joined them on the roof, and Faye kissed her. They tied their shoes around their necks, lest their footsteps give them away, and tore blankets into strips and tied them into rope for the perilous five-story drop. Descending to a flat roof about halfway down, they realized their plan was succeeding. John recalled Faye exclaiming, "We've done it!"

All of a sudden, the three escapees froze. Search-lights scanned the sky. Allied aircraft screeched overhead to bomb the industrial suburbs of Paris. John recalled that "as the R.A.F. came over, the flak started and woke everybody up." The guards inspected the cells as usual during raids and found John's and Khan's rooms empty. Flashlights from in-side 84 avenue Foch scanned the exterior walls. The three fugitives lay flat. When the lights passed, Faye led the way to a cast-iron fire escape. Below, guards were running from street to street. The escapees low-ered themselves again with their rope blanket and clung to the side of a mansion behind avenue Foch, 9-bis Square du Bois de Boulogne. Fearing immi-nent capture, Faye abandoned the truncheon John had given him. John hid his papers for London in a flowerpot on the ledge. He later wrote, "I went back to the protecting wall which hid me from the Gestapo windows and there got rid of my papers while Madeleine and Faye lay flat on the roof as the light shone from the rooftop windows."

Inside 84 avenue Foch, Major Kieffer was asleep. Guards woke him at about three o'clock to tell him that Bob and Madeleine were gone. Kieffer took charge. A check of all cells revealed that Colonel Faye was also missing. Kieffer recalled, "All three had broken through the iron bars in their cells leading to the windows of the ceiling and they climbed up on to the flat roof and by means of strips of blankets and sheets knotted together they let themselves down on to the balcony in the third storey of a neighbouring house and there smashed a window and entered the apartment."

Faye used his elbow to break the windowpane and the three clambered inside. With the lights off, they felt their way around the furniture to the stairway. They rushed downstairs and opened the front door. The street was a cul-de-sac with a high wall at one end and SS men at the other. Faye saw his only hope: a bold sprint into the dark. He made it past the guards, and they unleashed a flurry of automatic weapons fire.

John and Khan bolted back into the mansion and up two flights of stairs. They rested on a sofa. Khan erupted in tears, knowing their bid for liberty was ending. From the floor above came the voice of the owner of the house, Madame Esmerian, "Who are you? What are you doing? Are you thieves?" John looked up at the woman, who was peering back through the banister. Before he could answer, the Germans burst through the door.

The would-be escapees faced an irate Major Kieffer in the entryway of 84 avenue Foch. "You're all going to be shot!" Kieffer shouted. Guards hauled John, Khan, and a badly wounded Faye to the fourth floor for their summary executions. "I have only done my duty," Faye said. An SS soldier punched him in the face so hard that blood gushed out. The guards frisked the prisoners. In John's pocket was the photograph Kieffer had given him for the portrait. "A little souvenir," John explained, adding, "I left a letter for you. You'll find it in my cell." Kieffer sent a guard to fetch it, while the three awaited execution. The guard gave the letter to Kieffer, who read:

As you will have realized when you get this, we are trying to escape. Now that I hope we shall not be meeting again, I should like to thank you for the good treatment we have received here, and to say that we shall not forget it.

Wishing you the best of luck in the chase that will follow, but much better luck to ourselves,

"Bob"

As John watched Kieffer, he felt that "a terrible battle was going on inside him." Would he kill or

spare them? Kieffer turned to John. The terrible battle was over. He dismissed the firing squad.

Guards chained John's hands and feet and hauled
him to his cell. During the night, they beat him.
One of the guards used the truncheon that Faye
had left on the roof, irate that John might have used
it on him. In the morning, they moved him into
Faye's empty cell. John lay alone, shackled and defeated, for two weeks. Then Kieffer granted him an
audience and demanded an explanation. John, Kieffer later recalled, replied "that 'Madeleine' had approached him with the escape plan and that if as a
woman she had the courage to escape and had succeeded in doing so she would have made life impossible for him in England had he not displayed the
same courage as a man."

John's memory of their first meeting after the escape's failure differed from Kieffer's. He said that
Kieffer and von Kapri came to his cell ten days into
his solitary confinement and asked him to "give his
word of honour never again to attempt to escape
custody, not only whilst in the Avenue Foch but also
whilst in France." If he did not agree, they would
send him to Germany. He agreed. "Two or three
days later, he was again brought to the guard-room
in order to carry on with the work, and thereafter
he was afforded greater liberty than ever before the
abortive escape."

John added that he said to Kieffer, "So long as you keep me here, I give my word that I shall not attempt to escape. If I should be sent anywhere else, that promise will no longer be binding." He justified his decision to SOE, which recorded that he "would still have the chance of passing his information to another prisoner who had not been so bound and who might attempt escape with it to London or through any other manoeuvre chance might afford." Kieffer recalled that they shook hands after John gave his word of honor not to escape. Kieffer had a higher opinion of British than French officers, "since in contrast to the French officers no English officer had broken the word of honour he had given me during my work in France." He turned deadly serious at the conclusion of their meeting: if John reneged, twelve SOE agents would be shot.

Unlike John, Khan and Faye had declined to give their **parole**. Major Kieffer said, "'Madeleine' and 'Faye' were subsequently conveyed on the same day [November 26] to Strasbourg or Karlsruhe by order of the BDS [Befehlshaber der Sicherheitsdienstes, chief security officer Colonel Helmut Knochen] and assigned to a secure prison." The "secure prison" for each was a concentration camp, Khan at first to Pforzheim and Faye to Sonnenberg.

News of the aborted escape reached F-Section

in London through the socially prominent Emily Morin Balachowsky. She learned about it from Josef Placke, whom she had met in her endeavor to free her **résistant** husband, Alfred Serge Balachowsky of the Pasteur Institute, from German custody. The SD had arrested Professor Balachowsky, who worked for Francis Suttill's PHYSICIAN circuit, in July 1943 and sent him to the transit camp north of Paris at Compiègne. She met Placke first at avenue Foch and later at her home and in public places. When Placke told her about the escape attempt, she sent the information via an escape network to Spain and through Swiss intelligence to SOE in Berne. F-Section could no longer ignore the fact that the Germans were playing Noor Inayat Khan's radio. Madame Balachowsky's report confirmed one other detail: John Starr was alive.

Gilbert Norman, the radio operator John met on his arrival at avenue Foch, had also sworn not to escape from the building. When the SD needed his cell for a new prisoner, guards took him downstairs to a van for transfer to Fresnes. Outside, where his promise was no longer valid, he broke away and darted up the avenue. Corporal Alfred von Kapri took aim and shot him in the leg. The Germans picked him up and drove him, not to Fresnes, but to the Hôpital de la Pitié-Salpêtrière. In another bed, Norman saw the man to whom he had given his **parole d'honneur,** Ernest Vogt.

. . .

Two months of bureaucratic negotiation delayed Maurice Rouneau, Jeanne Robert, and the Duffoirs in Spain. On December 14, they crossed the no-man's-land from Spanish territory into Britain's Fortress Gibraltar, and just after midnight on December 29, a Dakota military transport flew them to Bristol. In London, Colonel Buckmaster congratulated them on their work and asked what they wanted to do next. Rouneau and Pierre Duffoir answered with one voice, "Return to France!"

At the end of December, London ordered George to destroy scores of railroad locomotives in Gascony. He could not wait for demolition expert Claude Arnault, who was still recovering in England from his crash injuries. With little time to undertake the sabotage himself, he taught others. George's knowledge of explosives was so thorough from his years in the mines that he claimed he could have taught his SOE instructors. This may have been what prompted one examiner to call him a "know it all." "I chose New Year's Eve, when the Germans would be celebrating and too drunk to pay too much attention," he said. Yvonne Cormeau claimed that he even sent the Germans in one train station a case of champagne to help them along. "We found out where all the locomotives would be, in roundhouses and sidings, and just blew them all up," George said. "In some places the railway workers helped. In others, they would not. On that night, we blew up 320 locomotives." Yvonne confirmed that sympathetic railroad workers, including a train inspector, assisted the saboteurs. The men placed the charges in the same place in each engine "so they couldn't take out a spare part from one engine to put it on the other."

By New Year's morning 1944, more than three hundred engines were useless. "It was a veritable New Year's Eve bash of locomotives," wrote George's security chief. "They danced like they never had; it was something monstrous, like the Elephants' Ball of which Kipling spoke; 28 machines [in one location] were left lying on the ground." In Bergerac, the saboteurs rendered twenty-five of thirty train engines inoperable. Despite the sweeping success, George regretted not doing it himself: "It's very difficult to send people away on dangerous jobs and wait there, wondering and hoping they're all right. I think it's more difficult than going and doing it yourself."

The destruction of the engines began a series of operations that would escalate in the new year with the arrival of Claude Arnault. There was no evidence, however, that the "concentrated attacks" George planned on "all Gestapo headquarters in his area" and for which London gave him permission on December 14 took place.

On January 4, 1944, Claude Arnault and Anne-Marie Walters made their second attempt to parachute into southwest France. George's ground team, led by a master carpenter named Gabriel Cantal, was standing by at the designated drop zone. The Halifax missed it and dropped Arnault and Walters a few miles off target. Cantal and the other **résistants** from the village of Gabarret found the pair caked in mud and burying their parachutes in marshland beside an irrigation channel. Scattered on the ground were fifteen containers and six boxes of supplies that the men collected before guiding the arrivals to a safe house. One of the reception committee later described Anne-Marie Walters:

> Colette looked like a Father Christmas in her flying suit, a shovel at her side, a knife on her sleeve, a [Czech .32 caliber] revolver in her pocket, lozenges, tablets, rum, food, maps of the area, compass, identity cards and ration coupons, well printed in England, [that] look better than those of many in France.

At sunrise, Walters and Arnault walked over frozen fields to Gabarret, and a day later drove to Condom to wait for George.

Walters was asleep the next morning when George's motorcycle sped into Condom. "**Le patron** is here," her hostess announced to the sleeping young woman. Walters's description of him at their first meeting was not flattering:

He was practically bald with a little moustache (the moustache was an irregular ornament, being shaved off when he visited certain parts of the region) and about forty-five. [George was thirty-nine.] He had a sly look, his eyes quickly avoiding yours when he spoke. He appeared to be in a frayed state of nerves as he bounced about the room and spoke in broken sentences. He spoke French with a strong foreign accent, not specifically English, but undefinable to German ears in the mix-up of regional accents.

To Walters, embarrassed to be seen in her blue pajamas, George was businesslike rather than friendly. "First," he said, "I am very strict on discipline." He would forgive a mistake once. "To put things plainly, you have to do what I tell you and we'll get along all right. If you don't, I shall have to shoot you." He advised her to remember her training, but to forget her cover story. No cover stood up to scrutiny. He advised her to deal only with people she knew by sight or through someone she trusted. "Passwords are poisonous traps," he said. He told her also not to smoke in public, because women in the region didn't. She noticed that "he couldn't spend five minutes without smoking. His fingers were stained with nicotine."

In what may have been a deception to frighten the young woman, George said the Gestapo had captured and tortured him. To prove the point, he showed her scars on his legs. Asked years later why he had lied to her, George said, "That was to impress the little bitch." Walters believed the story, as did many others.

He examined the identity card and ration coupons that London had issued her. The chits for food and clothing were first rate, but he spotted a flaw in the identity card: "London makes mistakes sometimes. This card shows that you've crossed the demarcation line illegally last year. It has the wrong stamp on it." He took the card with him when he left, saying he would bring her a replacement. She was indignant: "It seemed monstrous that I should stay any time at all without papers."

George returned seventy-two hours later with a new identity card. She asked when she could leave for northern France, where London had assigned her. George said, "You're better off here." Having initially resisted a courier from London, he said he needed her:

I've had to go everywhere myself all this time. Four or five months ago, the Boche put a heavy price on my head and it's been getting more difficult every day. The other day I came on a Gestapo barrage. I had a transmitter set in the back of my Simca car and my **canadienne** [coat] thrown over it. Fortunately, they didn't search the car.

The following Sunday, Walters accompanied George on rounds of senior agents to whom she would be his liaison. Her cover story was that she was "a student from Paris who just couldn't get on with her studies because Paris was so expensive and so difficult and who had come to seek refuge with the farmer who was supposed to be a friend of my father in the last war."

On the night of January 27, 1944, RAF Flight Lieutenant Maurice Southgate parachuted into George's area of operations on his second mission. His first assignment had concluded the previous November after ten months, during which he sabotaged factories and fought a pitched battle with French police. Buckmaster wrote of him that "he stuck to his job without any thought for his own safety or welfare. He worked long hours—sometimes as many as twenty a day—and he inspired the fiercest enthusiasm in all who worked with him." George sent Gabriel Cantal, who had received Walters and Arnault three weeks before, to meet Southgate and put him on a bus to Tarbes to resume his work with the STATIONER circuit.

Anne-Marie Walters traveled by train with Arnault, whom she called "Jean-Claude" in her memoirs, on missions for George. George, concerned that young Arnault "was in love with that Anne-Marie Walters," asked Gunzbourg to employ him north of the River Garonne. George and Gunzbourg told

Walters that "suspicious people who claimed to have come from England" were poking around the Gers and Arnault would be safer elsewhere. She missed the handsome young Frenchman "for many weeks."

Walters came down with a cough and high fever that confined her to bed. George sent a young physician and **résistant**, Dr. Jean Deyris, to treat her, and during her four-day illness, George "came almost every day," bringing her English tea and chocolate from a parachute drop.

While convalescing, Walters heard rumors of a mass breakout from the Maison Centrale d'Eysses. The former Benedictine monastery-turned-prison lay on farmland about forty-five miles away. On January 3, 1944, the day before she and Arnault parachuted into France, fifty-four inmates—led by SOE organizers Philippe de Vomécourt of VENTRILOQUIST and Major Charles Hudson of HEADMASTER—had escaped.

Vomécourt and Hudson, along with thirteen other escapees, took refuge not far from Eysses. Vomécourt needed help from the underground to reach Spain. He wrote, "The message was passed down to the **patron** of the Gascony circuit, who set about arranging our passage."

When George, **le patron**, visited them, he tallied their needs: civilian clothes, false identity cards, transportation to the Spanish frontier, and guides. He sent Walters to Roland Mansencal, George's representative in Mazères-de-Neste near Montréjeau, for information on the best escape route. Walters took buses from Condom to the market town of Tarbes, where Mansencal was waiting for her in an electricity shop owned by his nephew. While they ate lunch upstairs, Mansencal moaned about the obstacles— heavy snow, avalanches, German border guards. Walters held her tongue, recalling that George had told her Mansencal "fumed over everything but got things done better than anyone else."

Mansencal took her by train to Montréjeau and on foot about three miles through rolling meadows to his house in Mazères-de-Neste. To her delight, she found Arnault there. The young people, who had not seen each other since George sent Arnault north, argued and reconciled in the manner of young lovers. Mansencal left to seek the guides and, after bicycling up and down hills for thirty miles, returned at sunset. He told Walters the guides were leaving for Spain in the morning with thirty-five American airmen. They would not be back for two weeks. "This is the best I can do," he said. "The other guide working for us was caught by the Gestapo six weeks ago. I don't know anyone else I can trust."

Walters walked in darkness early the next morning to catch the 5:20 train to Toulouse and connected to another for Auch. She retrieved her bicycle and went to the farm of a family called Castagnos. Henri and Odilla Castagnos, along witht their son,

André, were providing her a room in their house at great risk to themselves. She rested there for a short time before cycling on to meet George. He told her to hide the ex-prisoners in Fourcès until their departure. Anne-Marie proceeded to Agen to relay **le patron**'s orders to Albert Cambon, who promised to arrange everything.

Cambon drove off in an old truck, picking up gendarme Raymond Aubin and handing the vehicle over to **résistant** Francis Peyrot to drive. The Eysses fugitives climbed under the tarpaulin on the truck bed. Peyrot drove them to Walters in Agen. She opened the canvas flap and climbed into a dark, five-by-seven-foot enclosure with fifteen sweaty men. Vomécourt remembered, "Just outside the town of Agen, a charming newcomer joined our cramped party in the back—an English girl called Anne-Marie Walters, who had dropped into Gascony and was operating under the code name of Paulette [**sic**]. She had cycled ahead to make sure the way was clear of Germans." F-Section Major Hudson introduced himself as if at a garden party and asked about SOE colleagues in London. He casually mentioned that he and the other men had broken rocks for fourteen hours a day in the prison, all the while dreading transfer to Germany.

The truck, running on wartime **gazogène** charcoal that produced less power than gasoline, struggled up the hills. At a steep incline, Anne-Marie and the fifteen men got out and pushed. They were trundling through the town of Nérac, when armed miliciens at a narrow bridge over the River Baïse ordered them to stop. "My heart was beating fast and I hoped no one could hear it," Walters wrote. Gendarme Aubin barked at one of the miliciens, "French police." He produced documents from his chief, clandestine **résistant** Captain Raymond Cosculuella, stating that he was on official business. When the miliciens tried to search the truck, Aubin nodded to Peyrot to drive on.

The miliciens screamed at Peyrot to stop. Aubin shouted to his passengers, "Lie flat!" The miliciens fired, but Peyrot made it over the bridge and drove as fast as his **gazogène**-powered engine could manage. When they were out of range, Major Hudson commented, "Boy, that was a neat job."

They settled in for the night inside a barn near Fourcès. Anne-Marie cycled back to the Castagnos farm the next morning. When George arrived, she told him what had happened. "You need not have been there at all," he said. "I don't want you to run any unnecessary risks. . . . It would bring awful trouble to us if you were caught. Anyway, I'm glad it's over." She felt his response "was a bit of a cold shower."

The escapees waited for the guides to return from Spain. "For a few days, we were able to relax," wrote Vomécourt, "eating well at the farm and enjoying freedom from alarms. All of us were fitter at the end of it." Finally, the fifteen men traveled to the border where **passeurs** were waiting to take them to Spain. The climb was grueling, but they made it over the Pyrenees through Spain to Gibraltar and, on March 8, to England. They said that they would not have made it but for the help they received from George Starr and his **résistants**.

ELEVEN

John's Cousin

Europe was not yet ablaze, but it was
beginning to smoulder.

MAURICE BUCKMASTER

––

While George Starr's domain expanded across the southwest, his brother John's world was contracting. The sole liberty he enjoyed was walking unescorted "between the guardroom and the lavatory." Worse, he had forfeited the prisoner's only hope: escape. His breakout on the night of November 25 might have succeeded if he had gone alone. The hours that he and Léon Faye spent extricating Noor Inayat Khan doomed his plan. Until that night, he had survived on the belief he would bring proof of the **Funkspiel** to London. Major Kieffer admitted, "Had the three managed to escape then it is to be assumed that all the radio plays which were in full swing would have been finished." That prospect vanished when he gave his word to Major Kieffer not to escape. Instead of a hero, John was a trusty of his German captors.

He justified his accord with Kieffer: "I thought it over and decided that if I refused I would never get a chance to escape again anyway, and that if I accepted there would still be a lot to learn, and that perhaps one day the opportunity to communicate my knowledge to London would arise." His conviction that he could confide details of the **Funkspiel** to another prisoner, who might escape to London, was a gamble at best, self-deception at worst.

"After the 'Escape' things began to change," wrote John. "To the extent that when Ernest returned [from the hospital] he had no longer his office on the top floor. It was his office which had become the 'Guard Room' & the 'guard room' had become my cell where I was <u>alone</u>." When Ernest Vogt recovered from his wounds in early January 1944, he took up his duties in a new office on the fourth floor, where SOE captives were brought to him for interrogation. Kieffer said that, with the rearrangement of rooms, "Bob himself was more closely guarded." Upstairs, John humored the staff by drawing caricatures and postcards. His work on maps and organizations taught him more about SD counterespionage, but the knowledge was useless.

A bizarre relationship developed between John

and his captors. The Russian guards, who had beaten him badly when he was recaptured, became friendly again, while August Scherer's widow, Ottilie, developed an attraction to him and tried to win him better treatment. Ernest Vogt wrote, "I knew that Millie Scherer fell in love with Starr, both have been surprised by a member of our service named [Second Lieutenant Stephan] Gutgsell when they kissed each other. Kieffer too knew it, because Gutgsell told him, and he told it to me." The office cleaner, Holwedts, swore that Frau Scherer was John's mistress. A report from another prisoner, who said that "STARR did not give anything away," corroborated Vogt's account, stating that a German woman "may have influenced the Gestapo to keep him there." He said the woman's name was "Odile," and "[h]er husband [August Scherer] had been shot by one of our agents."

When Master Sergeant Josef Placke mentioned one of his favorite restaurants in Paris to John, it gave John an idea. SOE recorded:

One day he said to the German, "Why don't you take me out for a meal?" meaning the whole thing as a joke. To his surprise the idea was taken seriously. Placke checked with Kieffer, who had no objection. So, one evening, the Germans took Starr to the restaurant.

As they left the building, Placke said to John, "I know you have given your parole to the Sturmbann-führer, but I should be glad if you would give it again, for tonight to me personally." John said his word to Kieffer was enough, and Placke did not insist. They arrived at the expensive restaurant, where the other diners did not appear to notice that one of the Germans' guests was a captured British agent. Among Placke's dining companions was a friend of Madame Balachowsky named Dr. Briault. Placke had turned Briault while interrogating him at Fresnes, although the doctor went on supplying intelligence to Madame Balachowsky for the British. Later, Dr. Briault told Madame Balachowsky about the dinner. Placke, he said, had boasted about running a bogus F-Section network north of Paris, ACROBAT, allegedly staffed by captured Canadian officers. It amused Placke that SOE was still parachuting supplies to the fictitious circuit. Madame Balachowsky passed Briault's information to London.

The Germans took John on a series of operations. Placke recalled that he "went out twice with BOB (or perhaps three times), once in Paris to take him to a restaurant, another time to Saint Quentin . . . following a message from London by radio, a message caught by our service, to find trace of two planes that had not returned to London at the end of their missions." One of these outings involved identifying the bodies from a downed British aircraft, and on another excursion, Dr. Goetz asked John to select a field where British agents could land. Knowing that Goetz planned to trap another SOE team, John dismissed the better sites as useless. While inspecting terrain he knew would be ideal, he pointed to German troops marching along the road. He said that their barracks must be near, which would rule out the area for an RAF landing. Goetz took him to another field, which was uneven and near a German radio listening post. Assuming that RAF reconnaissance planes had logged the station already, he assured Goetz it was perfect.

The SD next asked John to help thwart an F-Section attempt to discover whether Placke's ACROBAT network was genuine. It was ostensibly under two Canadian officers, Captains Frank Pickersgill, "Bertrand," and radio operator John McAlister, "Valentin." The SD had captured them when they parachuted onto a field ten miles north of Valencay on June 18, but their interrogators learned nothing from them and they were transported to concentration camps in Germany. The SD had been "playing" their radio since that time.

F-Section, probably in response to Madame Balachowsky's intelligence that Placke was bragging about running a fake circuit, was sending someone to fly over the **parachutage** terrain with an S-Phone to verify the Canadians' voices. Dr. Goetz asked John to speak on the S-Phone for him, because the SD officers' German accents would give them away. This crossed a line for John, who refused to offer genuine aid to the enemy. Nonetheless, he told Goetz he would consider doing it and needed time to think it over. Two weeks later, John announced his decision: no. It was too late for the SD to find someone else to speak English without a German accent. Placke took John to the site anyway. "He wanted to know the name of the officer who came to speak from the airplane," John said. "That is why he gave me the S-Phone to listen to the conversation and identify the voice of the speaker . . . I claimed to the Germans not to know the aviator."

John lied. He knew the voice of Major Gerry Morel, who the previous May had verified George Starr's identity by his prodigious profanity. Corporals Alfred von Kapri and Werner Ruehl spoke to Morel, but F-Section's operations chief recognized German accents when he heard them. The plane turned around. When Morel reported back to London, SOE cut communications with the Germans' Canadian circuit. However, Placke had others.

John drew Christmas cards for staff at avenue Foch. The one for Kieffer had the date 1944 on the front. When the major opened it, a paper British soldier popped up and pointed a rifle straight at him. "Do you think so?" Kieffer asked. John nodded.

227

The Allies had already taken North Africa, Sicily, and southern Italy. On the eastern front, the Wehrmacht was retreating from Ukraine. It was obvious even to a prisoner cut off from the world that the next battleground had to be France.

On New Year's Eve, Kieffer appeared in John's workspace with a tray of whisky and vodka for him and radio operator John Young. He drank a toast with them, saying in English, "Good health!" He returned to his office, leaving them the alcohol.

The SD accelerated its radio game in the new year. Dr. Goetz brought on three assistants for more support, remembering, "Each man had about three or four decoy transmissions on hand during the time when the majority of them were running." SOE sent more supplies. Goetz recalled, "I was present when, on two occasions, materials were dropped by parachute. That must have been in January or February."

In the seven months since John's arrest, his hair had grown down to his shoulders in the **zazou** style he had affected on his first mission to the south of France. To clean him up, the SD brought his old barber from Issy-les-Moulineaux to avenue Foch. The man, while clipping John's hair, offered to smuggle a message out for him. Suspecting entrapment, John declined.

· · ·

Yvonne Cormeau moved from house to house in Gascony, often a hundred miles apart, to prevent the Germans from locking onto her radio waves. Then, noted an SOE report on WHEELWRIGHT, "Yvonne CORMEAU lived in, and worked from, Col. STARR's house." The Germans were searching for her and her radio, but failed to pinpoint her location, because, SOE noted, "STARR's security section was invariably informed of the presence of any D/F [direction finding] car within 100 miles." Her steady flow of requests to London assured that George was one of the best supplied SOE organizers in France.

The weapons, however, were of little use until the Allies invaded France. The invasion that failed to materialize in 1943 had to come, George believed, sometime in 1944. In preparation, Castelnau-sur-l'Auvignon was becoming a fortress and mustering ground for **maquisards** from all over Gascony. George ordered his men to bring weapons from Miramont and Gabarret to Castelnau, and trucks delivered even more arms and explosives from Sainte-Maure-de-Peyriac and Condom. A French Resistance report, "**Le Batallion de Castelnau,**" reckoned, "This represented around fifteen tons of matériel." George and Mayor Larribeau buried the weapons under beehives, in the ancient castle dungeon, and in secret storehouses throughout the village.

While laying the ground for defense of his head-quarters, George remained closer to Yvonne Cormeau than to Anne-Marie Walters. Raymond Escholier, who knew and admired both women, thought that each was the "living contrast" of the other. He wrote of Yvonne Cormeau that "the rougher **maquisards** speak of her like a madonna" and that all Gascony called Walters "the true sister of the **maquisards**." To Philippe de Gunzbourg, Cormeau was "a woman of high culture."

On one of her many cycling expeditions, covering up to fifty miles a day, Cormeau strained a mus-cle. A doctor confined her to bed in the Larribeau house, where she and George were living at the time. She later told her SOE debriefer that "there was little danger of being D/F'ed when she was staying with Hilaire in March as the house was in a very small village, they knew the operator's cover story (that of refugee) and they were accustomed to her presence in the village, and they knew she had been ill and in hospital." She concealed her radio trans-mitter deep under bundles of straw at the top of the Larribeaus' barn.

George and Cormeau often bicycled together, and Cormeau later admitted that "this was against all their security training," but "it was unlikely that this would have led to difficulties as they usually travelled as brother and sister." One day, while cy-cling through a small village, they rested beside a house that was also, as in Castelnau, the school and the town hall. A wanted poster tacked to its shutters offered a reward for the capture of a man and a woman, and they were speechless to see that the images were of themselves. To Cormeau, the drawings were all too accurate: "The only thing that they couldn't give was the very piercing look of the grey eyes of Hilaire." The couple split up without a word, fearing they would be overheard. George sent a local courier to tell her to remain where she was until it was safe to move. Four days later, she bicycled to another safe house.

The danger of capture increased as George's network grew throughout the region. A leading **résistant** near Castelnau said that the Germans called George "the invisible man," whom they were exerting strenuous efforts to find. Cormeau was equally vulnerable. She learned that the Gestapo knew an Englishwoman was operating a clandestine radio in the Gers, and a Spanish communist, who had been turned by the Germans, told the Gestapo that the woman lived in a village called Castelnau. Luckily for her, there were eight villages in the region whose names began with "Castelnau." She said the reason the Gestapo did not seek her in Castelnau-sur-l'Auvignon was that it had no water or electricity: "And in their methodic way, they decided that no Englishwoman would live in such primitive conditions."

· · ·

George Starr's French followers grew more restive in the new year. When would the Allies land? They could not play at Resistance forever. Yvonne Cormeau observed their gloom with sympathy, noting that early 1944 was "a very, very hard period then, simply because the people were beginning to lose confidence. Enemy propaganda was very strong. It was said, 'Oh, the English will fight to the last Frenchman.'" In February, Cormeau sent an urgent communiqué to London, "Could you give us a sign that something is going to happen?" London responded in March by sending messages over the BBC to different groups in the southwest, telling them, in Cormeau's words, "to down tools and join whatever headquarters had been allocated to them. This put in a lot of courage . . . Unfortunately, this was a bit early, but it did encourage them."

March proved to be a good period for George after months of foul weather, ill health, and false hope. On March 11, London sent him a second radio operator, Lieutenant Dennis Parsons. Maurice Parisot received the young British officer, and the artist Maurice Poncelet gave him a radio from an earlier **parachutage**. Code-named "Pierrot," Parsons was, in Escholier's words, a "most pleasant boy. Physically, one hundred per cent English. Morally too, as well. As to his accent, it was imperceptible, it was more Swiss Roman than English." Like Anne-Marie Walters, Parsons had studied in Geneva before the war.

London promoted George to the rank of major ten days after Parsons's arrival. It also ordered fresh operations, raising Resistance morale at least as much as it damaged the Germans'. The first mission was to sabotage the **Poudrerie Nationale de Toulouse,** the National Gunpowder Factory, south of Toulouse on the River Garonne. The plant, established under royal warrant by King François I in 1536, had turned out tons of powder for use against the Germans in the First World War. Since November 1942, when the Germans occupied Vichy's Free Zone, the well-protected works had produced explosives for the country's enemy. London warned George that if he did not destroy the factory, the RAF would. "We didn't want them to do that," he said. "Too near the city." The factory employed six thousand workers, many of whom would die in a daylight raid by the RAF.

George assigned the task to his new lieutenant, Claude Arnault. The only way for the young French officer to disable the factory was by infiltrating it at night, when no employees would be harmed. Arnault took a train to Toulouse with Anne-Marie Walters and gendarme captain Raymond Cosculuella, who had helped the escapees from Eysses, and four explosives-filled suitcases. When they arrived, police and Gestapo agents at the station's exit seized Cosculuella. Walters and Arnault got through with three of the cases. They went to a safe house, where Cosculuella joined them in the evening. His police inspector's badge had dissuaded the Germans from searching his suitcase, and they released him with an apology.

A communist engineer at the factory provided Arnault with the facility's blueprints and a visiting engineer's pass. The two men smuggled explosives into the plant over the following week. The next stage fell to Arnault, who snuck alone at night, as Anne-Marie Walters recounted, into "a building 500 ft. long entirely lit and guarded by 10 men." He fixed fifteen charges, timed to blow after two hours, before proceeding to another building. As he was placing another fifteen devices, the bombs next door exploded. "The 2-hrs. pencils went off after 45 minutes," Walters said. Arnault nevertheless stayed to complete his work in the second building, while, Walters said, "the Boches were running madly after 'all' the saboteurs and guarding all exits."

Arnault fled, cutting through a barbed-wire fence and sliding down an embankment to a railway bridge. "The fools were only guarding the road bridge, next to the railway one; so I crawled along the tracks and got away," he told Walters. "From the opposite bank of the river I watched the last charges going up: it was so beautiful, Minou."

A Vichy police file for March 28, 1944, recorded "a series of explosions, thought to number 31 in the factory, between 0315 and 0730. The explosives were placed on the very powerful electric motors which served the grinding machines used to mix the gunpowder. Thirty out of 31 motors were destroyed." The factory was out of business for six weeks.

Soon afterward, the Germans captured Captain Raymond Cosculuella in Agen. Walters learned about it from George when they chanced upon each other on the road to Agen, he in his Simca with its bug-eye headlights and she on her bicycle. George said the Gestapo broke into a meeting above a restaurant in Agen: "Cyprien [Albert Cambon] jumped up, grabbed his gun and fired; he killed one of the Gestapo men and wounded another, but he received fifteen bullets in the chest and died immediately. Lépine [Cosculuella] was taken away manacled." George warned her to avoid Agen, and she reminded him that Cosculuella had a photograph of Claude Arnault for a false driving license. This gave the Gestapo the likeness of another SOE agent for their collection. The Gestapo tortured Cosculuella, who revealed nothing, before dispatching him to a concentration camp in Germany.

By early spring of 1944, the SD counterespionage headquarters at 84 avenue Foch was accommodating a parade of captured agents. One was a **résistant** named Pierre Brossolette, whom they brought to the fifth-floor guardroom on the morning of March 22, 1944. A socialist militant who had escaped to London, he had worked with Charles de Gaulle since April 1942. He not only wrote and presented radio speeches for de Gaulle, he was one of the few people from whom de Gaulle accepted criticism. Brossolette parachuted into the field in 1943. The SD captured him in Rennes and interrogated him for three days under torture that included the **baignoire,** a form of waterboarding, and expert beatings. As he sat on a bench in the guardroom at avenue Foch, he noticed an open window. It took him a second to run at it and jump.

Ernest Vogt was working in his office below when he heard a noise and saw Brossolette falling. He sprinted downstairs and out to the street, where the Frenchman was lying in blood. His bones were shattered, but he was breathing. "Don't move," Vogt said. The SD took him to the Hôpital de la Pitié-Salpêtrière, where he died. Vogt believed that Brossolette intended to escape rather than to kill himself. From then on, guards locked the windows.

Another captured agent, radio operator Adolphe Rabinovitch, entered the portals of avenue Foch at about the same time. John pretended not to know him, although they had trained together in 1941. A few days later, Rabinovitch whispered to John that he had escaped to Spain at the end of his first mission in June 1943 after transmitting for his brother, George. He parachuted back on the night of March 2, 1944, but Dr. Goetz was waiting for him. Rabinovitch was furious that London had sent him into the SD's hands, and John despaired that he had no means to prevent the entrapment of more agents.

On Sundays, Major Kieffer distributed chocolates, biscuits, and cigarettes to inmates in their cells. Sometimes, the cigarettes were English, undoubtedly from SOE consignments to Placke's false reception committees. Rabinovitch refused to accept presents from the Germans, but John gave the radio operator some of his. John observed that, while Kieffer knew Rabinovitch was Jewish, he did not single him out for ill treatment. That came a short time later, when Kieffer deported him to the Gross-Rosen concentration camp in Germany.

At the end of March, Parisot, the commander who had become George's closest friend, made the fortuitous acquaintance of a Spaniard named Tomás Guerrero Ortega. Known by his nom de guerre, "Camilo," the thirty-year-old was a legend among Spanish Civil War veterans. The youngest commander in the Republican forces, he lost a leg during the January 1939 retreat from Barcelona. Like a half million other refugees, Camilo, his men, and their families crossed the French border only to suffer internment in a concentration camp. The French government forced Spanish men of military age to labor under its **Main d'Oeuvre Immigré** (MOI) program, and when Germany invaded in 1940, Camilo fought in a Spanish regiment of the French Army. Vichy police again interned the Spaniards in a succession of camps. In April 1943, the Germans planned to deport them to Spain, where Franco was waiting to execute them. The men escaped with the help of Camilo's former commanding officer, communist general Luis Fernandez. Fernandez appointed Camilo chief of the **Groupe Espanol de Résistance dans le Gers,** also called the 35th Spanish Brigade of Guerrillas. Camilo moved to a house near Maurice Parisot in Saint-Gô and approached the Frenchman to request weapons and ammunition for more than three hundred men. Parisot introduced him to George Starr.

George's sympathies during the Spanish Civil War had been with his wife's conservative and religious family, who supported Franco. Although Camilo was a communist, George trusted the dashing "Red" with the Latin moustache and called him "a real character." Camilo's independent spirit— changing the gears of cars and motorcycles at breakneck speed with his only leg—appealed to the maverick British agent. The French called Camilo **uni-jambe,** one-leg, a fearless warrior with a rifle in one hand and his crutch in the other. The handsome bachelor lamented to Anne-Marie Walters that no woman would marry him as a one-legged man, although several women left testimonies to the contrary. Walters wrote that the Spaniard "had thick, long black hair shining with icy-blue lights. He wore it long down to his neck and usually said he had not time to have it cut, to excuse his secret pleasure at his romantic appearance." George armed Camilo's 35th Brigade, excusing his decision to help communists by calling them "a mixture of all sorts, anarchists, communists, liberal democrats."

In March, one of Hitler's most decorated armored formations, Das Reich 2nd SS Panzer Division, began arriving in southwest France. Das Reich's record included invading Yugoslavia in 1941 and defeating a Soviet armored division on the River Dnieper. Yet its reputation for massacres of partisans, Jews, and other civilians overshadowed its battlefield achievements. On April 6, the division established its headquarters about sixty-five miles east of Castelnau-sur-l'Auvignon, in the town of Montauban. The location was between two and four days' travel to the most likely landing beaches on the Mediterranean and the English Channel, giving the division flexibility to confront the Allies on either shore. Das Reich troops were dispersed among several Gascon villages, where they absorbed replacements for the thousands of men lost on the Russian front. The division recruited from Hungary, Romania, the Soviet Union, Alsace-Lorraine, and other conquered territories. Many did not speak German and lacked the customary SS fanaticism. WHEELWRIGHT's **maquisards** avoided Das Reich. George had no wish to provoke the reprisals for which the unit was notorious in the east.

On April 20, 1944, Dr. Goetz sent for John Starr. When John entered Goetz's office on the second floor, he noticed that the German staff, who normally wore civilian suits, were in full dress military uniforms with medals on their chests. The mood was somber. John did not know what was happening until Goetz explained it was Adolf Hitler's fifty-fifth birthday. John stood to attention, raised his arm in the Nazi salute, and blurted, "Heil, Churchill!" Dr. Goetz, Josef Placke, and their colleagues laughed. Afterward, Placke stopped by John's workspace and repeated, "Heil, Churchill!"

A few weeks later, on May 12, 1944, John saw seven women led into the guardroom. One was his former courier, Diana Rowden. The Germans had captured her with his former radio operator, John Young, on November 18, 1943. He also recognized Odette Sansom, whom he had seen briefly on her arrival with his brother in November 1942. John wanted to speak to the women, so he went to the guardroom with chocolates that Kieffer had given him. With the warders present, he and Rowden pretended not to know each other. She was unable to tell him that his comrades had tracked down Pierre Martin, the double agent who betrayed him. Harry Rée made the first, failed attempt to kill Martin in Dijon, and later two French **résistants** shot him dead in Dijon's Café de Belfort.

John gave the sweets to Rowden, Sansom, and the other women. There was nothing else he could do. The Germans took the women out of the guardroom and three weeks later sent them to Karlsruhe and on to concentration camps.

John observed so many SOE agents at avenue Foch that it seemed as if all of F-Section was in SD custody. "The door of my room was often open," John wrote, "as the guards were next door and at the top of the stairs or wandering about the corridors and could of course see me through the open door." The prisoners saw him, usually at work in shirt and tie and listening to the radio. One who recognized him was the childhood friend he had put forward for SOE, Maurice Southgate.

The Germans had captured Southgate, whom the RAF had promoted to squadron leader before his latest mission, on May 1, 1944. A radio detector van located the safe house in Montluçon, where his operator, René Mathieu, was transmitting. Southgate and Mathieu withstood violent interrogation in Montluçon and convinced the Germans that Southgate was a minor courier. The SD sent the two men by train to Paris for further questioning. Rather than hold them first at Fresnes Prison, they drove them straight to 84 avenue Foch. Southgate recalled that when he reached the top floor:

> I had the shock of my life on seeing opposite me in a little room Capt. JOHN STARR (BOB), sitting in a comfortable easy chair, smoking a cigarette in a very leisurely fashion. My immediate reaction was to think: "Oh . . . !", but pushed that idea from my mind immediately. He winked at me, but that was all.

John, having read a message in the guardroom a short time before referring to "**les amis de Hector,**" was expecting Southgate. Not only did he remember that Southgate's code name was Hector, he had recognized a photograph of his friend that Vogt had shown him. To Vogt, however, he had denied all knowledge of Southgate.

While the warders gave Southgate and Mathieu lunch in the guardroom, John's voice came from next door singing traditional British tunes like "It's a Long Way to Tipperary" and "Rule, Britannia." Southgate said the songs "cheered me up a lot."

After lunch, a Ukrainian guard took Southgate to the first floor and handcuffed him to a chair. Then "a German speaking fluent French, whose name I later found out was Ernest," came to question him. Southgate pretended to be "just a poor, miserable little courier," which Ernest Vogt did not contradict. Dr. Goetz, whom Southgate called "the second in command of all wireless transmitting activities," interrogated him afterward on the second floor.

Southgate spent the night at avenue Foch, and the SD moved him to Fresnes the next day. Two French cellmates there gave him coffee and biscuits from their Red Cross packages, and he fell asleep. A mere ten minutes later, guards woke him. A "French Gestapo man" roughed him up and threw him into the back of a black Citroën car.

At four thirty that afternoon, Southgate found himself back at avenue Foch without knowing why. He was, he said, "greeted by a large smile from ERNEST, Dr. GOETZ and a German colonel [Major Kieffer], head of that branch of the Gestapo [SD]." The three Germans were pleased to tell him that they realized he was not a "miserable little courier," but Squadron Leader Maurice Southgate, chief of SOE's STATIONER circuit. Southgate feared that John had betrayed him. As far as he was aware, no one else at avenue Foch knew who he was.

He felt that the "game was up," the end of three weeks' telling the Germans nothing, much longer than the forty-eight hours SOE required for his confederates to disappear. Southgate said:

I was considered as a gentleman, taken to a room where a table was set and offered dinner. I at first refused the offer, but they insisted, saying that they were soldiers and so was I, that I would be treated as a prisoner of war. . . . I accepted certain of the food, telling them that as it had originally been intended for the Maquis I felt justified in eating it. This was real coffee, chocolate, spam and American K-rations.

John was working upstairs, when the telephone rang. A guard answered and handed him the phone. Vogt asked if he had eaten lunch. John said no. "You'll have lunch with your cousin," the German said. John was puzzled. "Yes," Vogt said. " 'Hector,' Maurice Southgate. He **is** your cousin, isn't he?" John played along, assuming that Southgate had told Vogt they were related. Guards took him downstairs to the fourth floor, where he sat at the table with Vogt and Southgate. Kieffer came from his office next door and said something in German. Vogt translated, "Bob, we ought to shoot you."

"Why?"

"Because you knew perfectly well all the time who Hector was, and you didn't tell us."

"Well, would you expect me to?"

Kieffer, as John recalled, thought it over and said, "No."

After lunch, Vogt left John and Southgate together in the guardroom. Thinking that a hidden microphone might monitor their conversation, John spoke softly. This precaution may have been unnecessary, as Ernest Vogt revealed after the war "that there was never a single microphone in the whole building at 84 Avenue Foch." John told Southgate about his work for the Germans. Southgate remembered his justification: "If I don't do it somebody else will, and in doing it I am gathering very valuable information which may come in useful sometime."

Southgate attested to John's loyalty, recalling that "he used to run the German military and Nazis down, always boasting and [saying] 'Thumbs up for England,' telling the Germans they were doomed. . . ."

Kieffer asked John to take on the additional duty of writing summaries of the BBC's daily news broadcasts. Southgate felt the summaries had little significance, because Kieffer liked to read them "before he received the full list from the other office which also took them down." While listening to the BBC one day, John asked the guards, "Are you going to take us down to the cellars with you?" To their bewildered expressions, he explained that Radio Londres, which often warned civilians in advance of air strikes, had said the RAF was going to bomb avenue Foch. The RAF didn't bomb avenue Foch, but his practical joke sent the guards flying to the basement, while leaving the prisoners undisturbed in their cells, every time the air-raid sirens blared.

During one of Kieffer's interrogations of Southgate, the major, whom Southgate referred to as "the German colonel," showed him charts outlining the organization of SOE. He was shocked to see the names and photographs of Maurice Buckmaster, Gerry Morel, Nicholas Bodington, and several sergeants at commando school in Scotland. "They asked me numerous questions on our organisation, but I just said that it seemed to me they knew more about it than I did. The Colonel was very proud and excited, and laughed once this had been translated to him."

The SD had penetrated SOE more deeply than Southgate imagined. John showed him even more damning documents he had hidden in the hope of sending them with someone to London. According to Southgate, they included "wireless transmissions between LONDON and the German H.Q. Both of us were amazed at the ridiculous and foolish things done by LONDON H.Q. I would even go so far as to call them criminal." Southgate was enraged to learn that London asked SD wireless operators for security checks and that F-Section agents were parachuting into SD receptions.

In the weeks that followed, John learned more about Germany's counterespionage triumphs and still hoped to tell another prisoner who might escape with the information to London. But the prisoner he saw most often, Maurice Southgate, had also given his word not to escape. All this time, the SD was boring deeper into F-Section's networks. John's subsequent debriefing report to SOE stated, "The Germans kept adding new circuits to the map. In addition, they brought [the] source small printed maps showing ammunition dumps and others showing grounds."

One afternoon, John reported to Kieffer's office on the fourth floor without knowing what the major wanted. Kieffer showed him the map of France with F-Section's regions and operatives clearly indicated in John's beautiful hand. By now, the number of circuits known to the SD had increased from thirteen to thirty. A newly marked area, as large as Wales, stretched across southwest France from Périgord to the Pyrenees. Kieffer pointed at it and instructed him to write "Hilaire." John had no idea who Hilaire was.

Kieffer explained, "**Ihr Bruder.**"

"My brother?" John asked. "I haven't got a brother in France."

By the spring of 1944, George Starr was attacking the Germans when and where he could. F-Section compiled a "RECORD OF ACHIEVE-

MENTS OF COLONEL STARR'S WHEEL-
WRIGHT CIRCUIT" for the month of April:

April: German general is killed in attack on
German column in DORDOGNE.

April 22: Train containing munitions and
German war material attacked between Bergerac
and St. Foy.

April 26: Further 12 wagons from same train
destroyed in station at LAMONZIE.

April: 1,500 kgs of heavy submarine oil burned
at BOUSSENS. Factory temporarily stopped,
more oil and six transformers destroyed.

April: Further BOUSSENS information: 1
electric distributor destroyed, putting fire-pumps
out of action; 150 tons of synthetic lubricant set
on fire.

April 29: Petrol tanker train derailed at MON-
TREJEAU.

"It was the last day of April," Anne-Marie Walters
wrote, "and the sun was bright and hot: the cherries
were pink, the flowers in bloom, and the approaching summer seemed to burst out of every living
thing." Not everything was bright for her. Since the
killing of Albert Cambon in Agen and the capture
of another **résistant**, Aldo Molesini, in the town of

Tonneins, French police had been seeking a young Englishwoman courier in the Gers. She wrote that "no one was quite sure whether the Gestapo was in on the search or not, but it was quite probable." George ordered her to stay away from Tonneins, where the authorities had her description (along with those of himself and Yvonne Cormeau), and dispatched her to Paris to meet his old rival Maurice Rouneau, who had returned to France by sea.

Rouneau and his **Victoire** comrade Pierre Duffoir were now organizing SOE's RACKETEER circuit. Jeanne Robert stayed behind in England, waiting to give birth to her child by Rouneau. Lacking a radio operator, Rouneau turned to George for help in transmitting messages to London. Walters memorized London's answers to Rouneau's queries about **parachutage** sites and, using false identity papers, took a train to Paris to recount them in person. Rouneau was not there when she arrived, and she settled in to wait for him. The capital presented a vivid contrast to the southwest. Parisians were suffering more from shortages than Gascony's farmers, who grew their food and had firewood outside their doors. German counterintelligence in Paris was more thorough, severely restricting Resistance activity. "Paris was, of course," wrote Buckmaster, "far and away the most dangerous place to work: it was swarming with Germans and with security police of every description." Walters went one afternoon to the Gestapo headquarters in rue de Saussaies, "drawn by a sense of morbid curiosity." Watching it from outside, she wondered, "How many of my own friends, the men and women I had trained with in England, had spent endless and terrifying hours of cross-examination behind those black walls?"

Two weeks after Walters's arrival in Paris, Rouneau sent a courier to tell her "that his circuit was in the process of breaking up, and asking me to leave my messages at Vanves [just south of Paris]. I left a long coded letter to him, which he found when he came to Paris a few days later."

There could be no doubt, whether among the résistants in France or the German High Command in Berlin, that a sea and air invasion on an unprecedented scale was coming to France. The only questions were, where and when? The American and British air forces were decimating Luftwaffe squadrons in aerial duels over Germany, the better to ensure air dominance for the protection of troops pouring onto the beaches of France. The RAF and U.S. Army Air Forces (AAF) bombed rail lines, reducing Germany's power to reinforce frontline troops battling the Allied invaders. The Resistance and the French railway workers' union assisted with sabotage operations. Allied maneuvers up and down the British coast rehearsed amphibious assaults, causing casualties but teaching commanders what to avoid in real combat. American and British intelligence engaged in a monumental ruse to convince the Germans that General George Patton's fictitious First U.S. Army Group would lead the invasion with a landing at Calais from its nonexistent base in Dover. SOE and other intelligence agencies sent out thousands of radio transmissions to confuse the Germans, the signals version of the fog of war.

George Starr felt the time had come for him to do more. He sent Claude Arnault on May 13 to conduct another sabotage mission. The objective was the Lorraine-Dietrich factory, which produced parts for German planes and armored vehicles, at Bagnères-de-Bigorre near Lourdes. With three accomplices, André Coulom and two other men, Arnault broke into the Lorraine-Dietrich factory and planted charges in the machinery. When he detonated the explosives, shards of weapons-making equipment rocketed in every direction. "The only trouble was that we didn't get away quickly enough and received a shower of broken glass on our heads," he told Walters when she returned from Paris. The saboteurs made their getaway by train to Tarbes.

Arnault's first attack in Toulouse had cost one man in the factory his leg, but there were no casualties at the Lorraine-Dietrich plant. In comparison, RAF bombardments of factories in the area in April and May killed 67 civilians and seriously wounded

110 more. Sabotage was proving more effective than strategic bombing at destruction without killing and alienating civilians. The objective was to reduce Germany's capacity to withstand the Allied invasion, whenever it came, without losing the support of the French population.

SOE's official historian, M.R.D. Foot, wrote that George's accomplishments between January and May 1944 were among the finest F-Section could boast:

> In Gascony, WHEELWRIGHT flourished. Starr had several hidden Eurekas and reception committees well trained in their use. In five months, from 105 sorties, he received more than 1,200 containers, substantially more than PROSPER or SCIENTIST at their peaks.

The Resistance in the southwest had bloodied the Germans, blown up armaments factories, and derailed trains. Its **résistants** were armed and committed, but they could not liberate the country on their own. That required the might of the United States and the British Empire. "To tell the truth," reflected Raymond Escholier, "we thought of nothing but the landing." But when? Resistance fighters asked. When?

TWELVE
Das Reich

In almost every department of France our men
waited—waited for the signal that the great
day was at hand.

MAURICE BUCKMASTER

———

At the end of May 1944, George Starr was
struggling to hold his group together. Sabotaging the rails and destroying arms factories
hurt the Germans but did not end the occupation. The invasion on which they staked their lives
was delayed again and again. British and American
amphibious and airborne units planned to assault
the German forces in France on May 31, but bad
weather made that impossible.

"Underneath he was a person of great patience
and determination," Buckmaster wrote of George.
But as May turned to June, George's patience was

running low. It was a trying time of indecision and frustration. George used all his skills as a diplomat, which were few, and as a commander, which were many, to retain his group's loyalty.

On the night of June 5, armed men in berets, peasant wool clothing, and heavy boots crowded as they often did into the Larribeaus' farmhouse at the edge of Castelnau-sur-l'Auvignon. Beeswax candles and a wood fire lit the rustic kitchen, where George presided over an anxious conference of his chief lieutenants. The drinks were white wine and Armagnac, cigarettes the foul-smelling Baltos, and the talk of war. George had given up smoking and white wine, though that did not prevent the others from indulging themselves as they spent another night yearning for the long-promised invasion of France.

Outside, a full moon cast the farmyard in cool blue shadow. Most of the village, with no electric light, was asleep. At a little before nine o'clock, the hour for the BBC's **Messages personnels,** Yvonne Cormeau left the house alone. She walked to the barn, climbed up the hayloft ladder, and dug into the straw. Her wireless receiver lay in its familiar hiding hole. She assembled its four parts, hooked up the aerial, and put on her headphones. The radio sputtered static and German propaganda until she found the frequency of Radio Londres.

The announcer greeted listeners with the familiar preamble "**Les Français parlent aux Français,**" "The

French speak to the French." Next came a litany of apparently meaningless phrases that made sense only to selected **résistants**. "That evening, 306 messages were sent out by the BBC," wrote Buckmaster. And that night, for the very first time, "every single message was loaded with meaning."

"Wilma says yes" was code for destroying the Angoulême-Bordeaux railroad. "It's hot in Suez" decreed the cutting of telephone and telegraph cables. "The dice are on the table" and other doggerel told operatives from Calais to Marseille to demolish, rampage, and kill in a wave of terrorist violence to disrupt and distract the German occupiers. At last, Yvonne Cormeau heard, "**Il a une voix de fausset**," "He has a falsetto voice."

"I didn't even bother to go down the ladder," she said later, "but jumped down so as to tell everybody about it, because this was the culminating moment of our mission." She ran across the yard to the house and repeated the BBC's words, "**Il a une voix de fausset**." George turned to his lieutenants. "It's on," he announced. The French partisans were skeptical, but **le patron** was not to be contradicted: "They land at dawn tomorrow. Now, get cracking."

"Cracking" entailed heading into the night on missions he had assigned them over the previous weeks: demolishing rail lines, sawing telephone poles, closing roads, and blowing bridges to cripple German communications. Above all, his guerrilla teams had to delay nearby German forces, especially the Panzers of the SS's Das Reich armored division, from reaching the Normandy beaches. American, British, and Commonwealth troops were at that moment cruising toward shore as the cutting edge of Operation Neptune. More German troops tied down by the Resistance meant fewer Germans killing Allied soldiers. SOE signals chief Leo Marks wrote that "the Resistance was to act as Neptune's trident by attacking enemy troops, disrupting communications and blocking reinforcements." A Supreme Headquarters Allied Expeditionary Force (SHAEF) intelligence report noted that the Normandy landings "were synchronized with an appeal by General Eisenhower to the **Forces Française de l'Intérieur** (FFI), the French Forces of the Interior, to cease clandestine operations and come out into the open."

In Gascony, thousands did. As if by instinct, **résistants** were flocking to Castelnau-sur-l'Auvignon. Yvonne Cormeau remembered "terrific rejoicing":

They came up during the night; and we had been up all the time also, cleaning up what weapons we had. We didn't have many, but still quite a bunch, and they had been hidden under the beehives. We thought the bees would be good and protect them. And this was of course out of doors, so we had first of all put a lot of soft soap on them so that they would not rust. . . . Well, we had to get hold of the man himself, the beekeeper, to move his little hives a bit. We got all the stuff out, took it into the kitchen and spent the night cleaning these weapons.

"No arms were supplied before D-Day," George recalled. Now he supplied them in abundance, transforming underground **résistants** into guerrillas. Most were willing to risk their lives, but George urged caution to keep casualties to a minimum. SOE's model of the guerrilla leader, T. E. Lawrence, had written, "Our rebels were not materials, like soldiers, but friends of ours, trusting our leadership." Allied intelligence put total Resistance strength in the southwest at 4,500 men. Of these, only 2,500 had arms. Commanding irregulars, many of whom joined at the last minute, from disparate political creeds required a high caliber of leadership.

"Alone, two men kept their nerve," wrote Raymond Escholier, "Hilaire in Castelnau, Parisot in Saint-Gô." Captain Maurice Parisot, his wife, Jeanne, and Armagnac distiller Abel Sempé had also heard the BBC. They went straight to the town of Panjas, which Parisot and Abbé Laurent Talès had provisioned with stocks of food and six tons of SOE mortars, machine guns, rifles, ammunition, and bombs for the five hundred or so men assembling there. Like George's units, they launched assaults on roads, rails, fuel depots, telegraphs, and telephones throughout the long night.

Across fields and woodlands for miles around Panjas and Castelnau, Armagnac and WHEEL-WRIGHT fighters savaged Wehrmacht communications. North of the River Garonne, Philippe de Gunzbourg's **maquisards** blew bridges and blocked roads with felled trees and booby traps. **Résistants** in George's region alone rendered more than nine hundred sections of railway inoperable. Resistance sympathizers in the **Postes, Télégraphes et Téléphones** (PTT) smashed the exchanges and left them for the Germans to repair. Railway laborers, always the most pro-Resistance of France's trade unionists, destroyed the right-hand cylinders of their locomotives, smashed the points at junctions, and knocked out the signal lights. Tony Brooks's PIMENTO circuit stopped trains between Marseille and Lyon. The successful operations justified two years of hiding, acquiring weapons, learning to use them, and risking slow death in concentration camps.

For George Starr, the night of June 5 was an epiphany. Emerging at last from his long **guerre des ombres**, war of shadows, Gaston the Belgian collaborator declared himself as "Colonel" Hilaire, military commander in the FFI. "My role changed completely on D-Day," he said, "and I came into the open and could fight." In Escholier's words, "The supposed refugee from the north threw off his mask and was revealed as a war chief." When two peasants from another village rode by on bicycles, George heard one warn the other that Gaston the Belgian was a traitor working with the Germans. His disguise had served him well.

"Now Hilaire's organising genius was seen to its fullest advantage," wrote Buckmaster. "The disposition of his arms dumps was such that each village knew where it could arm itself and had qualified leaders to control and direct its effort." The destruction of the telephone and telegraph lines achieved an unstated objective: German reliance on their radios permitted the top-secret Government Code and Cypher School (GC&CS) at Bletchley Park, Buckinghamshire, to monitor the extra wireless traffic and break the German field codes. It was a service to Allied victory of which the **résistants** who made it possible remained ignorant during the war. The Germans' other option was to send written orders by hand. This had drawbacks, as George remarked: "They sent out motorcycle dispatch riders, but they didn't get very far. We didn't shoot them, unless they resisted and we had to." He claimed that his men did not stretch thin wire to decapitate the motorcyclists, "nothing naughty like that. Perhaps they were shot. I gave instructions not to, but . . ."

George blocked the main north-south and east-west highways, he said, "in spite of seven crack German divisions, including Das Reich, and other S.S.

troops in the area, who were attacking with double the number of men and the most elaborate modern equipment as well as planes and tanks."

George restored Castelnau-sur-l'Auvignon's historic role as a fortress from which medieval lords once dominated the plain below. He strengthened the hamlet's defenses, established forward outposts, and put French former military officers in command of different sections of fighters. Commandant Prost, a career officer since 1932 who had received several **parachutages** for George near Fourcès, directed the line of fire. Artillery captain Robert Bloch took charge of arms and ammunition. Captain Henry Solal commanded the antitank unit. Solal was a fortunate appointment, a seasoned veteran of the First World War and of colonial conflicts in Africa who, in Escholier's view, was "erudite, intelligent, artistic." Dr. Jean Deyris, who had treated Anne-Marie Walters, commanded the medical corps. German-speaking Théo Lévy became head of George's Deuxième Bureau, intelligence.

Just as important to George were the civilians, whose lives would be disrupted by war. He liaised with the heads of the butchers' and bakers' cooperatives, as well as government officials he knew to be pro-Resistance. They provided him with the means "for feeding not only the troops, but also the civilian population, one of my goals being that the civilian population should not suffer, because a Maquis cannot exist without the sympathy of the general population."

As the sun rose on D-Day, George raced out in his Simca to alert the followers who had yet to learn their war had begun. Reaching the Castagnos family's farm near Condom at eight o'clock, he shouted up to Anne-Marie Walters's bedroom window, "Haven't you heard? They've landed in Normandy."

Walters did not **go** downstairs, she wrote, "I **ran** downstairs." She and George tuned into the BBC to hear the national anthems of Britain, the United States, and France. Walters dashed into the vineyards to tell Henri and Odilla Castagnos and their son, André. The family rushed to the house, where neighbors joined their celebration. "Everybody kissed everybody else and wiped away the furtive tears of emotion," Walters wrote.

George asked her to wait at the farm for instructions, having previously warned her that the German Feldgendarmerie in Condom were seeking "a fair-haired woman who lived in the neighborhood." As he returned to Castelnau, boys from the surrounding towns and villages joined the great adventure. "The young men of Condom," Walters wrote, "rolled their fathers' old army kit and a few warm clothes in a blanket and started up to the **maquis**." Many, however, were "disappointed to see that the Allies were not going to land in the southwest right away."

Commandant Prost established a network of small posts to protect the routes into Castelnau and, during the night, dispatched patrols to cut all telegraph and telephone lines between Condom and neighboring villages. Solal praised the volunteers "assigned to blow the bridges, notably the Montrabeau-Losse-Condom. Mission accomplished without casualties." In one of his many detailed accounts of the war in the Gers, he added that the men who sabotaged the Germans all night "arrived at 8 in the morning in Castelnau-sur-l'Auvignon and immediately occupied the village. At nine, the tricolor flag was raised at the mairie [town hall]."

"The first job was getting out arms and equipping the men, forming them into sections, companies, feeding them and making arrangements," George said, "and preparing various immediate expeditions to carry out the destruction order received from London." His sappers escalated operations throughout D-Day, reporting back on the demolition of rail lines, telegraph wires cut, and roads denied to German vehicles. "Large numbers of [German] troops had then to be deployed to ensure the safety of communications," wrote Buckmaster. "And every man used for this purpose was one man less fighting the invading troops on the beachhead."

Resistance fighters in the north provided the Allies with intelligence on German fortifications and troop placements. When the forces came up from the beaches, the Frenchmen acted as guides and interpreters. They helped them find food, shelter, and people they could trust. Normandy was demonstrating the value of the Resistance.

The **résistants** in the south were no less effective, but the requirements were different. There were no Allied soldiers to help. Instead, the southern Resistance hobbled the Germans and thwarted their attempts to send reinforcements north. All they needed to keep fighting were supplies and encouragement from on high. George was with his **maquisards** on the evening of D-Day, when General Charles de Gaulle came on the radio from London to exhort his people:

> The supreme battle has been joined. It is, of course, the battle of France and the battle for France. For the sons of France, wherever they are, whatever they are, the simple and sacred duty is to fight the enemy by every means at their disposal.

To some, de Gaulle's speech validated their underground war. Others saw it as the general's attempt to co-opt a Resistance that was anything but united in support of him. George was one of only a few SOE organizers to gather under his command disparate factions—pro–de Gaulle, anti–de Gaulle, communist, socialist, royalist, and foreigners—into

a cohesive force. He armed, fed, clothed, and commanded them without regard to their political loyalties. One objective bound them, for the moment:
expelling the occupier.

An hour before sunrise on the seventh, Théo Lévy
raced into Castelnau on his motorcycle. Behind the
young Jewish partisan rumbled a convoy of about
two hundred men he had armed with weapons from
thirty-six containers that landed during the night.
Lévy told Escholier, "In the little square, Hilaire in a
canadienne with a submachine gun in his bandolier,
a Colt in his belt, received them with a big smile."

One **résistant** recalled seeing George "always in
espadrilles, threadbare trousers and shirtsleeves or a
pullover." Commandant Prost criticized his peasant
attire as inappropriate for a commander and advised
him to wear a British officer's uniform. This amused
George, who ignored him.

Castelnau grew like a Klondike town in the Gold
Rush. Every house became an armory. Family kitch-
ens served as mess halls. Barns became barracks.
The twelfth-century stone chapel was converted
into a prison for enemies that the **maquisards** were
capturing. Among them were members of the Milice, whom the **résistants** hated more than they did
the Germans.

George gave refuge on the night of June 7 to a
unit of the communist **Francs-Tireurs et Partisans**
(FTP). He regretted it in the morning, when Mayor

Larribeau told him "that these men of the FTP had broken into the prison (which was in the church), had knocked the prisoners about and had put them on their lorry to take them away no doubt to do away with them."

George remonstrated with the FTP chief, who relented and gave back the prisoners. "This incident caused somewhat of an upheaval amongst my own Maquis and I had to address them," George recalled. He explained to men thirsting for vengeance that "it was not up to us to administer rough justice, that was for the French courts later."

More visitors appeared during the day. Among them were the Spanish Republicans, with whom George came to an immediate understanding: "The arrangement was made then that I should provide as many arms as possible and they would execute any military orders that I might at any time transmit to them in order to carry out the orders of the High Command." Their chief, Camilo, moved into the command post of his friend Hilaire. Frenchmen and Spaniards, Jews and dissident Germans, peasant farmers and young deserters from German forced labor camps, communists and conservatives, all converged on the hamlet. Castelnau as the pre-eminent **maquis** garrison in the Gers was becoming a military target.

"The Germans tried to impose severer curfew and circulation restrictions, etc.," George's debrief stated, "but these were of no avail as after a short time if [German] patrols went out they were promptly ambushed by the F.F.I. and wiped out."

The German High Command put the Das Reich armored division on standby on June 7 to move north to Normandy. The division planned to transport its tanks and other tracked vehicles on purpose-built railroad flatcars. By rail, the vehicles and men could cover the five hundred miles to the front in three days. However, Tony Brooks's railroad workers drained the lubricating oil from the flatcars' axles and filled them with abrasive paste. This forced the division on June 8 to drive its tracked vehicles over asphalt roads. The SS's Panzer IV tanks' top speed was twenty-four miles an hour, much slower than the train. The drive wasted scarce fuel, damaged tanks, and shredded the roads. To avoid exposing massed armored vehicles to attack from Allied air forces and Resistance units, the column's 1,400 vehicles traveled one hundred yards apart. On the first day of its trek north, the division stopped to rescue a Wehrmacht garrison in the town of Tulle that was under Resistance siege. Das Reich routed the **maquisards** and, in revenge for forty German dead, hanged ninety-nine civilians from street lamps and balconies.

While the bulk of Das Reich proceeded north, elements of the division stayed in the southwest to deal with the **maquis**. George didn't risk confronting them by attacking or holding German garrisons. That was, to him, the opposite of mobile guerrilla war. His ragged warriors ambushed traveling Das Reich units, but they did not linger. He described his tactics:

> Pick a bend in the road, round a bend. Drop a bloody tree right across the road and they'd come. They'd have to stop. Choose a nice place and just fire into them with everything you've got. Drop another tree behind them so they can't go the other way. Give them ten minutes of hell, and then get the hell out of it.

Weakened by George's WHEELWRIGHT, Tony Brooks's PIMENTO, and the communist FTP, Das Reich came under fire from Philippe de Gunzbourg's fighters at a bridge over the River Dordogne. Gunzbourg had cut all the telephone lines out of Bergerac during the night of June 7 and made the Germans pay in lives for every mile of road they covered. "The region (Dordogne-Sud) became the center of a complete blockage," wrote Gunzbourg, "where the enemy had to dig in, bury his tanks and call for reinforcements from Périgueux and from the Gironde." Gunzbourg recalled that the Das Reich division "wanted to go to Agen from Montauban and to Normandy [but] found itself cut off by the positions occupied by the Resistance."

Generalfeldmarschall (Field Marshal) Gerd von Runstedt, commander of Germany's forces in the west, issued an order to Das Reich's commanding officer, General Heinz Lammerding: "For the re-establishment of order and security, the most energetic measures must be taken in order to frighten the inhabitants of this infested region, whom we have to make give up the taste for welcoming resistance groups and letting themselves be controlled by them. This will serve as a warning to the entire population." Warnings came one after another in savage retribution against civilians wherever **maquisards** fired on Das Reich or captured its personnel. But the reprisals wasted time, further delaying the division's march to Normandy.

On June 9, George's region went quiet. Das Reich was preoccupied farther north with other **maquis** groups, and the decisive battle raged five hundred miles away in Normandy. "After the first two or three days of enthusiasm were over, the men became terribly bored," recalled Anne-Marie Walters. "They had nothing to do all day: the Germans were scattered at great distances from Castelnau and expeditions were rare."

Philippe de Gunzbourg wrote that some **maquis** groups, particularly the communists, were attempting to conquer and control territory, as at Tulle:

British prime minister Winston Churchill established the Special Operations Executive (SOE) on July 6, 1940, to organize underground actions against the Axis powers from France to the Far East and, especially, "to set Europe ablaze."

Free French leader Charles de Gaulle escaped to London in 1940 and called on the French "to listen to my voice and follow me" in resistance to Nazi occupation.

French head of state Maréchal Philippe Pétain met Adolph Hitler at Montoire-sur-le-Loir, France, on October 24, 1940, to offer French "collaboration" with Germany. German interpreter Paul Schmidt stands between Hitler and Pétain, and German foreign minister Joachim von Ribbentrop is behind Hitler to the right.

George and John Starr volunteered in 1939 for the Royal Air Force, which rejected them because their father was American. They enlisted in the British Army and, due to their fluency in French, were recruited by SOE.

Entrance to the Port-Miou calanque (inlet) near Cassis in southern France, where SOE felucca **Seadog** dropped George Starr and repatriated John Starr on the night of November 3, 1944.

SOE French section intelligence officer Vera Atkins was devoted to her field agents, but she said of John Starr, "We feel he let the side down."

F-Section courier Odette Sansom arrived in France by sea on November 2, 1943, with George Starr, who disliked her and did not acknowledge her courage in resisting Nazi torture after her capture.

Baron Philippe de Vomécourt, one of F-Section's earliest French recruits, led the VENTRILOQUIST circuit. George Starr assisted his passage to Spain after a daring escape from German captivity in France on January 3, 1944.

F-Section radio operator Captain Marcus Bloom, code names "Urbain" and "Bishop," arrived in France by sea with George Starr. The affable north Londoner transmitted for Starr and Maurice Pertschuk. After his capture and torture, he refused to operate his radio for the Germans.

Left: Lieutenant Maurice Pertschuk, code name "Eugene," was of Russian Jewish origin and grew up in England. From the age of twenty-one, he ran F-Section's PRUNUS circuit in southwest France. Courier Denise Bloch said he "could easily pass as French, looks like an artist's model." **Right:** Yvonne Cormeau, code name "Annette," was George Starr's radio operator. F-Section regarded her as one of its best transmitters or "pianists."

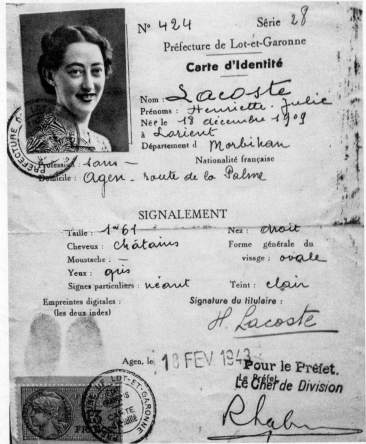

Yvonne Cormeau's false identity cards enabled her to evade detection at German checkpoints while on missions for George Starr.

Above, left: On November 29, 1944, French colonel Henri Monnet, who had served with George Starr in the field, presented the Croix de Guerre to Starr and Yvonne Cormeau. **Above, right:** Pilar Canudos Ristol—from Manresa, near Barcelona in Spain—wed George Starr in 1934 and worked for SOE in Spain. She did not know her husband was just over the border in the French Pyrenees.

Yvonne Cormeau brought this photograph of Alfred, Pilar, and Georgina Starr to George Starr in France in August 1943. "She was given a letter and photographs of the children," George recalled. "Of course, you're supposed not to look at them, but being a bloody woman, she bloody looked." Cormeau did not tell her SOE handlers that she and her late husband had known Starr in Brussels.

Anne-Marie Walters, code name "Colette," parachuted into occupied France in January 1944 at the age of twenty to become George Starr's courier. She would later accuse him of committing war crimes.

Philippe de Gunzbourg, a French Jewish aristocrat, code names "Philibert" and "Edgar," became one of George Starr's closest comrades. A colleague wrote that he was "a Frenchman, although due to his bearing, he was sometimes taken for an Englishman." Gunzbourg admired George Starr as "a great leader of the caliber of Lawrence [of Arabia]."

A French Jewish **résistante**, Denise Bloch, left, worked closely with George Starr as his first courier. Paul Sarrette, right, deputy to Henri Paul Sevenet of the F-Section's VENTRILOQUIST circuit, helped to save Bloch from capture by the Gestapo and later accused her of being George Starr's mistress.

Captain Adolphe Rabinovitch, an Egyptian-Russian-Jewish SOE radio operator for Peter Churchill's SPINDLE circuit, transmitted messages for George Starr and evaded capture on his first mission to France. When Germans captured him at the start of his second mission and took him to 84 avenue Foch, he complained to John Starr about SOE negligence.

At age twenty-eight, squadron officer Diana Rowden parachuted into occupied France on June 16, 1943, to work as courier for John Starr. She saw John Starr again when they were both imprisoned at 84 avenue Foch.

In August 1944, George Starr celebrated the liberation of Agen, the city where he had begun his secret mission in southwest France in November 1942. He is seen here with a cigarette, although he claimed to have given up smoking before D-Day.

This notice from 1941 reads: "The head of the German Military Administration in France warns that any person who offers help and assistance to a member of an English aircrew who has escaped, or any person who attempts to encourage his escape and help him in any way, will be brought immediately before a German court martial and will be punished with the death penalty."

AVIS AU PUBLIC

Le Chef de l'Administration militaire allemande en France avise que chaque habitant qui prête aide et assistance à un membre d'un équipage d'avion anglais à s'évader ou qui tenterait seulement de favoriser son évasion et l'aiderait de quelque manière que ce soit, sera traduit immédiatement devant une Cour martiale allemande et sera puni de la peine de mort.

Charleville, le 2 août 1941

Le Feldkommandant
signé : GROENEVELD
Général-Major

Mayor Roger Larribeau of Castelnau-sur-l'Auvignon provided George Starr with identity cards that permitted him to travel anywhere. Starr wore a moustache, which was easier to shave off than to grow when he needed to change his appearance. He said, "If somebody's used to a little dark man that wears a beret, and he's got a moustache and he always wears a brown suit, that's what they're looking for. They're not looking for a clean-shaven man wearing glasses and wearing a gray suit."

Below: Group photograph in Agen, 1944, of the Judex Mission to provide assistance to the French who had suffered for their support of SOE resistance. Yvonne Cormeau is in the front row, center, and George Starr, also in uniform, is fourth on her left.

Colonel George Starr—in the front row with his German shepherd, Lassie, at the Villa Hügel, near Essen—reorganized the German coal industry at the end of the war. Yvonne Cormeau, his wartime radio operator, sits to his left and, in her daughter Yvette Pitt's words, "was responsible for running the domestic side of the house."

Founders of the Réseau Victoire, Victory Network, in April 1942, the French nucleus of George Starr's WHEELWRIGHT circuit in southwest France. **From left to right:** Pierre Duffoir, who carried messages for Starr as far as Switzerland; his daughter, Josette; his wife, Paulette Duffoir, who worked ceaselessly for the Resistance; Gyl Al Carty; Maurice Rouneau, who introduced Starr to the network; and Rouneau's future wife, Jeanne Robert. Robert housed and fed Starr in her school in Castelnau-sur-l'Auvignon.

Castelnau-sur-l'Auvignon—George Starr's underground headquarters from 1942 to 1944—following its destruction by the German Army on June 21, 1944. Yvonne Cormeau wrote on the back of the photograph, "(Castelnau) main street after fighting June '44. Ruins of [Mayor Roger] Larribeau's house on right."

Below: John Starr and Michelle Vergetas shortly after their June 30, 1934, wedding in France. The couple moved into a flat in the Paris suburb of Issy-les-Moulineaux, while John worked as a commericial artist for Agence Yves Alexandre Publicité.

Right: Lieutenant John Starr at the British Army's Field Security Police base in Winchester, England, in 1940, following his escape from France in June. John, who was drawing propaganda posters for the army, accepted an invitation from SOE for an interview that led to his becoming agent "Emile."

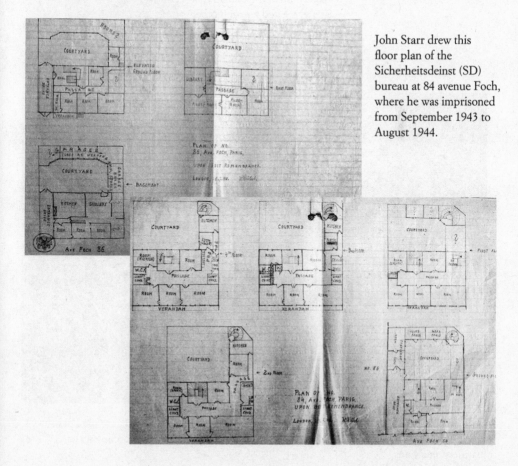

John Starr drew this floor plan of the Sicherheitsdeinst (SD) bureau at 84 avenue Foch, where he was imprisoned from September 1943 to August 1944.

Noor Inayat Khan, code name "Madeleine," was a radio operator for F-Section in Paris. Major Kieffer recalled, "We were pursuing her for months." Following her capture, she was interrogated at 84 avenue Foch and escaped from the building with John Starr and French officer Léon Faye.

Hans Josef Kieffer, counterespionage chief of the Nazi SD in Paris at 84 avenue Foch. John Starr testified that Kieffer treated him and other captured SOE agents humanely.

German occupation forces paraded from the Arc de Triomphe in Paris along avenue Foch, known as "avenue Boche" due to the number of German security services occupying its luxurious mansions.

General Charles de Gaulle arriving in Toulouse on September 16, 1944, to cement his support in the city. On this drive from the airport, a subordinate told him that George Starr was questioning his authority. De Gaulle responded, "And you didn't arrest him on the spot?"

Poster telling the people of Toulouse, "The enemy in flight has abandoned the city. . . . Toulouse is liberated."

RÉPUBLIQUE FRANÇAISE

LIBERTÉ · ÉGALITÉ · FRATERNITÉ

TOULOUSAINS

L'Ennemi en fuite a abandonné la ville.
TOULOUSE est libérée.
Libérée à la fois du joug allemand et de l'abjection Vichyssoise.

Libérée grâce aux offensives victorieuses de nos alliés, Anglais, Américains et Russes aux côtés de qui se battent tant de vaillants hommes de France, libérée par l'action héroïque des Forces Françaises de l'Intérieur, cette jeune armée de la République et des Milices Patriotiques, ces soldats citoyens.

Le peuple Français ne connaît qu'un seul gouvernement : le Gouvernement Provisoire de la République, présidé par le Général De Gaulle, l'homme qui pendant ces quatre années, a incarné la résistance et pris en mains les intérêts de la Patrie.

Ce Gouvernement est représenté, dans la région de Toulouse, par le Commissaire de la République, qui s'appuie sur les Comités de Libération.

La guerre continue pour la libération totale du territoire et l'écrasement définitif du nazisme, au dehors et au dedans.

Vous êtes tous mobilisés au service de la Patrie.

Vous maintiendrez l'ordre dans Toulouse. Cet ordre ne vous est pas imposé de l'extérieur : il est votre ordre, l'ordre populaire et national.

Nous faisons appel à l'union de tous les Français, à l'exclusion des traîtres qui seront châtiés en vertu des Lois de la République.

Dans la discipline et l'enthousiasme nous relèverons les ruines laissées par l'ennemi et nous construirons tous ensemble une France grande, libre et souveraine.

Vive la France, Vive la République, Vive la Liberté !

Le Commissaire de la République pour la région de Toulouse,
Le Comité Régional de la Libération,
Le Comité Départemental de la Libération.

In August 1944, the Wehrmacht abandoned Auch, capital of the Gers department. George Starr and Maurice Parisot's Armagnac Battalion secured the town.

As George Starr and Yvonne Cormeau drove into liberated Toulouse on August 21, 1944, an American officer lamented there was no American flag beside the French and British standards on their car. Cormeau pulled the patch from his uniform and put it on the windshield. They drove forward displaying the three Allied flags.

Serge Ravanel, Resistance leader in southwest France, met his chief, Charles de Gaulle, in Toulouse a month after he helped to liberate the city. De Gaulle, rather than offer congratulations, insulted the young man.

The officers and men of the Armagnac Brigade assembled in Auch for the funeral of their commander, Captain Maurice Parisot. Spanish commander "Camilo" is first in the front row with his crutch; George Starr is third to his left.

Memorial plaque to the men and women of SOE who trained at Beaulieu, the Montagu family estate in Hampshire that SOE used in secrecy throughout the war.

Memorial to the fighters and civilians who fell in the Battle of Castelnau-sur-l'Auvignon on June 21, 1944.

Telegram from F-Section intelligence officer Vera Atkins to Michelle Starr informing her of John Starr's return from the German concentration camps.

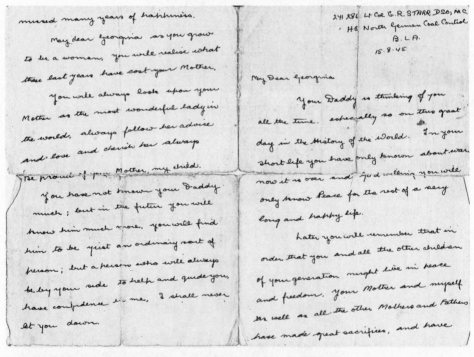

Letter from Lieutenant Colonel George Starr in Germany to his daughter, Georgina, on the day the Second World War ended.

"The tactic of grouping, protecting and defending did not work," he wrote, calling the policy "weak and bad." The Resistance's basic strategy of destroying German infrastructure and ambushing units on their way to Normandy was working. Yet General Eisenhower's SHAEF reduced **parachutages** to the guerrillas. Gunzbourg feared that the Allied command was losing faith in the Resistance. In fact, it was trying to save French civilians from German retribution. General Pierre Koenig, commander of the FFI, ordered his representatives in France, the **Délégués Militaires de Region** (Regional Military Delegates) to reduce their attacks:

CURRENTLY IMPOSSIBLE PREDICT NORMAL SUPPLY WEAPONS AND AMMUNITION YOU LIMIT TO A SIMMER ALL GUERRILLA ACTION STOP WHEN POSSIBLE BREAK CONTACT EVERYWHERE WHILE WAITING FOR PHASE OF REORGANIZATION STOP.

Koenig's order of June 10 arrived too late to save the civilians of Oradour-sur-Glane, which the SS visited that day. The ancient village lay 160 miles north of Montauban on Das Reich's route to Normandy. Unlike Tulle, where Resistance forces had attacked the German garrison, Oradour-sur-Glane had witnessed no violence. Yet German frustration with the hidden enemy that was killing, wounding, and capturing its men found an outlet in Oradour.

The 3rd Company, 1st Battalion of Das Reich's 4th Regiment, Der Führer, entered the village from the south at about two in the afternoon. It closed the roads and ordered the mayor to assemble the population. The Germans locked the women and children in the Saint-Martin Church. Outside, they slaughtered the men with machine guns. The SS then turned on the 400 women and children in the sanctuary, raking the interior with automatic weapons fire, lobbing hand grenades, and setting the church alight. A few villagers who had escaped to the fields heard their relatives' screams. Only one woman, Marguerite Rouffranche, survived the inferno that turned the church to ashes. The death toll was 642 men, women, and children, almost the entire population. At nightfall, the Germans looted and destroyed every building except one that they used as a command post.

In Castelnau-sur-l'Auvignon, no one knew about the events farther north. The morning of June 10 had dawned clear and warm enough for George to put the top down on his Simca and drive to the Castagnos farm. Anne-Marie Walters watched the car crawling up the road and smiled at the "sight of a pointed head sticking through in the most comic fashion." The passenger was Flight Sergeant Leslie Brown, whom George introduced as a "New Zealand pilot who has just joined us. He was shot down a month or so ago and has been moving from maquis to maquis. Now he will stay with us for awhile." Brown had been on the run since April 12, when German antiaircraft fire caught his Stirling heavy bomber over Anzex, about forty miles north of Castelnau. After hiding with various Resistance groups, he turned up at George's door. Rather than escape to Spain, the twenty-six-year-old New Zealander, whom the French called l'anglais, the Englishman, volunteered to stay and fight. George tasked him with instructing young maquisards in the use of weapons, although Brown spoke no French and had no infantry training.

George was weary, confessing to Walters: "I haven't had a single night's sleep since the maquis was started." He told her to come to Castelnau "to help with washing up and other fatigues 'proper for women.'" She obeyed the order with misgivings.

> I began to see the change that would take place in my life; he had his "staff" now, mostly young French officers who had been hiding for the past months and working with the Resistance. I would no longer be a confidante, he was too busy. And I was a woman, and not supposed to understand "military strategy."

George turned to counterespionage. His agents discovered a Frenchman with a gold medal awarded by Adolf Hitler "for exceptional services to the Führer." That was sufficient for his execution. A more complicated case involved two suspected spies, a German woman and her Polish husband, living near Castelnau on the road to La Romieu. During the night, George sent an anti-Nazi German refugee, whom Escholier called "Hans," to investigate. Hans, dressed in a German uniform, and two French officers reached the house in total darkness. He knocked on the door and announced himself as Oberst (Colonel) Rheinhardt. The woman said, "Come in. It's not good to be outside in this country. There are **maquis** everywhere around here. Very near us, in Castelnau, there is a formidable camp commanded by an English colonel." Hans entered the unlighted house and raised his Colt pistol. A struggle ensued that left the couple lying in blood on the floor. The three agents left. When they returned in the morning, only the man's body remained. The German woman had feigned her death and fled. Hans went out to track her down.

Later that morning, George assigned a local Resistance chief to sabotage the railroad bridge near Astaffort village. Using more than forty pounds of plastic explosives, the chief and his men blew up the line that carried ammunition from the arsenal at Tarbes to German troops in Agen.

Hans meanwhile captured the German woman, bound her hands with rope, and brought her to George's headquarters. The room was resplendent

with captured war trophies, including Milice arm-
bands and photographs of Vichy's Legion of French
Volunteers Against Bolshevism who had fought for
Germany on the Russian front. George sat as judge
in the ad hoc trial. Escholier wrote:

The German woman arrived at the HQ. She was
a strong blond woman with eyes the color of **Ver-
gissmeinnicht** [forget-me-not]. As she had struggled step by step against her kidnappers, she was
completely disheveled. Neither pretty nor gracious, yet the terror and the anger rendered her
beautiful. Her look was harrowing.

The woman claimed to be French from Lorraine, to hate the Germans, and to be working for
the Resistance. One of George's men tested her, saying, "We are miliciens. We are all volunteers against
Bolshevism. We are the Germans' friends. Don't be
alarmed." She relaxed for an instant, a mistake that
amounted to a confession. She struggled to wrench
the rope off her wrists, but, a moment later, yielded
to the inevitable. "Blindfold me, Monsieur Officer,"
she said. George did not speak. Escholier wrote, "In
truth, this inflexible man was looking above all for
a way to soften the end of this painful meeting, the
end of the life of this spy."

George offered the woman some water. She was
not thirsty. He ordered the men to bring her coffee.

Again, she refused to drink. George sipped the coffee to show it was not poisoned. She still declined. A doctor injected her with a sedative. When she was comatose, a "specialist team" took her away.

"I don't think anyone in high places could hold these two summary executions against Hilaire," Escholier wrote. "For the rest, one must recognize that in Gascony Hilaire's justice was swift. It always struck a severe blow and was **never** accompanied by torture sessions." Executions were taking place all over France as miliciens and **résistants** fought one another in a fratricidal bloodbath. Miliciens slaughtered captured **maquisards,** and ordinary Frenchmen and -women exacted revenge by murdering suspected collaborators and humiliating women accused of sexual relations with Germans by shaving their heads and stripping them naked in public. Maurice Buckmaster observed, "Hatred and violence burst through the length of France as the **Maquisards,** indeed nearly the whole population, rose to pay off the score of four years of barbarism, terrorism and tyranny." SOE-armed **résistants** took part, as Buckmaster admitted: "Germans were shot and their bodies floated down the canals."

The momentary lull in the Gers allowed George to accelerate training of the Castelnau battalion's six hundred or so fighters. Some of the older men were veterans of the Great War, but youngsters without combat experience took a crash course in Sten and

Bren guns, grenades, ambushes, and skirmish lines. Ammunition shortages, however, made target practice impossible. New Zealand flight sergeant Brown became a favorite with his young pupils, despite the lack of a common language. George's only battle-scarred contingent was the Spanish detachment under one-legged Commander Camilo. With three years' experience battling Franco's army, the Spaniards needed no lessons in guerrilla warfare. And they had a powerful motive: vengeance on the Nazis for turning their republic into a military dictatorship.

A French officer, Captain Georges Monnet, christened George's ragtag band of French peasants, Spanish **guérilleros,** German dissidents, and refugees from much of Europe "the Colonel's Hollywood Brigade." George loved the name. Escholier wrote that Hollywood's "biggest star" was the Spaniard Camilo. **Le Section Hollywood** turned out for its first formal parade on June 12 in Castelnau to salute Maurice Poncelet. Poncelet had just escaped, with George's and Maurice Parisot's help, from a Milice prison where he had been tortured. Escholier remembered that the Hollywood Brigade's "rough men, bearded, dressed in rags, but handsome under the burning sun, filled with emotion, rendered this military honor." Poncelet met George for the first time when **le patron** received the artist in his room at Larribeau's house. Poncelet was surprised to see

"Colonel Hilaire" in shirtsleeves: "A machine gun, a rifle, a dagger and some grenades surrounded photographs of his children."

On June 13, George and Cormeau returned to Castelnau at dawn from an all-night meeting in Condom with the town's subprefect, gendarmerie captain, and police commissioner. After stopping at Mayor Larribeau's house to discover whether any messages had arrived in his absence, he went to Jeanne Robert's former school. Camilo, two other Spaniards, and a Frenchman were inside beating a man they had just captured. "The prisoner was literally gushing blood out of his nose," George recalled. After scolding Camilo and his men for illegal and immoral behavior, he asked Dr. Deyris to give the prisoner first aid and to put him with the other prisoners in the church. George swore that Camilo did not torture any prisoner after that.

Later that day, the deceptive calm in the Gers ended when a Milice detachment from Agen ambushed one of George's French patrols near the village of Astaffort. Among the cornered **résistants** was André Castagnos, the teenage son of Anne-Marie Walters's hosts, Henri and Odilla Castagnos. About 150 miliciens ambushed André's detachment at the foot of a hill. "Meanwhile, at the top of the same hill, the first party was approaching in full fighting order," Walters recounted. "The miliciens ordered André and his friends to stand in a line, shoulder to shoulder, while they took cover behind them." The other **résistants,** seeing their friends in front of the enemy, fired over their heads. The miliciens panicked and shot their ten hostages in the back at point-blank range.

Nine of the **maquisards** died instantly. André, severely wounded in the right lung, lay bleeding for eight hours before someone took him to the nearest hospital in Lectoure. Physicians feared the Germans would find the young "terrorist" and punish the hospital staff, but a Spanish nun refused to leave his side until Dr. Deyris and his parents took him to a hospital in Condom. Surgeons there saved his life, making him, in Anne-Marie Walters's words, "the only survivor of a massacre organised by Frenchmen against Frenchmen."

While the Battle of Astaffort was raging, six of Camilo's **guérilleros** were battling a sixty-five-strong German detachment ten miles to the north near Agen. The Spaniards took cover behind an old stone tower and kept the Germans at bay for an hour and a half. When they exhausted their ammunition, the Germans rounded them up and murdered them. A bicycle messenger brought word of the killings to Castelnau. Camilo raced to the scene in his dilapidated Renault with the top down, followed by two trucks filled with his compatriots. The Germans had gone, but the bodies, some mutilated and all blood drenched, lay where they had fallen. Camilo carried them back to the village.

Castelnau staged its first military funeral. The French companies lined one side of the square, while the Spanish stood to attention on the other. A wooden cart bore the bodies of the six fallen Spaniards into the plaza. Seeing her comrades' naked and bloody corpses, one with a bloody stump where a foot had been, Walters recalled, "I couldn't help tears running down my cheeks." The men presented arms and remained immobile while Camilo delivered his eulogy. Although unable to understand Spanish, Walters sensed "that he spoke of hate, revenge and honour. His face, his gestures and his tone were more eloquent than words."

During this time, Walters's relationship with George Starr was deteriorating. Escholier wrote that George suspected Walters was having an affair with Claude Arnault. Angry at her late return from her mission to Gunzbourg and Arnault, he dismissed her as his liaison to Gunzbourg. This upset Walters, who longed to see Arnault again. Her replacement was Maguy Merchez, daughter of Antoine Merchez, the Belgian **résistant** in Agen. Walters asked Maguy to take a letter to her lover. Maguy hesitated, but Walters insisted and, Escholier wrote, "Reluctantly, Maggie [Maguy] finished by agreeing, then, at the last moment, she didn't have the courage to take the letter and confided in Annette [Yvonne Cormeau], the agent most devoted to Hilaire."

Cormeau showed George the letter, which Escholier quoted: "Everything is going badly in Castelnau. Terrible food supplies . . . Hilaire is an odious being." George swore in Gascon slang and told Cormeau to bring Walters to him. "A rather violent discussion erupted between Colette [Walters] and her chief," wrote Escholier. "She would never forgive him for violating the secrecy of her correspondence. Hilaire ignored it. He had other worries. The country was infested with spies, with disguised Boches and collaborators with the enemy." Walters remained in Castelnau, grudgingly doing work "proper for women." She and George avoided each other.

On June 17, Maurice Parisot destroyed a Luftwaffe fuel dump at Mont-de-Marsan and captured one German. One of his patrols then seized eight German soldiers, who had been transporting casks of Gascon brandy to German ambassador Otto Abetz in Paris. The Germans got on so well with their captors that, Escholier wrote, they "became comrades." Parisot's liaison officer suggested taking the prisoners to Castelnau, where the sight of them would raise the men's morale.

An open truck brought the Germans there in the evening. George received them in the orderly room and gave them cigarettes. "At this moment," he said, "I was called out for something else, and Theodore

Levy, a German Jew who had been for a long time [illegible word] with me (I knew in spite of his hate he would not touch them) was left in charge, because he could speak German." When George returned twenty minutes later, Lévy told him that the German Feldwebel (sergeant) spoke English and French. The sergeant stepped forward and said in English that he had left Paris just before the Allied landing in Normandy "to bring the alcohol from Tarbes to the officers' mess in Paris." The sergeant "swore by all the Gods that the only reason he was captured was because there were women and children in the streets of the town where they were captured and he had refused to give the order to fire for fear of hitting them." George promised to treat him and his men "as prisoners of war."

Maquisards took the Wehrmacht POWs to the chapel holding their nominal allies of the Milice. The Germans refused to enter and demanded to see the commander. George appeared, and they pleaded, "Imprison us where you like, but not with traitors to their country." George understood and installed them in a building beside Dr. Deyris's infirmary.

Operations gathered pace. On June 18, one of George's patrols spotted a German headquarters car driving toward the village of Fleurance. George dispatched a team to intercept it. The ensuing skirmish left one German wounded and showed again that the Wehrmacht had lost control of the roads.

Later that day, Abbé Boë bicycled from his rectory in Blaziert to Castelnau to say Mass for the Hollywood Brigade and its Catholic prisoners. Anne-Marie Walters wrote, "He had become famous in the region for his patriotic sermons. Already in 1942 he would curse and condemn the Germans from the height of his pulpit, in the simple and outspoken language of the district." The old priest's sermon of June 18, attended by most of the garrison as well as some of the prisoners, called the patriots to arms: "So, young men, go forward. God is with you."

The stirring sermon concluded, "Youth of France, youth of Armagnac, my brothers, remember Joan [of Arc]'s command: Kick them out of France!" At this injunction, wrote Escholier, "even the Reds of Spain applauded." The congregation burst into **La Marseillaise** with its refrain, "**Aux armes, citoyens!**" One of the Germans sang with them. The Milice prisoners, though French and Catholic, did not. Anne-Marie Walters watched as "the traitors turned to the wall in shame and humility and stood gazing at their feet." Suddenly, out of the summer sky burst a single German aircraft. Its pilot dropped no bombs, but he could not miss the armed men overflowing the ancient church.

June 19 brought another portent that Castelnau would not remain tranquil. George learned that a traitor in his headquarters had given the Germans his defensive order of battle. Escholier wrote that

281

"this betrayal was exposed and punished appropriately, [and] all our security measures were reversed." George's military advisers, Commandant Prost and Lieutenant André Herlin, abandoned defense from fixed positions in favor of "a series of small posts and a zigzag at sufficiently long distance with some machine guns and bazookas situated at points as nerve centers." Castelnau was not impregnable, but George was ensuring its conquest would not come cheap.

THIRTEEN

The Battle of Castelnau

Our job was, at all times, strictly military.

MAURICE BUCKMASTER

———

On June 6, 1944, as Allied soldiers poured onto the Normandy shore, the SD radio department on the second floor of 84 avenue Foch received a peculiar directive. Berlin ordered Dr. Josef Goetz to send a message, as he recalled, "through on the decoy transmissions then in progress which would reveal the existence of the decoy to the other side. BERLIN gave as a reason for this that the enemy would thus be frightened off." Goetz thought it was a mistake to tell SOE that the SD had been deceiving it for the previous year and a half, but disobedience was not an option. Major

Kieffer drafted a cable for Goetz to send to Buckmaster, spymaster to spymaster:

> WE THANK YOU FOR THE LARGE DELIVERIES OF
> ARMS AND AMMUNITION WHICH YOU HAVE BEEN
> KIND ENOUGH TO SEND US. WE ALSO APPRECIATE
> THE MANY TIPS YOU HAVE GIVEN US REGARDING
> OUR PLANS AND INTENTIONS WHICH WE HAVE
> CAREFULLY NOTED. IN CASE YOU ARE CONCERNED
> ABOUT THE HEALTH OF SOME OF THE VISITORS
> YOU HAVE SENT US YOU MAY REST ASSURED THEY
> WILL BE TREATED WITH THE CONSIDERATION
> THEY DESERVE.

As soon as Goetz sent the message, Berlin revoked the order. But it was too late—Buckmaster had read the cable. He was blasé, telling SOE signals chief Leo Marks, "They're trying to shake our confidence." He replied to Kieffer in equally jocular fashion:

> SORRY TO SEE YOUR PATIENCE IS EXHAUSTED AND
> YOUR NERVES NOT SO GOOD AS OURS. . . . GIVE
> US GROUND NEAR BERLIN FOR RECEPTION OR-
> GANISER AND WT OPERATOR BUT BE SURE YOU DO
> NOT CLASH WITH OUR RUSSIAN FRIENDS.

Berlin's next curious act was to dispatch military uniforms to avenue Foch's SD staff, who until then had worn civilian clothes. Ernest Vogt "felt I was putting on fancy dress." Kieffer assembled his newly uniformed cohort for an outdoor photograph on the steps of 84 avenue Foch. As they posed, someone behind Vogt whispered, "Is this to make sure the British will know us, to hang us?"

John Starr noticed Kieffer becoming depressed as the Allies secured beachheads in Normandy. On June 20, however, Kieffer's mood improved. Kieffer boasted to John and Maurice Southgate that Germany was unleashing its secret weapon, the V-1 rocket: "We can bomb your cities without sending airplanes, and one bomb is enough to wipe out a whole town." Corporal Alfred von Kapri added, "We've razed London. There's nothing left but rubble." John said that was impossible, but the German insisted, "London has been burned down. The Führer says so." Southgate became indignant.

> I got so fed up with their talk that I asked them the number of their secret weapon used against the Russian front. . . . I imagine that this reply rather upset them, so they got rid of me on the spot by sending me to Fresnes. I was put in a cell without permission to read, write, smoke or receive parcels until August of the same year, when I was sent to BUCHENWALD with 36 other agents.

Later, however, while listening to BBC reports mocking Germany's V-1 rockets over London as "doodlebugs," John realized that the secret weapon was more nuisance than game changer. It had not destroyed London and was not impeding Allied advances in France. He drew a flimsy, pilotless aircraft that looked like an insect and showed the squiggle to a disconsolate Kieffer. If that was the best Germany could do, its war was lost.

The same day Kieffer dispatched Maurice Southgate to Fresnes, the colonel's Hollywood Brigade in southwest France escalated its assault on the increasingly demoralized Germans. Camilo's Spaniards ambushed a German column near the village of Francescas, killed several German soldiers, and, in line with George's tactics, withdrew. The Spaniards lost five men and carried their corpses to Castelnau. As they prepared to bury them, another German reconnaissance plane overflew the village.

On June 20, Maurice Parisot's intelligence agents came to Panjas to inform him that the Germans were preparing to attack his friend Colonel Hilaire in Castelnau. With no radio to alert George, he ordered two companies to hasten to the fortress village. But Castelnau lay thirty-five miles away over rough country teeming with Germans and miliciens. During the night, a priest from the village of Saint-Martin-de-Goyne came to Castelnau and warned George that German troops were moving in his direction. George put the garrison of 150 French and 150 Spanish fighters on alert.

The sun rose over Castelnau at 5:45 on June 21. Anne-Marie Walters was slicing bread for breakfast in the Larribeaus' kitchen when Alberta Larribeau hurried in to say she had heard gunfire on the road from La Romieu. She asked Walters "if the Patron ought to be awoken, this is the first time he has slept for so many days." Walters went outside, where some of the inhabitants thought the noise came from **maquisards** practicing their marksmanship. Next, she recalled, "The Patron rushed out, zipping his cycling jacket, and vanished into the PC [**poste de commande**]." Leslie Brown, his shirt open on the sweltering morning, asked her, "What's all the fuss about?" Before she could answer, a **maquisard** told Brown to fetch the Bren gun under **le patron**'s bed. George then issued "orders that the German prisoners were to be taken to the village school and placed in a back room where the walls were extremely thick for their safety."

Camilo told Walters that his Spaniards were delaying the Germans along the road from La Romieu. He ordered her to assemble the village women for evacuation along the only route the Germans had not blocked, toward Condom. Castelnau's defenders took up their positions. It was nine in the morning.

"And this then," wrote Escholier, "would be the first great battle of Armagnac."

Sentries crouching in their outposts watched as more than 1,500 SS troops with artillery, mortars, and machine guns approached the hamlet from two directions. An eyewitness reported:

Some [units] of the Das Reich Division numbering several hundred came from Agen. 1,500 Germans from Auch began an all-out attack on Castelnau. Commandant PROST, Lieutenant [André] HERLEIN [Herlin], [and] PONCELET had arranged a series of little posts that stopped the Boches for a moment some three kilometers from Castelnau.

The Germans pushed through the outer defenses and, instead of encircling the village, "attacked only from two sides, from the east and from the south." German artillery shelled a post on the village outskirts and made a direct hit on George's headquarters in Larribeau's house. The accurate fire indicated that the Germans had local informers. One was the peasant whom gendarmerie Captain Fernand Pagès had chastised the previous September for accusing Jeanne Robert, Maurice Rouneau, and George of being spies. The turncoat, according to Rouneau, "took his revenge by informing the gendarmerie and the Milice who the patriots were. During a fight between the **maquis** and the SS, in which he did not fight, a German shot him in the head."

George asked Walters, "Evacuation going all right?" The village women were leaving in good order, but she insisted that she, Cormeau, and the Spanish women would stay to fight alongside the men. George did not object.

"At 9:30 A.M.," wrote antitank commander Captain Henry Solal in his hourly log of the conflict, "the encirclement seemed complete, except for the road to Condom which would permit an eventual retreat." George issued orders "to resist and to defend the village house by house." Solal rushed to plant grenades in every building "to assure the resupply of ammunition."

Five SS companies stormed the village. Abbé Boë, Anne-Marie Walters, and radio operator Lieutenant Dennis Parsons fired on them from windows and rooftops. Leslie Brown, assisted by Mayor Larribeau's eighteen-year-old son, positioned his Bren gun to protect the village water well. Firing the twenty-three-pound automatic weapon with single shots, he pinned down a whole German platoon. "What a sharpshooter and so calm!" wrote Escholier. "He fought the Boche methodically shot by shot."

Solal's diary picked up the story: "At 10:30, the situation was very critical." Castelnau's **Forces Mobiles** blew up a truckload of German troops and killed another twenty German infantry. German casualties were mounting, but reinforcements arrived in an attempt "to encircle Castelnau completely."

Escholier, in characteristic Gascon fashion, wrote the most colorful account of the Battle of Castelnau:

The unrelenting sun roasted the defenders, yet they fired on the green silhouettes advancing quickly in assault formation. A Gascon summer day, humming with insects, full of the cicadas' song. Pastoral harmony, bucolic, serene, brutally shattered by gunfire and explosions. . . . For the rest, the wheat of France finished the assailants. The Boches fell there like flies under the bullets of the maquisards, like green flies, those that gorge on garbage and are the most vicious.

He praised George, Dr. Deyris, Prost, Parsons, and Poncelet, as well as Anne Marie-Walters and the Spanish women, who "fought bravely with their rifles." Most impressive, he felt, was Yvonne Cormeau, who, "with admirable calm, assured under a hail of bullets the evacuation of her radio sets."

A messenger from Panjas stole through the German lines to tell George that Maurice Parisot's relief force would arrive within the hour. An hour, though, would be too late. The guerrillas could not hold for another fifteen minutes. George ordered a retreat. A sentry brought word that the imprisoned German sergeant wanted to speak to him. George ran to the Germans' cell, dodging "heaving shell and mortar fire." He said later,

I went and the Feldwebel sprang to attention and said to me that they all felt they would soon be released by their own people and he requested that I should allow him and his men to come up in turn and salute me. They then did so. He also said that if he had the good fortune to be rescued he would not fail to tell the officers of the attacking party how well they had been treated. . . . At the last minute when we were leaving the village I was able to stop two French hotheads from throwing grenades into the church where the [Milice] prisoners were.

"They freed their prisoners, who were terrified, and the miliciens," wrote Escholier. "Despite the pressing exhortations of certain maquisards, Colonel Hilaire and Poncelet observed the laws of war."

George abandoned all his personal possessions to lead one of the convoys out of Castelnau. A rear guard stayed to blow 400 pounds of high explosives and weapons that the **maquisards** could not carry. Nothing would be left for the Germans to use against them, as Solal reported: "At noon the Germans infiltrated the village. We thought about all the ammunition they would find in the houses, and after deliberating we decided to blow up the village."

Camilo and his Spaniards stayed to guarantee the withdrawal of their comrades in arms. The Germans burst into the hamlet, where they fought hand to hand with the rear guard. In their fury, they de-molished Jeanne Robert's school, the Larribeaus' house, the church, and the rest of the village. Solal wrote that "the Germans used their artillery to erase completely all that was saved after the explosion of the munitions." With sadness, he added, "Castelnau is destroyed; a large part of the livestock perished during the combat; the farms are devastated. . . . The small population of the commune (around 300 souls) has been left and no protest has been raised."

"No matter!" wrote Escholier. "The Gallo-Roman settlement played its great role of defense. It broke the advance of the barbarians. Castelnau of the Wolves fell on the field of honor."

The battle had lasted six hours. Casualty figures, difficult to assess in the confusion of combat, var-ied. One Resistance report stated, "On that day, the Germans suffered 380 losses, of whom 247 were killed; while the Maquis lost 160 men, of which 19 were killed." Raymond Escholier wrote that George's losses were "very light," 17 killed and 29 wounded to the Germans' 239 killed and 350 wounded. One of the wounded on the French side was radio op-erator Lieutenant Parsons. "The number of German losses may seem excessive," Solal wrote, "but it is correct, and the Germans acknowledged it in their verbal testimony."

The Germans fired on the Hollywood Brigade as

it retreated north, wounding Commandant Prost in both legs. Captain Solal carried him to the Château de Jansac, where they camped overnight. At sunrise, they left and, after passing by Condom, went another six miles west to the small hamlet of Larroque-sur-l'Osse.

Most of the Castelnau **maquis** regrouped in Condom before moving on to Parisot's headquarters in Panjas to treat their wounded and count those who died on the retreat: seven Spaniards and four French. For the eleven dead **maquisards** killed on the retreat, George's officers estimated that they had killed only five Germans.

The Spanish fighters paused long enough at La Romieu to destroy eight German trucks with hand grenades. When some of the force reached the village of Cazaubon, a physician named André Pitou treated the wounded from Castelnau in the local mayor's house. Although Dr. Pitou belonged to the Milice, he tended to Resistance patients without demur. This did not prevent the **maquisards** from arresting him afterward.

Many of George's combatants criticized him for sparing his prisoners. However, his fair treatment may have had a positive result. "After the battle of Castelnau," George said, "it was generally rumoured that a few of our wounded left behind had been spared by the Germans because the Feldwebel had intervened on their behalf pointing out the treatment he and the other German prisoners had received."

While the fighting was still under way in Castelnau that June 21, Philippe de Gunzbourg was fighting for his life eighty miles to the north. The Germans launched a surprise attack on his two thousand **maquisards** in the ancient Gascon town of Bergerac. The partisans lost the battle and retreated in disarray. While not as destructive as the Castelnau encounter, the engagement at Bergerac caused more French casualties—in Gunzbourg's accounting, "fifty partisans killed or finished off and more than 150 civilians, men, women and children." He added:

> That day had huge repercussions on the morale of the whole region, which was especially trying when I had no arms and ammunition to distribute. A state of panic and veritable mutiny stayed for a number of days, augmented by German [propaganda] tracts that were particularly well written.

Bergerac and Castelnau demonstrated that mustering large numbers of guerrillas in one place exposed them to attack and jeopardized civilians whose lives they could not protect. The Resistance was not a regular army. As a mobile guerrilla force, however, its achievements were growing.

. . .

"Prisoners" captured from the Second [SS] Panzer Division described its march north as one made through a practically hostile territory," reported the **New York Times** on June 23, 1944, "in which patrols constantly . . . had to be diverted to deal with the Maquis in central France. . . . These Maquis attacks and the sabotage of railways are reported to have been partly responsible, as well as the Allied air attacks, for the arrival of Field Marshal Gen. Erwin Rommel's armored divisions at the front in bits and pieces." The next day the **New York Times** published General Eisenhower's praise for the Resistance that "has increased both in size and in the scope of its activities. . . . The French were playing effectively their part in the war of liberation." The newspaper commented, "This lurking, powerful and secret foe is an ever-present danger to the Germans and its continuous exasperating work another threat to their morale as well as to their military operations." An internal SHAEF report stated that "FFI have fought exceedingly well with inadequate armament."

On June 24, three days after the destruction of Castelnau-sur-l'Auvignon, an exhausted and depleted Das Reich 2nd SS Panzer Division staggered into Normandy. This was eighteen days after the Operation Neptune landings, too late to repel the invasion. **Maquisards** from George's, Gunzbourg's,

Brooks's, and the other circuits had bought Eisenhower a crucial two-week respite from Das Reich's
attentions. Moreover, the division was so weak that
it had to regroup and replace the equipment, ammunition, and personnel lost on the perilous journey
before it could fight again. A shadow of what it had
been, Das Reich would go into battle as a reduced
force alongside other SS and Wehrmacht units that
slowed, but could not prevent, the Allied advance
through Normandy's dense and overgrown hedge-
rows.

"The extra fortnight's delay imposed on what
should have been a three-day journey may well have
been of decisive importance for the successful securing of the Normandy bridgehead," wrote M.R.D.
Foot in his authorized history of the SOE in France.
"Affairs in the bridgehead went so badly for the allies in the first few days that the arrival of one more
first-class fully equipped armoured division might
easily have rolled some part of the still tenuous allied front right back on to the beaches and sent the
whole of 'Neptune' awry."

On June 28, German units advanced from east
and west toward the safe house where Yvonne
Cormeau was transmitting George's messages. As
they neared her position, George appeared in his
open-top Simca and told her to get in. The pair
sped south for a few miles until a German armored

personnel carrier blocked the road. A sergeant and his troops ordered the pair out of the car and into a ditch. Cormeau recalled:

> With two soldiers in between us, both had a pistol, one in my back, one in Hilaire's back, we were back-to-back and these two were back-to-back too and therefore if the man's elbow, I gathered, had moved or something like that, the other who had felt his elbow on his body, on his back, would have shot Hilaire. . . .

The sergeant got on the radio to ask what he should do with a "tobacco inspector" and a "district nurse" he had detained. The radio crackled, but there was no answer. While they waited, Cormeau said, she sweated so much that flies stuck to her skin. "I couldn't move," she said, "because, if we'd moved, they would have shot immediately." The wait went on and on. An indistinct noise came from the Germans' radio. The sergeant walked toward them and said, **"Achtung!"** He ordered the two soldiers to move aside. Cormeau thought their execution was imminent. To her surprise, the sergeant told her and George to get back into their car. But their worries were not over. The sergeant saw her suitcase and asked to look inside. She opened it, exposing her radio transmitter. He asked what it was, and she replied, "Radio." In German, radio can mean "X-ray." "So, we got out very fast," she said. "The engine was already running."

That night, Philippe de Gunzbourg and Anne-Marie Walters greeted the first Jedburgh team to parachute into southwest France. The Jedburghs, three- or four-man units sent to assist and direct Resistance forces, landed in military uniform to avoid being shot as spies. SOE and the Special Operations (SO) section of America's wartime intelligence agency, the Office of Strategic Services (OSS), together ran the Jedburghs. Each team, with names like Team Frederick, Team George I, or Team Archibald, usually had one American, one British, and one French member. Flying into Dordogne-Sud from Algeria that night was Team Bugatti, commanded by thirty-six-year-old U.S. Marine Corps Major Horace "Hod" Williams Fuller, code name "Kansul." Harvard-educated Fuller had joined the French Army before America entered the war and in May 1940 fought the Germans. He returned to the United States, enlisted in the Marine Corps prior to Pearl Harbor, and landed at Guadalcanal with the First Marine Division in August 1942. Wounded and returned to the United States, he volunteered for the OSS rather than sit out the war behind a desk. OSS made Fuller the only Marine officer in the new Jedburgh units. The other members of Team Bugatti were two French officers, Captain Guy de la Roche du Rouzet and Lieutenant Marcel Guillemont.

When the Jeds landed, Walters and Gunzbourg took them to a farmhouse to await instructions from George Starr. Walters advised Fuller to change out of his Marine uniform into civilian clothes. Otherwise, informers would report the presence of an American officer to the Germans. Fuller, despite the risk of execution as a spy if captured, heeded her advice. George sent for Fuller a few days later. Walters wrote, "I brought KANSUL to HILAIRE who wanted to try and explain the various political entanglements of the region to him. From then on I continued liaison with them, mainly on bicycle." On July 4, Fuller "discussed the work with Hilaire . . . and Hilaire handed over the southern sector (Pyrenees)." Fuller and his Jedburgh colleagues worked with Philippe de Gunzbourg's **maquisards** to mount "many ambushes against the Germans leaving Tarbes and other towns in the region." They also captured a courier carrying Gestapo messages from Luchon to Toulouse, and their patrols sealed the Spanish border against fleeing German war criminals.

Walters thought "KANSUL's Jedburgh team was a terrific morale lifter on their arrival; they were immediately very popular and were backed by everyone in the 4th region, but the supplies they were promised and which they asked for were never sent

and bit by bit disappointment followed enthusiasm."
George was more cynical: "I sent him there [north
of the River Garonne] to get him out of my bloody
hair."

George took his Castelnau battalion forty miles
west of Castelnau to the tiny farming village of
Lannemaignan. German artillery and Luftwaffe
bombers attacked them there on July 2. The battalion retreated through heavily wooded country for
about ten miles to Panjas, where George and Parisot merged their forces into a single new **Bataillon
Armagnac**. Parisot became overall commander, and
George was his adviser. "After D-Day, I didn't give
orders. I made suggestions," George said.

The strength of the unified Armagnac Battalion, or **Demi-Brigade Armagnac**, was about 1,900
men. Escholier called them "a real society of nations. English, New Zealanders, American fly-
ers, some Belgians, many Spaniards, a Dane, some
anti-Nazi Germans, some Portuguese, some Poles, a
Czech, some Italians, some Russians—and above
all the French." The Panjas pastor, Abbé Laurent
Talès, circulated among the men, filling their glasses
with wine and blessing their enterprise. Parisot
based them in his new headquarters in the village of
Avéron-Bergelle.

Although no longer **le patron**, George did not
avoid combat. He felt he had to fight:

One of the chief reasons I lived with the Maquis and went into battle with them was the insidious propaganda which had been going on for a very long while to the effect that the British were making the French all sorts of promises to get them to rise up and then in the usual British manner would leave them high and dry. That is why, the Maquis knowing I was a British officer, I was always in view especially when there was action or trouble.

George was sleeping no more than an hour a night. It was a grueling ordeal for a soldier who three months before had turned forty. "He was becoming a little queer, the Patron," Walters wrote, "he went whole weeks without sleeping, and he took his **maquis** more seriously than a general his army group."

Lack of ammunition, however, was crippling the Armagnac Battalion's operations. The previous month of steady combat had exhausted their SOE supplies. George pleaded for more **parachutages,** but SHAEF ignored him. The RAF and AAF were concentrating their air power on support for Allied troops in the north. Complaints about lack of logistical support for the Resistance made their way into the press. "The men of the Maquis have every right to draw on Allied munition dumps and supply stores," raged London's **Observer** on June 25, "and the allies have every advantage to gain from establishing the closest possible liaison with the fighters of the French Forces of the Interior who have so generously and unsparingly offered themselves to the common cause."

Despite the supply shortage, London ordered George to attack SS and motorized Wehrmacht units entering his domain from the south. Exasperated, he told Yvonne Cormeau, "Take this message. 'Your message number and so on . . . I have taken good note, and I have given orders to the men under my command to manufacture bows and arrows. As soon as this is completed, we will attack and destroy these fucking divisions.' Send that!"

Cormeau refused. George shouted, "You bloody well send it!" She sent it, and the next night, George recalled, "there were bloody planes all over the bloody place. They bloody smothered us."

George's bow and arrow message jolted London into dispatching almost daily **parachutages** of weapons, ammunition, clothes, and food. One shipment contained four suitcases with six pairs of silk pajamas. "I just sat back and roared with laughter," George said. "I hadn't been in a bed for weeks. And [they sent] the same for Mrs. C. [Yvonne Cormeau], including a pair of pink bedroom mules with swansdown, marked, '**Maquis**—for the use of.'"

In addition to the silk pajamas, SOE sent George

a major's battle dress uniform. True to form, he did not wear it.

Weapons and clothes were arriving, but vehicles needed fuel. The Armagnac Battalion turned to an appropriate source, the Armagnac distillery that Abel Sempé had founded in 1934. Abel Sempé and another captain had previously "borrowed" the uniforms of George's Wehrmacht prisoners to infiltrate a German supply depot and steal 25,000 liters of gasoline. Now, Sempé mixed one part gasoline with nine parts 100-proof alcohol to run the cars. It worked, more or less. "The cars weren't much good," George remembered. "They were very difficult to start up. They ran them on pure alcohol, 90% alcohol. Once you started it up, you didn't shut it off."

The reconstituted Armagnac Battalion roared out in vehicles fueled with Sempé's concoction and in lightning combat captured fifteen miliciens. The **maquisards** took them back to Panjas and imprisoned them in a barn. The miliciens' handling in Panjas differed from George's treatment of captives in Castelnau. Anne-Marie Walters, daughter of a League of Nations diplomat, was incensed:

> It was also quite wrong in my opinion to lower ourselves to the standards of the Gestapo by torturing **miliciens** and collaborators to make them reveal the whereabouts of their colleagues—some were beaten until the blood spurted all over the

walls, others were horribly burnt; one man's feet were held in the fire 20 minutes and his legs slowly burnt off to the knee; other tortures were too horrible to mention. A good number of people were also shot.

The French were taking revenge on the French, but by any standard the practices constituted war crimes. While the war raged, however, no one sought to bring the culprits to justice.

FOURTEEN

The Germans Retreat

Hilaire's network totally dislocated, contained and
destroyed the German troops stationed
in the south-west of France.

MAURICE BUCKMASTER

O n July 3, scouts reconnoitering hilly terrain
about four miles north of Panjas spotted
1,000 German troops advancing on a hamlet called Estang. They dashed back to tell Maurice
Parisot, who left for Estang with George Starr and
four companies totaling 1,200 men. Two companies
hid in a pine grove where the road turned and laid
their ambush. The other two took up positions to attack the Germans if they retreated. The Armagnacs
outnumbered the Germans, but the **Boches** had bet-

ter arms and more combat experience. The German column moved toward Estang. As it closed on Parisot's position, his two forward companies opened up with Sten and Bren guns. The Wehrmacht regulars fought back and jumped into a ditch on the other side of the road. The two forces exchanged fire until evening. George reported, "Towards 19.00 hours the Germans retired to the North, intending to return to Mont-de-Marsan and fell into an ambush of [the other two] companies who held them the whole night." At the approach of dawn, the front fell silent.

Morning light found the Germans surrounded. The Armagnacs poured more fire into their position. The Germans sent out distress signals, bringing Luftwaffe reconnaissance planes over the battlefield. Focke-Wulf Condor and Dormier bombers followed, strafing and bombarding the Armagnacs. With no antiaircraft guns to protect themselves, the Armagnacs abandoned most of their trucks and cars and fled on foot. "We retreated without too great a loss and reformed at Maupas," George said. "Our losses were four men and the enemy approximately 150."

The "Battle of Estang," as the **maquisards** called it, was not the classic ambush that George had taught: "Give them ten minutes of hell, and then get the hell out of it." Instead, the irregulars fought all night and left themselves open to aerial attack. The Germans' revenge was swift: they executed nine civilians from Estang.

A few days later, the **maquis** sabotaged cables carrying electricity to Toulouse, which housed the notorious Saint-Michel Prison, important arms factories, and Germany's largest garrison in the region. The Wehrmacht was fortifying the city's defenses, and outlying units were pouring into Toulouse for their last stand in Gascony.

On France's national day, July 14, the Armagnac Battalion assembled about fifty miles west of Castelnau in the small village of Hontanx. George and Parisot staged a review of their forces. The now battle-scarred **maquisards**, in mismatched clothes and with an array of old and new weaponry, formed on the village square like a regular army. As Parisot addressed the men, a motorcyclist roared into the village, walked straight to his commander, and saluted. In a low voice that George overheard, the man told Parisot, "There are about 4,000 of the Das Reich Division approaching and they appear to be sweeping the countryside." Parisot calmly finished his speech, dismissed the men, and convened his officers in the temporary command post to question the dispatch rider. The man confirmed that he had seen Panzers emblazoned with Das Reich's distinctive, jagged **Wolfsangel** (wolf trap) insignia. There was no doubt. Das Reich was coming for them.

Combat with this remainder of the 2nd SS Panzer Division threatened the Armagnac Battalion's annihilation. "Capt. Parisot decided that our only hope was to lie low, keep an eye on the Germans and refuse battle at all costs," George said. "I suggested that a volunteer should be asked for to carry orders to the Maquis at Gabarret and to Gabriel's [Cantal's] Maquis that they should prepare mines and an ambush on the roads behind the column knowing that the column was likely to return on the same route." The Armagnacs secreted themselves beside the road and kept the Germans under close observation. The Panzers advanced, their huge cannons shining in the sunlight. George watched, dreading the assault. As the German column came within range, it stopped. George watched it, knowing its armory could wipe out his Armagnacs in a few minutes.

Suddenly, the massive Panzers stopped in the middle of the road. Their officers scanned the route ahead. Without warning, the tanks turned and rumbled off in the opposite direction. George called it "a miracle."

George feared that the German garrison in Tarbes would come from the south to "squash us between themselves and Das Reich." He organized a reconnaissance to the southwest. Parisot, worried for George's safety, made him attach two Bren guns to his car, one pointed forward and the other back. He also sent two escorts for protection. One of them, named Buresie, was a huge Russian with previous service in the French Foreign Legion, which did not inquire into the past of its volunteers. They scouted the countryside until eight that night, when George realized that his fears of an attack from Tarbes "were unfounded."

As they returned to Hontanx, a Citroën car sped toward them. Buresie aimed the forward Bren and asked George for permission to fire. George ordered him to wait. The car sped away, and George pursued it until it plunged into a ravine. The driver was "a typical German" male, aged about fifty, and the passenger a pregnant woman in her early twenties. The man made no attempt to reach for the revolver on his seat. "What bad luck," he said to the woman, "we've fallen into the hands of the Maquis." The couple had almost made good their escape to Spain. A quick search turned up badges showing that they belonged to the Gestapo. George took them to his command post.

The German refused to answer George's questions. Buresie led him away and brought in the woman. When she too said nothing, George told Buresie to lock her in a cell. "Don't give me to the French," she pleaded. "You are a British officer and a gentleman, spare my unborn child." The young woman broke down in tears. George, dressed as a **maquisard**, hadn't revealed himself to be a British officer, and replied to the woman, "You are mistaken for once. I am not a British officer and a gentleman." If the woman escaped or was rescued, George wanted to prevent her from revealing who and where he was.

George returned to Armagnac Battalion head-quarters in Avéron-Bergelle at two o'clock in the morning. "Capt. Parisot was still waiting up for me," he recalled. "We were friendly indeed and generally waited up for each other." Parisot urged him to accept someone "to be always on tap when you want to go out and to act as your bodyguard." George was unenthusiastic, but Parisot insisted, "Then you won't have to come along to me every time you want to go out and ask me to detail somebody to go with you." He proposed Buresie, whom George accepted, believing the muscular ex-Legionnaire "was a good fighting man to be relied on in an emergency."

Three days later in Avéron-Bergelle, George chanced upon the German prisoner he had captured on the road. "I spoke to him," he said, "and that is when he told me that he would have treated me as I had treated him, had the positions been reversed." The implication was that the **maquisards** had abused him, but George saw no marks of torture. "I never saw him again," he said.

In the following days, rumors reached George that Buresie had tortured the German. He made "discreet inquiries":

I found out the man had been tortured, and the Doctor DREYIS [Deyris] confirmed this. I had learnt that BURESIE . . . had suspended by one foot the Gestapo agent on a rope round a pulley. . . . I also learnt that another torture that might have been used on the Gestapo agent was to stick a knitting needle into the penis and heating the outside end with a flame. I had also heard that people had had their feet burnt.

More followed. George recalled, "I was informed that the two Gestapo agents had been shot that evening and that [Serge] TAESCH had been wounded by a ricochet." Parisot sent Taesch to his small château in Saint-Gô, where Jeanne Parisot oversaw his recovery and hid him from the Germans.

Some of the French officers who had fought with him at the Battle of Castelnau gave George a watch. Having lost his own along with all his other belongings in Castelnau, he accepted. However, he said, "I recognised it as having seen it on the wrist of the Gestapo agent when I was interrogating. They did not say it belonged to the Gestapo man but simply asked me to accept it. I did so." Refusal would have given offense. They also handed him a lady's wristwatch for Yvonne Cormeau. They did not tell him whether it had been the Gestapo woman's, and he did not ask.

"At the beginning of July 1944," Major Kieffer said, "it transpired (during the course of a radio deception plan) that a dropping operation was to take place south of Paris." His radio department was expert at organizing **parachutages** and receiving weapons from SOE north of Paris. The south, however, was the responsibility of the Kommandos der Sicherheitspolizei und SD (KDS) rather than Kieffer's bureau. The KDS asked Kieffer to assign his men to the operation "so that the reception lights and signals should be shown correctly." He sent Sergeants Haug and Stork, along with a lieutenant.

In the early hours of July 5, the SD men saw, rather than the supply containers they expected, the parachutes of twelve commandos from the 1st Regiment of Britain's Special Air Services (SAS). The SAS unit was on a sabotage mission. The commandos wore full battle dress uniforms and SAS red berets. Descending onto the drop zone in a wheat field, they were as surprised as the Germans. Instead of a friendly Resistance reception, they faced a barrage of automatic weapons fire. "Suddenly it occurred to me that we had dropped into an ambush," wrote Czech-born French commando Serge Vaculik. "The Germans were expecting us." Vaculik had time to tie notes to carrier pigeons saying, "Hard luck! Germans were waiting for us. God help us." The commandos fought back with Stens, but the Germans killed four of them, wounded three, and captured the rest. They took the wounded to Hôpital de la Pitié-Salpêtrière and delivered the uninjured prisoners to Major Kieffer for interrogation.

Kieffer, with Alfred von Kapri interpreting, received the Britons in his office at avenue Foch. The men declined to answer his questions about their communications and links to the Resistance. One man, probably Vaculik as he was the team's only French citizen, admitted he spoke French and would have been the group's liaison to the **maquis,** if the **maquis** had been genuine. Kieffer, who had hopes of using the men for his **Funkspiel,** concluded that "they were not able to give the necessary details for carrying out a radio deception plan." He ordered Erich Otto's radio department to interrogate the men more thoroughly and sent a team to the hospital to debrief the wounded. "Not one was fit for interrogation," he said.

In the evening, Colonel Helmut Knochen, the SD commander in Paris, ordered Kieffer to keep the five healthy commandos at avenue Foch rather than send them to Fresnes. Kieffer's cells were full, so he transferred them to another German security office nearby at 3 place des États-Unis. While Kieffer claimed afterward that he assigned Master Sergeant Stork to ensure the prisoners "were properly accommodated and fed," interrogators drenched them in the **baignoire** and burned cigarettes into their skin. The men's refusal to speak made it clear to Kieffer that "a radio deception plan or further interrogation reports could not be expected."

One of the wounded prisoners died in the hospital, while the other two recovered sufficiently for the Germans to move them to the place des États-Unis. Kieffer's secretary said that Kieffer proposed "that they should be transferred to the Luftwaffe POW camp." For the time being, however, they languished in handcuffs until Kieffer's superior, Knochen, received orders from Berlin.

Berlin was preoccupied with losses in both Russia and Normandy that pointed to certain defeat. Some Wehrmacht officers wanted to negotiate, despite the Allies' "unconditional surrender" policy, to save Germany from annihilation. On July 20, Lieutenant Colonel Claus Schenk von Stauffenberg secreted a bomb in the **Wolfsschanze,** the Wolf's Lair, in East Prussia, while Adolf Hitler was conferring with military staff. Hearing an explosion as he left, Stauffenberg believed the Führer was dead. His Wehrmacht coconspirators purged the Nazi leadership. In Paris, anti-Hitler plotters took Helmut Knochen and other senior SD and Gestapo officers prisoner. Kieffer's own arrest appeared imminent that night. "Kieffer was alone at 84 avenue Foch," wrote Ernest Vogt, "and I was at home while this was taking place."

When news reached Paris that Hitler, though lightly wounded, had survived, the SD and Gestapo turned on their Wehrmacht captors and arrested them. On the top floor of avenue Foch, though, John Starr and the other SOE prisoners remained unaware of the drama that nearly set them free.

THE GERMANS RETREAT

. . .

One day before Stauffenberg's putsch, twenty-four-year-old Serge Asher, who went by the cover name Serge Ravanel, went to Avéron-Bergelle to meet George Starr and Maurice Parisot. The dynamic Ravanel was one of the Resistance's more intrepid leaders. Of mixed Jewish-Catholic-Protestant and Swiss background, he was on track to be an artillery officer when the Germans invaded in 1940. He joined the Resistance early, and in March 1943 the Germans captured him in Lyon. Berty Albrecht, who committed suicide at Fresnes Prison just before John Starr was interned there, extricated Ravanel from a prison hospital. He organized resistance and, despite his youth, became a colonel and regional commander of the FFI. "I actually met Ravanel in person on (approximately) the 19th of July," George Starr said. "From the 19th of July Ravanel was living practically entirely at my HQ." Like Philippe de Gunzbourg before him, Ravanel saw in George another "Lawrence of Arabia, a dyed-in-the wool Intelligence Service professional." Ravanel appointed George his liaison to SOE.

Toward the end of July, SOE affirmed its confidence in Major Starr by promoting him to lieutenant colonel. This achievement was unique for clandestine officers, and only two other F-Section field agents would attain that distinction. "Colonel Hilaire" was, at last, a real colonel.

Meanwhile, the feud between George Starr and Anne-Marie Walters was escalating. On July 25, two days before George's promotion, his Russian bodyguard, Buresie, arrested Walters. She wrote that he locked her all night in a makeshift jail with Milice prisoners. In the morning, guards dragged her to George. **Le patron** unleashed his anger, accusing her of indiscipline, love affairs, and spreading false rumors about his relationship with Yvonne Cormeau. Walters, who had just turned twenty-one and had served George for a year, resented the charges. George did not punish her, but she understood that their quarrel was compromising her position in the **maquis.**

On July 31, George ordered Anne-Marie Walters back to England. The woman irritated him, but, more important, he wanted someone who had worked in the field to present his situation report to SOE and answer any questions. In his view, her mission was crucial:

I wanted London to have a Frenchman's point of view and this is a paraphrase of a report which I asked Col. [Henri] Monnet to write. When I gave it to Colette [Walters], I impressed on her that it was urgent and must be delivered to Col. Buckmaster. I told her this was a chance for her to show what she is worth. I told her that it must be delivered and that she must be there to explain that it was a Frenchman's point of view and also to give her own impressions (she travelled a lot and would collect impressions).

Walters confided in Hod Fuller that she preferred to remain in France. Sympathetic to the young woman's plea, he asked, "Do you think you could go to Algiers on a mission for us? I have a long report to send to H.Q. and Bouboule [Martial Sigaud, a member of Fuller's team] has too much work to pass it on by radio." She needed London's permission to proceed to Algiers, and Buckmaster later said that "permission was given from H.Q. London, but not by my section, so far as I know." She sewed Fuller's report into her shoulder pads with the one from George. As she readied to depart, Camilo and six of his Spaniards kissed her good-bye. She cried over the friends she would miss.

"She did not forgive Hilaire for tearing her away from the battle and her dear Armagnacs," wrote Escholier, who respected both George and Walters. Within hours of her departure for Spain, George transmitted his Message Number 48 to F-Section:

Have had to send Colette [Walters] back because she is undisciplined in spite of my efforts to train her since arrival. Most indiscreet. Very man-mad,

also disobedient in personal matters. She consti-
tutes a danger to security, not only her own but
of everyone. On the other hand she does not lack
courage, never hesitated to go on any mission.
Totally unsuitable for commission. She should
never be sent back to France to work for our organization.

Spanish guides led Walters and some American
airmen on foot over the Pyrenees to Spain. From
Barcelona, she flew to Algeria with Fuller's report rather than follow George's orders to proceed
to London and advocate his cause. When she met
Fuller's commanding officer, Major F. N. Marten,
at OSS headquarters in Algiers, he offered to send
her back to France to liaise with his Jedburgh teams.
"I was to help rounding up the Jeds which I could
easily do in the S.W. and help in their debriefing,"
wrote Walters. SOE, however, recalled her to London. George's Message Number 48 had by then
prejudiced F-Section against her. In London, she defended herself and accused George of overseeing the
torture of miliciens and suspected collaborators.

On August 3, an informer told the Germans that
the "terrorists" had hidden machine guns in a village
about three miles west of Maurice Parisot's house.
A German column searched the cemetery, only to
learn that **maquisards** had already made off with the
weapons. The furious Germans seized five hostages.

The same informer produced more precious intelligence: the chief of the Resistance, Maurice Parisot, lived nearby in Saint-Gô.

A force of forty-eight German officers and men boarded cars and trucks and sped to the village. Parisot had been away since D-Day, and Jeanne Parisot was in Auch on a mission for her husband. The Parisots' twenty-year-old Polish housekeeper, Josépha Mikolajazyck, saw the troops coming and ran inside to move Serge Taesch, still recuperating from his foot wound, to the attic of the house next door. She returned to the Parisot château, where a German officer declared in pidgin French, "**Ici, maquis . . . Monsieur Parisot, chef de maquis . . . Ici, réunion maquis.**" He had orders to arrest Jeanne Parisot and Serge Taesch, indicating that the informer knew arrangements in the house. The other people they found were the Parisots' nine-year-old daughter, Françoise, and a family friend named Yvonne Collin. Some of the Germans interrogated Françoise, Yvonne, and Josépha, while others ransacked the house. They seized hidden parachutes, family papers, and photographs.

"They set fire to the house with incendiary grenades in the attic and scattered gasoline in all the rooms," Jeanne Parisot told Escholier. "They used the wool harvest for kindling."

A messenger raced to Parisot's headquarters a mere eight miles away. "My husband knew I was not there that day, but he did not know the time of my return and had every reason to believe our little daughter was in the house," Jeanne Parisot said. "Not a muscle in his face flinched. . . . He continued dictating his orders calmly and only when he finished did he decide to pay attention . . . to this small incident." Parisot's 1,400 men could have saved the house from 48 Germans. Remembering the massacre at Oradour-sur-Glane, he allowed it, with the family treasures, to burn to ash.

No day passed without combat between the Resistance and Germans. United Press reported on August 8:

In southwestern France near Bayonne, one group of patriots attacked a German munitions train moving toward Normandy front, the [SHAEF] communiqué said. Twenty-two cars were blown up and the explosion set off forty-seven others standing in the station. North of Toulouse in southern France, FFI units attacked a German column, killing seventy-two officers and men and wounding fifty-four others. Two vehicles were captured and nine were destroyed.

George, Parisot, and the Armagnac Battalion seized every opportunity to harass the Germans. The next battle came on August 12, when Parisot attacked units of the Edelweiss Division who were withdrawing from Aire-sur-l'Adour. George re-called, "The attack was most successful, liberating the town with scarcely any damage, inflicting losses on the enemy who finally retreated to Mont de Mar-san, and only losing four of our men."

Parisot's courier notified George about the Aire-sur-l'Adour victory. George sent his friend a return message from their headquarters:

You are there. You see better than I do.

After breaking off, go into Aire and see if there is materiel worth taking.

If you need anything, send me word.

Bonne chance et merde.

Hilaire.

Starr's sign-off echoed SOE's friendly valediction to agents departing for France, "**Merde alors.**" Youthful FFI leader Serge Ravanel went from group to group throughout southwestern France to unify rival Resistance groups. His charm and intel-ligence convinced most of them that it was better to fight the Germans than one another, however opposed their postwar visions for France. He re-turned to George and Parisot in Avéron-Bergelle on August 14. They discussed their next major objec-tive: Toulouse, the most important metropolis in the Midi-Pyrénées. Liberating the city required seizing the towns and villages surrounding it. Working out of George and Parisot's headquarters, Ravanel devised their strategy.

SHAEF, however, assigned the **résistants** in the south a more important mission: to support Operation Dragoon, the landing of American and French forces on the beaches of the Riviera. At last, the Allied war that began in Normandy on June 6 was coming to the south. The southern Resistance was a vital component of the campaign. By the time the French and Americans hit the Côte d'Azur at dawn on August 15, Resistance attacks had severely weakened their German opponents. The Allies moved inland, while the Resistance assaulted the Germans to speed the advance of American general Alexander Patch's Seventh Army from the Mediterranean up the Rhône Valley. It became one of the fastest Allied offensives of the war, with logistics units struggling to keep up with the infantry.

A U.S. Army study of the Resistance observed, "They made the occupation of FRANCE a continual hell for the Germans." Eisenhower again thanked the native guerrillas for saving his soldiers' lives. The Allies moved north and east, but the southwest was not part of their battle plan. The **résistants** there were left to face the Germans on their own.

The Armagnac Battalion moved slowly, step by step, toward Toulouse. It conquered nearby towns and took possession of others after the Germans evacuated. When it entered Montréjeau, about sixty miles west of Toulouse, the inhabitants turned out for an ecstatic welcome. Women kissed the partisans, and musicians played patriotic tunes. There were the inevitable speeches, including one in American-accented French by Colonel Hod Fuller: "**Je ne suis pas un orateur. Je suis un soldat. J'ai une dette de reconnaissance envers la France qui a aidé la libération de mon pays.**" While Fuller was acknowledging America's debt to the Marquis de Lafayette during the War of Independence, a German unit drove into town. Fortunately for the celebrants, it bypassed the main square on its way to Tarbes without firing a shot.

Local gendarmes informed George that the German garrison in the departmental capital of the Gers, Auch, was abandoning the town. The Wehrmacht column departed on August 19, and the Armagnac Battalion moved in. During George's many missions there before D-Day, he had avoided suspicious eyes and kept to the shadows. At last, he donned his British officer's uniform and drove straight into town at the head of a column of victorious Armagnacs. While the populace acclaimed the ragtag fighters riding Abel Sempé's motley vehicles, one woman spotted George's uniform. She handed him a basket of tea and marmalade that she had saved since 1940 to give to the first British soldier she saw. A little later, a young Frenchman asked him, "Tell me, old man, you don't know where the commander hangs out?" George answered in French with his strong British accent, "No. You'll have to look for him." George and Parisot established their headquarters in Auch's gendarmerie.

The Germans fled east from Auch in two columns along the Bayonne-Toulouse highway. Damaged bridges and roads slowed their momentum, and they trudged ahead into increasingly hostile territory. Local fighters erected a makeshift barricade to block them on the outskirts of L'Isle-Jourdain at a bridge over the River Save. The Wehrmacht convoy paused to determine the size of the **maquis** force on the opposite bank. Camilo's Spaniards went behind the Germans to block reinforcements from Montauban. The rival forces faced each other across the river without firing a shot. The sun went down and at nine o'clock Parisot gave the order to attack. The defenders held their ground. Battle raged through the night, neither side gaining ground.

Shortly after sunrise on August 20, Captain Parisot slung a rifle over his back and walked toward the German line. Speaking German, he called on his opponents to surrender. A German colonel shouted, "**Nein!**" Parisot returned to his men. The Germans used the momentary cease-fire to move troops into a meadow beside the railroad tracks, threatening to turn the French line. Parisot sent an urgent message to George in Auch asking for additional fighters.

George dispatched two companies, about six hundred men. While awaiting their arrival, Parisot's machine gunners in a water tower and the steeple of Saint Bernard's Church rained heavy fire on the Germans below. The two companies that George sent reached the front, and the opposing forces fought into a second night.

At daybreak, forty-eight hours into the combat, the shooting stopped. Nine Frenchmen lay dead. The Germans raised the white flag. Parisot took 192 Germans, including two colonels, prisoner. George's account of L'Isle-Jourdain noted, "We captured several lorries, also petrol and other stores." Four German officers escaped, only to stumble on a Resistance checkpoint. They unholstered their revolvers, yelled, "**Heil, Hitler!**" and shot themselves.

George's report to London on Parisot's victories at Estang, Aire-sur-l'Adour, and L'Isle-Jourdain ended with fulsome praise for his friend: "By his continual gallantry, devotion to duty and leadership of his men, the Bataillon became a terror to the German forces in the region." George celebrated the triumph at a sumptuous banquet with Parisot, Cormeau, and forty Armagnac comrades. While they drank before dinner, **maquisards** led three German soldiers they had just captured into the room. Captain Gabriel Termignon, who said he spoke German, questioned them in front of everyone. The prisoners were slow to answer. George, who believed the prisoners had trouble understanding Termignon's ungrammatical German, described the encounter:

> Termignon lost his temper and started striking them and also taking their belongings from them and offering them to the ordinary troops who were round about. After a bit I could not stand it any longer. I was in British uniform in the rank of Major [colonel] and I got up and went over to him and in front of everybody told him that that was not the way to treat prisoners of war who were soldiers and were under orders whatever they had done. I said the proper way was to hand them over to the Gendarmerie who were charged with looking after the prisoners.

George later said that Termignon had suffered at German hands in Toulouse's Saint-Michel Prison, from which he had just escaped, and was "naturally overwrought."

The Battle of L'Isle-Jourdain was the last in the Gers, where George Starr had set up shop in November 1942. The entire department was now liberated.

The **Forces Française de l'Intérieur** acknowledged Captain Parisot's accomplishments by promoting him to colonel, an honor he declined. "I have only the stripes I wear," he declared. The FFI chief in the Gers appealed to Jeanne Parisot: "I am writing to your husband to give him an order to wear colonel's stripes. He cannot command 2,000 men as a captain!" Parisot remained a captain and went on commanding.

In the Haute-Garonne department, isolated German units were retreating into Toulouse. FFI brigades filled the void in each town they abandoned. On August 18, Colonel Hod Fuller's Jedburghs with Philippe de Gunzbourg's **maquisards** captured Tarbes. Fuller sent a message to his Algiers headquarters: "What a spectacle, our maquis has liberated Tarbes and Lubon. The Germans are fleeing to Spain. I have a German general [Major General Leo Mayr] and his general staff prisoners."

The **New York Times** trumpeted the FFI's conquests under the headline FFI MASTERS OF PYRENEES:

The entire Pyrenees region of southwestern France from the Atlantic to the Mediterranean is now in the hands or under the control of the FFI. . . . All the German forces just north of the Spanish border have withdrawn north towards Germany and the FFI immediately took possession, appointing new civil administrators.

Toulouse, the Germans' last and largest bastion in the region, was next. Conquering the city entailed risks to the attackers, the civilians, and the fabric of

327

the city the FFI hoped to liberate. They proceeded with caution. Early on August 19, **maquisard** units moving into Toulouse's suburbs were joyously received by the inhabitants. Inside the city, the Germans were burning documents and setting fire to their headquarters. They packed their provisions and loot, and they abandoned the city. The FFI moved in, capturing the Saint-Michel Prison and liberating more than four hundred political prisoners, including the French writer André Malraux. The **maquisards** burned German trucks, clashed with the German rear guard, and erected barricades to block departing columns on the roads and rails. The Germans escaped along the main highway toward Carcassonne, pursued by ecstatic **maquisards**. By morning, the city was free. A dispatch of August 21 to the **New York Times** informed the American public, "The French Forces of the Interior have captured Toulouse."

The French tricolor flew over the city's monuments, and the **maquisards** controlled the major governmental buildings. More than thirty thousand Toulousians flooded the place du Capitole to welcome their liberators. Every faction of the Resistance shared the adulation of the newly freed populace. George Starr and Yvonne Cormeau drove into the city with two thousand victorious Gascons and their foreign comrades. A French officer on motorcycle stopped their convoy and asked to speak to the British colonel. Yvonne Cormeau, sitting in George's old Simca between him and a six-feet-five American Jedburgh officer called Tiny, remembered:

He stopped the whole column and explained that, as we were at the point of entering the town of Toulouse, he would very much like the colonel who was driving to put a Union Jack on the car to indicate that it was a friendly car, you see. And he brought out of his pocket a Union Jack his wife had made out of parachute material.

They placed the homemade standard on the car, and Tiny said, "Oh, if only Old Glory was there." Cormeau pulled the flag patch from his uniform and put it on the car's windshield. Bearing the improvised colors of Great Britain and the United States, Starr and Cormeau led their comrades into the liberated city. The surviving combatants of Castelnau and Panjas received rapturous applause, kisses, and wine from the people of Toulouse. The rejoicing and drinking went on all night.

In the morning, the Armagnac Battalion settled into the Niel Barracks. The FFI issued them military uniforms and declared them a regular unit of the French Army. This was not a welcome development to many of the independent fighters. Escholier said one man complained, "Maquisards, my brothers, here we're in a cage. The maquis is finished: here

is our barracks and our splendid new khaki uniforms. The change is complete." The guerrillas were
now soldiers.

The FFI by this time controlled, as the United
Press reported, "more than 50,000 square miles in
southern France," but their war was not over. Within
a few days, the Armagnac Battalion deployed to
Villefranche-de-Lauragais in pursuit of retreating
German units. George Starr did not go with them.

On August 6, John Starr's thirty-sixth birthday,
something unexpected happened at 84 avenue
Foch. His debrief to SOE recorded:

> On his birthday, source was given presents by the
> Germans and flowers were placed in his room. In
> the evening they had a party and the Comman-
> dant came up to the cell and brought a bottle of
> champagne and a bottle of cognac.

German officials in Paris, like the British and
French in June 1940, were putting their files to the
torch. Evacuating the French capital was a logistical
headache. **Résistants** of the last hour attacked German patrols. Railway workers sabotaged trains. The
British and American air forces bombed the Germans' escape route east. There was the additional
problem of prisoners, hundreds of whom were sum-

marily executed at Fresnes Prison and in the Jardin du Luxembourg.

A day after John's birthday, Colonel Helmut Knochen ordered Major Kieffer to report to his headquarters on avenue Foch. Berlin had made a decision about the British SAS commandos imprisoned at the place des États-Unis. Kieffer recalled that Knochen

> . . . read out to me a teleprint which had just arrived, the contents of which were to the effect that by order of the Führer and Supreme Commander of the Wehrmacht the death penalty was to be carried out against the prisoners from the SAS-Commando Operation. Before execution they were to be dressed in civilian clothes. The BDS [Knochen] was held personally responsible for the strictest secrecy.

Berlin's decree accorded with Adolf Hitler's infamous "commando order" of October 18, 1942, that prescribed "all men operating against German troops in so-called Commando raids in Europe or in Africa are to be annihilated to the last man." Hitler ordered his troops to kill commandos "whether they be soldiers in uniform" or were "giving themselves up as prisoners." Obedience to the order was a war crime, and Knochen sought to keep it secret. Kieffer recalled Knochen's insistence that "members of my section who already knew about the case had to be used." Two of the men he assigned, Haug and Stork, "asked why they in particular had been detailed for the operation." They were not offered a choice. Nor were the SAS prisoners, whom the SD forced to change into civilian clothing during the night of August 7.

The operation began before sunrise on the eighth, when guards handcuffed the commandos and drove them to avenue Foch. A driver from the SD motor pool, Fritz Hildemann, arrived in his truck to collect them. "I was not able to see whether they were chained but I saw that sandwiches for them were taken too," Hildemann said. "I assumed that these men were to collaborate in some way or other in connection with a comb-out operation or at the reception of parachute drops as usual, so I understood from other comrades who had made previous such trips." The convoy drove northwest out of Paris for over forty miles. Hildemann was ordered to stop north of the town of Noailles, "near a projecting piece of woodland." A few yards off the road, two of the SD officers walked through the forest toward a nearby cornfield. They returned and told the prisoners, "Get out." Hildemann wondered about the purpose of the operation: "Since the big column was not very far from us, I thought that perhaps the prisoners were to show us something in the wood which was to help in the comb-out operation."

A second truck with a tarpaulin-covered bed backed into the field.

Hildemann went into the cornfield and saw the handcuffed prisoners standing in a row. Hauptsturm-führer (Captain) Richard Schnurr of Kieffer's staff read out a long statement in German that began, "In the name of the Führer." When Alfred von Kapri's English translation reached "will be shot," the commandos bolted, dispersing through the cornfield to the woods. Commando Serge Vaculik wrote, "Startled, the Germans did not open fire at once and that was my salvation." The moment's hesitation gave Vaculik and Thomas "Ginger" Jones time to run. The Germans fired Sten guns from SOE arms drops at the fleeing prisoners. Vaculik later stated:

I opened my handcuffs with my watch spring and I ran away down the hill. Some firing occurred. I was not hit. Von KAPRI was carrying an English sten gun. HAUG was carrying an American repeating rifle. The others were carrying automatic pistols. . . . As I ran I did not see any of my comrades. Later I made my way to a French village and afterwards I joined the French Resistance.

Jones similarly recalled, "I made a run for it. I got 10/15 yards away and I fell. I lost my balance as my hands were handcuffed." The Germans wounded Jones, who crawled into the brush, where he saw the bodies of four of his comrades. Jones evaded the Germans and, like Vaculik, was not recaptured.

The Germans killed five commandos, some while they ran, the others as they lay wounded. They buried their bodies in an orchard of the Château de Parisis-Fontaine. If anyone revealed what happened, the cover story would be that they had shot escaping spies in civilian clothes. Hildemann recalled that they had to ask for trucks from a nearby Luftwaffe base to remove the corpses. Too many people outside the SD knew what happened, from the two surviving SAS commandos to the Luftwaffe burial detail, to keep the massacre secret forever.

Kieffer heard what had occurred that evening:

I was not present at the departure of the squad or during the execution and I can only state what was reported to me by Schnurr. According to this all the prisoners are said to have escaped after the order for execution was made known to them. One [two] of the SAS men in fact succeeded in escaping. Hauptsturmführer Schnurr was very depressed when he reported to me that the execution had been carried out. From the beginning he as well as Haug and Stork were depressed by this task.

The SD staff had also to deal with their own prisoners at 84 avenue Foch before they left Paris.

They could not permit the Allies to liberate people, especially John Starr, who knew everything about the **Funkspiel**. Kieffer and Goetz intended to send more false signals to SOE after they left Paris, despite the joking exchange of messages with Buckmaster. Then, recalled the radio department's Corporal Werner Ruehl, "a telegram had arrived from Berlin instructing us to liquidate all agents held in Paris." The orders infuriated radio department chief Erich Otto. Ruehl said that Otto "came into the office and slammed some papers on the desk and said 'This is a Schwenerie [disgrace],' saying that he would refuse to carry out this order. GOETZ and OTTO were greatly excited and I believe that no agents were shot in Paris at that time." Kieffer, who had obeyed the order to facilitate the SAS commandos' murders, did not execute "his" prisoners. Instead, he arranged to send them to Germany.

He bade farewell to John Starr. Neither man left a record of their parting, but the two enemies had a mutual respect. John felt that Kieffer had behaved correctly throughout his confinement. Kieffer respected John for refusing to betray his comrades and keeping his word not to attempt another escape. Later, Corporal Ruehl told John, "Now that you are going, there's something I think you ought to know. Kieffer three times received an order to have you shot, and each time he refused to comply with it." It was too late to thank Kieffer for his life.

John left Paris under guard on a train bound for Germany. Eight days later, the train stopped outside Saarbrücken. The Neue Bremm concentration camp was too full of Russian, Polish, and other prisoners to admit new arrivals. John and the rest of the detainees waited for four days in sealed wagons with only one tin can for body waste and a scrap of bread each. A new train arrived to take them to Buchenwald. Indicative of the chaos overtaking the Third Reich, Buchenwald was also full. John's next destination was the Sachsenhausen concentration camp north of Berlin in Oranienburg. It was at capacity with sixty-five thousand inmates, but it admitted the new prisoners anyway.

John sat on a bench outdoors amid two thousand other arrivals. A few of the men became so thirsty that they scrambled for foul water from a standpipe that gave them dysentery. After waiting several hours, guards stripped, shaved, and deloused them before distributing them among huts already bursting with starving men. John lodged in Block 49, where an SS guard looked him up and down and pronounced, "You are not so tall for an Englishman." His reply was, "Yes, and you're not so fat for a German." When prison work details were assigned, John found himself with Strafe Kommando, or Punishment Command. The other Strafe Kommando inmates were naval officers, most from Norway, and lived in the Strafe Block. The Norwegians shared their Red Cross food parcels with the British, who were not allowed to receive anything. John lived in a separate blockhouse, but went out each morning with the Norwegians to test boots made of ersatz leather by marching around and around a stony square of land. The Germans did not permit them to rest during daylight hours, and they walked scores of miles each day without going anywhere.

John distracted himself from the camp's savagery by painting the interior walls of his block in a trompe l'oeil of hills, forests, and rivers around a panorama of Nuremberg. Rather than punish him, guards ordered him to paint other huts. The Elysian vision contrasted with the reality of Sachsenhausen's mud, filth, vermin, lice, work details, and torture. The prisoners' only hope of an end to the torment came from rumors that the Soviets were advancing from the east and the Western Allies were penetrating Germany from Belgium. If the rumors were true, would any of them live to witness the camp's liberation?

FIFTEEN

"I Said 'Shit' to De Gaulle"

The Resistance was a vital factor in the recovery of the French national spirit.

MAURICE BUCKMASTER

=====

In liberated Toulouse, revolutionary fervor reigned. Crowds rounded up collaborators as well as innocents suspected of cooperating with the Germans. Communist partisans seized government buildings and raised the red flag. FFI commander Serge Ravanel suspended the gendarmerie, the national police force that had collaborated with the occupier from the beginning. The gendarmes had also been instrumental in the oppression of the city's ancient Jewish community and in gathering young men to serve in the forced labor battalions of the STO. **Résistants** whom the gendarmes had arrested and tortured supported Ravanel. To Charles de Gaulle, however, Ravanel's action constituted a challenge to his authority. He wrote:

> Around Ravanel, leaders of the armed units constituted something like a soviet. The members of this council claimed to carry out the necessary purges with their own men, while the gendarmerie and the garde mobile were confined to remote barracks. . . . Furthermore, a Spanish "division" was forming in the region with the loudly publicized purpose of marching on Barcelona. To top it all, an English general known as "Colonel Hilary" and introduced into the Gers maquis by the British services, held several units under his command and took orders from London.

The **Forces Aériennes Françaises Libres** (FAFL), the Free French Air Forces, sent two Hudson light bombers from Algiers to Toulouse in early September, part of the process of establishing de Gaulle's provisional government in the region. The American-made aircraft had flown countless sorties over France, but these would be the first FAFL planes to land at Toulouse. Serge Ravanel sent Maurice Parisot and George Starr to welcome them at the Francazal military airfield near the city.

On the night of September 6, George, Parisot,

and their men formed an honor guard beside the runway. Two aircraft appeared in the heavens, and the **maquisards** snapped to attention. The first plane landed, and its crew received the Armagnacs' salute. The second approached the tarmac. As it touched down, one of its twin engines jettisoned its propeller. The blade spun like a Catherine wheel. The honor guard dived and rolled out of the way. George recounted:

> I was as close to him [Parisot] as I am to you now, and the other bloke, in fact closer. It was the three of us talking, and I saw this bloody thing and I said, "Down!" and dropped like a bloody bullet. It took the bloody cap off my head, but it didn't touch me. And it killed the other two standing bloody dead.

"Parisot did not hear his men scream, 'Get down!'" wrote Escholier. "As for Parisot, faithful to his tradition as a leader, he stayed up, the last of all, and it was then he was struck, standing up." Parisot, his followers' beloved Caillou, **résistant** before the first hour and one of the most respected **maquis** leaders, was cut to pieces. He and George had survived nearly three years of clandestine and open warfare at each other's side. George, a stoic not known for tears, wept at the sight of his closest comrade dying in a senseless accident.

Parisot's funeral took place in Auch two days later. The somber mood was the opposite of what it had been in August, when Parisot, George, and their comrades liberated the town. Escholier wrote that George looked pale. Beside him stood Camilo and Parisot's successor, Henri Monnet. The departmental chief of the FFI, Colonel Marcel Lesur, delivered the eulogy: "He was a leader of men. He possessed courage with self-control, nerve with clarity, marked with an exceptional zeal, it was his goodness, it was his magnificent brilliance which those who served him would not deny. And that is why my comrades see him as the pure face of the French Resistance." Philippe de Gunzbourg said that Parisot was "the most durable, the most courageous, who did splendid work, the most remarkable person in the Gers." George's homage was no less heartfelt: "Captain Parisot was not only a brave soldier, but a good man for whom I had a great admiration." His death was a loss for his friends, but also for France.

Two days afterward, Camilo attended another ceremony, his wedding. The Spanish commander, who had told Anne-Marie Walters that no woman would marry someone like him with only one leg, wed Eva Odette Berrito, a young Spanish woman he had met while fighting in the Gers. There was no time for a honeymoon. The war was not over, and some of Camilo's **guérilleros** were agitating to take their struggle to Spain against dictator Francisco

Franco. Camilo refused. He would not rekindle the civil war in Spain, but he would battle the Germans until they were out of France. Then, he said, he would raise his family in the adopted country that he had fought for.

George Starr, whose loyalties to Britain and France had not conflicted during the occupation, was clashing with Frenchmen everywhere after the liberation of Toulouse. In a city teeming with fifty thousand armed men at odds with one another, the absence of regular police and army made the reimposition of law seem a vain hope. Yet George and his men expelled the communists from the city hall, lowered their red flag, and handed the building to Charles de Gaulle's representatives. They assisted in bringing order to districts where rival **maquis** bands vied for control and assumed legal powers, like fining wartime profiteers and punishing collaborators. George forced the **maquisards** to release prisoners he knew were blameless, "people who had been high-handedly arrested by the F.F.I. and other French people" and who were "absolutely innocent." To him, that was simple justice. To de Gaulle's men in Toulouse, it was British interference in their country's affairs.

London had more missions for George. The first was to commandeer one of two new Heinkel He-177A-5 bombers that the Luftwaffe had left behind at Toulouse's Blagnac Airfield. The British and French both wanted to study the revolutionary jet engine technology, but the French were denying access to their British allies. George's **maquisards** were happy to help the British who had helped them. They descended on the airbase and daubed "**Prise de Guerre**" on one of the aircraft. George turned it over to the RAF's chief test pilot, Wing Commander Roland Falk, who flew the war prize to Farnborough in England. The Gaullists were furious, again resenting British perfidy on their soil.

In mid-September, de Gaulle descended on southern France. His objective was to establish his provisional government in defiance of both the Americans, who planned to impose an American Military Government for Occupied Territories (AMGOT), and French **résistants**, who were organizing a new, leftist order. On his arrival in Toulouse on the morning of September 16, his **Commissaire de la République**, a socialist-leaning **résistant** named Pierre Bertaux, met him at the airport. Their conversation during the drive into town turned to the ranking British officer in Toulouse, Lieutenant Colonel George Starr.

Bertaux claimed to de Gaulle that George had told him, "I am Colonel 'Hilaire,' I have 700 men under arms, I have in my pocket an order signed by Churchill and de Gaulle and, in this bloody mess, I bang the table and say, 'Here it is I who commands.'" De Gaulle is said to have responded, "And you didn't arrest him on the spot?" Bertaux couldn't arrest a man who commanded 700 armed men. De Gaulle asked, "You haven't, at any rate, invited him to lunch with me?" Bertaux admitted he had, because George had fought in de Gaulle's name. De Gaulle told him to cancel George's invitation. He would grant the English colonel a tête-à-tête after the lunch.

When George arrived at the Prefecture for the banquet, an officer informed him he was not welcome and told him to wait for the end of lunch. George's anger grew with every passing minute in the prefect's office. At last, de Gaulle came in. Without shaking George's hand, he called him a mercenary and ordered him to leave the country. George responded in French, "**Je suis un militaire britannique en opération. J'ai un commandement à exercer. Je ne le quitterai que sur ordre de mes supérieurs à Londres. Je vous emmerde. Vous êtes le chef d'un gouvernement provisoire que les Alliés n'ont pas reconnu!**" ("I am a British soldier on duty. I have a command to exercise. I will not leave except on the order of my superiors in London. I shit on you. You are head of a provisional government that the Allies have not recognized!") George stormed out in a fury. The men in the antechamber heard George grumble as he passed, "I said 'shit' to de Gaulle." French historian of the liberation Robert Aron wrote that de Gaulle told Pierre Bertaux, "You will give him twenty-four hours to leave French territory. If he stays, you will arrest him."

De Gaulle's memoirs did not mention the argument. All the general wrote was "Lastly 'Colonel Hilary.' Within two hours he had been sent to Lyons, and from there immediately returned to England." That was false. George did not leave "within two hours." He returned to the Niel Barracks, where Yvonne Cormeau observed that he was "very, very upset. He was called a mercenary and that upset him above all." He dictated a message for her to encode and transmit to London, telling SOE of the encounter and requesting instructions. They also drafted "a letter in French for the General to explain that we had to obey the orders and we were awaiting the reply of the telegram I'd sent and would be excused if we could not get away within the twenty-four-hour limit. We never heard another thing. We stayed for over forty-eight."

George was not the only victim of de Gaulle's tongue. When Serge Ravanel reported to the general in his colonel's uniform, de Gaulle said, "Ah, it's Second Lieutenant Asher." De Gaulle questioned Ravanel's right to wear the Liberation Cross that his own provisional government had awarded the young officer. Ravanel, who had spent two years fighting in occupied territory while the general lived in London, had admired de Gaulle as a hero. Some said that after de Gaulle insulted him, he went outside and cried.

The next day, de Gaulle went to Bordeaux and abused the famed F-Section organizer Roger Landes, code name "Aristide," as he had George and Ravanel. Rather than thank Landes for liberating Bordeaux, the general banished him. When another SOE agent, Peter Lake, went to the town of Sainte, north of Bordeaux, to meet de Gaulle, the general ordered him out of the country. The purging of British agents from French soil presaged their erasure from the Gaullist version of Resistance history.

George was in no hurry to leave France while important business in the southwest remained unfinished. "Hilaire decided then it was about time," said Yvonne Cormeau, "as we had some money left, to go back on our tracks if there was anyone we should help of the people who had helped us." They went to the Bouchou family farm at Saint-Antoine-du-Queyret near Bordeaux, where Cormeau had parachuted into France in August 1943. The Bouchous' daughters, aged fourteen, sixteen, and seventeen, were living in poverty with their grandmother. The Germans had deported their mother and father to concentration camps. "And therefore we were glad that we could give them some money to feed them," said Cormeau. "They'd been on their own since September '43."

· · ·

On September 25, George Starr and Yvonne Cormeau flew from Bordeaux to England, where Cormeau was reunited with her young daughter, Yvette. But George's homecoming was bitter. Having survived constant danger and privation since November 1942, all he wanted was to see Pilar and the children. But they were stuck in Spain, where the Franco regime was denying them exit visas. George was underweight and tired. He had lost friends in France, most recently the closest, Maurice Parisot. The leader of Free France had insulted him. Most painful of all, he did not know whether his younger brother was alive or dead.

Colonel Maurice Buckmaster gave George a hero's welcome at Orchard Court and asked him to write a report on his work in France. George recalled the conversation: "And I said, me? I don't write reports." His compromise was to answer questions from SOE debriefing officers. Major Bourne-Patterson wrote in the first official account of F-Section's work, "Hilaire himself, unfortunately for posterity, is a most unvocal person and his own reports on his activities are of the briefest. (He indeed once expressed to the writer the view that, once an action was over, it was not worth reporting on.)" Buckmaster recommended him to British counterintelligence, MI5, for further clandestine work.

Although George's deeds remained a secret from the public, his reputation earned him the esteem of

SOE staff. Colleagues at Beaulieu, the Group B Special Training School (STS) in Hampshire, invited their star alumnus to dinner a month after his return. George went there on the night of October 30 in low spirits: "I was very tired, suffering rather from exhaustion and very worried about my wife and children because I had been told that morning that Franco was causing trouble as she was suspected of being a British agent."

It was good to see friends from his training course in 1941, but most of the officers were new to him. "I arrived at the mess about 8 P.M. and was met by Major Follis who acted as my host there and I went into the mess and we had drinks," George wrote. Peter Follis, a famously handsome actor in civilian life, taught the art of disguise. (Follis had said to F-Section's Noreen Riols, "Forget the false beards, they're too obvious. Instead dye your hair, change your hair parting, wear glasses and put a pebble in your shoe as that will give you a limp.") Follis asked George about his brother and his "cousin," undoubtedly Maurice Southgate. If they were alive, George said, they were in concentration camps. Follis wondered whether the Germans had tortured them. "I said I did not know but it was most likely," George wrote, "because I know from hearsay what the Gestapo did to anybody they caught." He remembered Follis saying, "You must have been damn lucky to have lasted so long without any trouble."

The camp commandant, Lieutenant Colonel Stanley H. C. Woolrych, entered the room. A short, balding officer in his midfifties, Woolrych had been the chief instructor during George's term at Beaulieu. He had a drink with George and, like Follis, raised the subject of torture. Beaulieu's curriculum included techniques for surviving interrogation. George, who knew more about Gestapo methods than the teachers, answered that the most common practices were hanging prisoners upside down by the feet and inserting red-hot needles into the urethra. Woolrych asked if the Resistance also employed torture. George replied, "Well, they don't have to invent anything. They just copy the Gestapo."

When Woolrych asked George whether he had experience with the Gestapo, George mentioned the male and female Gestapo agents he and his Russian bodyguard, Buresie, had captured in July. He believed the couple had been tortured, but he had not witnessed it. Major Follis then remarked on George's unusual wristwatch, which George said had belonged to the Gestapo man. The officers made their way to dinner, and Woolrych asked George to deliver a lecture afterward. "This was the first I knew that I was to give a formal talk," George said. "I had of course prepared nothing." He asked what he should discuss. Woolrych suggested his work in France, his circuit, and the torture of the Gestapo man and woman. "I did not think torture had any

349

bearing on the work and wanted to confirm that he really meant that." He did. George and his fourteen fellow officers then sat down to eat.

"After dinner we went back into the mess and the first person I saw was Captain Harris," George said. "We began to chat. While we were talking, Captain Harris said, 'We must stop chatting. You must go over to the Colonel who is getting fidgety.'" Starr approached Colonel Woolrych, who said, "There is a lady present. Will her presence embarrass you? Shall I ask her to go?" The lady was Lieutenant Violet Dundas of the First Aid Nursing Yeomanry (FANY). George did not want her to leave, but he assumed that Colonel Woolrych mentioned her because the torture of the Gestapo couple might upset a woman.

George, who had regaled his **résistants** with stories around Jeanne Robert's kitchen table, disliked giving formal talks. He spoke anyway about his arrival at Port-Miou in November 1942, his WHEELWRIGHT circuit in Gascony, recruiting volunteers, **parachutages**, avoiding capture, betrayals, fallen comrades, and post-D-Day combat. As he concluded, he discussed the Gestapo couple: "I said that I believed that the man had been tortured, and I described the torture of hanging by the leg. I didn't repeat the torture of the heated pin, because of the lady's presence."

The talk lasted, according to Colonel Woolrych,

"a couple of hours," after which batmen served drinks. George recalled that "the atmosphere was informal and friendly. . . . I was bombarded with questions right and left." He did not notice that one officer, Captain F. Lofts, left early. Lofts explained, "After the talk, I was disgusted by the incident with regard to the woman. This was what made me leave the mess. I felt I wanted to hear no more." When the evening drew to a close at eleven o'clock, Major Follis showed George to his room.

In the morning, George met Colonel Woolrych and some of the staff for breakfast in the officers' mess. Woolrych was "very cordial" and asked George's opinion of the training at Beaulieu, especially which courses had helped him most in the field. Although Normandy, Paris, and the south of France had been liberated, SOE was still sending agents to unliberated areas of the Continent. Feedback from an experienced operative like George was invaluable. After breakfast, they went to Major Follis's office, where Woolrych, Follis, and Major H. S. Hunt "were very friendly and said they would be very pleased to see me any time I liked to go down." At nine thirty, a car took George to London.

After George's departure, Beaulieu was anything but friendly to him. "As a consequence of this talk," Captain F. W. Rhodes said, "I went to see Major Hunt, then assistant chief instructor, and told him I felt Colonel Starr's actions were despicable in so far as the torturing was concerned." Rhodes was not alone. Captain Lofts said, "On the following afternoon at 1830 hours, I saw Colonel Woolrych and Major Hunt in the lounge. I expressed the opinion I held—this was one of disgust at the story of the woman in particular. . . . I think I said to Colonel Woolrych that I thought it was a horrible story and such a story would never bear exposure." Lofts said that he and other officers discussed the tale for days. But, he said, "a few days after the talk Maj. Hunt . . . instructed us that the Commanding Officer Colonel Woolrych did not want the matter to be the subject of further discussion."

Colonel Woolrych, urged by his staff, referred George's speech to higher authority. "Two days later I wrote a report, dated 1 November," Woolrych stated, "addressed to Air Commodore [Archibald "Archie" Robert] Boyle [head of SOE Intelligence and Security Directorate], with reference to what Colonel Starr had said." Woolrych continued:

In it I said we were all impressed by the fact that Colonel Starr had done a magnificent job in the field for which he deserved every possible credit, but that his mission did appear to have been tainted by a streak of sadism in view of what he had told us. I narrated the incident about the Gestapo man and woman and said that it had caused a certain consternation among some of my officers, two of whom had approached me in the matter.

George was unaware of the stir his lecture was causing. "The next I heard was late one evening when I had a phone call saying Colonel Buckmaster wanted to see me immediately and I was to bring Annette [Yvonne Cormeau] with me." He and Cormeau visited Buckmaster, who asked about torture in the **maquis**. The questions outraged George, but his venom was not directed at Buckmaster: "I can remember my immediate reaction was that Colette [Anne-Marie Walters] had said something against me. I said to myself it was a frame-up by her, as when I had got back to England she had made a scene, said her father was influential, she had friends and would get me."

In November, George and Cormeau flew to France to assist Buckmaster on the Judex Mission to find and help those who had worked for SOE during the German occupation. They met old friends and attended a formal military parade on November 29. Their battlefield comrade Colonel Henri Monnet presented the Croix de Guerre to both George and Cormeau in the name of George's antagonist, General Charles de Gaulle.

When they returned to England, George discovered that the case against him was gathering momentum. Buckmaster, who refused to believe that

George could torture anyone, urged him to spend the Christmas holiday with his parents in the north of England. "Anyway, I'd spend Christmas at home," George said. "That was important." Morose that Pilar and the children were trapped in Spain, he went north to Newcastle-under-Lyme on Christmas Eve. "It was my daughter's [eighth] birthday," he said. "That's when I arrived home." To his astonishment, Pilar, Georgina, and Alfred were there. Buckmaster and the British Consulate in Barcelona had arranged their Spanish exit visas. George's happiness had a tinge of melancholy as he reflected, "They didn't know me. Five years. That ached." His son, Alfred, at the age of six was seeing his father for the first time in five years. "The thin man with the moustache did scare us kids," he remembered. "In Manresa, we had one photo of father clean-shaven and slightly better nourished. It was years before I really got to know him."

While the Starrs celebrated Christmas, the bureaucracy of military justice ground on in London. On December 28, Buckmaster rose to George's defense in a memo to Colonel Woolrych:

I have formed the impression that the work of WHEELWRIGHT's circuit was only possible thanks to his infinite capacity for taking pains and his very great diplomacy and ready wit. He was easily one of the three most popular Organisers we had.

Woolrych and his staff remained indignant that a Beaulieu-trained officer would order or condone torture. Torture was the policy of the Nazis, whom the Allies planned to prosecute for it after the war. Added to Anne-Marie Walters's accusations ("It was also quite wrong in my opinion to lower ourselves to the standards of the Gestapo . . .") on her return from Algiers, George's Beaulieu lecture generated demands for an official investigation. Buckmaster stepped up his defense of George, writing on December 30 to SOE operations chief Brigadier E. E. Mockler-Ferryman that he had "carefully investigated the charges against Lt. Col. G. R. Starr in connection with the incident of alleged torture of German officers and find quite definitely that the charge is totally unsubstantiated." He added that it was "a travesty of the facts to impute sadism to Col. Starr."

When Walters reported three months earlier that George was responsible for torturing prisoners, F-Section officers decided there was no case to answer. The Beaulieu incident forced their hand. SOE director Major General Colin Gubbins wrote to Mockler-Ferryman on January 5, 1945, that "fairness to Colonel Starr" required SOE to question

Anne-Marie Walters, George's accusers from Beaulieu, and George himself. He added, "Unless this is
done I cannot regard Colonel Starr as being clear of
these allegations which would naturally have an effect upon our putting him forward for any further
employment."

Three days later, Buckmaster wrote another
memo to Mockler-Ferryman in which he referred to
Walters as "an unreliable witness because she suffered from the deluded idea that every man she came
across fell in love with her and she bore a grudge
against Starr because he did not comply." This did
not spare George further scrutiny. On January 20,
Woolrych provided investigators the names of the
fourteen officers who heard George speak about torture on October 30. Most of them would be available to testify.

George was seeking work with MI5, but the allegations against him were delaying his appointment.
As certain of his innocence as Walters and Woolrych were of his guilt, he could clear his name only
in a court of inquiry. He said later:

> Well, I asked for it. Walters had started it. So after
> France, I sent her home. Of course, she never for-
> gave me when she got back. That got to my ears
> when I was back in London, so I said, "Okay,
> bastards, we'll have a court of enquiry."

The court was a gamble. It could restore his reputation or lead to dishonorable discharge and prison. The inquiry commenced on January 26, 1945. The president of the court was Lieutenant Colonel J. W. Munn of the Royal Regiment of Artillery, and its members were Lieutenant Colonel John M. Gray and Major Frank Soskice. A court document stated its terms of reference were to "investigate the conduct and activities of Lieut/Colonel G.R. Starr . . . towards any enemy prisoners that may at any time during the course of the said Mission have been under his control or under control of troops or resistance forces under his immediate command or control." It would also determine whether George "permitted or connived with BURESIE or other persons under the immediate command or control of Lieut/Colonel G.R. Starr, the torture of two German Gestapo agents, namely a man and woman who were proceeding from FRANCE to SPAIN."

At ten o'clock on Monday morning, February 5, 1945, the court convened in the boardroom at SOE headquarters in Norgeby House, Baker Street, London. Although entitled to legal representation, George said, "I opted not to have a defending officer. I can defend myself."

The first witness was Colonel Woolrych, who was sworn in and testified that he had been present at George's talk on October 30. Colonel Starr, he said, had

> told us that on one occasion after D-Day he was out in a car with his Russian bodyguard—the man's name is Buresie—and they met a large German car going southwards. Believing it to contain Germans, they chased it for a number of miles and finally forced it into a ditch. . . . He handed them [the man and woman] over to Buresie for the exaction of torture. . . . The girl, Colonel Starr said, "spoilt it all" by breaking down in the end and asking that her life be spared if not for her sake, then for the child's. The request was refused. The girl said to Colonel Starr, "I thought British officers were gentlemen." He replied, "Well, you have met one who is not."

Woolrych added that the torture involved inserting a pin into the man's penis and hanging him upside down, brutality that outraged Beaulieu's officers. Court member Lieutenant Colonel John Gray asked a question that was not recorded, to which Woolrych answered, "I got the impression from what he said that torture was not repugnant to him."

George, acting as his own counsel, leaped into the cross-examination: "Is it the case that since I had spoken no English for over two years, I used turns of phrase which might have given rise to misunderstanding?" Woolrych replied, "I think it is very unlikely you were misunderstood. Most of my instructors are French-speaking." George's next question was "Is it not the case that my nervous smile, even when recounting unpleasant detail, might have given the impression that I treated these matters lightly?" Woolrych answered, "Yes."

Captain Rhodes, the first to raise concerns about George's speech, was next in the witness box. He repeated Woolrych's account of the evening and added details about the Gestapo couple, "He [Starr] said that as they refused to talk he had them shot and that just prior to being shot the woman appealed to him for mercy on account of her unborn child." Rhodes echoed Woolrych's contention that George's reply to her statement that British officers were gentlemen was "You have met one who is not." Rhodes said George also told them about Buresie "putting a man's legs into a fire and burning them off up to the knees."

These damning indictments from two officers strengthened the case against George. Rhodes took the testimony further, saying, "From the expression of his [Starr's] face, I gather he rather enjoyed it." George cross-examined him, and Rhodes repeated the accusation: "If I had not seen the leering expression on your face, I should not have thought you had taken pleasure in the torture." Sadism was a serious charge. It was bad enough to permit torture in the heat of war, when obtaining information from suspects might have an operational rationale. But perpetrating it for pleasure lacked even a prima facie justification. No one who worked with George in France had ever hinted that he was sadistic, but the judges knew only what was presented in the confines of the court.

George posed a question whose relevance was not obvious to the court but was crucial to his defense: "Didn't I say that at that time I had no uniform?" Rhodes: "I don't remember your doing so."

The third witness was Captain F. Lofts, whose revulsion had compelled him to walk out of George's talk. His testimony supported Woolrych and Rhodes on George's response to the Gestapo woman's plea, adding, "At that stage, I left the mess and heard no more." To a question from court member Major Soskice, Rhodes answered, "My disgust with regard to the story of the woman was only in the fact that she had been shot in spite of her appeal to Colonel Starr for the sake of her unborn child."

Lofts's appearance concluded the first day's proceedings. What happened in the days following is a matter of conjecture. The handwritten record kept by lawyer Sam Silkin, who would later become Britain's attorney general, stopped on page 17 with Lofts's testimony. Pages 18 to 172 went missing from government files. Seven crucial days, from February 6 to 9 and February 12 to 14, included evidence from George's radio operators, Yvonne Cormeau and Lieutenant Dennis Parsons, and New Zealand flight sergeant Leslie Brown. All three had fought beside George during the Battle of Castelnau on June 21. Given the esteem in which they held their former commander, it is likely that their evidence was in his favor.

The surviving transcript resumes at page 173 with the session of Thursday, February 15. Anne-Marie Walters was delivering her concluding remarks, undoubtedly after cross-examination by George. His subsequent statement hinted that his questions were hostile: "Mary [sic] Walters came, and I tied her up in bloody knots. I knew that a defending officer wouldn't know. [Walters said] I'd been torturing people and Christ-what-have-you. It's not in my nature to hurt anybody." His disregard for her was absolute. In the same interview, he called her "unscrupulous" and said, "She was the stupidest bitch, and bitch is the word."

The prosecution was unraveling. Walters's answer to an unspecified question from court member Lieutenant Colonel Gray undermined the case against George:

I didn't write my report [of September 18, 1944] with any intention of making an accusation against Hilaire. I did not know he was not head of the **Maquis,** in spite of the fact that I was his personal courier. I therefore considered him responsible for allowing these tortures. . . . I did mean to say that Hilaire was responsible for not trying to stop the tortures. I wish to stress that I thought he was head of the **Maquis**. . . . I agree that what I said might easily be construed as an accusation against Hilaire. I feel I ought to have been told that Hilaire was not head of the **Maquis** and about administrative changes.

A decisive element in George's defense was that he was no longer in command when the crimes took place. He did not order torture, because he could not order anything. He had ceased to command when the Castelnau and Panjas formations united as the Armagnac Battalion under Parisot. As Parisot's adviser and arms supplier, George had influence but not authority.

Walters stepped down, and George took the stand. He swore to tell the truth. Over three grueling days, he presented his statement and answered the court's questions. His testimony covered more than thirty pages of Silkin's handwritten notes. It was, in essence, the report on his thirty-four months in the field that he had declined to provide Colonel Buckmaster. George's **tour d'horizon** took the court through his life in Castelnau-sur-l'Auvignon, organizing clandestine cells, comrades in arms, intrigues, sabotage, and battles. His thorough abhorrence of torture and mob rule emerged from his many interventions, not to harm people, but to spare them. He mentioned two local miliciens, sons of men he knew, named Caille and Rizon:

> Fearing that summary justice or lynch law would be applied to these men, I had them arrested for their own safety, taking the view that neither the **maquis** nor the FFI had any right to mete out summary justice. . . . I myself interviewed alone the **fils** Rizon. I said to him, "You need not be afraid. I am not here to judge or to punish. I am pointing out to you that you have been misled by Pétain and his propaganda. The real duty of a Frenchman is to fight for his country against our common enemy. . . . I will give you time to think it over. If you are willing to fight and prove yourself a good Frenchman, I will give you the chance to prove you are a good Frenchman and you can join us." . . . After that, I saw Caille, to whom I said exactly the same thing. That night, i.e., 7/8 June, we had a visit from a party belonging to an FTP **maquis** of Lot-et-Garonne (of which I of course had no authority, having never worked for the FTP).

On the evening George made his offer to Caille, June 7, he said that men of the communist FTP stayed overnight in Castelnau. In the morning,

Mayor Larribeau told George they had broken into the church, attacked the prisoners, and loaded them onto a truck, "no doubt to do away with them." George told the court:

> I rushed out and after very heated arguments I persuaded the chief of this FTP party that he was wrong, and he gave me back the prisoners. I remember distinctly that I actually apologized to the prisoners for the treatment they had received. I think this is the incident to which Brown or Parsons referred [in the missing testimony].

He added that saving the miliciens had angered his **maquisards,** but they accepted his argument that their fate was a matter for the courts and not for rough justice. He sent Rizon and Caille, the two miliciens whose families he knew, to serve in another Resistance group, where they fought against the Germans. Friends in France told him later that a French court sentenced Caille to twenty years at hard labor for his earlier Milice service.

George turned to the Spanish contingent under Commander Camilo, whom he praised but who beat a prisoner they had captured. "The prisoner was literally gushing blood out of his nose," George said.

> I had a hell of a row with Camilo and told him that Spanish independence did not mean this

sort of thing in my house. He promised he would not do it again. I would stress the great difficulty of maintaining discipline, because [there] was no means of punishment.

George continued his story from the Battle of Castelnau to his interrogation of the two Gestapo agents. "I wish to point out," he said of the interrogation, "that I was dressed in my normal manner as a **maquisard**, that is, not in British uniform." When the German woman said he was British, he feared that she recognized him from a description the Gestapo had of "Colonel Hilaire." To her comment that she thought he was a British officer and a gentleman, he insisted his response was "You are mistaken for once. I am not a British officer and a gentleman." That was significantly different from his telling her, as the officers from Beaulieu alleged, that he was a British officer who was not a gentleman.

Major Soskice interrupted to ask a question, to which George replied that the woman was about seven months pregnant. "The woman's French was very good," he added. "She said she was German. Her papers said so, and she spoke with a strong German accent." He had heard that the man, but not the woman, had been tortured and both had been executed. He then told the court about the questioning of other German prisoners by Captain Gabriel Termignon. When Termignon battered them,

George "went over to him and in front of everybody told him that that was not the way to treat prisoners of war who were soldiers and were under orders whatever they had done." Later, in liberated Toulouse, he said, he saw many prisoners in FFI custody.

In quite a few cases I intervened to have them released knowing perfectly well they were absolutely innocent and the victims of mass hysteria and vengeance. For example I caused to be released the director of the **Puits de Petrole** [oil wells] **de Saint-Gaudens**.

George turned to the talk at Beaulieu that had led his colleagues to accuse him. He felt they had misunderstood him. The exact words he exchanged with the Gestapo woman proved that he was hiding from her the fact he was a British officer rather than authorizing her mistreatment. His defense hinged on the fact that he was not in charge of the **maquis** when torture took place. When he was able, he had prevented torture. He produced documents proving that control of the **maquis** after the Battle of Castelnau had passed to Captain Parisot and Colonel Ravanel. His concluding words, however, were a defense of his friend Parisot:

I wish to say that Captain Parisot was not only a brave soldier, but a good man for whom I had great admiration. I feel that he would not have allowed any serious misdoings to go on in his **maquis** of which he had knowledge.

The court of inquiry adjourned on February 17 to consider its verdict. Deliberations lasted eleven days, while George Starr's fate and reputation hovered between vindication and disgrace. At last, on February 28, the court announced its decision:

Undoubtedly, Lieutenant Colonel STARR was aware, as a matter of general knowledge, as were other organizers and resistance leaders, that on occasion enemy prisoners were ill-treated and even subjected to torture in various **maquis**. He himself, however, was never party to, nor did he authorize, approve or condone such ill-treatment or the inflicting of torture . . . there is no justification whatsoever for any imputation against Lieutenant Colonel STARR of inhumanity or cruel treatment to any enemy prisoner at any time under his control or under the control of troops or resistance forces under his immediate command or control.

The court went further and condemned George's accusers for slandering him. Of Anne-Marie Walters's statements, it said, "The Court finds that each and every one of these detrimental allegations are wholly and utterly unfounded and false." It criticized Lieutenant Colonel Woolrych for making "serious charges against another officer in unqualified terms encouraging the impression that there was no room for doubt or mistake, when he (as he admits) had made no enquiry of Lieutenant Colonel STARR or anyone else."

The court's decision and robust condemnation of George's accusers amounted not only to his acquittal but to the vilification of everyone who had testified against him. MI5, however, did not hire him as an agent. Its reasons for withholding the appointment went unrecorded, but rumors reaching London about his brother's conduct at 84 avenue Foch may have played a part.

The Nazis commenced the mass executions at Sachsenhausen concentration camp in January 1945. Among the victims of the elimination program were John Starr's Norwegian friends from Strafe Block, who were hanged on February 5. John was the only member of the Strafe Kommando to survive, because he was not living in their block-house when the warders came for them. A German kapo named Jakob, who had served more than ten years in the camp, warned John that the authorities planned to kill him next. His only chance was to leave with French inmates the Germans were evacuating to camps farther east.

As the French prisoners marched through the gates, Jakob advised him, "Slip yourself into that column. This place is no good to you." John smuggled himself into the line of men and onto a waiting train. Squalid boxcars carried 2,500 prisoners for three days, while overcrowding, lack of air, and dehydration killed 800 of them. On February 17, 1,700 men stumbled out of the train at Mauthausen in Austria. Guards whipped them through heavy snow toward the forced labor camp, while Mauthausen's citizens looked away in shame and, John said, "openly wept."

The motto over the camp's entrance left prisoners in no doubt about their fate: **Du Kommst, Niemals Raus**. "You arrive, but never leave." The regime at Mauthausen made Sachsenhausen's barbarity seem mild. John recalled:

> On arriving at the camp, those who were ill were lined up separately and made to undress. It was very cold and they were kept in a state of complete nudity for the whole day. Towards the evening, they were forced, by brutal beatings of truncheons, into the shower baths, where they were made to take a hot shower. After that they were forced in the same way, out into the open again and kept there until well in the night,

still without any clothes. In the early hours of the morning, they were thrust down to the showers again and then made to take a cold shower, which lasted for about half an hour. Again they were brutally urged out into the open, and only a mere handful survived the treatment. The other prisoners, in the meantime, after much brutal handling, were made to take a shower and given a pair of underpants and a vest . . . As befits such a place, all the members of the staff, without exception, were absolute brutes.

John was housed with a thousand other prisoners in one of Number 3 Camp's timber huts. His bed was a plank in the mud floor. Breakfast was warm water, lunch a kind of soup. John, like all his fellow inmates, endured beatings and inhuman abuse. Guards executed prisoners who collapsed on labor details or were too weak to stand at morning roll call. They murdered others for no reason at all.

The killing intensified as winter snows thawed, turning the camp's walkways from ice to mud. With the Third Reich disintegrating, the authorities sought to leave no witnesses to their crimes. In April, however, negotiations involving the Swiss Red Cross, Swedish intermediaries, and Nazi officials led to evacuations of prisoners from many of the camps. At Mauthausen, the Swiss Red Cross took female inmates away in white buses. French and Belgian male prisoners were scheduled to follow. John, as a Briton of American origin, did not qualify for the humanitarian rescue. A French prisoner came to his aid by tearing up his British identity card and replacing it with a forgery stating he was French.

On the day of the French and Belgian evacuation, an SS warder who had been at Sachsenhausen recognized John and said, "But you're not a Frenchman." John replied, "Yes, but in a very short while now the war will be over, and you can help yourself best by saying nothing, and maybe I could put in a good word for you." The guard said nothing. John fell in with the French and Belgian detainees who were boarding a convoy of trucks, and they rolled through the gates. Free at last of their German tormentors, the men sang **La Marseillaise** under the spring sky. Along their route through Austria, villagers offered food to the starving evacuees.

The Red Cross convoy crossed the Swiss border three days later. The men waited in Switzerland for five days until a train came to take them to France. In the first village over the French border, the inhabitants swamped the evacuees with all the wine and food they could spare.

The next day, John staggered off a train in Paris and returned to his apartment in Issy-les-Moulineaux. The concierge let him into the empty flat he had last seen while collecting paintbrushes for his portrait of Major Kieffer. Home at last, he lay on his bed, emaciated, exhausted, and alone.

In the morning, he called on his prewar work-mates at the Agence Yves Alexandre Publicité. They barely recognized the haggard figure who had some-how survived the camps from which most did not return. John then walked to the military attaché's office at the British Embassy in the rue du Faubourg Saint-Honoré. The attaché was out, and an embassy official told him to try the Hotel Bristol a short walk away. In the Bristol bar, British officers gath-ered around their traumatized comrade. His skeletal frame was enough to tell them where he had been. The Intelligence Corps issued him cash and some coupons for a new uniform. John stepped outside into the warming air of a bright spring morning. On his promenade toward the Champs-Élysées, he saw thousands of Parisians waving flags and singing as they streamed through the avenues and boule-vards toward the Arc de Triomphe.

It was May 8, 1945. Germany had just surren-dered.

The next day, John went to Paris's Le Bourget Air-port to fly to England. The plane was full, but the pilot offered to stow him in the cargo hold. John said he was too weak from Mauthausen to make it that way. Hearing "Mauthausen" and seeing John's condition, the pilot seated him in the cockpit and gave him headphones so he could listen to the BBC. As Dover's white cliffs loomed up from the English shore, the BBC played "God Save the King." John could not stop himself from bursting into tears. The ordeal was over. Another was beginning.

F-Section officers met him when he landed and drove him to Tyting House, known as STS 28, near Guildford, Surrey. The seventeenth-century farm was one of SOE's debriefing centers for agents returning from the Continent. His handlers ordered him to write a full report about his experiences in France and Germany. He said he first wanted to see his wife, Michelle, their children, and his parents in Newcastle-under-Lyme. The officers insisted he complete the report before he went anywhere. Unlike his brother, George, he lacked the self-confident bravado to declare he did not write reports. He compromised by dictating a three-page "Rough Report." The truncated account gave highlights of his time in the field and his captivity in Dijon, Paris, and Germany. "During my 11 months there [84 avenue Foch] I had either seen or heard all our agents who were arrested in France," he said. "I am in a position also to relate how long, and how several circuits continued to work long after the arrest of our agents." The suggestion that circuits went on working "after the arrest of our agents" was certain to cause controversy, especially among superior officers he held responsible for succumbing to German deception. He signed the typescript and wrote below his signature, "A full report with all details will take several weeks to write. I realise the necessity of such a report and am only too willing to write it. Nevertheless I do feel that above all, I would like to see my family if only for a few hours first."

John did not leave an account of the family reunion at his parents' house, but years later his daughter, Ethel, had not forgotten it. Her grandmother, also named Ethel, roasted a chicken for her favorite son's return. Young Ethel said her father looked at the bird and, without pausing, ate the whole thing. He did not stay long. Ethel wrote that her father said, "I'm going to see Oncle George in London. I will be back soon." The brothers met in London, but no record of the encounter survived. Each Starr had experienced a different war. George's had been the excitement of field work and liberation. John's was betrayal, torture, compromise, and isolation. John recounted in his postwar letters the brothers' enduring friendship and mutual loyalty. Each always rose to the defense of the other.

After seeing George in London, John returned to STS 28 in Surrey and wrote a lengthy document that he said included everything he knew about Germany's penetration of F-Section and the sacrifice of agents parachuted into German hands. His candid account, as well as many subsequent debriefs, described his work for Major Kieffer and Ernest Vogt. He maintained that his cooperation had enabled him to learn everything that he nearly escaped with to London in November 1943.

He submitted the report to the War Office, which claimed to be satisfied with it. SOE's only comment came from F-Section's formidable intelligence chief, Vera Atkins, when John called at her office in Orchard Court: "There were some quite amusing things in your report." He waited to hear more, but it was as if he had never written it.

Suspicion of John Starr was mounting within the halls of SOE. A "NOTE ON CAPTAIN J.A. STARR'S INTERROGATION" stated, "Certain rumours had been current with regard to his conduct which, if true, might justify his being classified as a renegade." Other captured SOE agents who survived their detention were bringing stories back to England about "Bob" at avenue Foch, a man at ease in German company, enjoying privileges and wearing comfortable civilian dress.

No one told John about the accusations until he chanced upon the brothers Alfred and Henry Newton in a Soho pub frequented by former agents. The Newtons had trained with him at Wanborough Manor and saw him at avenue Foch. Like John, they had endured the concentration camps and were lucky to survive. The brothers told him, "When we got back we were told that none of us was to speak to you if we met you." John asked why, and they said they didn't know. "But," they added, "your word is good enough for us."

The Newton brothers, unknown to John, had been among his accusers. One SOE report stated that they were "extremely critical [of John], yet, on the other hand, agents of higher standing and experience, such as [Peter] Churchill and [Maurice] Southgate, saw nothing particular to criticise in STARR's conduct and are unlikely to go further than to say he was not as clever as he thought he was."

Henry Newton's statement to SOE implied that John had helped the Germans to deal with other prisoners. On May 2, he told a debriefer that John had said to him at avenue Foch, "Do not lead them up the gun. It is quite useless to do so. They know everything." The debriefer acknowledged that neither of the Newtons believed John had betrayed them: "The brothers had been operating under the name of NORMAN, and so far as they are aware, STARR never gave away their real name, or said anything that he knew about them."

Peter Churchill defended his old comrade during questioning on May 21. Churchill, here called "source," referred to John as "Emile," his code name during their time together in Cannes:

Asked his opinion about EMILE, source said that he thinks EMILE is perfectly innocent. So far as source knows he gave away no information about him (source) or his organisation. The explanation of EMILE's presence at the Avenue Foch may well be the German vanity and love of having their portraits painted, and photographs taken. If EMILE, under interrogation, had said he was an artist, source thinks it quite likely that the Germans might have suggested to him that he should come and paint pictures of them at the Avenue Foch.

As the investigation into John's conduct proceeded, testimony from French collaborators awaiting trial in France weighed against him. However, the statements of men and women in Parisian prisons contained too many mistakes to be reliable. One accuser was Pierre Bony, a former policeman who had worked with a criminal named Henri Lafont in the Bony Lafont Gang doing the Gestapo's dirtiest work in Paris against Jews and **résistants**. He had never met John but claimed he was:

Devoted to the German cause, his role consisted in taking morse messages from London and sending them out. . . . Gifted with prodigious memory, he was able to reproduce by pencil drawings, the portraits of English and French agent [sic] whom he knew, which enabled the person wanted to be identified at first sight.

A note on Bony's affidavit cautioned, "This statement was made by a man who was at the time on trial for his life, and therefore cannot be regarded as reliable. Source has since been executed."

Kieffer's chauffeur and odd-job man, Michel Bouillon, also testified from a prison cell: "When he [John Starr] got to Paris, he told them all he knew, helped with the messages, identified agents, and in fact worked with them a great deal." Bouillon claimed that he and John were "like brothers." One incredible assertion was that he had assisted John's escape, but the story did not stand up. Bouillon said John fled alone from avenue Foch, with no mention of Noor Inayat Khan and Léon Faye. "STARR was discovered on the roof," he added, although the SD had captured John inside the mansion next door. Bouillon also claimed to have been waiting in Josef Placke's car to drive John to Gibraltar. Like Pierre Bony, he was executed for treason soon after making his statement.

The cleaner from avenue Foch, Rose Marie Holwedts, also testified from prison while awaiting trial. "She was particularly bitter about Bob STARR," British lieutenant colonel Warden wrote from Paris. She claimed that John betrayed both Maurice Southgate and Noor Inayat Khan, although Southgate himself denied it and Noor's attempt to escape with John demonstrated her trust in him.

The prima facie evidence against John Starr

grew, but it amounted to nothing. Lieutenant Colonel E.J.P. Cussen of MI5 wrote to Lieutenant Colonel T. G. Roche on July 4, 1945:

> Many thanks for your letter of June 13th, with which were enclosed in a folder STARR's own report as to his activities on the Continent, your Department's interrogation report, a note of your interrogator's impressions and extracts from certain relevant interrogations of other of your agents. . . .
>
> You say: "I am doubtful whether any Court Martial would feel able to reach that degree of certainty necessary for conviction. . . ."
>
> I respectfully agree with the conclusion to which you have come. I note that you do not propose to advise your Department to initiate any action against STARR.
>
> It might be a very bad thing if it were to be thought among prospective agents that any efforts to double-cross the enemy after capture were tolerably likely to result in a trial by Court-Martial upon their return.

F-Section intelligence officer Vera Atkins nonetheless insisted, "We feel he let the side down. And he was the only one who did."

John's chance meeting in Soho with the Newton brothers led to a commercial partnership. The three men, having grown up with show business parents, opened a nightclub in Hanley, Staffordshire. The venture failed though, in no small part because the concentration camps had traumatized them all. Alfred Newton had, in the words of British MP Dennis Walters to Parliament, "suffered appalling treatment following their capture and he consequently receives a 100 per cent. disability pension and has received the maximum in compensation paid to any individual out of the fund for victims of Nazi persecution."

John Starr eventually moved with his wife and children back to Paris. They resettled in their Issy-les-Moulineaux flat, where John had rescued his wife's pots and pans from the Germans. Resuming his career as a commercial artist with Agence Yves Alexandre Publicité, John sought nothing more than to leave the war behind. It would not be easy.

On July 19, 1945, Britain awarded Lieutenant Colonel George Starr the Distinguished Service Order to add to his Military Cross and the French Croix de Guerre. France, despite George's confrontation with General de Gaulle, also conferred on him the Medal of the Resistance and the Legion of Honor. The United States granted him the Medal of Freedom with Silver Palm. His war had ended with distinction, and he went on to rebuild some of what the war had destroyed by reorganizing the German coal industry in the British zone of occupation. As a former miner and mining engineer, he was the right man for the job.

George took up residence outside Essen at Villa Hügel, the palatial country mansion of the German industrialist Krupp family, arms makers for all their country's modern wars. Living with him in the villa's nearly three hundred rooms above the River Ruhr were scores of other British male officers. The only woman on the staff was Yvonne Cormeau. Cormeau, recalled her daughter, "was responsible for running the domestic side of the house."

George was at Villa Hügel on August 15, V-J Day, when Japan surrendered. Unable to celebrate the end of the Second World War with Pilar and the children in England, he wrote a letter to his eight-year-old daughter, Georgina Ethel Margarita Starr:

15.8.45

My Dear Georgina,

Your Daddy is thinking of you all the time, especially so on this great day in the History of the World. In your short life you have known only about war. Now it is over and God willing you will only know Peace for the rest of a very long and happy life.

Later you will remember that in order that you and all the other children of your generation might live in peace and freedom, your Mother and myself as well as all the other Mothers and Fathers have made great sacrifices, and have missed many years of happiness.

My dear Georgina as you grow to be a woman, you will realise what these last years have cost your Mother.

You will always look upon your Mother as the most wonderful lady in the world, always follow her advice and love and cherish her always. Be proud of your mother, my child.

You have not known your Daddy much; but in the future you will know him much more. You will find him to be just an ordinary sort of person, but a person who will always be by your side to help and guide you, have confidence in me, I shall never let you down.

I want you to keep this letter so that as you grow up, you can read it from time to time.

I will give you one golden rule for all your life:

"Do unto others as you would have them do unto you."

> Au revoir Georgina
> All my love & kisses,
> Daddy

A short time later, George wrote another letter. It asked Colonel Buckmaster why F-Section treated his brother, John, differently from other returning agents and why John had received no decorations. Buckmaster did not reply.

The government officially disbanded SOE on January 15, 1946, although the organization had a short second life as the Special Operations Branch of MI6 until the new Labour government of Prime Minister Clement Attlee liquidated it later in the year.

SIXTEEN

Starrs on Trial

In no other department of war did so much
courage pass unnoticed.

MAURICE BUCKMASTER

═══

With the end of the war came the reckoning. The Allies established tribunals to prosecute those who had perpetrated war crimes and crimes against humanity. The most notable were the Nuremberg Trials, whose chief British prosecutor, Hartley Shawcross, wrote:

At Nuremberg the Defendants, the leaders of Nazi Germany, were charged not only as common murderers, as they all were, but also with the crime of aggressive war. It is the crime of war which is at once the object and the parent of the other crimes: the crimes against humanity, the war crimes, the common murders.

The trials of some of the Nazi "common murderers" took place at Wuppertal, Germany, in March 1947. It may have been less significant than the prosecution of men who had massacred millions at Auschwitz, Treblinka, and the other death camps, but it represented an important precedent for both the Allied military and international law. The premeditated killing of five SAS commandos by the Sicherheitsdienst on August 8, 1944, near Noailles, France, could not be left unpunished. The British owed it to their personnel in uniform and future combatants needed to know that there were sanctions for murdering captured soldiers.

Former SS Major Hans Josef Kieffer was one of the defendants. The others were his superior, Helmut Knochen, and some of the men Kieffer had commanded, including Richard Schnurr and Karl Haug. Kieffer's counsel, Dr. Lauterjung, based his client's defense on the fact that he had merely relayed Knochen's command to kill the British soldiers. Kieffer maintained, "I had to obey because the whole affair took place during the time after the attempt on Hitler's life, when every opposition was impossible. . . . If I had refused, I would not have survived the prisoners."

Dr. Lauterjung asked John Starr to come to Wuppertal and testify on Kieffer's behalf. Although John knew nothing about the SAS victims, he could attest to Kieffer's humane treatment of SOE prisoners at avenue Foch. He flew to Wuppertal in northwest Germany on March 12, the last day of Kieffer's trial. He rode to the tribunal through the battered city, where Allied bombardment had killed more than 25,000 civilians and left another 350,000 homeless. It was two o'clock when he arrived at the court. He took the stand a half hour later, following the massacre's two survivors, Serge Vaculik and Thomas Jones, who testified for the prosecution. Unlike them, he was there to save the life of the man who had spared his. Dr. Lauterjung asked for his sworn statement. John said:

I know the accused Kieffer and identify him. I knew him at 84 Avenue Foch. I was his prisoner. He treated me very well indeed. The food I received was the same as that of my guards. Other prisoners at the Avenue Foch were treated in the same way. My good treatment did not change after I had tried to escape. Kieffer often distributed chocolate and cigarettes to the prisoners. I gave Kieffer my word of honour that I would not escape again as long as I was at the Avenue Foch. After that, my door was not locked any longer. From his behavior, I do not think that he would take part in the deliberate murder of British prisoners.

The court adjourned. Two hours later, Serge Vaculik remembered, the justices returned. The president of the court addressed Kieffer, "The court martial at Wuppertal has found you guilty of wilful murder against the persons of five British soldiers and condemns you to death by hanging." When Kieffer's sentence was translated into German, Vaculik wrote, "Kieffer's eyelids blinked, but he did not falter." A guard ordered, "Right turn! Quick march!" Vaculik watched Kieffer march out, "his head held high and his face and neck as red as ever." John was also watching Kieffer, who paused, looked at his former prisoner, and bowed his head.

Kieffer wrote an appeal for clemency: "Even to-day I feel innocent before God, Christ and my conscience, because I was not aware of the illegality of the order given to me." He asked the court to reduce his sentence to imprisonment "in view of my three minor children who, since the death of my wife 18 months ago, are without a mother." The court denied his request. The British executioner hanged Kieffer, along with Schnurr and Haug, at the prison of Hamelin on June 26, 1947. The court commuted the death sentence of Helmut Knochen, overall commander of the massacre, reducing his sentence to life, then to twenty years. He served fifteen.

The past pursued John Starr to Paris, where French investigators were reviving the case that the British had abandoned. Denunciations came from French former inmates of 84 avenue Foch, who remembered a well-dressed Englishman fraternizing with the enemy. Former SD officials Dr. Josef Goetz, Josef Placke, and Werner Ruehl added German voices to the chorus of recrimination. Over a period of more than one year, policemen of the **Direction de la Surveillance Territoire** (DST) at 13 rue des Saussaies in Paris interviewed witnesses. Placke told a police inspector on April 1, 1946, that John "was completely all right about working with us. He helped our service strongly in the transmission of messages to London." His tales of John accompanying him to a Paris restaurant and on outings to the field sounded to the investigators like collaboration.

Dr. Goetz was even less helpful to John during his interrogation on December 13:

> It was he [John Starr] who corrected certain mistakes in my spelling, in editing, who let me know the correct way to edit a technical message . . . he enjoyed a certain liberty, returning to his cell on the fifth floor every night.

His account of John's cooperation in drawing maps and organizational charts for Major Kieffer constituted evidence for a potential prosecution. But, Goetz admitted, John had provided no useful information and betrayed no colleagues.

John drove to the rue des Saussaies the same day. Police Superintendent René Gouillaud asked him about his childhood, marriage, and prewar life before moving on to his missions for SOE in France. Subsequent questions dwelled on his eleven months at avenue Foch. John admitted drawing maps of "Gaullist and Giraudist organisations." Yes, he had gone to Saint-Quentin with Josef Placke "to assist in an S-Phone operation" and on other trips. The strongest factor in his favor was the attempt to escape with Léon Faye and Noor Inayat Khan in November 1943. The examiners, who did not appear hostile, kept a record of his responses.

The process resumed on January 6, 1948, again at the DST bureau in rue des Saussaies. John answered more questions from Superintendent Gouillaud about his relationship with Placke, who had lured SOE and Resistance personnel to their deaths. "It's true that I went out on several outings with PLACKE," John again admitted, "but never in his service." He elaborated on his dinner with Placke in the restaurant, adding that "he took me another time to an apartment where he had a housewarming." He denied assisting the **Funkspiel:** "I never took part in their editing or their transmissions, as he [Placke] seems to claim." And he protested against Dr. Goetz's assertion that he had "corrected certain mistakes in my spelling, in editing":

> To tell the truth, I never worked for Goetz. Only, it happened that he called me to his bureau on different occasions and asked me to correct certain spelling in messages sent or received. For him, at his instruction, I received messages from the BBC; but if I had not done it, the Germans would have had it anyway, because during the broadcast times, there were six or seven radios for listening . . . I repeat, I never drew likenesses of agents that I knew. I knew very few of them at the time and I could not have done it.

Two days later, John was back in the chair at rue des Saussaies. Superintendent Gouillaud asked about the period before his arrest. He wanted to know about Pierre Martin, the Frenchman who had betrayed John. John told him what he remembered about the double agent whom the Resistance assassinated. He continued with the long tale of the torture he endured in Dijon, his experiences at Fresnes and avenue Foch, and, finally, the ordeal of the concentration camps.

The next witness, ten days later, was Werner

Ruehl. The former corporal stated that John had made "a tour of inspection in the region of Le Mans to find objectives and emplacements that we could use in the radio game as possible sites for demolition." Ruehl thought that John, who "had been sent to France to undertake sabotage," was qualified to serve as "our expert" in convincing London that the sham "Resistance" was blowing up bridges and rail lines.

Evidence from Placke, Goetz, and Ruehl, alongside John's own admissions, were tipping the scales against him. In June, investigators questioned the German who knew John best, Ernest Vogt. Vogt had been on the move for nearly four years. "Following our retreat from Paris in August 1944," he wrote, "we brought one [radio] link with us, and we fruitfully continued our transmissions with London from Nancy, then from Offenburg, from Freiburg . . . and then from the shore of Lake Constance." When the war ended, he went into hiding. He was working in a dairy on May 29, 1946, when the American Army tracked him down. It took the Americans a year to determine that they had no case against him. They passed him to the British, who incarcerated him for three months before returning him to the Americans. The new government of West Germany took charge of him and confined him at Dachau camp until it issued his Certificate of Denazification. Western intelligence services attempted to recruit him, as they did many other German spies, but he declined.

He returned to France seeking the release of his wife from French detention. On June 19, 1948, he answered questions about John Starr:

As far as I know BOB only corrected the text of the transmissions devised by Dr. GOETZ so that it was not known that they were German translations . . . so far as I know, BOB did not devise the texts himself, but only corrected those that Dr. GOETZ gave him. . . . As far as I know BOB never denounced any members of the "French Section" Organisation nor any members of any other organisation or resistance movement. Nobody was captured owing to a statement or denunciation of BOB's as far as I know. BOB always declared to me that he would never become an agent or informer of our Dienststelle [Department] and on no account would denounce anyone else.

The French informed London about the investigation and requested corroboration. The British complied, but they were unenthusiastic about bringing the case to trial. A senior officer in Military Operations at the War Office wrote to Miss J. Russell King of MI5 on September 28, 1948, "I, too, hope that the STARR case may peter out—certainly the present testimony does not provide a very hopeful basis for a successful prosecution, but, as you say, the processes of French justice are unpredictable."

The DST weighed the pros and cons of **l'affaire Starr** and came to no conclusion. They turned his dossier over to the Permanent Military Tribunal of Paris. The tribunal studied the evidence and, on December 13, 1948, officially indicted Captain John Ashford Renshaw Starr under Article 75 of the Penal Code for "intelligence with the enemy." The maximum penalty was death.

The case fell to a conscientious young officer named Captain J. Mercier, described by one British observer as "tall, blond, very smart." Mercier cast a wide net, seeking evidence in France, England, and Germany. As **juge d'instruction**, investigating judge, his role was not that of prosecutor so much as adjudicator. His word would determine whether John had to face a French court-martial and, possibly, the guillotine.

Mercier requested a character assessment of John from the local gendarmerie in Issy-les-Moulineaux. The response, dated December 23, 1948, affirmed that "his conduct and morality are excellent. To our knowledge he has no prior history [i.e., criminal record]."

The interrogations and examination of documents proceeded throughout 1949. In the midst of the investigation, John acquired an unexpected ally in the person of British author Jean Overton Fuller. Fuller was writing a biography of her friend and London neighbor, Noor Inayat Khan, whom the Germans had murdered in Dachau. Vera Atkins, F-Section's former intelligence officer, told Fuller that John had been at the avenue Foch when Khan was imprisoned there. Not knowing how to contact him, she put Fuller in touch with George Starr in Brussels. George sent her his brother's address in Paris. Fuller wrote to John, and on September 14, 1949, she met him, along with his wife, Michelle, at home in Issy-les-Moulineaux.

John told her all he could remember about Khan, her courage at avenue Foch, and their near escape. He mentioned the **Funkspiel,** but he warned Fuller that the former SOE officials assisting with her biography might disown her if she wrote about Germany's successful deception of SOE. Back in London, Fuller saw Colonel Buckmaster to discuss Khan. Toward the end of the interview, she asked, "What do you think of Starr?"

The vehemence of Buckmaster's answer startled her: "Nothing! After he'd been taken by the Gestapo, he did everything they asked him for a year! . . . Well, almost everything." Fuller defended her new friend. Buckmaster conceded that John probably gave no information to the Germans, but he wondered why he had not tried to escape with Khan and Faye. "But he did," she said.

As Fuller recalled the conversation, he responded,

"You've only got his word for that. And that's worth nothing." A moment later, he added, "I never trusted him from the beginning."

John was convinced that F-Section's former staff had a vendetta against him, because his report had revealed their mortal errors. The report he gave the War Office disappeared, and he was convinced that SOE had suppressed rather than lost it. But that was not germane to his case in France.

At ten in the morning on November 15, 1949, John reported to the headquarters of the Permanent Military Tribunal in its barracks at 20 rue de Reuilly in Paris. Captain Mercier told him he was entitled to a lawyer but John, like his brother at the court of inquiry in England, believed in his innocence so strongly that he declared, "I do not deem it necessary to have the presence of an attorney, and I am ready now to answer all your questions." The interrogation was brief, running a mere two typed pages. John corrected minor errors in documents Mercier presented to him relating to the degree of movement he enjoyed at avenue Foch and his cooperation with the SD. "It is necessary," he said, "to understand that I made it appear I was working for them, and that in reality I worked there, but with the exclusive intention of learning everything they knew about our organization."

Mercier showed him Ernest Vogt's statement and asked for his response. John read it and said,

VOGT confirms what I told you. I rendered to the Germans little, inoffensive services. I denounced no one. I gave no useful information on either the transmissions of messages or the organization of French-Section. . . . I am convinced that I always acted loyally.

Captain Mercier located two of John's cellmates from Fresnes, Jean-Claude Comert and Jean Argence. Both confirmed everything John had told him about their discussion over whether John should cooperate with the SD at avenue Foch in order to gather information. Comert testified on November 22 to the tribunal that they had discussed German infiltration of British operations in France and London's dispatch of weapons to the SD. Comert added, "He [John Starr] confided at the time that there was treason that was so well organized that he thought it must have originated in London."

The next day, Mercier wrote to the French ambassador in London, René Massigli. He outlined the case and hinted at doubts about John: "He pretends that his services were never anything but of a purely material character with no chance of harming Allied interests and that his functions permitted him to understand what the Germans knew about the British networks with a view to alerting the Allied services so they could stop it." Mercier admitted a troubling aspect of the case, "It seems difficult to hang the honor and an eventual penal sentence on a British officer [based] on German testimony. . . ." He asked the ambassador, "in the absence of direct testimony, French or Allied" that John had betrayed F-Section, to ask Colonel Buckmaster whether John's actions had harmed his organization. The tribunal's file contains no response from Buckmaster.

The British Consulate in Paris advised John to leave the country. He refused, explaining to Fuller, "If I were to leave the country now, with a thing like this pending, I should never be able to show my face again either here or anywhere else in the world."

The investigation dragged into the new year. Mercier achieved a breakthrough on January 3, 1950, when he went to 84 avenue Foch in order, he wrote, "to reconstruct in its location the attempted escape made by Captain STARR accompanied by Colonel FAYE and 'MADELEINE' [Noor Inayat Khan]." The Germans had executed Khan on September 13, 1944, at Dachau and Faye in Sonnenberg on January 30, 1945. John was the escape's only survivor, and Mercier needed more than his word for what happened. Mercier went to the former SD headquaters with John, Jean Overton Fuller, and his lawyer adjutant. As they drove into the broad expanse of the avenue Foch, John blurted, "Avenue Boche!"

They rang the bell of number 84 and went inside. The fourth and fifth floors had become a separate maisonette, whose owner allowed them to make an inspection. There had been changes since the German departure, a new door where a wall had been, and a wall in the once familiar corridor between the guardroom and the lavatory. John described the old layout and guided the others through the scene of his drama. Mercier wrote, "Captain STARR showed us the room that served as his cell and also the cells that held Colonel FAYE and 'MADELEINE' and the clear skylights lighting the rooms and by which the three detainees left to meet one another on the roof." The iron bars that John, Faye, and Khan had struggled to remove were gone. Jean Overton Fuller recalled:

> Starr took us into the guardroom. . . . Starr had become really alive now, even excited, darting here and there with great interest, in search of things he had known before as keen as a terrier sniffing holes. . . . Starr showed us the basin under which they had hidden the notes and the screwdriver, and we bent down and put our fingers into the crevice.

The party went to 9-bis Square du Bois de Boulogne, the adjoining house where the would-be escapees had broken in and where the SD captured John and Khan. "Look!" said John. "They haven't even put a new pane in the window we broke." A strip of corrugated iron filled the hole where Faye had smashed the glass to enter the building. Mercier wrote, "The proprietress, Madame ESMERIAN, allowed us to go to the roof and Captain STARR showed us his route." Fuller wrote four years afterward that Esmerian exclaimed:

Why, it was you who broke into my house one night during the war! You were sitting with a young lady on a couch in the room on the first floor when I came down and saw you. I asked you if you were thieves, and then I saw the lady was crying and realised that you must be prisoners who had escaped from the Avenue Foch.

Mercier, however, in his report dated the same day, stated that Madame Esmerian "did not recognize Captain STARR but did recall the arrest in her house of a man and a woman, then that another man (Colonel FAYE) went out of the building and had been shot by rifle fire." While Fuller's and Mercier's recollections disagreed on whether Madame Esmerian recognized John, they concurred that the physical evidence supported John's version of events.

Mercier continued his inquiries, which included more meetings with John. He told John that he had asked Colonel Buckmaster for information about him. He had not received Buckmaster's reply. John said, "I don't think you will."

There was no formal court session in which John,

as his brother had had in England, confronted his accusers. Under the French system, Mercier sifted the evidence, studied it, took his time, and recalled witnesses for additional testimony in order to arrive at a judgment. John had been waiting since December 13, 1948, when the tribunal indicted him, for exoneration or court-martial. On June 19, 1950, Captain Mercier finally issued his decision.

Mercier's office mailed it to John, who received it a week later, on June 27. The **Ordonnance de Non-Lieu** declared that "there is no case to pursue against the above named."

Jean Overton Fuller returned to Paris that day and called on Captain Mercier, who told her, "I do believe that Starr is a very good, very loyal and devoted Englishman. And he loves France too." Though his name was cleared, suspicion among some colleagues that he had collaborated followed him for the rest of his life.

Jean Overton Fuller later pursued SOE's failures in a series of books. Vera Atkins wrote to her on July 17, 1954, "It is, of course, true that London made mistakes and in war mistakes involve the lives of men and women." But Buckmaster never admitted that the SD's **Funkspiel** succeeded in deceiving him, writing in his memoir, "We could not afford to risk our men being betrayed, and we severed contact with all wireless operators and section heads who seemed to us to be suspect."

Neither Vera Atkins nor Colonel Buckmaster thanked John Starr for exposing those mistakes.

When George met Buckmaster in London, he demanded an answer to the question he had posed in his letter months earlier. Why had his brother been denied awards for his war service? Buckmaster answered, "You have quite enough decorations yourself to suffice for one family."

George never returned to southwest France, although veteran **résistants** invited him to attend commemorations and reunions. "You've got to think about it this way," he said. "I didn't liberate the southwest of France. The French did. Why should I go poking my nose in?" He died in Senlis, France, on September 2, 1980, aged seventy-four. John, after divorcing Michelle, married again and retired to Switzerland. He was eighty-eight years old when he died there in 1996.

After the war, the people of Castelnau rebuilt their stone hamlet as it was before the SS demolished it. They renamed the central square place Roger Larribeau for the mayor who had befriended the foreigner called "Gaston le Belge" and sacrificed all he owned to liberate his country. On June 21, 2016, Jeanne Robert, by that time aged

102, attended the annual remembrance of the Battle of Castelnau in the village that had given her a home during the dark years of occupation. At the ceremony, the French government promoted her to Chevalier of the Legion of Honor. She died fifteen months later, the last veteran of the **Réseau Victoire,** out of which George Starr created a legendary Resistance army that drove the German occupiers out of Gascony.

At Madame Delattre's old school, they were still teaching children the story of "Colonel Hilaire."

ACKNOWLEDGMENTS

On completion of my previous Second World War book, **The Deserters: A Hidden History of World War II,** I decided to write about combatants who fought in darkness, away from comrades, on their own behind enemy lines, living by their wits. My friend Colonel Tim Spicer, a Falklands War veteran who served in Britain's Scots Guards Regiment, suggested I look at the career of the late Anthony Brooks. In 1942 at the age of twenty, Brooks became the youngest agent that SOE F-Section sent into occupied France. His career, mentioned in these pages, was spectacular even by SOE standards for the ingenuity and success of his sabotage operations and his survival of Gestapo interrogation to return to the field. I researched Brooks's eventful life in France and during the postwar era with British intelligence. This led me to historian Mark Seaman, who had worked on SOE at the Foreign Office and the Imperial War Museum. When we met, Seaman informed me that he was completing his own biography of Brooks. Seaman had exclusive access to Brooks's personal papers to add to his professional acquaintance with SOE lore. He mitigated my dejection by asking whether I had heard of the Starr brothers. That was the genesis of this book, for which I thank Tim Spicer and Mark Seaman.

Without the assistance and encouragement of countless friends, colleagues, relations, hosts, hostesses, researchers, and editors, I would not have been able to complete this book. I owe the greatest debt to my gallant agent, Ed Victor, who recognized from the moment I mentioned the Starr brothers saga that their story needed telling. Moreover, he gave moral and editorial support throughout the research and writing. He was reading the final draft two days before he—to the dismay of clients, friends, and family alike—died. Charlie Brotherstone of Ed's literary agency took over from the master to see this book through to publication. I am grateful to him and his agency colleagues Edina Imrick, Linda Van, Hitesh Shah, Georgina Le Grice, and Burt Salvary. Ed Victor, among his other fine qualities, left behind a first-class team to carry on his work.

The strenuous exertions of two formidable women proved invaluable: Parisian researcher Lisa Vapné and my editor at Penguin Press, Ann Godoff. Among Mlle. Vapné's dogged accomplishments was leading me to local archives throughout Gascony, to which **résistants** and **résistantes** left their memoirs, diaries, and correspondence. This treasure trove of information informs this book as much as the documents in the national archives of Paris, London, and Washington. She introduced me to George Starr's wartime collaborator, Jeanne Robert, in her retirement home near Bordeaux and participated fully in our discussion. She also put me in touch with the mayor of Castelnau, Maurice Boison; local historians Alain Geay, president of the Association des Amis du Réseau Victoire; and Jacqueline Geay. Thanks to her, I also met Robert Darroux. Aged twelve in 1943, he began assisting his father, local café proprietor Joseph Darroux, in Resistance actions with George Starr, and he shared many amusing reminiscences. These French people, of whom their country can be proud, spent hours in the mayor's office telling me about George Starr, Yvonne Cormeau, Anne-Marie Walters, Roger Larribeau, and the other heroes and heroines of this tale.

Ann Godoff, who demonstrated her faith in this saga from the moment Ed Victor presented it to her, kept a close eye on its progress. When I submitted the first draft in the form of an overlong manuscript, she forced me to turn it from a scholarly account of the Starr brothers' activities into the taut tale of ambiguity, romance, and danger that it needed to be. Her meticulous editing, redolent of publishing's Golden Age, compels me to acknowledge her as not only an editor, but as a coauthor. The differences I had along the way with both Lisa and Ann merit apologies, which I offer them here, while thanking them for all they did.

It would be remiss of me not to single out David Hewson, historian of SOE in the Gers and former Household Cavalry officer with whom I share a love of Ireland's Blackwater Valley, for his advice, expertise, contacts, and fact-checking. Without his assistance, this book would contain egregious errors and lack stories that his sources provided. He put me in touch with David Harrison, another SOE authority whose wise counsel guided me much of the way, and whose expertise far outweighs my own. Both Davids gave generously of their time and knowledge.

I must also offer profound thanks to Jeanne Robert, who gave me hours of her time to tell me about life in Castelnau-sur-l'Auvignon with George Starr. Her energy and enthusiasm were boundless, despite her advanced years and the recent loss of her daughter, Michèle. I am grateful as well to members of the Starr family for weeding out errors in the manuscript, providing photographs and letters, and giving insights into the characters of both brothers: George Starr's son, Alfred Starr; his grandson, David Cochu; and John Starr's daughter, Ethel Starr Lagier. This book would not have been possible without them.

Thanks must go also to an old friend, Rupert Scott, for guiding me through the old training grounds at Beaulieu, Hampshire, where the Starrs and nearly three thousand other SOE agents studied, and to Beaulieu's archivist, Sue Tomkins. Phil Tomaselli assisted me through the labyrinth of SOE files at the British National Archives in Kew, which he knows better than anyone else living. He was unfailing in his assiduous determination to root out every detail of the Starr story. I must also thank researchers Stephen Kippax, Steven Tyas, and R. W. O'Hara for their help.

Others to whom I owe debts are my old friends and colleagues Jonathan Randal, Sarah Helm, and Allan Massie, as well as SOE specialists Elspeth Forbes-Robertson, Paul McCue, Noreen Riols, Anne Whiteside, Yvette Pitt, and Rosy Frier. In Paris, I am thankful to Eliza Peynel and Marcello Simonetta. My gratitude extends to Francis J. Suttill, son of SOE organizer Major Francis Suttill and author of a fascinating biography of his father, **Shadows in the Fog**. In London, I owe Lauren Smith a debt for the hours she spent printing, without complaint, scans of thousands of archival documents.

Archivists in Britain and France made valuable contributions: Neil Cobbett of the British National Archives; Madame Rey at the Archives Départementales du Gers in Auch; Amelia Briaris of the Imperial War Museum Research Room in London; Julie Baffet and the rest of the staff at the Musée de la Résistance Nationale in Champigny-Sur-Marne; Daniel

Korachi-Alaoui, archives assistant at the Canterbury Cathedral Archives; Chantal Pagès of the Archives Départementales de Haute-Garonne; Claire Landais, Direction des Affaires Juridiques, Ministry of Defense, Paris; Belgian Diplomatic Archives Documentalist Didier Amaury; and Priscilla de Schaetzen of the Belgian Embassy, London. I am grateful also to the directors and staffs at the Centre d'Etude et de Recherche de la Résistance Toulousaine; the Comité de Résistance pour l'Histoire de la Libération de Toulouse et de sa Région; the Archives du Comité d'Histoire de la Seconde Guerre Mondiale; the Amicale du Réseau Hilaire-Buckmaster au Mairie de Losse in les Landes; and the Service Historique de la Défense, Paris.

Anyone who has lived and worked in France cannot help but come up against the occasional obstinacy and obstructiveness of its bureaucracy. Some of my research met with the determined resistance of certain officials to releasing documents that belonged in the public domain. Without the strong intervention of a French former journalist and ex-spokesman of the Defense Ministry, Pierre Bayle, the Ministry of Defense would not have released records of the investigation into charges of collaboration against John Starr. The ministry held out for five years before releasing seventy-year-old files that mentioned no living persons and posed no national security is-

ACKNOWLEDGMENTS

sues. I am grateful to Pierre Bayle for achieving what French friends called a "miracle."

I would like also to thank the directors and staff of the Special Forces Club, London, for granting me access to their extensive library and other facilities. The members of the Special Operations Executive Yahoo! group were informative with their many posts on almost every aspect of SOE operations.

Anarchic conditions in the Provençal village where I bought a house in which to write left me unable to work in peace. Official indifference was a reminder of the behavior of much of the French establishment during the occupation, actions that were redeemed by the courage of a then unpopular minority. That and my peripatetic life left me at times dependent on the kindness of, not strangers, but good friends. Many made me welcome in their country houses to write out of season and undisturbed. They are Chris Whittle and Priscilla Rattazzi-Whittle in East Hampton, New York, whose hospitality knew no bounds and whose generosity was unlimited; John and Ania Borrell at Kania Lodge, Sytna Góra, Kartuzy, Poland, the most beautiful site imaginable to retreat from a troubled world; Barone Alessandro and Baronessa Caterina de Renzis at Castello Sonnino, Montespertoli, Italy, whose fine wines and good humor made writing a pleasure; Natasha Grenfell, who afforded me a brief stay near the beach in

ACKNOWLEDGMENTS

Hampshire, England; and Rupert and Vanessa Fairfax at their superb spread in Lincolnshire, England, where I passed many happy hours in their company and from which they kindly took me to the races nearby. All of my hosts and hostesses were unfailingly tolerant, generous, and gracious, and my hope is one day to repay them in kind, somewhere.

While exploring the Gers, I stayed at the Lacassagne Maison d'Hotes in Larressingle. Its proprietress, Maïder Papelorey, provided me with the excellent Gascon food that George Starr praised in an earlier time, and shared her knowledge of the region's history. I do much of my writing in cafés rather than in isolated rooms and would like to acknowledge the kind service and good coffee of, in France, Café du Midi and Café des Cerises in La Roque d'Antheron; Café de l'Etang in Cucuron; Café Gaby in Lourmarin; and Café du Cours in Reillanne. In Italy, my congenial workspaces were Florence's Caffè Ricchi and Pasticceria Paolini, and Lo Chalet and Jack's Bar in Montespertoli. In Long Island, I frequented, happily, Sagtown Coffee and the American Hotel Bar in Sag Harbor, the Poxabogue Fairway Restaurant in Wainscott, and John Papas Café in East Hampton. The garden of the Crown Hotel in Stamford, Lincolnshire, offered tranquillity, decent coffee, and good service in abundance. In Beirut, work would have been impossible without strong coffee and liberty to smoke at Caffeine in Zareef, Younes in

ACKNOWLEDGMENTS

Hamra, and Dar Bistro in Wardieh Square. Thanks to all of you.

Finally, the staff at Penguin Press—assistant editor Casey Denis, copy editor Jane Cavolina, and production editor Ryan Boyle—carried the project through the home stretch to the finish line. While they share credit for the book's strengths, its flaws are mine.

Charles Glass
Castello Sonnino
Montespertoli, Florence, Italy

NOTES

The following abbreviations are used in the notes section.

BNA: British National Archives
FNA: French National Archives
IWM: Imperial War Museum
IWMSA: Imperial War Museum Sound Archive
Tribunal Militaire: Tribunal Militaire de Paris, Ordre d'Informer 1546, 19 juin 1950, Dépôt central d'archives de la justice militaire, Division des Affaires Penales Militaires, Ministère de la Defénse

PROLOGUE

1 **"Courage was their":** Maurice Buckmaster, **They Fought Alone: The True Story of SOE's Agents in Wartime France** (1958; repr., London: Biteback Publishing, 2014), 268.

3 **He moved to France:** Ibid., 3.

3 **he was a "tall man":** Patrick Howarth, **Undercover: The Men and Women of SOE** (New Haven, CT: Phoenix Press, 2000), 186–87.

3 "was for the safety": Leo Marks, **Between Silk and Cyanide: A Codemakers's War** (New York: HarperCollins, 1998), 75.

3–4 **More infiltrations, of men and women, followed:** Anthony M. Webb, ed., **The Natzweiler Trial** (London: William Hodge, 1949), 17. Webb wrote, "From the spring of 1941 ever-increasing numbers of British and British-trained men dropped by parachute or landed from aircraft or submarines in occupied countries and in Germany and Italy."

4 **"Only the English":** Jean Overton Fuller, **The German Penetration of SOE: France, 1941–1944** (Maidstone, UK: George Mann, 1975), 50.

6 **"In the eyes of the French people":** Olivier Wieviorka, **The French Resistance,** trans. Jane Marie Todd (Cambridge, MA: Belknap Press of Harvard University Press, 2016), 30.

CHAPTER ONE: AN UNEXPECTED ENCOUNTER

9 **"It was no use trying":** Maurice Buckmaster, **They Fought Alone: The True Story of SOE's Agents in Wartime France** (1958; repr., London: Biteback Publishing, 2014), 134.

10 **Lieutenant George Reginald Starr:** BNA, Kew, Richmond, Surrey, HS 9/1407/1. Starr received his second lieutenant's commission on July 18, 1942, and was promoted to lieutenant on Octo-

ber 15, 1942. His military identification number was P/241286.

11 "It was more than a hunch": George Starr, IWMSA, Recording 24613, 1978, Reel 4, www .iwm.org.uk/collections/item/object/80022295.

11 "too rough even for the Polish navy": M.R.D. Foot, **SOE in France: An Account of the Work of the British Special Operations Executive in France, 1940–1944** (London: Her Majesty's Stationery Office, 1966; rept., London: Whitehall History Publishing with Frank Cass, 2004), 65. The **Seadog**'s sister ship was the felucca **Seawolf,** under another Polish naval officer, Lieutenant Marian Kadulski.

12 "It turned every way": George Starr, IWMSA, Reel 14.

13 **Watremez had been George's classmate:** George Starr, IWMSA, Reel 15. Starr explained, "The Watremez family were from Vendôme. They had a factory, and they made gloves or something. There was the father and the mother and the two sons, and we all went to school together, Lycée Vendôme. And I took his name because I thought well, if I'm checked, they'll never give me away. That's why I took it."

13 "My family motto": The Starr family motto is **Vive en Espoir.** Email from Alfred Starr to the author, September 19, 2016.

13 "Rodolphe is expecting you": BNA, HS 9/1407/1.

13 **Baron Philippe de Vomécourt:** Philippe de Vo-

mécourt, **Who Lived to See the Day: France in Arms, 1940–1945** (London: Hutchinson, 1961), 24–25. After the fall of France, Vomécourt escaped to England, trained with SOE, and parachuted back to his homeland. His brother Pierre, code name "Lucas," had established SOE's first circuit in France, AUTOGYRO. See Buckmaster, **They Fought Alone,** 21.

13 **"an extremely courageous officer":** BNA, HS 9/1346/2.

14 **"I swear I had the surprise":** George Starr, IWMSA, Reel 2.

14 **Sansom was a beautiful young woman:** Ibid. Odette Sansom told the interviewer that Jan Buchowski "refused to take me. He said, 'What am I going to do with women onboard?' 'Well,' I said, 'we'll do anything. Wash apples, something. We had all day.' The fact was, if he liked it or not, he was supposed to take us to France. And so he did. It didn't make things terribly easy, but we did manage to get there." See also Jerrard Tickell, **Odette** (1949; repr., London: Headline Review, 2007), 126.

15 **Sansom was born:** Tickell, **Odette,** 28.

15 **Odette sent her letter:** Ibid., 47.

15 **This led to an interview:** Odette Marie Céline Sansom, IWMSA, Catalogue number 9478, Reel 1. Odette Sansom recalled, "As far as I was concerned I thought, 'Well, this is the end of it,' because, of course, I should never get my photographs

back. And they were very innocent photographs. Most, I should say, were of no use at all to anybody, because they were photographs of my brother [Louis] and myself, taken on the beaches of France. But I was very surprised, because a few weeks after I had a letter thanking me and asking me if it would ever be possible for me to come to London and have an interview at an address given."

16 **Sansom cruised from Glasgow:** BNA, HS 9/648/4. See also Squadron Leader Beryl E. Escott, **The WAAF** (London: Shire Publications, 2001), 64–68.

16 **"Arriving at the position":** Brooks Richards, **Secret Flotillas: The Clandestine Sea Lines to France and French North Africa, 1940–1944** (London: Her Majesty's Stationery Office, 1996), 569.

17 **John Ashford Renshaw Starr:** BNA, HS 9/1406/8.

18 **"Are you going now?":** George Starr, IWMSA, Reel 14.

18 **Lieutenant Buchowski recorded:** Richards, **Secret Flotillas,** 569.

18 **"It was your fault":** George Starr, IWMSA, Reels 14 and 20.

CHAPTER TWO: CALLED TO THE COLORS

20 **"Most of our agents":** Maurice Buckmaster, **They Fought Alone: The True Story of SOE's Agents**

in Wartime France (1958; repr., London: Bite-back Publishing, 2014), 122.

20 **Dr. Starr donated land:** http://news.harvard .edu/gazette/1998/01.29/TwoSchoolstoBen.html and https://ia802604.us.archive.org/16/items/his toryofstarrfa00star/historyof starrfa00star.pdf.

21 **lifelong phobia of heights:** Alfred Starr, email to the author, November 1, 2016.

22 **"Those men, they were salt of the earth":** George Starr, IWMSA, Recording 24613, 1978, Reel 1, www.iwm.org.uk/collections/item/object/ 80022295.

23 **briefly married to:** Alfred Starr, email to the author, August 22, 2016.

23 **John studied art:** Ibid.

24 **"During the civil war":** George Starr, IWMSA, Reel 1.

24 **volunteer for the Royal Air Force:** BNA, KV 6/29, letter from A. D. Starr to the Chief Constable, Newcastle, Staffordshire., December 18, 1941.

24 **"We heard Chamberlain":** George Starr, IWMSA, Reel 2.

25 **"all hell broke loose":** Ibid.

25 **to work with Phantom:** Andy and Sue Parlour, **Phantom at War: The British Army's Secret Intelligence and Communication Regiment of WWII** (Essex, UK: Cerberus and Ten Bells Publishing, 2003).

25 **"direct line to Downing Street":** Ibid.

NOTES

27 **"I spoke last night"**: Pétain's speech can be heard at http://wartimespeeches.net/content_04/1940-06-20%20announcement%20of%20french%20surrender.mp3.

27 **"I remember him sitting"**: George Starr, IWMSA, Reel 16.

28 **friend named Maurice Southgate**: BNA, HS 9/1395/3.

28 **"His father and mother"**: George Starr, IWMSA, Reel 15.

29 **Southgate was born**: BNA, HS 9/1395/3. Flight Lieutenant Southgate was promoted to squadron leader on June 17, 1945.

29 **German dive bombers sank his ship**: Raye Dancocks, "The 'Lancastria'—a Secret Sacrifice in World War Two," BBC History, www.bbc.co.uk/history/worldwars/wwtwo/lancastria_01.shtml.

29 **"I go in there"**: George Starr, IWMSA, Reel 2.

30 **"[t]he use of codes"**: Buckmaster, **They Fought Alone**, 47.

31 **"He brought his brother"**: BNA, HS 9/1407/1.

32 **His destination was**: IWM, File 03/541/1, Folder 09/18/2.

32 **"the first hour"**: BNA, HS 9/1223/4. The villa belonged to a Jewish resident who put his property in Malval's name to avoid confiscation under Vichy's anti-Jewish edicts. Malval's SOE code name was "Antoine."

33 **"Churchill was here, there"**: Buckmaster, **They Fought Alone**, 76.

35 "He accomplished this mission": BNA, HS 9/1406/8. "France Combattante," report on J.A.R. Starr, 1.

35 his promotion from second lieutenant: Ibid., "Training Reports."

35 "London let him down": BNA, KV 6/29, "Interrogation of RAOUL (real name Peter CHURCHILL) dated 21.3.45."

36 S-Phone and a Eureka homing device: "This completely portable ground station, complete with all batteries, is designed in the form of personal equipment to be worn by the operator. Communication is between the ground station and a ship or aircraft." The War Office, **The British Spy Manual: The Authentic Special Operations Executive (SOE) Guide for WWII** (repr., London: Aurum Press, 2014), 158.

36 followed André Marsac from the shore: Lieutenant Colonel E. G. Boxshall, "WHEELWRIGHT Circuit," in E. G. Boxshall and M.R.D. Foot, "Chronology of SOE Operations with the Resistance in France During World War II," December 1960, IWM, 05/76/1.

36 "We had at six in the morning": George Starr, IWMSA, Reel 3.

37 In Cannes, Peter Churchill: M.R.D. Foot, **SOE in France: An Account of the Work of the Special Operations Executive in France, 1940–1944** (London: Her Majesty's Stationery Office, 1966; rept., London: Whitehall History Publishing with

Frank Cass, 2004), 187. The **resistante** who ran the beauty salon was named Marie-Lou Blanc, and her SOE code name was "Suzanne."

37 **Churchill explained, "I want her":** George Starr, IWMSA, Reel 3.

38 **George told a different story:** Ibid.

38 **"one of these organdy blouses":** Ibid.

39 **Vichy police had penetrated the circuit:** Foot, **SOE in France,** 189.

39 **"Lyon was blown sky high":** George Starr, IWMSA, Reel 3.

40 **"And we got out of the train":** Ibid.

40 **"I remember one morning":** Ibid.

40 **"An Italian officer":** Ibid.

41 **He gave the list to Marsac:** IWM, File 03/54/1, Folder 09/18/2, Colonel M. J. Buckmaster, "André Marsac (END) a member of the CARTE organization lost an attaché case full of lists of names in a train on his way to Paris. This found its way into the hands of the Gestapo in consequence of which massive arrests followed." See also BNA, HS 6/426, and John Goldsmith, **Accidental Agent** (New York: Charles Scribner's Sons, 1971), 49.

41 **immigrating to the United States:** Thomas Rabino, "André Girard," **Dictionnaire historique de la Résistance** (Paris: Robert Laffont, 2006), http://dictionnaire.sensagent.leparisien.fr/Andr%c3%a9%20Girard%20(peintre)/fr-fr.

42 **George left for the remote Gascon:** Foot, **SOE in France,** 189.

42 "That's where it all started": George Starr, IWMSA, Reel 3.

CHAPTER THREE: A BEAUTIFUL FRIENDSHIP

43 "Hilaire typifies the sort of person": Maurice Buckmaster, **They Fought Alone: The True Story of SOE's Agents in Wartime France** (1958; repr., Biteback Publishing, 2014), 133.

44 **résistant named Maurice Henri Rouneau:** BNA, HS 9/1285/7, "Rouneau alias Albert."

44 **Having spied before the war:** Letter from Maurice Rouneau to Philippe de Gunzbourg, April 9, 1952, Archives départementales du Gers, 16 J, Folder "Colonel Starr (Hilaire)."

44 **a "curious contrast" between them:** Raymond Escholier, **Maquis de Gascogne** (Geneva: Editions du Milieu de Monde, 1945), 27.

44 **George's "profound gaze:** Jeanne et Michèle Robert, **Le Réseau Victoire dans le Gers: Mémoires du 19 mai à la liberation** (Saint-Cyr-sur-Loire: Editions Alan Sutton, 2003), 51. The book includes the complete text of Maurice Rouneau's wartime memoire, **Quatre ans dans l'ombre** (Rennes les Bains: A. Bousquet, 1948).

45 **"Henri Sevenet asked me":** Rouneau to Gunzbourg. Rouneau added, "Hilaire, for his part, helped us with his knowledge and furnished us with the materials we needed."

45 "How many times": Robert, **Le Réseau Victoire dans le Gers,** 43.

47 "Age 47," stated an SOE report: BNA, HS 9/1285/7, "Interrogation of Maurice Rouneau (real name)," 14.

47 **Rouneau's girlfriend, an attractive:** Jeanne Robert was born on August 11, 1914. FNA, File 16 J 58, "Dossier de Gunzbourg, Philippe, Liquidateur du Réseau Hilaire."

47 "So I went in": Author's interview with Jeanne Robert, EHPAD, 240 chemin du Port d'Hourtin, 33140 Cadaujac, France, January 22, 2014. (Unless otherwise indicated, all quotes from Jeanne Robert are from this interview.)

50 "I was hunted": Robert, **Le Réseau Victoire dans le Gers,** 169.

50 **She stopped in Castétis:** Ibid.

51 **The teachers' residence:** George Starr, IWMSA, Recording 24613, 1978, Reel 2, www.iwm.org .uk/collections/item/object/80022295.

51 **Villagers called her Madame Delattre:** FNA, File 16 J 58, "Dossier de Gunzbourg, Philippe."

51 **The preeminent patriot:** Yvonne Cormeau, IWMSA, September 2, 1984, Catalogue number 7369, www.iwm.org.uk/collections/item/ob ject/80007171. Unless indicated, other statements from Yvonne Cormeau are from this comprehensive interview. The Larribeau children were Simone, Arnaud, Paul, Yves, and René.

52 **Rouneau took "most of his meals":** Report by

Captain Steward, February 3, 1945, BNA, HS 9/1285/7.

52 **A group of noncommissioned officers:** Alain Geay and Jeanne Robert, **"Association les Amis du Réseau VICTOIRE—Réseau S.O.E. Hilaire-Buckmaster,"** www.7juin44.fr/spip.php?article85&lang=fr. Also author's interview with Alain Geay in Castelnau-sur-l'Auvignon, January 24, 2014.

53 **"the soul of that clandestine military action":** Archives départementales du Gers, 42 J 134, **"La Résistance à Castelnau sur l'Auvignon."**

53 **"My house, my buildings":** Ibid.

53 **"Jumped with both feet":** Ibid.

53 **Alsatian refugee Maurice Jacob:** Ibid.

54 **(Sergeant) Fernand Gaucher:** "Témoignage de M. Philippe de Gunzbourg," FNA, 72 AJ 39 I.

55 **"Among ourselves, we say":** Alexandre Dumas, **The Three Musketeers** (Ware, UK: Wordsworth Editions, 1993), 187.

CHAPTER FOUR: "I WAS A HUMAN BEING"

57 **"Hilaire built up his series":** Maurice Buckmaster, **They Fought Alone: The True Story of SOE's Agents in Wartime France** (1958; repr., London: Biteback Publishing, 2014), 126.

57 **"I feel good here":** Author's interview with Jeanne Robert, January 22, 2014. Starr told the

Imperial War Museum interviewer that he lived with Robert in the school. Maurice Rouneau, however, wrote in his memoir that Starr slept at Mayor Larribeau's house and used Jeanne Robert's as his restaurant. (See Jeanne and Michèle Robert, **Le Réseau Victoire dans le Gers: Mémoires du 19 mai à la liberation** [Saint-Cyr-sur-Loire: Editions Alan Sutton, 2003], 47. The book includes the complete text of Maurice Rouneau's wartime memoir, **Quatre ans dans l'ombre** [Rennes les Bains: A. Bousquet, 1948].) This contradicted what he wrote to Philippe de Gunzbourg on April 9, 1952, "And Hilaire found Castelnau-sur-l'Auvignon much more secure than Agen, so much that he asked me if he could stay. It was then that he moved into the house with my wife [Jeanne Robert]." Robert was not then his wife; FNA, 16 J, Folder: "Résistants de la 1ère heure."

58 **"No one was more unobtrusive"**: Raymond Escholier, **Maquis de Gascogne** (Geneva: Editions du Milieu du Monde, 1945), 31.

58 **"We'd go to bed like"**: George Starr, IWMSA, Recording 24613, 1978, Reel 4, www.iwm.org.uk/collections/item/object/80022295.

58 **"He was a man who"**: Robert, **Le Réseau Victoire dans le Gers**, 51.

58 **"If somebody's used to"**: George Starr, IWMSA, Reel 4.

59 **They called him Gaston**: When I visited

Castelnau-sur-l'Auvignon in 2014, people there referred to Starr with affection as "Tonton."

59 **"I had deliberately given"**: George Starr, IWMSA, Reel 4.

59 **"In this little village"**: BNA, HS 9/1285/7.

59 **"I never locked anything"**: George Starr, IWMSA, Reel 17.

60 **"All these eight people"**: Ibid.

60 **The team comprised George:** Author's interview with Jeanne Robert, January 22, 2014.

60 **"set on the table"**: Robert, **Le Réseau Victoire dans le Gers**, 44.

61 **"all of a sudden, at one o'clock"**: Ibid.

62 **an air-raid siren:** Archives départementales du Gers, 42 J 134, **"La Résistance à Castelnau sur l'Auvignon."**

62 **"That was the first disappointment"**: George Starr, IWMSA, Reel 2.

62 **The fault was not his:** S-Phone malfunctions were rare. See BNA, HS 8/422, 5.

62 **"Hilaire went out slowly"**: Robert, **Le Réseau Victoire dans le Gers**, 45–46.

63 **"the population as a whole"**: BNA, HS 9/1407/1, "Lt.-Col. Starr interviewed by Major [R. H.] Angelo on 20–21 September 1944."

64 **"That put an end to"**: Robert, **Le Réseau Victoire dans le Gers**, 47.

64 **Sergeant Pierre Wallerand, was leaving France:** Rouneau wrote that Wallerand was among the

first soldiers to land in Normandy on June 6, 1944, when he was killed in action, ibid., 48.

64 "who said he was a refugee": Ibid.

64 "they became full Resistance": George Starr, IWMSA, Reel 14.

64 Some hid their weapons: Escholier, **Maquis de Gascogne**, 49.

66 "Then you protect your people": George Starr, IWMSA, Reel 4.

66 "I never wrote anything": Ibid., Reel 16.

66 "No paper. No pen.": Escholier, **Maquis de Gascogne**, 31.

66 "There was a very strict code": BNA, HS 9/1407/1.

66 Sergeant Maurice Dupont: BNA, HS 9/460/1.

67 deputy, Paul Sarrette: Documents supplied to the author by Paul McCue, www.paulmccuebooks.com/capt-paul-sarrette. See also BNA, KV 6/18 and HS 9/1346/2.

67 "The school had become": Robert, **Le Réseau Victoire dans le Gers**, 49.

68 Gaucher's more imaginative spots: Ibid., 56.

68 George did not use dead letters: BNA, HS 9/1407/1.

68 Having fled the Nazi anti-Jewish regime: BNA, HS 9/1407/1. An SOE report noted: "All family in France, except one uncle in U.S.A."

68 Denise Bloch's beauty: BNA, HS 9/165/8.

69 A telegram she had sent: Denise Bloch admitted

to her F-Section interrogator that she "had sent a cable to her mother addressed to the office at 2 Rue St. Helene [SOE safe house, which police had penetrated], in which she had said she was arriving [in Lyon] on Tuesday"; ibid.

69 "Sevenet not impressed": Ibid.

69 "After discussing the matter": BNA, HS 9/1364/2.

69 "But DUPONT was stopped": Ibid.

70 "I installed her": Robert, **Le Réseau Victoire dans le Gers**, 171.

70 "they don't eat vegetables": George Starr, IWMSA, Reel 9.

71 "An experienced woman": Robert, **Le Réseau Victoire dans le Gers**, 171.

71 "SARRETTE says that": BNA, KV 6/18. See also BNA, HS 9/165/8: F-Section's interrogation report on Denise Bloch states that neither Sevenet nor Sarrette "appears to have had much use for her."

71 "DENISE disliked both 'RODOLPHE'": Ibid.

73 "He has plenty of guts": BNA, HS 9/166/7. See also Martin Sugarman, "Marcus Bloom: A Jewish Hero of SOE," **Jewish Historical Studies** 39 (2004): 186. Some reports stated that Eugène/ Pertschuk and Bloom, while on their SOE course in England, had agreed to meet at the house of Odette Larocque when they got to Toulouse. See BNA, HS 9/1223/4, "Interrogation of Catalpha [Rabinovitch]," October 1, 1943. Adolphe

Rabinovitch claimed that the divorced Madame Larocque was Pertschuk's girlfriend. That meeting, if it took place, delayed Bloom's planned rendezvous with Brooks and posed the danger of connecting Brooks's PIMENTO with Pertschuk's PRUNUS circuit. To Brooks, these were unpardonable breaches of security. See Anthony Brooks, IWMSA, Catalogue number 16568, Reel 16.

73 "I don't need a wireless operator": Brooks, IWMSA, Reel 16. SOE files on George Starr's activities in 1943 stated that Pertschuk "agreed to help by allowing Bloom to transmit for George also" in March. Maurice Rouneau recalled that the connection had begun in January, which is when Brooks said they met at the Trouffe de Quercy restaurant. George made no mention of the meeting in postwar debriefs or interviews. See Lieutenant Colonel E. G. Boxshall, "WHEELWRIGHT Circuit," in E. G. Boxshall and M.R.D. Foot, "Chronology of SOE Operations with the Resistance in France During World War II," December 1960, IWM, London, 05/76/1, and Robert, **Le Réseau Victoire dans le Gers**, 56. According to SOE official historian M.R.D. Foot, Bloom appeared in Toulouse for his first meeting with Brooks wearing a bright check jacket, smoking a pipe, and greeting Brooks in English: "'Ow're you, mate?" Foot may have heard the story from Brooks, although his version differs slightly from Brooks's own to the Imperial War Museum. See M.R.D.

Foot, **SOE in France: An Account of the Work of the Special Operations Executive, 1940–1944** (London: Her Majesty's Stationery Office, 1966; rept., London: Whitehall History Publishing with Frank Cass, 2004), 274. However, Brooks's recollection years after the events may not have accorded with the facts. Pertschuk did not know Odette Larocque before he arrived in France, according to Anne Whiteside, Pertschuk's niece, in an email to the author, November 7, 2016.

74 **"Starr recruited, mainly in Condom"**: "Réseau WHEELWRIGHT," Archives départementales du Gers, 42 J 186.

74 **Denise Bloch described him**: BNA, HS/9/165/8.

74 **Pertschuk found Gunzbourg**: "Lady Berlin— obituary," **Telegraph**, August 26, 2014, www .telegraph.co.uk/news/obituaries/11056990/Lady -Berlin-obituary.html. See also FNA, 72 AJ 39 I, pièce 8a.

75 **"He regarded two groups"**: FNA, 72 AJ 39 I, pièce 8a.

75 **Gunzbourg "was a Frenchman"**: Maurice Loupias, dit Bergerac, **Messages personnels** (np: Amicale Bergeret Résistance, Dordogne-Sud, 1999), 83.

75 **They lived in hiding**: FNA, 72 AJ 39 I, pièce 8a.

76 **"established contacts, housed agents"**: Archives départementales du Gers, 42 AJ 186.

76 **Marie-Louise Lac, though, concealed**: Escholier, **Maquis de Gascogne**, 35.

76 **build that his SOE file called "solid":** BNA, HS 9/1223/4.

76 **Rabinovitch's friends called him Alec:** Archives de la Haute Garonne, 16 J 58, Fondes Daniel Latapie, Réseau WHEELWRIGHT.

76 **Rabinovitch repaired Bloom's radio:** "L'OrganisationAliée:LeSOE,"http://sdonac32.pagesperso -orange.fr/1944.htm.

77 **George and Bloch took turns:** BNA, KV 6/18 and HS 9/165/8.

77 **Morrisse bicycled twenty miles:** Jeanine Morrisse, **Là d'où je viens . . .** (Portet-sur-Garonne, France: Editions Empreinte, 2007), 15–16. See also www .ladepeche.fr/article/2011/10/02/1181636-niquou -combattante-de-l-ombre.html.

78 **The strain on George emerged:** George Starr, IWMSA, Reel 15.

78 **"one of the biggest bloody smugglers":** Ibid., Reel 16.

79 **some of the messages she relayed:** Pilar Starr, IWMSA, Catalogue number 24614, www.iwm .org.uk/collections/item/object/80022296.

79 **"A superior Armagnac":** Robert, **Le Réseau Victoire dans le Gers,** 51.

80 **Robert urged George:** Jeanne Robert told me in 2014 that she pleaded with Mayor Larribeau, "I don't dare leave him, but I'm tired." She said that the mayor convinced Starr that it was time for bed, and he followed her home.

80 "the agent never lost": Robert, **Le Réseau Victoire dans le Gers**, 51.

80 "I decided to ring the bloody church bells": George Starr, IWMSA, Reel 4.

CHAPTER FIVE: A CURSED DAY

81 "**You had to use your head**": Maurice Buckmaster, **They Fought Alone: The True Story of SOE's Agents in Wartime France** (1958; repr., London: Biteback Publishing, 2014), 135.

82 "**The elimination of German**": Leon V. Sigal, **Fighting to a Finish: The Politics of War Termination in the United States and Japan, 1945** (Ithaca, NY: Cornell University Press, 1988), 91.

82 **George's reception committee hid the matériel**: George Starr, IWMSA, Recording 24613, 1978, Reel 4, www.iwm.org.uk/collections/item/object/ 80022295.

83 **Bloom proved ingenious**: Martin Sugarman, "Marcus Bloom: A Jewish Hero of SOE," **Jewish Historical Studies** 39 (2004): 188.

83 **He helped to receive 35 tons**: BNA, HS 9/166/7.

83 "**He assisted in many acts**": Ibid.

83 "**The place was spotted**": Philippe de Gunzbourg, **Souvenirs du sud-ouest**, privately printed reminiscence (provided to the author by David Hewson), 7.

84 "**Nous, officers RAF**": M.R.D. Foot, **SOE in France: An Account of the Works of British Spe-**

cial Operations Executive in France, 1940–1944 (London: Her Majesty's Stationery Office, 1966; rept., London: Whitehall History Publishing with Frank Cass, 2004), 92.

85 **his daughter, Maguy, had already scouted:** Archives départementales du Gers, 16 J, "Annexe au formulaire modele 3."

85 **guide the two men to Spain:** Jeanne and Michèle Robert, **Le Réseau Victoire dans le Gers: Mémoires du 19 mai à la liberation** (Saint-Cyr-sur-Loire: Editions Alan Sutton, 2003), 60–61. The book includes the complete text of Maurice Rouneau's wartime memoir, **Quatre ans dans l'ombre** (Rennes les Bains: A. Bousquet, 1948). For transportation, Merchez recommended a businessman in Sainte-Livrade named Ordy, who promised Rouneau, "In two days, I will take the two men within four kilometers of the Spanish border."

85 **"at the Café Regina":** Ibid., 56.

86 **a résistant from the lower Pyrenees:** Ibid., 57–58. See also FNA, 72 AJ 40 III, pièce 2a. The **résistant**'s name was Albert Ascaso.

87 **"They want to do great things":** Ibid., 57.

87 **semiautomatic German Mauser:** George Starr, IWMSA, Reel 15.

88 **"some fat Boche officers":** Robert, **Le Reseau Victoire dans le Gers,** 59.

88 **George installed a line of Eureka:** George Starr, IWMSA, Reel 16.

88 **RAF Halifaxes made two more deliveries:**

Lieutenant Colonel E. G. Boxshall, "WHEEL-WRIGHT Circuit," in E. G. Boxshall and M.R.D. Foot, "Chronology of SOE Operations with the Resistance in France During World War II," December 1960, IWM, London, 05/76/1. See also FNA, 72 AJ 39 I, pièce 8a.

89 **"RODOLPHE [Sevenet] went to pick up":** BNA, HS 9/1407/1, "Notes on Hilaire, 12th July 1943."

89 **"he had seen at Agen":** BNA, KV 6/18, "Interrogation of Henri Sevenet, 28 May 1943."

90 **"Before he left":** Robert, **Le Réseau Victoire dans le Gers,** 71.

90 **The Pat Escape Line:** BNA, HS 9/1328.

90 **Sevenet and Sarrette decided to flee:** BNA, HS 9/1346/2.

91 **Pertschuk was living at:** Archives départementales du Gers, 42 J 185.

91 **"Lieutenant 'Denis' would turn":** Robert, **Le Réseau Victoire dans le Gers,** 61. See also BNA, HS 9/288/3: "His mission was to be lieutenant to an Organiser [Pertschuk] in the Toulouse area."

92 **"decided English (or Canadian) accent":** BNA, HS 9/288/3.

92 **Labayle had worked for PRUNUS:** BNA, HS 9/128/7.

92 **Duchalard hid in one:** Robert, **Le Réseau Victoire dans le Gers,** 68. See also BNA, KV 6/19.

93 **rendezvous at the Café Riche:** BNA, HS 9/165/8. There are discrepancies in official accounts of this meeting. Paul Sarrette told SOE that Denise and

Starr together met Pertschuk in the café on April 12. Denise stated that she met him on her own.

93 **"PRUNUS's days were numbered":** Archives départementales du Gers, 42 J 185.

93 **Bloom's wife had left:** Germaine attempted to obtain her husband's release from Fresnes Prison near Paris and visited him there before he was transported to concentration camps in Germany; Sugarman, "Marcus Bloom," 191.

94 **"BLOOM and a Spaniard":** BNA, HS 9/166/7, "Interview with M. Colle, 17 July 1945."

94 **"In BLOOM's opinion":** Ibid.

94 **"URBAIN [Bloom] was seen shortly":** BNA, HS 9/1223/4.

95 **a cactus plant in the window:** Jeanine Morrisse, **Là d'où je viens . . .** (Portet-sur-Garonne, France: Editions Empreinte, 2007), 16.

95 **Gestapo had discovered Vuillemot's name:** BNA, HS 6/422. The F-Section cable of July 11, 1943, added, "Gestapo at first did not realize importance of affair."

95 **Although Bardet was a double agent:** IWM, Private Papers of Cecile Pearl Cornioley, Documents, 16594.

96 **Buchowski visited a flat:** Brooks Richards, **Secret Flotillas: The Clandestine Sea Lines to France and French North Africa, 1940–1944** (London: Her Majesty's Stationery Office, 1996), 225.

96 **"made enquiries of the proprietress":** BNA, HS 9/165/8.

97 **Bloch drew the obvious conclusion:** Starr's report, November 20/21, 1944, BNA, HS 9/1707/1. George claimed that he rather than Bloch went to meet Pertschuk in the café. A report in his SOE file stated: "Meanwhile, HILAIRE on 15th April, went to a pre-arranged rendezvous with EUGENE at TOULOUSE. EUGENE did not turn up and HILAIRE later discovered that he, together with his W/T operator and at least 10 others, had been arrested." Philippe de Gunzbourg supported the view that Starr had gone to Toulouse to see Pertschuk on April 15 and realized he had been arrested. See Archives de la Haute Garonne, 16 J 58, Fonds Daniel Latapie, Réseau WHEEL-WRIGHT.

97 **"And when I went in":** Tony Brooks, IWMSA, Reel 16.

97 **large cache of Pertschuk's papers:** BNA, HS 9.1223/4. Hanon added that the Germans had also seized 200,000 francs from Pertschuk. Anne Whiteside, niece of Maurice Pertschuk, doubted that Hanon would have known that Pertschuk's papers were in the WC. "Another doubt for me is how Hanon knew that the Germans got lots of info from this supposed basket in the WC . . . Hanon is interviewed Nov. 43, 7 months after the arrests, when he might not remember the difference between theory and fact." Anne Whiteside, email to the author, January 23, 2016.

98 **To notify London:** Archives de la Haute Garonne,

16 J 58, Fonds Daniel Latapie, Réseau WHEEL-WRIGHT.

98 "Mind your own business": Jean Overton Fuller, **Doubt Agent?: Light on the Secret Agents' War in France** (London: Pan, 1961).

CHAPTER SIX: "IT LITERALLY RAINED CONTAINERS"

99 We could never have functioned: Maurice Buckmaster, **They Fought Alone: The True Story of SOE's Agents in Wartime France** (1958; repr., Biteback Publishing, 2014), 65.

99 Major Hermann Josef Giskes: Christer Jorgensen, **Spying for the Führer: Hitler's Espionage Machine** (Guilford, CT: Lyons Press, 2004), 85–86. Huub Lauwers's SOE code name was "Ebenezer."

100 **Englandspiel, "England game":** H. J. Giskes, **London Calling North Pole** (London: William Kimber, 1953).

100 "SOE's most regular penfriend": Leo Marks, **Between Silk and Cyanide: A Codemakers's War** (New York: HarperCollins, 1998), 143. Giskes ran the **Englandspiel** for twenty months during which the Germans captured sixty-one SOE agents.

100 "Goetz, the famous German": Anthony Brooks, IWMSA, Reel 16. In Holland, Lauwers had cooperated with the Abwehr, believing his deliberate mistakes, including the code for CAUGHT

and the omission of his security checks, would convince SOE he was acting under duress. See Marks, **Between Silk and Cyanide**, 114–22, and Paul Leverkuehn, **German Military Intelligence** (London: Weidenfeld and Nicholson, 1954), 114.

100 **"allowed to disclose"**: Marks, **Between Silk and Cyanide**, 319.

101 **"London refused to believe"**: BNA, HS 9/1407/1.

101 **SOE asked Bloom personal questions**: BNA, HS 6/422.

101 **"The decoy transmission"**: BNA, WO 208/4679, "VOLUNTARY STATEMENT BY PW, ID 1424 Civ Josef Goetz, 26 June 1946."

103 **John landed without entangling**: BNA, KV 6/29, "Interrogation of J.A.R. Starr, 28th and 30th May, 1945."

104 **Buckmaster regarded Southgate**: Buckmaster, **They Fought Alone**, 174.

104 **"made frequent use"**: BNA, HS 9/1395/3, "Interrogation of Hector, 28.10.43."

104 **the captain "was English"**: BNA, KV 6/29, "Interrogation of J.A.R. Starr, 28th and 30th May, 1945."

105 **Madame Neraud peered out**: The Gestapo arrested the Neraud family on September 2, 1943. They were sent to concentration camps in Germany, from which only the daughter, Colette, returned. BNA, KV 6/29, "Report of Mlle. Neraud." She blamed John Starr for the family's arrest, because an interrogator read a statement allegedly

438

written by Starr with a description of the house. However, SOE doubted this. If Starr had betrayed the Nerauds in July, the SD was unlikely to have waited until September to apprehend them.

105 "ISIDORE [Jones] transmitted for many circuits": Ibid.

105 "In the case the police": BNA, HS 9/1406/8.

106 "I'd arrived with a suitcase": George Starr, IWMSA, Recording 24613, 1978, Reel 2, www .iwm.org.uk/collections/item/object/80022295.

106 "They [the Gascons] wash their teeth": Ibid., Reel 9.

107 "the skin goes all white": Ibid., Reel 15.

107 "When it got to Agen": Ibid., Reel 9.

108 George's appointment as **Inspecteur**: BNA, HS 9/1407/1.

108 "This was an ideal cover": Ibid., "Lt.-Col. Starr interviewed by Major [R.H.] Angelo on 20–21 September 1944." See also Lieutenant Colonel E. G. Boxshall, "WHEELWRIGHT Circuit," in E. G. Boxshall and M.R.D. Foot, "Chronology of SOE Operations with the Resistance in France During World War II," December 1960, IWM, London, 05/76/1.

108 "The position grew so serious": Boxshall, "WHEELWRIGHT Circuit," 2.

109 lured Peter Churchill: M.R.D. Foot, **SOE in France: An Account of the Works of British Special Operations Executive in France, 1940–1944** (London: Her Majesty's Stationery Office, 1966;

rept., London: Whitehall History Publishing with Frank Cass, 2004), 275; Peter Churchill, **The Spirit in the Cage** (London: Hodder and Stoughton, 1954), 242. Churchill wrote, "Roger Bardet was the French double agent who betrayed us in the Resistance . . ." Surviving colleagues accused Roger Bardet, the French double agent called **le Boiteaux,** the Lame, of betraying Pertschuk as well.

109 **London advised the wireless operator:** Boxshall, "JOCKEY Circuit," 1.

109 **"she always travelled everywhere":** BNA, HS 9/165/8.

110 **"a terrible mess":** Ibid.

110 **George asked Maurice Dupont:** George Starr appeared to have doubts about Dupont. An SOE report of 1943 noted, "HILAIRE told source that YVAN [Dupont] was very sincere, but was too young and talked too much, and should not be sent back into the field." See BNA, HS 9/1223/4. See also Boxshall, "WHEELWRIGHT Circuit," 2: "She was accompanied by Sgt. Maurice DUPONT (who in Oct. 1943 as Major DUPONT (Abelard, Yvan) expanded the Troyes circuit . . .)." Dupont had an honorable war record before and after his association with Starr. He would be promoted to captain and receive Britain's Military Cross and the Croix de Guerre and Médaille de la Résistance Française from France. See **Supplement to the London Gazette,** HMSO, August 30,

NOTES

1945, 4372, available at www.thegazette.co.uk/London/issue/37244/supplement/4372/data.pdf.

110 "We were at the end": Jeanne and Michèle Robert, **Le Réseau Victoire dans le Gers: Mémoires du 19 mai à la liberation** (Saint-Cyr-sur-Loire: Editions Alan Sutton, 2003), 43. The book includes the complete text of Maurice Rouneau's wartime memoir, **Quatre ans dans l'ombre** (Rennes les Bains: A. Bousquet, 1948).

110 "guides were excellent": BNA, HS 9/165/8.

111 **At last, she and Dupont reached:** Ibid.

111 **seize George's report:** Archives de la Haute Garonne, 16 J 58, Fonds Daniel Latapie, Réseau WHEELWRIGHT.

111 **"the loss of her papers in Spain":** BNA, HS 9/1407/1, "Danielle Wood, May 24th, 1943."

111 **frontier guards in Bausen:** Ibid. The border guards were carabineros of Spain's Real Cuerpo de Carabineros de Costas y Fronteras, who sent the report to the Guardia Civil in Lerida. The records do not indicate what happenend to it afterward.

111 **Franco was a friend of Abwehr chief:** Léon Papeleux, **L'Admiral Canaris entre Franco et Hitler: Le rôle de Canaris dan les relations germane-espagnoles, 1915–1944** (Tournai, Belgium: Casterman, 1977), 134–40.

112 **Dupont, who was reunited with Bloch:** Boxshall, "WHEELWRIGHT Circuit," 2: "She was accompanied by Sgt. Maurice DUPONT. . . . They

441

reached England on 21 May 1943, but unfortunately the report had been confiscated in Spain."

112 **furious to be kept waiting:** BNA, HS 9/1407/1. The report stated, "DANIELLE [Bloch] met RODOLPHE at Gibraltar . . . RODOLPHE was not working with HILAIRE, and will explain himself, why." See also BNA, HS 9/1346/2.

112 **journey took twenty days:** BNA, HS 9/165/8.

112 **"He needs someone":** Ibid.

112 **"Apparently his position is":** Ibid.

113 **"would like his Mother":** Ibid.

114 **He evaded German surveillance:** Jean Overton Fuller, **The Starr Affair** (London: Victor Gollancz, 1954), 36–39. John Starr assisted the author in the writing of the book from its inception through correction of galleys. Fuller wrote (194), "We have been careful to include in this book only what Starr is sure of." See also John Starr's letter to Fuller, April 4, 1954: "I sent the galley proof back to Gollancz some time ago." IWM, J. V. Overton Fuller Collection, Box 8, File 2.

114 **George Starr sent London:** BNA, HS 9/1407/1.

115 **"there was no mistaking me":** George Starr, IWMSA, Reel 3.

115 **"He was a very brave man":** Archives de la Haute Garonne, Fondes Daniel Latapie, 16 J 58.

116 **"a leaf out of the communists' book":** George Starr, IWMSA, Reel 2.

116 **His seven-member cells:** BNA, HS 9/1407/1.

116 **subprefect of Bergerac provided:** Archives de la

Haute Garonne, Fondes Daniel Latapie, 16 J 58, and Archives Municipales de Toulouse, 82 Z 6. George liaised with Loupias through Philippe de Gunzbourg and met him "only two or three times, not in his command post which was in Condom, but at a hardware store in Condom." See Maurice Loupias, dit Bergerac, **Messages personnels** (np: Amicale Bergeret Résistance, Dordogne-Sud, 1999), 85. Loupias wrote, "The password was, '**Je viens de chercher les trois pipes Rops.**' ["I have come in search of three Rops pipes."] That phrase opened the door to a comfortable apartment, where Colonel Hilaire received us."

117 **"The English colonel"**: Archives departementales du Gers, 42 AJ 186.

117 **Rabinovitch emerged from hiding**: BNA, HS 9/1223/4. One SOE report on Rabinovitch stated, "In April 1943, as the result of the arrest of his organizer and several others, Rabinovitch was left in a position of the utmost peril. He nevertheless carried on, and endeavoured to gather together the remaining healthy elements of the organisation." The same file added, "A tireless worker, Rabinovitch sent nearly 200 messages from the field, a feat involving long hours of operating almost daily under difficult and dangerous conditions. He showed courage of a very high order and the greatest disregard for his own personal safety. He never shirked responsibility, and was frequently called upon at great risk to himself to

assist other circuits whose communications had broken down."

117 "After the RAOUL [Peter Churchill] affair": BNA, HS 9/1407/1, "Notes on Hilaire, 12th July 1943." The report added, "Arnaud [Rabinovitch] is now on his way out with another member of that circuit, GERVAIS [Victor Hazan], and will be able to give full details on the HILAIRE set up, as he and Gervais passed through Hilaire's headquarters on the night of 21/22 June. Also, Hilaire at present keeps in touch with us through BERNE, and by that means let us know that he now has 28 teams ready for action on JOUR 'J.'"

118 **Despite brutal torture:** Yvette Pitt, email to the author, October 18, 2016: "I can confirm that GRS [George Reginald Starr] never liked Odette, after the war even saying (to me) that she had not really had her toenails pulled out."

118 **"embryo of the arsenal":** Robert, **Le Réseau Victoire dans le Gers,** 59.

118 **"war matériel had arrived":** Ibid., 60.

119 **"We had a German section":** George Starr, IWMSA, Reel 8.

119 **Escholier imagined George's thoughts:** Raymond Escholier, **Maquis de Gascogne** (Geneva: Editions du Milieu du Monde, 1945), 39.

121 **I refuse to be complicit":** Ibid., 45.

121 **"the men from Flanders":** Ibid., 50. Parisot suc-

ceeded the Armagnac Battalion's first commander, car mechanic Louis Dales, when the latter died in a motorcycle accident in September 1943.

122 **first consignment to Parisot's:** Ibid., 65.

122 **Lévy brought Parisot to meet George:** George Starr, IWMSA, Reel 16.

122 **Lévy vanished rather than risk:** Escholier, **Maquis de Gascogne,** 66.

123 **"two men with the same idea":** In 2014, the mayor of Castelnau-sur-l'Auvignon, Maurice Boison, said, "The provider was Gaston [Starr], the soldier was Parisot."

123 **"Freedom of thought":** Jean-Louis Colonna Cesari, **Ruhe, Le silence des âmes** (np: The Book Edition, nd), 72, https://books.google.co.uk/books?id=P0rckWhdIOgC&printsec=frontcover&source=gbs_ge_summary_r&cad=0#v wopage&q=edition&f=false.

123 **"The abbé was a jovial old boy":** George Starr, IWMSA, Reel 6.

123 **hiding tons of SOE weaponry:** Escholier, **Maquis de Gascogne,** 53. Escholier wrote that Abbé Talès "transformed his church into an arsenal. . . ."

124 **Abbé Boë's loyalty was:** David Hewson, introduction and notes to Anne-Marie Walters, **Moondrop to Gascony,** foreword by M.R.D. Foot (1946; rept., Petersfield, UK: Harriman House, 2009), 261. In his notes, Hewson wrote: "Abbé Boë took up his post as **curé** of Blaziert, near Castelnau-

sur-l'Auvignon, in 1932. A professor of theology, former priest of the Vatican, a poly-glot and water-diviner, he was well known throughout the Gers . . . Boë joined the Resistance after the total occupation of France and subsequently became a recruiting agent and courier for the **maquis** at Castelnau."

124 **"the classic poilu"**: Escholier, **Maquis de Gascogne,** 95.

124 **"He tore about the countryside"**: Walters, **Moondrop to Gascony,** 170 [1946 edition].

124 **"so badly compromised"**: BNA, HS 9/1223/4.

125 **"All means of communications"**: BNA, HS 9/1407/1.

125 **Duchalard, who had complained:** BNA, KV 6/19, "INTERROGATION OF DENIS, 4.10.43."

125 **Duchalard spent a third of the 100,000:** Ibid.

125 **Duchalard "not remain long"**: Robert, **Le Réseau Victoire dans le Gers,** 72.

126 **"In the middle of 1943"**: Buckmaster, **They Fought Alone,** 225.

127 **"troops, machines for transporting light tanks"**: FNA, 72 AJ 39 I, pièce 8a, "Témoignage de M. Philippe de Gunzbourg, Liquidations du Réseau Hilaire, 21 avril 1947."

127 **Allied headquarters "decided not to use"**: Ibid.

128 **acquired a second master:** Buckmaster, **They Fought Alone,** 225.

128 **"28 teams for railway destruction"**: Boxshall, "WHEELWRIGHT Circuit."

128 Its area of operations: BNA, HS 9/1407/1, "Court of Enquiry re Lt. Col. G.R. STARR (SOE), Feb. 1945."

CHAPTER SEVEN: ARRESTS AND ARRIVALS

129 "War is no exact science": Maurice Buckmaster, **They Fought Alone: The True Story of SOE's Agents in Wartime France** (1958; repr., London: Biteback Publishing, 2014), 72.

129 "I should have been suspicious": Henri Raymond, "Experiences of an SOE Agent in France, alias César (Harry Rée)," in Michael Elliot Bateman, ed., **The Fourth Dimension of Warfare: Volume I: Intelligence, Subversion, Resistance** (Manchester, UK: Manchester University Press, 1970), 117–18.

129–30 "told BOB [John Starr] that he had grounds": BNA, KV 6/29, "Interrogation of CESAR @ STOCKBROKER, dated 24.7.44."

130 "rather too much facility": Ibid., "Interrogation of J.A.R. Starr, 28th and 30th May, 1945."

130 two other female agents: These were Noor Inayat Khan and Cecily Lefort. Khan, code name "Madeleine," went to Paris as the PROSPER circuit's radio operator. SOE assigned Lefort, code name "Alice," to the Drôme as courier for DONKEYMAN organizer Francis Cammaerts.

131 sabotage operation "near DIJON": BNA, KV

6/29, "Interrogation of J.A.R. Starr, 28th and 30th May, 1945."

131 **"Operation Husky was"**: Lieutenant Colonel Jon M. Swanson, "Operation Husky, the Campaign in Sicily: A Case Study" (USAWC Military Studies Program Paper, U.S. Army War College, Carlisle Barracks, PA, 1992), ii.

132 **Schutzstaffel (SS) troops ordered them**: Jean Overton Fuller, **The Starr Affair** (London: Victor Gollancz, 1954), 39.

132 **"MARTIN had given me away"**: BNA, KV 6/29, "Rough Report by Capt. J.A.R. STARR, dictated to C.S.M Goddard at Stn. XXVIII commencing 9 May 1945."

132 **"sold by a French double agent"**: British Foreign and Commonwealth Office, Knowledge Management Department, FO 950/1299.

133 **"got out, pretended to be stiff"**: BNA, KV 6/29, "Interrogation of J.A.R. Starr, 28th and 30th May, 1945."

133 **A bullet pierced**: British Foreign and Commonwealth Office, Knowledge Management Department, FO 950/1299.

133 **"I continued to run"**: BNA, KV 6/29, "Rough Report by Capt. J.A.R. STARR, dictated to C.S.M Goddard at Stn. XXVIII commencing 9 May 1945."

133 **"Bob, contagious illness"**: Tribunal Militaire, Testimony of Ernest Vogt, June 19, 1948.

133 **"I was thrown into a cell"**: Ibid.

NOTES

134 **"his reserve cover story"**: BNA, KV 6/29, "Interrogation of J.A.R. Starr, 28th and 30th May, 1945."

134 **"my wounded thigh was beaten"**: Ibid.

135 **"about five feet nine"**: Fuller, **The Starr Affair**, 46.

135 **time for his comrades to disappear**: BNA, HS 9/1406/8: On September 23, 1943, a returning agent informed F-Section: "BOB was arrested one day as he was going by car to DIJON. The car was stopped as it was about to enter the town and BOB was about to enter the town and BOB was taken off by the Gestapo. There was a man with him in the car and it is believed this man denounced him."

136 **"He used to come to see STARR"**: BNA, KV 6/29, "Interrogation of J.A.R. Starr, 28th and 30th May, 1945."

136 **The plane was about to jettison**: Archives départementales du Gers, 42 J 18 G, **"Dossier: SOE. Actions menées (parachutages),"** 1943–1944.

137 **Maurice Rouneau had been**: Jeanne and Michèle Robert, **Le Réseau Victoire dans le Gers: Mémoires du 19 mai à la liberation** (Saint-Cyr-sur-Loire: Editions Alan Sutton, 2003), 79. The book includes the complete text of Maurice Rouneau's wartime memoir, **Quatre ans dans l'ombre** (Rennes les Bains: A. Bousquet, 1948).

137 **a sudden crisis**: Ibid., 106.

138 **"Quick, my old Albert" . . . "I said Albert only"**:

Ibid., 83–86. Rouneau's full account of Gaucher's arrest is missing in other narratives.

140 **"I gave my hand"**: Ibid, 77.

141 **"Paul Revere ride"**: George Starr, IWMSA, Recording 24613, 1978, Reel 17, www.iwm.org.uk/collections/item/object/80022295. Starr said he ordered, "Everybody disappear!"

141 **"cease all activities"**: Lieutenant Colonel E. G. Boxshall, "WHEELWRIGHT Circuit," in E. G. Boxshall and M.R.D. Foot, "Chronology of SOE Operations with the Resistance in France During World War II," December 1960, IWM, London, 05/76/1.

141 **"If he'd waited"**: Starr, IWMSA, Reel 14.

141 **Germans arrested a journalist**: Robert, **Le Réseau Victoire dans le Gers**, 86. The arrested journalist was Roger Banabera.

142 **Gunzbourg ran into the post office**: Anne-Marie Walters, **Moondrop to Gascony**, foreword by M.R.D. Foot, introduction and notes by David Hewson (1946; rept., Petersfield, UK: Harriman House, 2009), 68. Walters wrote that Gunzbourg had come down the stairs when the Gestapo asked him if he was Albert Cambon, another **résistant**. He told them he wasn't and rode off on his bicycle.

142 **Marie-Louise Lac opened her door**: Archives départementales du Gers, 42 AJ 186, Madame Lac, 14, rue Cassaignolles, Vic-Fezensac, **"Souvenirs de la Résistance."** Madame Lac gave the date of Gunzbourg's escape from the Gestapo as May 9,

1943, but all other sources, including Gunzbourg himself, confirmed that he fled his château following Fernand Gaucher's arrest in August 1943.

142 **remained in hiding at Madame Lac's:** Ibid.

142 **"He was interrogated":** Boxshall, "WHEEL-WRIGHT Circuit."

142 **sent a résistant to evacuate:** Robert, **Le Réseau Victoire dans le Gers,** 92.

143 **"total hospitality and relative security":** Ibid., 87.

143 **German security personnel had raided:** Ibid., 87–88.

144 **Vera Atkins reported to:** Sarah Helm, **A Life in Secrets: The Story of Vera Atkins and the Lost Agents of SOE** (New York: Little, Brown, 2005), 426.

145 **"I was willing to do":** Yvonne Cormeau, IWMSA, September 2, 1984, Catalogue number 7369, www.iwm.org.uk/collections/item/object/80007171.

145 **"I did not take it":** Ibid.

145 **silver powder compact:** Yvette Pitt, email to the author, October 18, 2016.

146 **"I had to slide through the hole":** Cormeau, IWMSA, September 2, 1984.

147 **"The landing was perfect although":** BNA, HS 6/658.

147 **a falling canister grazed her leg:** Yvette Pitt, email to the author, October 16, 2016.

147 **"It was the first operation":** Cormeau, IWMSA, September 2, 1984.

148 **Rouneau recalled, "Hilaire astonished us":** Robert, **Le Réseau Victoire dans le Gers,** 53.

149 **regaling Rouneau with technical details:** Ibid., 91.

150 **his radio operator, Annette:** BNA, HS 6/658.

150 **George arranged to meet her:** Starr had requested a male radio operator, preferably one too old to be subject to forced labor in Germany under Vichy's **Service du travail obligatoire** (STO) law. Cormeau recalled, "London's answer was to send him a woman. He must have cursed." Cormeau, IWMSA, September 2, 1984.

150 **"I've known this lady":** Liane Jones, **A Quiet Courage: Women Agents in the French Resistance** (New York: Bantam Books, 1990), 181. The author wrote that Starr met Cormeau in the station and said, "**Je connais Madame.**" ["I know Madame."] She does not cite a reference.

150 **"Physically he was small":** Cormeau, IWMSA, September 2, 1984.

151 **on a long walk:** BNA, HS 6/658: In Yvonne Cormeau's SOE debrief, she said that she and Starr "went out for a ride on bicycles, to discuss arrangements, etc. . . ." The differences between Cormeau's and Starr's recollections of minor details in this encounter are reminiscent of the lyrics in "I Remember It Well" from the Lerner and Loewe musical **Gigi.**

151 **photograph of his wife:** Alfred Starr, email to the author, August 24, 2016.

151 "She was given a letter": George Starr, IWMSA, Reel 15.

151 "what the hell are you doing here?": Ibid., Reel 17.

152 "about this other chap": Cormeau, IWMSA, September 2, 1984.

152 made her first transmissions: Douglas Boyd, **Voices from the Dark Years: The Truth About Occupied France, 1940–1945** (Stroud, UK: Sutton Publishing, 2007), 185–86.

152 "The owner of this house": BNA, HS 6/658.

153 "nine men were shot": Boxshall, "WHEELWRIGHT Circuit."

153 "Look, if you are found": Cormeau, IWMSA, September 2, 1984.

153 "Knowing that my husband": Ibid.

CHAPTER EIGHT: AVENUE BOCHE

155 "In secret wireless work": Maurice Buckmaster, **They Fought Alone: The True Story of SOE's Agents in Wartime France** (1958; repr., London: Biteback Publishing, 2014), 60.

155 penitentiary was by then notorious: BNA, KV 6/29, "Interrogation of J.A.R. Starr, 28 and 30th May, 1945" states, "After roughly five weeks in DIJON (i.e., about the end of August 1943) both STARR and MICHEL were taken together by car to FRESNES, where STARR was placed in a cell with three other prisoners, and MICHEL was

[placed] in another cell a few doors away." Michel was one of the code names for Peter Churchill, but there is no record of Churchill being held at Dijon. He had been arrested in Saint-Jorioz and taken to Annecy before Fresnes. Just before John's arrival at Fresnes, a French prisoner who had endured weeks of torture had hanged herself. She was Berty Albrecht, who helped found the **Combat** network with her husband, Captain Henri Frenay.

156 **cellmates were "a Polish officer":** BNA, KV 6/29, "Interrogation of J.A.R. Starr, 28th and 30th May, 1945," 5. See also Jean Overton Fuller, **The Starr Affair** (London: Victor Gollancz, 1954), 51. Fuller and some documents spelled the student's name "Commert," but official postwar documents use the spelling "Comert." By 1949, he had become a journalist at **France Soir**. See Tribunal Militaire, statement of Jean-Claude Comert, November 22, 1949. After the war, Comert married Anne-Marie Walters. The name Argence is spelled Argens in this statement and other documents.

156 **Germans had penetrated PHYSICIAN:** Jean Overton Fuller, **The German Penetration of SOE: France, 1941–1944** (Maidstone, UK: George Mann, 1975), 46. Francis Suttill's code name was "Prosper."

156 **double agent Henri Déricourt:** Ibid., 89 and 118. See also Jean Overton Fuller, **Déricourt: The Chequered Spy** (Norwich, UK: Michael Russell Publishing, 1989).

157 Parisians called it "avenue Boche": Charles Glass, **Americans in Paris: Life and Death Under Nazi Occupation** (New York: Penguin Press, 2009), 181 and 245.

157 "It was incongruous": Peter Churchill, **The Spirit in the Cage** (London: Hodder and Stoughton, 1954), 53.

158 Vogt's chief, Sturmbannführer Hans Kieffer: BNA, WO 208/4679, "NOTES ON THE INTERROGATION OF WERNER EMIL RUEHL, BORN ON 5.6.1905 IN MARXLOH, BY SQUADRON OFFICER V.M. ATKINS AT L.D.C. ON 24.10.16." Ruehl said Kieffer's three children were "a boy Hans and two girls." The girls were Hildegarde and Gretel. Kieffer wrote of his duties in France, "Until about January 1943 I was employed in the building of the Ministry of Interior (Sûreté) and afterwards at 84 Avenue Foch, where in addition to Counter Intelligence and Sabotage matters, the execution of radio deception plans with fake messages in particular was among the tasks of my section." See BNA, WO 235/560, "Statement of Hans Kieffer, 29 November 1946."

158 "square-headed, not tall": BNA, HS 9/1395/3, "Report by S/LDR. M. SOUTHGATE."

158 John "had the sense": BNA, KV 6/29, Testimony of Ernest Vogt, June 19, 1948.

159 "He made it appear": Fuller, **The Starr Affair**, 54n.

159 **another prisoner, Major Gilbert Norman:** Fuller, **The German Penetration of SOE,** 46.

159 **Norman believed Suttill had given:** Francis J. Suttill, **Shadows in the Fog: The True Story of Major Suttill and the Prosper French Resistance Network** (Stroud, UK: The History Press, 2014).

160 **"there was a leak":** BNA, KV 6/29, "Interrogation of J.A.R. Starr, 28th and 30th May, 1945."

160 **brought him to Vogt:** There is a discrepancy between Starr's statement to SOE in BNA, KV 6/29 and his account to Jean Overton Fuller for her authorized biography of him, **The Starr Affair,** about whether Vogt and Kieffer showed him the map on his first or second day at avenue Foch.

160 **suspicion that the SD had a mole:** Fuller, **The Starr Affair,** 55.

161 **"He likes the way":** Ibid., 56.

161 **"decided to comply":** BNA, KV 6/29, "Interrogation of J.A.R. Starr, 28th and 30th May, 1945."

161 **a few years later, he claimed:** Fuller, **The Starr Affair,** 56.

161 **"to glean a lot of information":** BNA, KV 6/29, "Interrogation of J.A.R. Starr, 28th and 30th May, 1945."

161 **"That's what's waiting":** Tribunal Militaire, statement of Jean-Claude Comert, November 22, 1949.

162 **on the second floor:** The European and British method of numbering floors makes the ground

floor zero, or **rez de chaussée,** making the first floor the American second floor.

162 **"BOB was given various":** BNA, KV 6/29, Testimony of Ernest Vogt, June 19, 1948.

163 **"The charts consisted of":** BNA, HS 9/1395/3, "Interrogation of S/Ldr Maurice Southgate @ HECTOR, 13 June 1945."

163 **"Sometimes, he would be taken":** BNA, KV 6/29, "Interrogation of J.A.R. Starr, 28th and 30th May, 1945."

164 **"Prisoners were better fed":** BNA, HS 9/1395/3, "Interrogation of S/Ldr Maurice Southgate @ HECTOR, 13 June 1945."

164 **"I was amazed at H.Q. GESTAPO":** BNA, HS 8/422, "COMMENTS. Squadron Leader SOUTHGATE makes the following comments."

164 **The coffee, tea:** Paul Leverkuehn, **German Military Intelligence** (London: Weidenfeld and Nicholson, 1954), 115.

164 **John came to know:** Jean Overton Fuller, **Madeleine: The Story of Noor Inayat Khan** (London: Victor Gollancz, 1952), 147. Fuller wrote, "The guards were mainly Rumanians and Russians (prisoners of war) and could hardly speak a word of German, let alone French or English. It was very difficult, even for the Germans, to make them understand anything, and the staff were always anxious lest a mistake should occur because the guards had not been able to follow their instructions."

165 "dark, dirty and very vulgar": BNA, HS 9/1395/3, "Interrogation of S/Ldr Maurice Southgate @ HECTOR, 13 June 1945."

165 mistress of . . . Master Sergeant Karl Haug: BNA, KV 6/29, "NOTE OF INTERVIEW IN FRESNES PRISON WITH ROSE-MARIE HOLWEDTS, nee CORDONNIER." See also BNA, WO 311/933, "Affidavit, Captain Starr, 4 October 1945."

165 "When I came back": BNA, WO 208/4679, "VOLUNTARY STATEMENT BY PW, ID 1424 Civ Josef Goetz, 26 June 1946."

166 "Dr. Goetz was furious": IWM, J. V. Overton Fuller Collection, Box 8, File 2, letter, Ernest Vogt to Jean Overton Fuller, September 12, 1954.

166 "You have forgotten": Fuller, The German Penetration of SOE, 58. See also IWM, J. V. Overton Fuller Collection.

166 "When STARR arrived": BNA, KV 6/29, "Interrogation of J.A.R. Starr, 28th and 30th May, 1945."

CHAPTER NINE: WORD OF HONOR

167 "Our men were lonely": Maurice Buckmaster, They Fought Alone: The True Story of SOE's Agents in Wartime France (1958; repr., Biteback Publishing, 2014), 136.

167 "Thanks to the patriotism": Jeanne and Mi-

chèle Robert, **Le Réseau Victoire dans le Gers: Mémoires du 19 mai à la liberation** (Saint-Cyr-sur-Loire: Editions Alan Sutton, 2003), 92. The book includes the complete text of Maurice Rouneau's wartime memoir, **Quatre ans dans l'ombre** (Rennes les Bains: A. Bousquet, 1948).

168 **He and Robert risked:** Ibid., 95.

169 **"You never knew which man":** Yvonne Cormeau, IWMSA, September 2, 1984, Catalogue number 7369, www.iwm.org.uk/collections/item/object/80007171.

169 **"I shook the hand warmly":** Robert, **Le Réseau Victoire dans le Gers,** 99. The mayor of Castelnau-sur-l'Auvignon, Maurice Boisou, told me in January 2014 about Captain Pagès: "He worked for [Maurice] Papon, but when he saw that it was beginning to turn into a massacre and that they were making people disappear, Pagès asked to be posted outside the occupied zone, a zone that was forbidden because it was forbidden to us; and he was deployed to the gendarmerie brigade in Condom and there he went into the Resistance and met Gaston [George Starr]." Maurice Papon, general secretary of the Gironde Prefecture under Vichy, was responsible for the arrest of more than fifteen hundred Jewish men, women, and children, who were sent to the death camp at Auschwitz. Papon, who survived the war under the fiction that he had supported the Re-

sistance, became police chief in Paris in 1958 and detained thousands of Algerians and oversaw the murder of at least two hundred of them.

170 "I know now what calumnies": Ibid, 100.

171 "the security section reported": Lieutenant Colonel E. G. Boxshall, "WHEELWRIGHT Circuit," in E. G. Boxshall and M.R.D. Foot, "Chronology of SOE Operations with the Resistance in France During World War II," December 1960, IWM, 05/76/1.

171 "ordinary work of finding": Cormeau, IWMSA, September 2, 1984.

172 George broke into Labayle's office: Robert, Le Réseau Victoire dans le Gers, 101.

172 "without his presence of mind": Archives Départementales du Gers, 42 AJ 186.

173 "you had to go through the snow": Cormeau, IWMSA, September 2, 1984.

173 turned the matériel over: Robert, Le Réseau Victoire dans le Gers, 105. For the Milice, see Robert O. Paxton, Vichy France: Old Guard and New Order, 1940–1944 (New York: Alfred A. Knopf, 1972), 298.

174 "worse than the Gestapo": Cormeau, IWMSA, September 2, 1984.

174 "It was amusing to hear": Ibid.

175 "A true patriot": BNA, HS 9/1407/1.

175 "During his subsequent interrogation": Boxshall, "WHEELWRIGHT Circuit."

175 "As regards this man": Ibid.

176 "tall man of maybe forty": Peter Churchill, **The Spirit in the Cage** (London: Hodder and Stoughton, 1954), 53.

177 "They're a very well-known couple": Jean Overton Fuller, **The Starr Affair** (London: Victor Gollancz, 1954), 59.

177 "freed the Russian guard": Jean Overton Fuller, **Conversations with a Captor** (West Sussex, UK: Fuller d'Arch Smith, 1973), 26–27.

177 "I suggested to Kieffer": Ibid., 27.

178 On the brothers' arrival: BNA, HS 9/1096/8 and HS 9/1097/1. In January 1944, the SD transferred the brothers to Buchenwald concentration camp in Germany.

178 "he would never become an agent": BNA, KV 6/29, Testimony of Ernest Vogt, June 19, 1948.

179 Kieffer let him go: BNA, HS 9/836/5, "A Report About Captain John Starr (by Kieffer)." Kieffer testified, "I myself established that during his interrogation he had not broken his word of honour which he had given, as was originally believed, since at this time he had given it only for a quite specific case (namely transport to his flat in Paris to fetch his painting equipment)."

180 "Dr. Goetz obtained the help": Ibid.

180 "this wireless traffic": Ibid.

181 flown Khan with Diana Rowden: BNA, HS 9/836/5.

181 "We were pursuing her": BNA, HS 9/836/5, "Translation of the Voluntary Statement Made

by the Commandant of the Paris Gestapo, Hans Kieffer."

181 **"It was, naturally, of the greatest interest"**: BNA, HS 9/836/5, "VOLUNTARY STATEMENT OF CIVILIAN INTERNEE LD 1424 (formerly St. Ustuf.) Josef Goetz." Goetz also said, "I first learnt of the existence of MADELEINE [Khan] at the beginning of July 1943, at the time of ARCHAM- BAUD's [Gilbert Norman's] arrest. We then had a personal description of her and knew she was a W.T. operator of the reseau PROSPER [Francis Suttill]."

181–82 **in return she would hand over**: Jean Over- ton Fuller, **Madeleine: The Story of Noor Inayat Khan** (London: Victor Gollancz, 1952), 145. This Frenchwoman's use of names known only to the SD and F-Section convinced Vogt that she could deliver. A subsequent interview with Vogt stated that the women, who was called Renée, took him to the place "where Madeleine was staying, and showed him her radio-set and the drawer in which she kept a complete set of all the back messages exchanged between herself and London since she arrived in the field." See Jean Overton Fuller, **The German Penetration of SOE: France, 1941–1944** (Maidstone, UK: George Mann, 1975), 109. Fuller added, "A colleague had asked her [Khan] to destroy these, but she insisted her instructions from London were to preserve them. Miss [Vera] Atkins has asked me to make plain that the instructions were, on the contrary, to destroy them; nevertheless Professor [M.R.D.] Foot found instructions to another radio operator to be 'extremely careful with the filing of your messages.' Apparently, this was intended to mean only that they should be given sequential numbering."

182 **Haug and I followed her:** BNA, HS 9/836/5, Testimony of Werner Ruehl, November 1946. See also Shrabani Basu, **Spy Princess: The Life of Noor Inayat Khan** (Stroud, UK: Sutton Publishing, 2006), 153–54. Noor Inayat Khan was born on January 2, 1914, in Russia.

183 **"Another few days":** Fuller, **Madeleine**, 146. Corporal Ruehl later stated, "About two hours later I heard that Madeleine had, all the same, been arrested, I believe, by [Corporal Alfred von] Kapri. Kieffer and the whole office were obviously delighted."

183 **"You know who I am":** Ibid., 147.

184 **"Madeleine, after her capture":** BNA, HS 9/836/5, "Extract from a deposition on oath of Hans KIEFFER, Commandant of the Gestapo, sworn before a War Crimes Investigative unit on 19.1.47."

184 **"she was the best human being":** Fuller, **The German Penetration of SOE**, 109.

184 **"light brown hair":** Fuller, **Madeleine**, 163.

185 **"more than forty or so":** IWM, J. V. Overton Fuller Collection, Box 8, File 2, letter, John Starr to Jean Overton Fuller, July 12, 1953.

185 **Faye also secreted notes:** Ibid., letter, John Starr to Jean Overton Fuller, May 26, 1953.

185 **"He asked me if I thought":** Ibid.

186 **They too needed a screwdriver:** There are various accounts of the escape plan, most of them based on information provided by John Starr. BNA, KV 6/29, "Rough Report by Capt. J.A.R. Starr, dictated to C.S.M. Goddard at Stn. XXVIII commencing 9 May 1945"; IWM, J. V. Overton Fuller Collection, Box 8, File 2, John Starr letters to Jean Overton Fuller; Fuller, **The Starr Affair,** 69–77; Fuller, **Madeleine,** 164–71; Basu, **Spy Princess,** 162–65; Sarah Helm, **A Life in Secrets: The Story of Vera Atkins and the Lost Agents of SOE** (New York: Little, Brown, 2005), 116–18.

188 **John noticed a truncheon:** IWM, J. V. Overton Fuller Collection, Box 8, File 2, letter, John Starr to Jean Overton Fuller, January 15, 1954.

189 **"a great insight":** BNA, HS 9/836/5, "A Report About Captain John Starr (by Kieffer)." Kieffer added, "It was at precisely this time that the capture of the W/T operator, 'Madeleine,' of the French Section and of Colonel 'FAYE' of the French Resistance Movement took place."

190 **interrogators in Dijon tortured him:** Fuller, **The German Penetration of SOE,** 119.

CHAPTER TEN: SABOTAGE

191 **"Women were as brave":** Maurice Buckmaster, **They Fought Alone: The True Story of SOE's**

Agents in Wartime France (1958; repr., Biteback Publishing, 2014), 232.

193 "Now I'm going": Jeanne and Michèle Robert, **Le Réseau Victoire dans le Gers: Mémoires du 19 mai à la liberation** (Saint-Cyr-sur-Loire: Editions Alan Sutton, 2003), 115. The book includes the complete text of Maurice Rouneau's wartime memoir, **Quatre ans dans l'ombre** (Rennes les Bains: A. Bousquet, 1948).

193 "I looked in vain": Letter from Maurice Rouneau to Philippe de Gunzbourg, April 9, 1952, Archives départementales du Gers, 16 J, Folder "Colonel Starr (Hilaire)."

194 **Maurice Jacob, head of:** Maurice Jacob died in Bergen-Belsen on April 18, 1944. See originals of Paul Blasy's testimony at www.7juin44.fr/spip .php?article88&lang=fr.

196 **house of Marius Sorbé:** BNA, HS 6/456.

197 "He fell out with me": George Starr, IWMSA, Recording 24613, 1978, Reel 14, www.iwm.org .uk/collections/item/object/80022295.

198 **Rain beat down:** Robert, **Le Réseau Victoire dans le Gers,** 119.

198 "The slightest misstep": Ibid., 125.

199 **George arranged for Roland Mansencal:** Lieutenant Colonel E. G. Boxshall, "WHEELWRIGHT Circuit," in E. G. Boxshall and M.R.D. Foot, "Chronology of SOE Operations with the Resistance in France During World War II," December 1960, IWM, London, 05/76/1.

200 "These are the days": Raymond Escholier, **Maquis de Gascogne** (Geneva: Editions du Milieu du Monde, 1945), 73.

201 "permission to make concentrated attacks": BNA, HS 9/1407/1.

201 "We had our courier service": Yvonne Cormeau, IWMSA, September 2, 1984, Catalogue number 7369, www.iwm.org.uk/collections/item/object/80007171.

201 Walters's field code name: For their flight to France, Walters's temporary code name was "Hairdresser" and Arnault's "Milkmaid."

201 Gray's aircraft crashed: Carpetbagger Aviation Museum, Harrington, Northamptonshire. Archive at http://harringtonmuseum.org.uk/Aircraft%20lost%20on%20Allied%20Forces%20Special%20Duty%20Operations.pdf.

202 "suffered shock and concussions": BNA, HS 9/339/2.

202 But the RAF: George Starr, IWMSA, Reel 10.

202 "I went out in the dark": Ibid.

203 "When both our pistols": Jean Overton Fuller, **The German Penetration of SOE: France, 1941–1944** (Maidstone, UK: George Mann, 1975), 119–20.

203 Stork called only "Untersturmführer X": BNA, WO 311/933 and WO 208/4679. In his postwar "voluntary statement," Kieffer's driver, Josef Stork, provided a contradictory account of the Vogt-Dubois encounter. He claimed it took place

in early 1944, although Vogt, Starr, and other sources insisted it took place on November 19, 1943. He also said he drove Vogt, Scherer, and other SD men to a place in Paris, although other sources said it was a farmhouse outside Paris. "I remained on the road near the car. SCHEERER [sic] then went to the flat again where, as VOGT told me later, the man who was to be arrested was waiting for them. After some minutes I heard a wild exchange of shots. Fearing the worst I ran to the flat and there on the staircase I met Untersturm-fuehrer X who was also hurrying up to the third floor where the shooting came from. As we got there VOGT who had been injured by six shots came out of the flat and the door was shot from inside. VOGT told us that SCHEERER [sic] had been seriously wounded. The three of us pushed upon the door whereupon a man jumped into the doorway from inside. I could not see him as I was on the blind side of the doorway. This man was immediately shot in the head by Untersturm-fuehrer X. Then we rushed into the flat and found SCHEERER [sic] dying but no one else was there except the dead man. . . . I with the help of the German Field Police had the wounded man taken to La Pitie hospital in a French Red Cross car. Some weeks later, after his recovery, he was taken from there to the prison. VOGT too was taken to hospital."

204 **"You should not have fired"**: Jean Overton Fuller,

Conversations with a Captor (West Sussex, UK: Fuller d'Arch Smith, 1973), 52.

204 "After [a] three months stay": BNA, KV 6/29, "Rough Report by Capt. J.A.R. STARR, dictated to C.S.M Goddard at Stn. XXVIII commencing 9 May 1945."

205 "as the R.A.F. came over": Ibid.

205 "I went back to": IWM, J. V. Overton Fuller Collection, Box 8, File 2, letter, John Starr to Jean Overton Fuller, May 26, 1953.

206 "All three had broken": BNA, HS 9/836/5, "A Report About Captain John STARR (by Kieffer)."

206 Khan erupted in tears: Jean Overton Fuller, **Madeleine: The Story of Noor Inayat Khan** (London: Victor Gollancz, 1952), 173–75, and **The Starr Affair** (London: Victor Gollancz, 1954), 178–80.

207 "As you will have realized": Fuller, **The Starr Affair**, 76.

208 "'Madeleine' had approached him": BNA, HS 9/836/5, "A Report About Captain John Starr (by Kieffer)."

208 Kieffer and von Kapri came: BNA, KV 6/29, "Interrogation of J.A.R. Starr, 28th and 30th May, 1945."

209 "So long as you keep me here": Fuller, **The Starr Affair**, 82.

209 he "would still have the chance": Jean Overton Fuller, **Doubt Agent?: Light on the Secret Agents' War in France**, (London: Pan, 1961), 10–11.

209 "in contrast to the French officers": BNA, HS

9/836/5, "A Report About Captain John Starr (by Kieffer)."

209 " 'Madeleine' and 'Faye' were subsequently conveyed": Ibid.

210 arrested Professor Balachowsky: The Germans sent Balachowsky to Buchenwald concentration camp on January 17, 1944. At Madame Balachowsky's request, Placke had her husband transferred to the scientific block at the camp, giving him a better chance of survival.

210 John Starr was alive: Fuller, **The German Penetration of SOE**, 86–87 and 121.

210 von Kapri took aim: IWM, J. V. Overton Fuller Collection, Box 8, File 2, letter, Ernest Vogt to Jean Overton Fuller, September 12, 1954.

210 In another bed, Norman saw: Fuller, **The German Penetration of SOE**, 123.

211 "Return to France!": Robert, **Le Réseau Victoire dans le Gers**, 142–43.

212 Yvonne confirmed that sympathetic: Cormeau, IWMSA, September 2, 1984.

212 "New Year's Eve bash of locomotives": Maurice Loupias, dit Bergerac, **Messages personnels** (np: Amicale Bergeret Résistance, Dordogne-Sud, 1999), 110.

212 "It's very difficult to send people": George Starr, IWMSA, Reel 7.

213 found the pair caked in mud: Archives départementales du Gers, 42 J 18 G. The reception committee listed for the night of January 3–4, 1944,

included the names "Cantal, Dumartin, Daubin, Fiton." The BBC personal message signaling the drop was **"La vertu est une qualité rare"** (Virtue is a rare quality).

213 **"Colette looked like"**: Archives départementales du Gers, 42 J 18 G, **"Histoire de parachutage dans l'Armagnac," La Gascogne**, April 10, 1945. See also Anne-Marie Walters, **Moondrop to Gascony**, foreword by M.R.D. Foot, introduction and notes by David Hewson (1946; rept., Petersfield, UK: Harriman House, 2009), 33.

214 **"He was practically bald"**: Walters, **Moondrop to Gascony**, 50.

214 **"I am very strict on discipline"**: Ibid.

215 **"to impress the little bitch"**: George Starr, IWMSA, Reel 4.

215 **Walters believed the story**: The mayor and residents of Castelnau-sur-l'Auvignon said to me during interviews in January 2014 that Starr had been tortured before his arrival there. When I asked Jeanne Robert whether the Germans tortured him, she said, "On his skin, yes. He had a triangle on his arm from a branding iron. And on the back. He showed it to us. And on the leg, but to me, he did not show that." When I pressed her, she explained, "Lies are necessary in war." Marie-Louise Lac wrote, "Before coming to the Gers, he had been taken by the Gestapo in Lyon. He was tortured, and his torso bore the scars of the ill-

treatment that had been inflicted on him by the Nazi torturers, but he never spoke of it." See Archives départementales du Gers, 42 J 134, "Souvenirs de la Résistance." In fact, George Starr was neither captured nor tortured.

215 **I've had to go everywhere:** Walters, **Moondrop to Gascony,** 58.

216 **"a student from Paris":** BNA, HS 9/339/2, "Para girl," BBC interview with Anne-Marie Walters, January 16, 1945.

216 **Maurice Southgate parachuted into:** BNA, HS 9/1395/3. See also Susan Ottoway, **Sisters, Secrets and Sacrifice: A True Story** (New York: HarperCollins, 2013), 90.

216 **"he stuck to his job":** Buckmaster, **They Fought Alone,** 174.

216 **resume his work with the STATIONER circuit:** Archives départementales du Gers, 42 J 18 G.

216 **young Arnault "was in love":** George Starr, IWMSA, Reel 17.

216–17 **told Walters that "suspicious people":** Walters, **Moondrop to Gascony,** 136. See also note 6, 260: David Hewson wrote, "The 'suspicious people' turned out to be Jacques Poirier (Nestor) and members of his SOE DIGGER circuit. There was some rivalry between Starr and Poirier over control of the Dordogne and very little cooperation between the two organisations."

217 **"came almost every day":** Ibid., 72–73.

217　**led by SOE organizers:** BNA, HS 9/1539/5. Vo-mécourt's debrief on the affair stated: "When the rest of the prisoners were being marched back from roll-call in groups of seven, each group was accompanied by a 'friendly' gaoler who took them through the gate, whereupon they all separated and ran, making for a fixed meeting point. The sentries on the walls were completely taken by surprise and when they had started firing it was getting dark and they lost sight of the prisoners." See also André Brissaud, **La dernière année de Vichy (1943–1944)** (Paris: Librairie Académique Perrin, 1965), 587.

217　**"The message was passed":** Philippe de Vomé-court, **Who Lived to See the Day: France in Arms, 1940–1945** (London: Hutchinson, 1961), 150.

218　**"fumed over everything":** Walters, **Moondrop to Gascony,** 73.

218　**He told Walters the guides were leaving:** Ibid., 75.

219　**"a charming newcomer":** Vomécourt, **Who Lived to See the Day,** 150–51.

220　**"For a few days":** Ibid., 152.

221　**they would not have made it:** BNA, HS 6/583. Walters wrote in her "Report on Mission in France" of September 18, 1944, for SOE: "I also accompanied the escapees from the prison of Eysses (Lot et Garonne) to their escape line contacts and a number of people pursued by the Gestapo, and a few allied air crews."

CHAPTER ELEVEN: JOHN'S COUSIN

222   "Europe was not yet ablaze": Maurice Buckmaster, **They Fought Alone: The True Story of SOE's Agents in Wartime France** (1958; repr., Biteback Publishing, 2014), 101.

222   "between the guardroom": IWM, J. V. Overton Fuller Collection, Box 8, File 2, letter, John Starr to Jean Overton Fuller, May 26, 1953.

222   "Had the three managed": BNA, HS 9/836/5, "A Report About Captain John Starr (by Kieffer)."

223   "After the 'Escape'": IWM, J. V. Overton Fuller Collection, Box 8, File 2, letter, John Starr to Jean Overton Fuller, July 12, 1953.

224   "I knew that Millie Scherer": Ibid., Box 6, File 7.

224   Holwedts, swore that Frau Scherer: BNA, KV 6/29, "NOTE OF INTERVIEW IN FRESNES PRISON WITH ROSE-MARIE HOLWEDTS, nee CORDONNIER."

224   report from another prisoner: BNA, HS 9/1395/3, "Interrogation of S/Ldr Maurice Southgate @ HECTOR, 13 June 1945."

224   "One day he said": BNA, KV 6/29, "Interrogation of J.A.R. Starr, 28th and 30th May, 1945."

225   Placke had turned Briault: Jean Overton Fuller, **The German Penetration of SOE: France, 1941–1944** (Maidstone, UK: George Mann, 1975), 139.

225   "went out twice with BOB": BNA, KV 6/29, Procès-Verbal, April 1, 1946, Joseph Pierre August Placke.

226 **asked John to help thwart**: BNA, HS 9/1186/2 and HS 9/954/2.

227 **"He wanted to know"**: Tribunal Militaire, PROCES-VERBAL, John Starr, December 17, 1947.

227 **SOE cut communications**: Fuller, **The German Penetration of SOE**, 139; and Jean Overton Fuller, **The Starr Affair** (London: Victor Gollancz, 1954), 92.

228 **"I was present when"**: BNA, WO 208/4679, "VOLUNTARY STATEMENT BY PW, ID 1424 Civ Josef Goetz, 26 June 1946."

229 **"STARR's security section"**: Lieutenant Colonel E. G. Boxshall, "WHEELWRIGHT Circuit," in E. G. Boxshall and M.R.D. Foot, "Chronology of SOE Operations with the Resistance in France During World War II," December 1960, IWM, London, 05/76/1. See also Archives de la Haute Garonne, 16 J 58.

229 **"Le Batallion de Castelnau"**: Archives départementales du Gers, 42 J 193.

230 **"the rougher maquisards speak of her"**: Raymond Escholier, **Maquis de Gascogne** (Geneva: Editions du Milieu du Monde, 1945), 84.

230 **"a woman of high culture"**: FNA, 72 AJ 39 I, pièce 8a, "Témoignage de M. Philippe de Gunzbourg," 2.

230 **"there was little danger"**: BNA, HS 6/658.

230 **"it was unlikely"**: Ibid.

230 **whilecyclingthrough:**YvonneCormeau,IWMSA,

September 2, 1984, Catalogue number 7369, www
.iwm.org.uk/collections/item/object/80007171.

231 "The only thing": Ibid. Although Cormeau wrote
that George Starr's eyes were gray, his SOE file
stated they were brown. His son, Alfred, wrote,
"My father's eyes were described as brown, but
were more of a light brown to grey, they could be
quite light in certain lights and probably became
lighter with age." Alfred Starr, email to the author, June 1, 2017.

231 "the invisible man": IWM, 09/11/13—16-24,
Collection: Lieutenant Colonel F. C. Cammaerts,
7.

231 "And in their methodic way": Cormeau, IWMSA,
September 2, 1984.

232 "a very, very hard period": Ibid.

232 a second radio operator: Boxshall, "WHEEL-
WRIGHT Circuit."

232 "most pleasant boy": Escholier, Maquis de Gascogne, 86.

233 "We didn't want them to": "Les moulins à poudre
de Toulouse: un patrimoine à conserver," Fédéra-
tion des Moulins de France, July 1, 2012, www
.fdmf.fr/index.php/documentation/histoire/474
-les-moulins-a-poudre-de-toulouse-un-patrimoine
-a-conserver.

234 "the Boches were running madly": BNA, HS
9/1407/1.

234 "it was so beautiful, Minou": Anne-Marie Walters, Moondrop to Gascony, foreword by M.R.D.

Foot, introduction and notes by David Hewson (1946; rept., Petersfield, UK: Harriman House, 2009), 116.

235 **"a series of explosions":** Ibid.

235 **the Gestapo broke into a meeting:** Ibid., 110.

236 **Brossolette intended to escape:** Having heard the story from Vogt, SOE historian Jean Overton Fuller wrote in a letter to General de Gaulle, "As all the floors had balconies, there was no question of doubt for him that he had tried to escape and in descending from one balcony to another, and that he fell only from one balcony to a lower floor . . . Ernest climbed back upstairs, after the accident, to find this guard, and said to him in anger, 'I suppose you were asleep when he arrived.' The guard, who looked terrified and denied it, and as is natural declared that the prisoner threw himself out of the window with such speed and violence that he could not prevent him from committing suicide . . . [Brossolette] did not end his life by suicide." IWM, J. V. Overton Fuller Collection, Box 6, File 6, letter to General de Gaulle, November 11, 1955.

236 **Rabinovitch whispered to John:** BNA, HS 9/1223/4.

239 **The handsome bachelor lamented:** Archives départementales du Gers, 42 J 134, Tomas Guerrero Ortega, age thirty-two, married Eva Odette Berrito, September 10, 1944.

239 **"had thick, long black hair"**: Walters, **Moondrop to Gascony**, 144.

239 **"a mixture of all sorts"**: George Starr, IWMSA, Recording 24613, 1978, Reel 16, www.iwm.org .uk/collections/item/object/80022295.

240 **On April 20, 1944**: Fuller, **The Starr Affair**, 95.

240 **John saw seven women**: Fuller, **The German Penetration of SOE**, 144.

241 **Harry Rée made the first**: Henri Raymond, "Experiences of an SOE Agent in France, Alias César (Harry Rée)," in Michael Elliot Bateman, ed., **The Fourth Dimension of Warfare: Volume I: Intelligence, Subversion, Resistance** (Manchester, UK: Manchester University Press, 1970), 123–24.

241 **"The door of my room"**: IWM, J. V. Overton Fuller Collection, Box 8, File 2, letter from John Starr to Jean Overton Fuller, July 17, 1953.

241 **the childhood friend**: Before his capture, Southgate had one of the most successful careers in F-Section. See BNA, HS 9/1395/3. F-Section chief Maurice Buckmaster wrote in an internal memo on April 8, 1944: "Out of 120 British officers under my orders in France at the moment he has the most efficient and the most disciplined organisation which has carried out the most daring and fruitful attacks on the German armed forces and on industry turning out products (particularly aircraft parts) for the G.A.F. [German Air Force]. He is in direct command of 6,000 men

nearly all of whom he has armed as a result of parachute operations in pursuance of his orders. He is the uncrowned king of five large departments in France."

242 **"I had the shock of my life"**: BNA, HS 9/1395/3, "Report by S/LDR. M. SOUTHGATE." See also IWM, J. V. Overton Fuller Collection, Box 8, File 2, letter from John Starr to Jean Overton Fuller, July 12, 1953.

243 **"a German speaking fluent French"**: BNA, HS 9/1395/3, "Report by S/LDR. M. SOUTH-GATE."

243 **"greeted by a large smile"** . . . **"American K-rations"**: Ibid.

244 **"Bob, we ought to shoot you"**: Fuller, **The Starr Affair**, 98–99.

245 **"was never a single microphone"**: IWM, J. V. Overton Fuller Collection, Box 8, File 2, letter from Ernest Vogt to Jean Overton Fuller, August 8, 1954. Vogt added, "The best proof that there was no listening device is that Starr, Madeleine and Faye were able over some weeks to communicate among themselves by Morse signals tapped on the walls of their cells without anyone of us noticing a thing."

245 **"If I don't do it"**: BNA, HS 9/1395/3, "Report by S/LDR. M. SOUTHGATE."

245 **"he used to run"**: Ibid. Although Southgate recalled hearing John Starr play the accordion, his nephew, Alfred Starr, wrote, "No one in the fam-

ily could play, though most tried at family gatherings." Alfred Starr, email to the author, August 22, 2016.

245 "before he received the full list": BNA, HS 9/1395/3, "Report by S/LDR. M. SOUTHGATE." See also BNA, KV 6/29, Testimony of Ernest Vogt, 19 June 1948: "This was only so that KIEFFER and Dr. Goetz were more quickly informed which sentences came through each evening, because all the messages which were given by Radio London were received by a German wireless station and KIEFFER was notified."

245 "Are you going to take us": Fuller, **The Starr Affair**, 95.

246 "They asked me numerous questions": Ibid.

246 "wireless transmissions between": Ibid. See also BNA, HS 8/422, "COMMENTS. Squadron Leader SOUTHGATE makes the following comments."

247 "The Germans kept adding new circuits": BNA, KV 6/29, "Interrogation of J.A.R. Starr, 28th and 30th May, 1945."

247 number of circuits known to the SD: Fuller, **The Starr Affair**, 101.

247–48 "RECORD OF ACHIEVEMENTS": Boxshall, "WHEELWRIGHT Circuit."

248 "It was the last day of April": Walters, **Moondrop to Gascony**, 119.

249 "Paris was . . . the most dangerous place": Buckmaster, **They Fought Alone**, 226.

250 "How many of my own friends": Walters, **Moondrop to Gascony**, 158 [1946 edition].

250 "that his circuit was": Buckmaster, **They Fought Alone**, 134.

251 "The only trouble was": BNA, HS 9/53/5.

252 "In Gascony, WHEELWRIGHT flourished": M.R.D. Foot, **SOE in France: An Account of the Works of British Special Operations Executive in France, 1940–1944** (London: Her Majesty's Stationery Office, 1966; rept., London: Whitehall History Publishing with Frank Cass, 2004), 332.

252 "nothing but the landing": Escholier, **Maquis de Gascogne**, 86.

CHAPTER TWELVE: DAS REICH

253 "In almost every department": Maurice Buckmaster, **They Fought Alone: The True Story of SOE's Agents in Wartime France** (1958; repr., Biteback Publishing, 2014), 239.

253 "a person of great patience": Ibid., 133.

254 George had given up smoking: George Starr, IWMSA, Recording 24613, 1978, Reel 10, www.iwm.org.uk/collections/item/object/80022295.

255 Next came a litany: Leo Marks, **Between Silk and Cyanide: A Codemakers's War** (New York: HarperCollins, 1998), 521. Marks, who undoubtedly had the best sense of humor in all of SOE, wrote, "Despite the competition from air raids, the ugliest sounds in June were the voices of the

NOTES

BBC announcers. They stopped reading 'Stand by' messages on the 4th, and began broadcasting 'Action' messages on the 5th."

255 **"That evening, 306 messages"**: Buckmaster, **They Fought Alone**, 240.

255 **"I didn't even bother"**: Yvonne Cormeau, interview, "Gladiators of World War II—Special Operations Executive," directed by Charles Messenger (2001; Nubus Martin Productions, 2002), available at www.youtube.com/watch?v=_po7wOf84pc&index=2&list=PLLN3wp0-uPSjrApvf37HcwOVBNwVSdSNU.

255 **"They land at dawn"**: Geoffrey Lucy, "George Starr's Secret War," **Reader's Digest**, June 1978, 181. Lucy interviewed Starr for the article, but he provides no sources for many of the assertions in it. Lucy's article states that Starr himself went into the hayloft and heard the radio transmission. However, Starr made no such claim to Lucy in the rambling interviews lodged at the Imperial War Museum. Yvonne Cormeau's IWM interview makes it clear she heard the message, which was more likely for her as radio operator than for Starr as organizer.

256 **"act as Neptune's trident"**: Marks, **Between Silk and Cyanide**, 520.

256 **Normandy landings "were synchronized"**: BNA, WO 219/112, "Special Report (France), No. 10."

256 **"They came up during the night"**: Yvonne Cormeau, IWMSA, September 2, 1984, Cata-

481

logue number 7369, www.iwm.org.uk/collections/item/object/80007171.

257 **"No arms were supplied"**: BNA, HS 9/1407/1, "Lt.-Col. Starr interviewed by Major [R. H.] Angelo on 20–21 September 1944."

257 **only 2,500 had arms**: BNA, WO 219/112, headquarters, Seventh Army, APO 758, July 26, 1944.

257 **"Alone, two men kept their nerve"**: Raymond Escholier, **Maquis de Gascogne** (Geneva: Editions du Milieu du Monde, 1945), 97.

258 **"My role changed completely"**: George Starr, IWMSA, Reel 7.

258 **"The supposed refugee"**: Escholier, **Maquis de Gascogne**, 117.

259 **"Now Hilaire's organising genius"**: Buckmaster, **They Fought Alone**, 245.

259 **German reliance on their radios**: Marks, **Between Silk and Cyanide**, 519.

259 **"They sent out motorcycle"**: George Starr, IWMSA, Reel 7.

259 **"in spite of seven crack German divisions"**: BNA, HS 9/1407/1, "Lt.-Col. Starr, interviewed by Major [R. H.] Angelo on 20–21 September 1944."

260 **"erudite, intelligent, artistic"**: Escholier, **Maquis de Gascogne**, 120–21. In some documents, Bloch is listed as a lieutenant rather than as captain. Prost appears in different accounts as commandant, captain, and lieutenant. See Archives départementales du Gers, 42 J 134.

260 **Dr. Jean Deyris, who had treated**: Archives

départementales du Gers, 42 J 134, "Combat de Castelnau sur l'Auvignon," 1/2/70.

260 "**for feeding not only**": BNA, HS 9/1407/1, "Court of Enquiry re Lt. Col. G.R. STARR (SOE), Feb. 1945."

261 "**The young men of Condom**": Anne-Marie Walters, **Moondrop to Gascony**, foreword by M.R.D. Foot, introduction and notes by David Hewson (1946; rept., Petersfield, UK: Harriman House, 2009), 139.

262 "**assigned to blow the bridges**": Archives départementales du Gers, 42 J 136, "Testimony of Commandant Solal of the Military Justice to Monsieur Vila, 11 May 1945."

262 "**the tricolor flag was raised**": Archives départementales du Gers, 42 J 134, "Activities of the Castelnau Battalion from 6 June to 3 July 1944."

262 "**The first job was**": BNA, HS 9/1407/1, "Court of Enquiry re Lt. Col. G.R. STARR (SOE), Feb. 1945."

262 "**And every man used for this purpose**": Buckmaster, **They Fought Alone**, 244.

263 "**The supreme battle**": Charles de Gaulle, **The Complete War Memoirs of Charles de Gaulle**, trans. Jonathan Griffin and Richard Howard (New York: Carroll & Graf, 1998), 560.

263 **To some, de Gaulle's speech**: Among some former **résistants**, resentment of de Gaulle outlived the war. Jeanne Robert said to me in 2014, "**Nous, nous dépendions de Buckmaster, et non de Mon-**

sieur de Gaulle, hein, excusez-moi." ("Us, we depended on Buckmaster and not on Monsieur de Gaulle, so, excuse me.")

264 **Théo Lévy raced into Castelnau:** Escholier, **Maquis de Gascogne,** 119.

264 **"always in espadrilles":** Archives départementales du Gers, 42 J 134, "Combat de Castelnau sur l'Auvignon," 1/2/70.

265 **"it was not up to us":** BNA, HS 9/1407/1, "Court of Enquiry re Lt. Col. G.R. STARR (SOE), Feb. 1945."

265 **the Spanish Republicans:** Ibid.

265 **"The Germans tried to impose":** BNA, HS 9/1407/1, "Lt.-Col. Starr interviewed by Major [R. H.] Angelo on 20–21 September 1944."

266 **railroad workers drained:** M.R.D. Foot, **S.O.E.: The Special Operations Executive, 1940– 1946** (1984; rept., London: Arrow Books, 1993) 232–34.

266 **Das Reich routed the maquisards:** Horst Boog, Gerhard Krebs, Detlef Vogel, eds., **Germany and the Second World War,** vol. VII (Oxford: Oxford University Press, 2006), 644.

267 **"Pick a bend in the road":** George Starr, IWMSA, Reel 7.

267 **"The region (Dordogne-Sud) became":** FNA, 72 AJ 39 I, pièce 8a, "Action d'Hilaire lui-même."

267 **"wanted to go to Agen":** Ibid.

268 **"For the reestablishment":** Sarah Farmer, **Mar-**

tyred Village: Commemorating the 1944 Massacre at Oradour-sur-Glane (Berkeley: University of California Press, 1990), 48.

268 "After the first two or three": Walters, **Moondrop to Gascony**, 169 [1946 edition].

269 **Gunzbourg feared that:** FNA, 72 AJ 39 I, pièce 8 a. "Témoignage de M. Philippe de Gunzbourg," 405. See also Arthur L. Funk, "Churchill, Eisenhower and the French Resistance," **Military Affairs** 45, no. 1 (February 1981): 29–35. The United States made three large drops to the Resistance on June 25, July 14, and August 1, 1944.

269 **"CURRENTLY IMPOSSIBLE PREDICT":** FNA, 3 AG 2 562, "Telegrams à ELLIPSE [Eugène Déhelette]," quoted in Benjamin F. Jones, "Freeing France: The Allies, the Résistance, and the JEDBURGHS" (MA thesis, University of Nebraska, 2008), 186–87, www.dtic.mil/dtic/tr/fulltext/u2/a488406.pdf.

269 **civilians of Oradour-sur-Glane:** Farmer, **Martyred Village**, 20–24.

270 **"New Zealand pilot":** Walters, **Moondrop to Gascony**, 140.

271 **"I began to see the change":** Ibid.

272 **sabotage the railroad bridge:** Alain Beyneix, **Les combats d'Astaffort du 13 juin 1944** (Biarritz, France: Atlantica Editions, 2011), 12.

273 **"The German woman":** Escholier, **Maquis de Gascogne**, 129.

273 "this inflexible man": Ibid.

274 "Hatred and violence burst through": Buckmaster, **They Fought Alone**, 253.

274 "Germans were shot": Ibid., 158.

274 **allowed George to accelerate training**: Archives départementales du Gers, 42 J 134, "Activities of the Castelnau Battalion from 6 June to 3 July 1944."

274–75 **a crash course in Sten and Bren guns**: Ibid. Solal recorded Captain Weber's company of 100 to 140 men; Lieutenant Hornoga's company of 100 to 140; Lieutenant Herlin's company of 100; Commandant Camilo's Spanish company of 150; Lieutenant Lalanne's 25 to 30 irregulars; and an antitank section under Solal himself.

275 "the Colonel's Hollywood Brigade": George Starr, IWMSA, Reel 16.

275 **Hollywood's "biggest star"**: Escholier, **Maquis de Gascogne**, 122.

275 "rough men, bearded": Ibid., 116.

276 "The prisoner was literally": BNA, HS 9/1407/1, "Court of Enquiry re Lt. Col. G.R. STARR (SOE), Feb. 1945."

276 **150 miliciens ambushed André's detachment**: Walters, **Moondrop to Gascony**, 146.

277 **Physicians feared the Germans**: The hospital had reason to fear German reprisals. The Gers newspaper **La Dépêche** wrote on October 1, 2013: "Another affair, that of Astaffort, which saw the **maquis** confronting the Milice and then the Ger-

mans on 13 June, was the probable cause of the machine-gunning, two days after, of the victims at Lectoure where the bodies of the victims had been taken by the Red Cross."

277 "the only survivor": Walters, **Moondrop to Gascony**, 147.

278 "I couldn't help tears": Ibid., 147–48. She also wrote, "It was a painful parade: for the first time in our safe and secure maquis, death had been brought right before our eyes."

278 **Walters's relationship with George:** Walters's memoir, **Moondrop to Gascony**, did not mention that George had seized her pistol and dispatched her to Gunzbourg's camp. She wrote only that she spent some nights with the Castagnos family at Mamoulens and others in Castelnau. In George's interviews, he similarly did not refer to the incident. The only record of the encounter was in **Maquis de Gascogne** by Raymond Escholier, who was in the Gers and knew the participants. His account had Anne-Marie returning late to Castelnau, but her memoir placed her there in time to witness the funeral on June 13. That was within the three days George had allotted her to spend with Gunzbourg.

278 **This upset Walters:** Walters, **Moondrop to Gascony**, 231.

278 "Reluctantly, Maggie [Maguy] finished": Escholier, **Maquis de Gascogne**, 124.

279 "A rather violent discussion": Ibid.

279 they "became comrades": Ibid., 131.

280 "swore by all the Gods": BNA, HS 9/1407/1, "Court of Enquiry re Lt. Col. G.R. STARR (SOE), Feb. 1945." See also BNA, WO 219/112, in which SHAEF acknowledged, "The French have seen [German] troops which committed these atrocities taken prisoner, at times put to work, quite happily chewing gum and eating sweets, while little or no attention has been paid to the atrocities committed."

280 "Imprison us where you like": Escholier, **Maquis de Gascogne**, 132. He wrote, "These last, having demanded by reason of their status as soldiers not to be held with traitors, were incarcerated in a room beside the infirmary in the Command Post and the Miliciens in the church."

280 beside Dr. Deyris's infirmary: Archives départementales du Gers, 42 J 136, "Testimony of Commandant Solal of the Military Justice to Monsieur Vila, 11 May 1945. " Solal wrote that on June 17 the Spanish unit captured the eight Germans, who were on their way to requisition gasoline.

280 **Wehrmacht had lost control of the roads:** Ibid.

281 "He had become famous": Walters, **Moondrop to Gascony**, 169 [1946 edition].

281 "God is with you": Escholier, **Maquis de Gascogne**, 132–36.

281 "the traitors turned to the wall": Walters, **Moondrop to Gascony**, 170 [1946 edition].

282 "this betrayal was exposed": Escholier, **Maquis de Gascogne**, 149.

CHAPTER THIRTEEN: THE BATTLE OF CASTELNAU

283 "Our job was": Maurice Buckmaster, **They Fought Alone: The True Story of SOE's Agents in Wartime France** (1958; repr., London: Biteback Publishing, 2014), 95.

284 "WE THANK YOU": Leo Marks, **Between Silk and Cyanide: A Codemakers's War** (New York: HarperCollins, 1998), 522.

284 "SORRY TO SEE": M.R.D. Foot, **SOE in France: An Account of the Works of British Special Operations Executive in France, 1940–1944** (London: Her Majesty's Stationery Office, 1966; rept., London: Whitehall History Publishing with Frank Cass, 2004), 307; and Jean Overton Fuller, **The German Penetration of SOE: France, 1941–1944** (Maidstone, UK: George Mann, 1975), 145. Leo Marks, M.R.D. Foot, and Jean Overton Fuller date the exchange of telegrams as June 6, 1944. Josef Placke and Ernest Vogt stated that it took place in July. Josef Placke recalled that Dr. Goetz sent the message, which said, "WE THANK YOU FOR ALL THE ARMS YOU HAVE SENT US SIGNED GESTAPO." Vogt wrote about the incident, "It is true that Dr. Goetz sent in July 1944 a message to Buckmaster thanking him for everything he sent us and the information that it was we who had sent the transmissions. . . . In sending that message Goetz hoped to provoke

confusion in London and not knowing any longer which line to trust. He received the response from Buck: 'You have lost your nerve.'" IWM, J. V. Overton Fuller Collection, Box 8, File 2, letters, Ernest Vogt to Jean Overton Fuller, October 10, 1954, and November 2, 1957.

285 "Is this to make sure": Jean Overton Fuller, **Conversations with a Captor** (West Sussex, UK: Fuller d'Arch Smith, 1973), 36.

285 "We've razed London": Jean Overton Fuller, **The Starr Affair** (London: Victor Gollancz, 1954), 103.

285 "I got so fed up": BNA, HS 9/1395/3, "Report by S/Ldr. M. Southgate."

286 Camilo's Spaniards ambushed: Archives départementales du Gers, 42 J 136, "Testimony of Commandant Solal of the Military Justice to Monsieur Vila, 11 May 1945."

287 "orders that the German prisoners": BNA, HS 9/1407/1, "Court of Enquiry re Lt. Col. G.R. STARR (SOE), Feb. 1945." Starr added, "I thought it would be bad luck for any fighting man to be bumped off by his own people."

287 assemble the village women: Anne-Marie Walters, **Moondrop to Gascony**, foreword by M.R.D. Foot, introduction and notes by David Hewson (1946; rept., Petersfield, UK: Harriman House, 2009), 149–50.

287 "first great battle of Armagnac": Raymond Es-

cholier, **Maquis de Gascogne** (Geneva: Editions du Milieu du Monde, 1945), 147.

288 **more than 1,500 SS troops:** Archives Municipales de Toulouse, 85 Z 6, "Historique de l'Organisation." (See blue notebook, 86.)

288 **"Some [units] of the Das Reich":** Archives départementales du Gers, 42 J 134, "LA RESISTANCE A CASTELNAU SUR L'AUVIGNON: Recits et renseignements recueillis par M. HOUTH."

288 **"took his revenge":** Jeanne and Michèle Robert, **Le Réseau Victoire dans le Gers: Mémoires du 19 mai à la liberation** (Saint-Cyr-sur-Loire: Editions Alan Sutton, 2003), 100. The book includes the complete text of Maurice Rouneau's wartime memoir, **Quatre ans dans l'ombre** (Rennes les Bains: A. Bousquet, 1948), 100.

289 **"What a sharpshooter":** Escholier, **Maquis de Gascogne,** 152.

290 **"fought bravely with their rifles":** Ibid., 150.

291 **"I went and the Feldwebel":** BNA, HS 9/1407/1, "Court of Enquiry re Lt. Col. G.R. STARR (SOE), Feb. 1945."

291 **"They freed their prisoners":** Escholier, **Maquis de Gascogne,** 154.

291 **A rear guard stayed:** Walters, **Moondrop to Gascony,** 153.

291 **"blow up the village":** Archives départementales du Gers, 42 J 134, "Activities of the Castelnau Battalion from 6 June to 3 July 1944."

292 "Castelnau is destroyed": Ibid.

292 "Castelnau of the Wolves fell": Escholier, **Maquis de Gascogne**, 155.

292 "the Germans suffered 380 losses": Archives Municipales de Toulouse, 85 Z 6, "Historique de l'Organisation." SOE recorded the same totals. See Lieutenant Colonel E. G. Boxshall, "WHEELWRIGHT Circuit," in E. G. Boxshall and M.R.D. Foot, "Chronology of SOE Operations with the Resistance in France During World War II," December 1960, IWM, London, 05/76/1. Another French account was equally lopsided in favor of the colonel's Hollywood Brigade: Germans, 253 killed and 149 wounded; French, 17 killed and 6 wounded.

292 George's losses were "very light": Escholier, **Maquis de Gascogne**, 155.

292 radio operator Lieutenant Parsons: Archives Municipales de Toulouse, 85 Z 6, "Historique de l'Organisation." Parsons had by then transmitted eighty-four coded messages for Starr. Philippe de Gunzbourg, who was not present but spoke to many of the combatants, wrote that about twenty of George's fighters were killed but that "German losses were much heavier." See FNA, 72 AJ 39 I, pièce 8a, "Témoignage de M. Philippe de Gunzbourg," 7.

293 "it was generally rumoured": BNA, HS 9/1407/1, "Court of Enquiry re Lt. Col. G.R. STARR (SOE), Feb. 1945."

294 "fifty partisans killed": FNA, 72 AJ 38 I, pièce 8b, "Rapport de l'activité de la résistance dans les arrondissements de Bergerac, Barlat, et quelques communes du Nord du Lot-et-Garonne à partir du 7 juin 1944 par Philippe de GUNZBOURG."

294 "That day had huge repercussions": Ibid.

295 "Prisoners captured from the Second": "Patriots in France Snarl Foe's Lines," New York Times, June 23, 1944.

295 Resistance that "has increased both in size": "Army of the Interior," New York Times, June 24, 1944.

295 "FFI have fought exceedingly well": BNA, WO 219/112, "Special Report (France) No. 10."

296 "The extra fortnight's delay": Foot, SOE in France, 350.

297 "With two soldiers" . . . "engine was already running": Yvonne Cormeau, IWMSA, September 2, 1984, Catalogue number 7369, www.iwm.org.uk/collections/item/object/80007171.

298 greeted the first Jedburgh team: Walters, Moondrop to Gascony, 177.

298 Team Bugatti, commanded by: Olivier Matet, "Bataille du maquis de Campels, Juillet 1944, Commune d'Arbon, 31," http://passion.histoire.pagesperso-orange.fr/bataille_maquis_campels.pdf. See also Major Robert E. Mattingly, USMC, "Herringbone Cloak—GI Dagger: Marines of the OSS" (Occasional Paper, History and Museums Division, Headquarters, U.S. Marine Corps,

Washington, D.C., 1989), 135, available at https://
ia601304.us.archive.org/2/items/Herringbone
CloakGIDaggerMarinesOfTheOSS-nsia/Herring
boneCloakGIDaggerMarinesOfTheOSS.pdf.

299 "I brought KANSUL": BNA, HS 9/1407/1,
"Miss A. M. Walters, COLLETTE, WHEEL-
WRIGHT, 18th September, 1944, REPORT ON
MISSION IN FRANCE."

299 Fuller "discussed the work": BNA, HS 6/658,
Yvonne Cormeau, interrogated by Captain Howard, 5.1.45.

299 "many ambushes against": Archives Municipales de Toulouse, 85 Z 6, "Historique de
l'Organisation," 7. See also Colin Beavan, Operation Jedburgh: D-Day and America's First
Shadow War (New York: Viking Penguin, 2006).

299 captured a courier: Archives Municipales de Toulouse, 85 Z 6, "Historique de l'Organisation," 7.

299 "a terrific morale lifter": BNA, HS 9/1407/1,
"Miss A. M. Walters, COLLETTE, WHEEL-
WRIGHT, 18th September, 1944, REPORT ON
MISSION IN FRANCE."

300 "I sent him there": George Starr, IWMSA, Recording 24613, 1978, Reel 16, www.iwm.org.uk/
collections/item/object/80022295.

300 farming village of Lannemaignan: Archives
départementales du Gers, 42 J 134, "Activities of the Castelnau Battalion from 6 June to 3
July 1944." See also BNA, HS 9/1407/1, "Court
of Enquiry re Lt. Col. G.R. STARR (SOE),

Feb. 1945," in which Starr stated, "The night of 21/22 June Capt Parisot and myself and the various officers went into consultation and it was decided that the whole should become one as quickly as possible and the whole should be under the command of Capt Parisot and I should devote myself to my real job, thus relinquishing command of the Maquis which I had commanded between 6 June and 21 June. This did cause some concern to the Castelnau Maquis as they said they wanted to serve under me. They threatened to go home if I didn't command them. A few went home but the others did agree to serve under Capt Parisot. From then on I lived at the PC of Captain Parisot."

300 "I didn't give orders": George Starr, IWMSA, Reel 15.

300 "a real society of nations": Escholier, **Maquis de Gascogne**, 158.

301 "One of the chief reasons": BNA, HS 9/1407/1, "Court of Enquiry re Lt. Col. G.R. STARR (SOE), Feb. 1945."

301 "becoming a little queer": Walters, **Moondrop to Gascony**, Hewson edition, 172.

301 "The men of the Maquis": "Call for Arms for French Patriots," **Observer**, June 25, 1944.

302 "Take this message": George Starr, IWMSA, Reel 14.

302 "roared with laughter": Ibid.

303 Abel Sempé had founded: Armagnac Sempé,

whose motto is **Sempé it Semper,** was still in business in 2016. www.armagnac-sempe.fr/en.html#.

303 **"The cars weren't much good"**: George Starr, IWMSA, Reel 7.

303 **"It was also quite wrong"**: BNA, HS 6/583, Anne-Marie Walters, "Report on Mission to France, 18 September 1944."

CHAPTER FOURTEEN: THE GERMANS RETREAT

305 **"Hilaire's network totally dislocated"**: Maurice Buckmaster, **They Fought Alone: The True Story of SOE's Agents in Wartime France** (1958; repr., London: Biteback Publishing, 2014), 126.

306 **"Towards 19.00 hours"**: BNA, HS 7/122, Major R. A. Bourne-Patterson's "British Circuits in France, 1941–1944, Appendix B, Report of Hilaire on Post-D-Day Activities."

306 **"Give them ten minutes"**: Archives Municipales de Toulouse, 85 Z 6, "Historique de l'Organisation," 7.

307 **the maquis sabotaged cables**: "Sabotage Darkens Toulouse," **New York Times,** July 9, 1944.

307 **"There are about 4,000"**: BNA, HS 9/1407/1, "Court of Enquiry re Lt. Col. G.R. STARR (SOE), Feb. 1945."

307 **"Capt. Parisot decided"**: Ibid.

310 **"was a good fighting man"**: Ibid.

310 **"I never saw him again"**: Ibid.

310 "I found out the man": Ibid.

311 "I was informed that": Ibid.

311 "I recognised it": Ibid.

311 "a dropping operation": BNA, WO 235/560, "Statement of Hans Kieffer, 29 November 1946." Unless otherwise indicated, Kieffer's comments on the British prisoners are from this nine-page sworn document.

312 "we had dropped into an ambush": Serge Vaculik, **Air Commando** (New York: Dutton, 1955), 194.

313 "they were not able": BNA, WO 235/560, "Statement of Hans Kieffer, 29 November 1946."

313 interrogators drenched them: Vaculik, **Air Commando,** 202–7.

314 "Kieffer was alone": IWM, J. V. Overton Fuller Collection, Box 8, File 2, letter, Ernest Vogt to Jean Overton Fuller, August 28, 1954.

315 "I actually met Ravanel": BNA, HS 9/1407/1.

315 "Lawrence of Arabia": FNA, 13 AV 53, Serge Ravanel interview, January 17, 1992. Quoted in Robert Gildea, **Fighters in the Shadows: A New History of French Resistance** (London: Faber and Faber, 2015), 363.

315 Ravanel appointed George: BNA, HS 9/1407/1, "Court of Enquiry re Lt. Col. G.R. STARR (SOE), Feb. 1945." Starr added, "I produce copies of three signals, two from London to me, and one from me to London dated respectively 22nd July, 21st July and 23rd July."

315 **promoting him to lieutenant colonel:** Ibid.

316 **"I wanted London":** Ibid.

317 **"Do you think you could go":** Anne-Marie Walters, **Moondrop to Gascony,** foreword by M.R.D. Foot, introduction and notes by David Hewson (1946; rept., Petersfield, UK: Harriman House, 2009), 286 [1946 edition].

317 **"permission was given":** BNA, HS 9/1407/1, "Court of Enquiry re Lt. Col. G.R. STARR (SOE), Feb. 1945."

317 **"She did not forgive Hilaire":** Raymond Escholier, **Maquis de Gascogne** (Geneva: Editions du Milieu du Monde, 1945), 171.

317 **"Have had to send Colette":** BNA, HS 9/1407/1.

318 **"I was to help rounding up":** BNA HS 9/1407/1, "Miss A. M. Walters, COLLETTE, WHEELWRIGHT, 18th September, 1944, REPORT ON MISSION IN FRANCE."

319 **"They set fire to the house":** Escholier, **Maquis de Gascogne,** 179–80.

320 **Remembering the massacre:** Ibid., 181. Madame Parisot said to Escholier that a woman from the village told her, "We will never forget that M. Parisot sacrificed all he had and risked his family's life so the Germans would not cause us trouble. That was beautiful, that!"

320 **"In southwestern France":** "French Guerrillas Cut Germans' Lines," **New York Times,** August 9, 1944.

321 **"The attack was most successful":** BNA, HS

7/122, Major R. A. Bourne-Patterson's "British Circuits in France, 1941–1944, Appendix B, Report of Hilaire on Post-D-Day Activities."

321 **"You are there":** Escholier, **Maquis de Gascogne,** 186.

321 **Starr's sign-off echoed:** Leo Marks, **Between Silk and Cyanide: A Codemakers's War** (New York: HarperCollins, 1998), 45.

321 **next major objective: Toulouse:** Pierre Bertaux, **Le Bataillon d'Armagnac: Un groupe de résistants pas comme les autres** (Paris: Printemps, 1944), 9.

322 **"They made the occupation":** "OSS Aid to the French Resistance in World War II: Operational Group Command, Office of Strategic Services: Company B—2671st Special Reconnaissance Battalion," FNA, 72 AJ 84 I, Pièce, 9.

323 **"Je ne suis pas":** "Les réseaux de résistance Eugène-Prunus et Hilaire-Wheelwright du SOE à Montréjeau sous l'occupation allemande de 1942 à 1944," www.mairie-montrejeau.fr/fr/notre-bastide/histoire/doc_view/728-le-soe-a-montrejeau-sous-l-occupation-allemande-de-1942-a-1944.html. Fuller said, "I am not an orator. I am a soldier. I have a debt to acknowledge to France which aided the liberation of my country."

324 **Camilo's Spaniards went behind:** Archives départementales du Gers, 42 J 35, "Témoignage A. Ruiz et Manuel Fernandez."

324 **A German colonel shouted, "Nein!":** Escholier, **Maquis de Gascogne,** 189.

325 "We captured several lorries": BNA, HS 7/122, Major R. A. Bourne-Patterson's "British Circuits in France, 1941–1944, Appendix B, Report of Hilaire on Post-D-Day Activities." See also La Commission Départementale du Gers de l'Information Historique, "1944: Les Années de Combat," http://sdonac32.pagesperso-orange.fr/1944.htm.

325 Four German officers: Escholier, **Maquis de Gascogne,** 191.

325 "By his continual gallantry": BNA, HS 9/1407/1, "Nr. 87 of 21st July 1944."

326 "Termignon lost his temper": Ibid., "Court of Enquiry re Lt. Col. G.R. STARR (SOE), Feb. 1945."

327 "I am writing to your husband": Escholier, **Maquis de Gascogne,** 192.

327 "What a spectacle": Major Robert E. Mattingly, USMC, "Herringbone Cloak—GI Dagger: Marines of the OSS" (Occasional Paper, History and Museums Division, Headquarters, U.S. Marine Corps, Washington, D.C., 1989), 145, available at https://ia601304.us.archive.org/2/items/Herring boneCloakGIDaggerMarinesOfTheOSS-nsia/ Herring boneCloakGIDaggerMarinesOfTheOSS .pdf.

327 "The entire Pyrenees region": "FFI Masters of Pyrenees," **New York Times,** August 21, 1944.

328 "The French Forces": "French Liberate Toulouse, Hendaye," **New York Times,** August 22, 1944.

329 "He stopped the whole column": Yvonne Cormeau, IWMSA, September 2, 1984, Cata-

logue number 7369, www.iwm.org.uk/collections/item/object/80007171.

329 "Maquisards, my brothers": Escholier, **Maquis de Gascogne**, 195.

330 "more than 50,000 square miles": "FFI Gain Control of 14 Departments," **New York Times**, August 23, 1944.

330 "On his birthday": BNA, KV 6/29, "Interrogation of J.A.R. Starr, 28th and 30th May, 1945."

331 "read out to me a teleprint": BNA, WO 235/560.

331 "so-called Commando raids": Ibid., "Statement of Hans Kieffer, 29 November, 1946."

332 "I was not able to see": Ibid., "Statement of Fritz Hildemann, 30 December 1946."

333 "Startled, the Germans did not": Vaculik, **Air Commando**, 232.

333 "I opened my handcuffs": BNA, WO 235/560, "Proceedings of the Military Court (War Crimes) Trial, NOAILLES case, Deputy Judge Advocate General, 22 April 1947." See also Lorna Almonds Windmill, **Gentleman Jim: The Wartime Story of a Founder of the SAS and Special Forces** (London: Constable, 2011), 202–3.

333 "I made a run for it": BNA, WO 235/560, "Proceedings of the Military Court (War Crimes) Trial, NOAILLES case, Deputy Judge Advocate General, 22 April 1947."

334 "I was not present": Ibid., "Statement of Hans Kieffer, 29 November 1946."

335 " 'This is a Schwenerie' ": BNA, WO 208/4679,

"NOTES ON INTERROGATION OF WERNER EMIL RUEHL, BORN ON 5.6.1905 IN MARXLOH, BY SQUADRON OFFICER V.M. ATKINS AT L.D.C. ON 24.10.46."

335 "Now that you are going": Jean Overton Fuller, **The Starr Affair** (London: Victor Gollancz, 1954), 182.

CHAPTER FIFTEEN: "I SAID 'SHIT' TO DE GAULLE"

338 "The Resistance was": Maurice Buckmaster, **They Fought Alone: The True Story of SOE's Agents in Wartime France** (1958; repr., London: Biteback Publishing, 2014), 269.

339 "Around Ravanel, leaders": Charles de Gaulle, **War Memoirs: Salvation, 1944–1946**, trans. Richard Howard (London: Weidenfeld and Nicholson, 1960), 19.

340 "I was as close to him": George Starr, IWMSA, Recording 24613, 1978, Reel 15, www.iwm.org .uk/collections/item/object/80022295.

340 "Parisot did not hear": Raymond Escholier, **Maquis de Gascogne** (Geneva: Editions du Milieu du Monde, 1945), 199.

341 "He was a leader": Ibid., 200–1. Lesur's Resistance name was "Marceau."

341 "the most durable": FNA, 72 AJ 39 I, pièce 8a, "Témoignage de M. Philippe de Gunzbourg," 7.

341 "a brave soldier": BNA, HS 9/1407/1, "Court

of Enquiry re Lt. Col. G.R. STARR (SOE), Feb. 1945."

341 **Camilo attended another ceremony**: Archives départementales du Gers, 42 J 134.

342 **fifty thousand armed men**: "The Commissaires Challenged by Resistants: Toulouse and Poitiers," **Journal of Modern History** 53, no. 1 (March 1981): D-1102–14.

342 **"people who had been high-handedly arrested"**: BNA, HS 9/1407/1, "Court of Enquiry re Lt. Col. G.R. STARR (SOE), Feb. 1945."

343 **"I am Colonel 'Hilaire'"**: Henri Amouroux, **La grande histoire des Français sous l'occupation** (Paris: Robert Laffont, 1998), 162. Amouroux quoted Starr's Resistance colleague Pierre Peré, who said Starr had repeated the words to him. See also Robert Aron, **Histoire de la libération de la France: juin 1944–mai 1945** (Paris: Librairie Arthème Fayard, 1959), 603–4. Aron quoted Starr as telling Bertaux he had more than a thousand men under his command.

344 **"I said 'shit' to de Gaulle"**: Ibid., 162. See also E. H. Cookridge, **They Came from the Sky** (London: Heinemann, 1965), 584.

344–45 **"You will give him twenty-four hours"**: Aron, **Histoire de la libération de la France**, 606. In one version of the encounter, de Gaulle relented and told Starr, "I see that you really know how to use the word **merde**." In a second, Geoffrey Lucy wrote in "George Starr's Secret War," **Read-**

er's Digest, June 1978, 199, that de Gaulle said, "I've heard two things about you, and now I know they're true. They say you're frightened of nobody, and that you can swear like a Frenchman." There is no primary source for either. Lucy went further in expanding on history with another uncon-firmed story that King George VI, when he pre-sented the Distinguished Service Order to Starr, said, "Ah, you're the grand little chap who told de Gaulle off. Thank you."

345 "Lastly 'Colonel Hilary' ": de Gaulle, War Mem-oirs: Salvation, 1944–1946, 20.

345 he was "very, very upset": Yvonne Cormeau, IWMSA, September 2, 1984, Catalogue num-ber 7369, www.iwm.org.uk/collections/item/object/80007171.

345 When Serge Ravanel reported: Robert Gildea, "De Gaulle Makes Officers Cry and the General Poli-tics of the Liberation," January 13, 2014, https://exampleliberation.wordpress.com/2014/01/13/de-gaulle-makes-officers-cry-the-general-politics-of-the-liberation-by-robert-gildea. See also de Gaulle, War Memoirs: Salvation, 1944–1946, 20: "Before leaving Toulouse, I rescinded the order that kept the gendarmerie in barracks and restored these brave men to their normal duties." Restoring the gendarmes' authority without purg-ing those who had oppressed them angered the maquisards as much as de Gaulle's maltreatment of Serge Ravanel and George Starr. The Tou-

louse gendarmerie had arrested the city's Jews in August 1942, three months before the Germans occupied the city. In 1943, when the Germans demanded the names of all Jews still living there, the police chief, Jean Philippe, resigned. He went underground with the Resistance, but the Germans captured, tortured, and executed him. He was a notable exception to the rule of the Toulouse gendarmerie's collusion with the Third Reich.

346 **Rather than thank Landes:** Roger Landes, foreword to David Nicholson, **Aristide: Warlord of the Resistance** (London: Leo Cooper, 1994), i.

346 **another SOE agent, Peter Lake:** "Peter Lake," obituary, **Daily Telegraph,** July 12, 2009, www.telegraph.co.uk/news/obituaries/military-obituaries/special-forces-obituaries/5811738/Peter-Lake.html.

346 **"And therefore we were glad":** Cormeau, IWMSA, September 2, 1984.

347 **"Hilaire himself, unfortunately":** BNA, HS 7/122, Major R. A. Bourne-Patterson's "British Circuits in France, 1941–1944," 94.

348 **"Forget the false beards":** Jane Clinton, "Love and Training Spies," **Daily Express,** September 1, 2013, www.express.co.uk/news/uk/426006/Love-and-training-spies-WWII-secret-army-member-tells-how-she-learnt-to-be-a-good-liar.

348 **"I said I did not know":** BNA, HS 9/1407/1, "Court of Enquiry re Lt. Col. G.R. STARR (SOE), Feb. 1945." Quotes from the following

two pages are all drawn from this trial transcript.

350 **George and his fourteen fellow officers:** Ibid.
The file, marked PERSONAL AND CONFIDENTIAL,
20TH JANUARY 1945, provided this list of the offi-
cers who "dined in the Mess on the occasion of
Colonel Starr's visit on October 30th and listened
to his talk afterwards": Lt. Col. S.H.C. Woolrych,
Intelligence Corps; Major P.L.A. Follis, Intel-
ligence Corps; Major H. S. Hunt, King's Royal
Rifle Corps; Major R. H. Angelo, Intelligence
Corps; Captain C. C. Howard, General List; Cap-
tain R.J.L. Steward, Intelligence Corps; Captain
P. B. Whittaker, Royal Artillery; Captain J. H.
Walker, East Lancashire Regiment; Captain J. D.
Taylor, Royal Artillery; Captain J. M. Lonsdale, In-
telligence Corps; Captain H.R.F. Burr, Intelligence
Corps; Captain F. Lofts, General List; Captain
F. W. Rhodes, Pioneer Corps; and Lt. V[iolet] Dun-
das, First Aid Nursing Yeomanry. The list does not
include the Captain Harris to whom Starr referred.

354 **"They didn't know me":** George Starr, IWMSA,
Reel 5.

354 **"The thin man":** Alfred Starr, email to the author, August 22, 2016.

354 **"I have formed the impression":** BNA, HS
9/1407/1.

355 **"carefully investigated the charges":** BNA, HS
9/1407/1, letter from Colonel Buckmaster to
AD/E, December 30, 1944.

356 **"Unless this is done"**: Ibid., letter, "Personal and Confidential, To: AD/E [Mockler-Ferryman] From: A/CD [Gubbins], 5 January 1945."

356 **"an unreliable witness"**: Ibid., letter, "Personal and Confidential, To: AD/E [Mockler-Ferryman], From: Col. Buckmaster, 8 January 1945."

356 **"Well, I asked for it"**: George Starr, IWMSA, Reel 3.

357 **Major Frank Soskice**: Frank Soskice, a career barrister, became solicitor general and home secretary in postwar British Labour Party governments.

357 **"investigate the conduct"**: BNA, HS 9/1407/1, "Court of Enquiry re Lt. Col. G.R. STARR (SOE), Feb. 1945."

357 **Monday morning, February 5, 1945**: Ibid. The court of inquiry produced 213 handwritten pages of evidence and testimony, including Starr's sworn statement, but pages 18 to 172 of the official transcript went missing from government files. Court testimony in the rest of this chapter is from the surviving pages in this file. The handwritten transcript, taken in haste while witnesses testified, contains spelling and punctuation errors. I have corrected these, but made no other changes to the original.

361 **"Mary [sic] Walters came"**: George Starr, IWMSA, Reel 20. Jeanne Robert, although she was in England during the events discussed in the court of inquiry, knew of the allegations. Seventy years later, she defended Starr: "Oh, no. I don't believe it."

363 **"Fearing that summary justice"**: Jeanne Robert to the author, January 24, 2014: "The principal collaborator was a notaire, Rizon, Maître Rizon. Collaborator at heart, he was the first to receive the Legion of Honor in Condom. His brother was with de Gaulle, so there you go."

369 **"On arriving at the camp"**: BNA, WO 311/933, "Name of Source: J.A.R. STARR, Date of Capture: 18th July 1943."

373 **"During my 11 months there"**: BNA, KV 6/29, "Rough Report by Capt. J.A.R. STARR, dictated to C.S.M. Goddard at Stn. XXVII, commencing 9 May 45."

374 **"I'm going to see Oncle George"**: Ethel Starr Lagier, email to the author, November 8, 2016.

375 **"some quite amusing things"**: Jean Overton Fuller, **The Starr Affair** (London: Victor Gollancz, 1954), 136.

375 **"NOTE ON CAPTAIN J.A. STARR'S"**: BNA, HS 9/1406/8.

375 **"When we got back"**: Fuller, **The Starr Affair**, 135.

376 were **"extremely critical"**: BNA, HS 9/1406/8, "NOTE ON CAPTAIN J.A. STARR'S INTERROGATION."

376 **"The brothers had been operating"**: Ibid., "Interrogation of the NEWTON Brothers dated 2nd May 1945."

376 **"Asked his opinion"**: Ibid., "EVIDENCE OF

ARRESTED AGENTS WHO SAW STARR AT
AVENUE FOCH."

377 "Devoted to the German cause": BNA, HS
9/1406/8, "STATEMENT MADE BY PIERRE
BONY OF THE RUE LAURISTON GANG
IN PARIS."

378 "When he [John Starr] got to Paris": Ibid.,
"STATEMENT MADE BY MICHEL BOUIL-
LON TO LT. COL. WARDEN IN PARIS."

378 "She was particularly bitter": Ibid., memo to
Commander Senter, RNVR, London from
Lt. Col. Warden Paris, April 21, 1945. See also
BNA, KV 6/29, "NOTE OF INTERVIEW IN
FRESNES PRISON WITH ROSE-MARIE
HOLWEDTS, nee CORDONNIER."

379 "Many thanks for your letter": BNA, HS
9/1406/8, letter, E.J.P. Cussen to Lt. Col. T. G.
Roche, July 4, 1945.

379 "he let the side down": Fuller, The Starr Affair,
144.

380 "suffered appalling treatment": Commons Sitting, June 5, 1967, Hansard, vol. 747, cc753–62,
accessed online at Hansard, http://hansard
.millbanksystems.com/commons/1967/jun/05/
special-operations-executive-mr-alfred.

381 Krupps, arms makers: William Manchester, The
Arms of Krupp: The Rise and Fall of the In-
dustrial Dynasty That Armed Germany at War
(Boston: Little, Brown, 1964), 701.

381 **"was responsible for running"**: Yvette Pitt, email to the author, November 8, 2016.

381 **"My Dear Georgina"**: Letter provided to the author by Alfred Starr.

382 **George wrote another letter**: IWM, J. V. Overton Fuller Collection, Box 8, File 2, letter, John Starr to Jean Overton Fuller, September 29, 1953.

383 **Special Operations Branch**: Sanchia Berg, "Churchill's Secret Army Lived On," BBC, December 13, 2008, http://news.bbc.co.uk/go/pr/fr/-/today/hi/today/newsid_7780000/7780476.stm.

CHAPTER SIXTEEN: STARRS ON TRIAL

384 **"In no other department of war"**: Maurice Buckmaster, **They Fought Alone: The True Story of SOE's Agents in Wartime France** (1958; repr., Biteback Publishing, 2014), 249.

384 **"At Nuremberg the Defendants"**: Anthony M. Webb, ed., **Trial of Wolfgang Zeuss et al. (The Natzweiler Trial)**, foreword by Sir Hartley Shawcross (London: William Hodge, 1949), 13.

385 **"I had to obey"**: BNA, WO 235/560, "Statement of Hans Kieffer, 29 November 1946."

386 **attest to Kieffer's humane treatment**: IWM, J. V. Overton Fuller Collection, Box 8, File 2, letter, John Starr to Jean Overton Fuller, April 4, 1954.

386 **where Allied bombardment:** OSS Numbered Bulletins, MR 12, Section 2, June, July, August 1943, OSS Official Dispatch, Stockholm, "Germany: Air Bombardment and Morale," Declassified, CIA 006687, April 3, 1975.

386 **"I know the accused Kieffer":** BNA, WO 235/560, "SYNOPSIS OF CASE [Noailles Case] Being concerned near NOAILLES, OISE, FRANCE on or about 9 August 1944."

387 **"The court martial":** Serge Vaculik, **Air Commando** (New York: Dutton, 1955), 301.

387 **The court commuted:** BNA, WO 235/560, "SYNOPSIS OF CASE [Noailles Case] Being concerned near NOAILLES, OISE, FRANCE on or about 9 August 1944." SD driver Fritz Hildemann, who had been unaware of the purpose of the operation until a moment before the firing squad fired, was sentenced to five years.

388 **"was completely all right":** Tribunal Militaire, PROCES-VERBAL, Léon Jega, Inspecteur de Police à la Direction de la Surveillance Territoire, Paris, 13 rue des Saussaies. Interrogation of Josef Pierre Auguste Placke, age forty-nine, prisoner of war, April 1, 1966.

388 **"It was he":** Ibid., PROCES-VERBAL, René GOUILLARD, Commissaire de Police à la Direction de la Service de la Surveillance Territoire, 13 rue des Saussaies. Josef Gotz [sic].

390 **"I never worked for Goetz":** Ibid., PROCES-

VERBAL, René GOUILLARD, Commissaire de Police à la Direction de la Service de la Surveillance Territoire, 13 rue des Saussaies. John Starr.

391 "a tour of inspection": Ibid., PROCES-VERBAL, Werner Ruhl [sic], January 18, 1946.

391 "Following our retreat": IWM, J. V. Overton Fuller Collection, Box 8, File 2, letter, Ernest Vogt to Jean Overton Fuller, September 12, 1954.

391 He was working in a dairy: Jean Overton Fuller, The German Penetration of SOE: France, 1941–1944 (Maidstone, UK: George Mann, 1975), 157. See also Tribunal Militaire, letter, A. P. Le Man, Le Chef d'Escadrons, to Monsieur le Chef d'Escadrons de ROUGEMENT, London, April 13, 1948.

392 "As far as I know": Tribunal Militaire, Testimony of Ernest Vogt, June 19, 1948.

392 "I, too, hope that the STARR case": BNA, KV 6/29, "Letter, To: Miss J. Russell King, M.I.5., From: M.O.1 (S.P.) War Office, 73 Upper Berkeley Street, W.1., 28 September 1948."

393 indicted Captain John Ashford Renshaw Starr: Tribunal Militaire, letter, Le Capitaine MERCIER, Juge d'Instruction près le Tribunal Militaire Permanent de Paris à Son Excellence Monsieur L'Ambassadeur de France à Londres, Paris, 23 novembre 1949.

393 maximum penalty was death: Henry Rousso, The Haunting Past: History, Memory, and Justice in Contemporary France (Philadelphia: Uni-

NOTES

versity of Pennsylvania Press, 2002), xiii. See also Caroline Fournet, **Genocide and Crimes Against Humanity: Misconceptions in French Law and Practice** (London: Bloomsbury, 2013), 8.

393 "tall, blond, very smart": Jean Overton Fuller, **The Starr Affair** (London: Victor Gollancz, 1954), 176.

393 "his conduct and morality": Tribunal Militaire, RAPPORT, MDL Chef Commandant de Brigade, Issy-les-Moulineaux, December 23, 1948.

394 **Fuller wrote to John:** Fuller, **The Starr Affair,** 145.

395 "I never trusted him": Ibid.

395 "I do not deem it necessary": Tribunal Militaire, PROCES-VERBAL DE PREMIERE COMPARUTION, STARR, John Ashford, Alias "Bob," November 15, 1949.

395–96 "VOGT confirms what I told you": Ibid.

396 **John's cellmates from Fresnes:** Ibid., PROCES-VERBAL, Jean-Claude Comert, November 22, 1949.

396 "He pretends that his services": Ibid., letter, Le Capitaine MERCIER, Juge d'Instruction près le Tribunal Militaire Permanent de Paris à Son Excellence Monsieur l'Ambassadeur de France à Londres, Paris, 23 novembre 1949.

397 "If I were to leave": Fuller, **The Starr Affair,** 164.

397 "to reconstruct in its location": Tribunal Militaire, PROCES-VERBAL DE TRANSPORT, Captain Mercier, January 3, 1950.

398 "Captain STARR showed us": Ibid.

398 "Starr took us into the guardroom": Fuller, **The Starr Affair,** 178.

399 "Why, it was you": Ibid., 179.

399 "did not recognize Captain STARR": Tribunal Militaire, PROCES-VERBAL DE TRANSPORT, Captain Mercier, January 3, 1950.

400 "I do believe": Fuller, **The Starr Affair,** 190.

400 "We could not afford": Buckmaster, **They Fought Alone,** 68.

401 "You have quite enough": IWM, J. V. Overton Fuller Collection J, Box 8, File 2, letter, John Starr to Jean Overton Fuller, September 29, 1953.

402 **French government promoted:** "Décret du 25 Mars 2016 portant promotion et nomination," **Journal Officiel de la République Française,** 4, in which Jeanne Robert is nominated for the Legion of Honor, www.legiondhonneur.fr/sites/default/files/promotion/lh20160327.pdf.

402 **She died fifteen months later:** "Grande figure de la Résistance, Jeanne Robert n'est plus," **La Dépêche,** September 8, 2017, www.ladepeche.fr/article/2017/09/08/2641446-grande-figure-de-la-resistance-jeanne-robert-n-est-plus.html.

CREDITS

Insert page 1 (top left): Prime Minister Winston Churchill of Great Britain. 1942. Library of Congress, Prints and Photographs Division, LC-USW33–019093-C; (top right): Charles de Gaulle, half-length portrait. 1942. Library of Congress, Prints and Photographs Division, LC-USZ62–96046; (bottom): Pétain shakes hand with Hitler. 1940. Bundesarchiv, Bild 183-J28036, via Wikimedia Commons

Insert pages 2 (top), 5 (top right and bottom), and 16 (bottom): Courtesy of Alfred Starr

Insert pages 2 (bottom) and 15 (bottom): Courtesy of the author

Insert page 3 (top left): Vera Atkins, WAAF squadron officer. 1946. United Kingdom Government, via Wikimedia Commons; (top right): Lieutenant Odette Marie-Céline Sansom, George Cross, MBE. 1939–1945. Imperial War Museum, HALLOWES G M (MR), HU 3213; (bottom left): All rights reserved, Musée départemental de la Résistance et de la Déportation de Lorris

Insert pages 3 (bottom right) and 4 (top left): Courtesy of Anne Whiteside

CREDITS

Insert page 4 (top right): Yvonne Cormeau. 1941–1945. Imperial War Museum, CORMEAU Y (MRS), HU 47367

Insert pages 4 (bottom), 5 (top left), 8 (top), 9 (bottom), 10 (top and bottom), and 14 (bottom): Courtesy of Yvette Pitt

Insert page 6 (top): Courtesy of Jean-Pierre Comert

Insert pages 6 (bottom) and 9 (top and middle): Courtesy of Archives départementales du Gers

Insert page 7 (top left): Photograph of Denise Bloch, no known author, via Wikimedia Commons; (top right): Retrieved from http://www.specialforcesroh.com/gallery .php?do=view_image&id=28453&gal=gallery; (middle): Captain Adolphe Rabinovitch, SOE. Imperial War Museum, SPECIAL FORCES CLUB COLLECTION, HU 98879; (bottom): Diana Hope Rowden. 1942. Records of Women's Auxiliary Air Force, United Kingdom Government

Insert page 8 (bottom): Produced by French government, no known source

Insert page 10 (middle): Courtesy of Alain Geay

Insert pages 11 and 16 (top): Courtesy of Ethel Starr Lagier

Insert page 12 (top left): Hon. Assistant Section Officer Noor Inayat Khan (code name Madeleine), George Cross, MiD, Croix de Guerre avec Etoile de Vermeil. Imperial War Museum, DEPARTMENT OF DOCUMENTS VC-GC FILES/CARROLL F(WING COMMANDER), HU 74868; (middle right): Retrieved from http://www.redcap70.net/A%20History%20of%20 the%20SS%20Organisation%201924-1945.html/K/

CREDITS

KIEFFER,%20Hans.html; (bottom): Paris, Avenue Foch, Siegesparade. 1940. German Federal Archives, via Wikimedia Commons

Insert page 13 (top and middle): © Private Archives of Serge Ravanel, donation to AERI. Courtesy of Musée de la Resistance, via http://www.museedelaresistance enligne.org; (bottom): Courtesy of Archives départementales du Gers, 42 J 385, Fonds Guy Labédan

Insert page 14 (top and middle): By Jean Dieuzaide, courtesy of Michel Dieuzaide

Insert page 15 (top): SOE memorial plaque at Beaulieu, Hampshire. 2014. By Ericoides, via Wikimedia Commons

INDEX

INDEX

INDEX